Handbook of Psychology of Investigative Interviewing

Handbook of Psychology of Investigative Interviewing

Current Developments and Future Directions

Edited by Ray Bull, Tim Valentine and Tom Williamson

WILEY-BLACKWELL

A John Wiley & Sons, Ltd., Publication

This edition first published 2009
© 2009 John Wiley & Sons Ltd.

Wiley-Blackwell is an imprint of John Wiley & Sons, formed by the merger of Wiley's global Scientific, Technical, and Medical business with Blackwell Publishing.

Registered Office
John Wiley & Sons Ltd, The Atrium, Southern Gate, Chichester, West Sussex, PO19 8SQ, UK

Editorial Offices
The Atrium, Southern Gate, Chichester, West Sussex, PO19 8SQ, UK
9600 Garsington Road, Oxford, OX4 2DQ, UK
350 Main Street, Malden, MA 02148-5020, USA

For details of our global editorial offices, for customer services, and for information about how to apply for permission to reuse the copyright material in this book please see our website at www.wiley.com/wiley-blackwell.

The right of the editors to be identified as the authors of the editorial material in this work has been asserted in accordance with the Copyright, Designs and Patents Act 1988.

Library of Congress Cataloging-in-Publication Data

Handbook of psychology of investigative interviewing : current developments and future directions / edited by Ray Bull, Tim Valentine and Tom Williamson.
    p. cm.
  Includes index.
  ISBN 978-0-470-51267-8 (cloth) – ISBN 978-0-470-51268-5 (pbk.) 1. Interviewing in law enforcement–Psychological aspects. 2. Police questioning–Psychological aspects. 3. Criminal investigation–Psychological aspects. I. Bull, Ray. II. Valentine, Tim, 1959– III. Williamson, Tom.
  HV8073.H258 2009
  363.25′4019–dc22

                                           2009013396

A catalogue record for this book is available from the British Library.

1 2009

Contents

About the Editors

Ray Bull is Professor of Forensic Psychology at the University of Leicester, England. In July 2008 he received an 'Award for Life-time Contribution to Psychology and Law' from the European Association of Psychology and Law. In June 2008 he received the 'Award for Distinguished Contributions to Academic Knowledge in Forensic Psychology' from the British Psychological Society. In 2005 he received a Commendation from the London Metropolitan Police for 'Innovation and Professionalism whilst Assisting a Complex Rape Investigation'. He was part of a small team commissioned by the Home Office in 2000 to write the 2002 government document *Achieving Best Evidence in Criminal Proceedings: Guidance for Vulnerable or Intimidated Witnesses, Including Children* (ABE). In 2002–3 he led a small team commissioned by the government to produce an extensive training pack relating to ABE. In 1991 he was commissioned by the Home Office (together with a law professor) to write the first working draft of the *Memorandum of Good Practice on Video Recorded Interviews with Child Witnesses for Criminal Proceedings*. He has advised a large number of police forces in several countries on the interviewing of witnesses and suspects, and has testified as an expert witness in many trials. He has co-authored and co-edited many books, including *Investigative Interviewing: Psychology and Practice* (1999; a second edition is now being written) and *Witness Identification in Criminal Cases* (2008). In recognition of the quality and extent of his research publications in 1995 he was awarded a higher doctorate (Doctor of Science).

Tim Valentine is Professor of Psychology at Goldsmiths, University of London. Previously he was a member of the scientific staff at the Medical Research Council Applied Psychology Unit, Cambridge, and has held academic appointments at the University of Manchester and the University of Durham. His PhD was awarded by the University of Nottingham in 1986. He has authored more than 70 articles on cognitive models of face processing and eyewitness identification, and has provided advice on eyewitness identification and facial identification from CCTV to government, the courts and the Criminal Cases Review Commission in both England and Scotland. He is a member of the editorial board of *Applied Cognitive Psychology* and is author (with T. Brennen and S. Brédart) of *The Cognitive Psychology of Proper Names* (1996) and editor of *Cognitive and Computational Aspects of Face Recognition* (1995). He is a Fellow of the British Psychological Society.

Tom Williamson – readers please see the preface.

About the Contributors

Charles J. Brainerd is Professor of Human Development and Psychology at Cornell University, USA. He holds BS, MA and PhD degrees in experimental and developmental psychology. He has published over 200 research articles and chapters, and more than 20 books. His research covers human memory and decision-making, statistics and mathematical modelling, psychological assessment, learning, intelligence, cognitive development, learning disability and child abuse. His current research programme centres on the relation between memory and higher reasoning abilities in children and adults, and also focuses on false memory phenomena. He is the co-developer of fuzzy-trace theory, a model of the relation between memory and higher reasoning, which has been widely applied within medicine and law. He is a Fellow of the Division of General Psychology, the Division of Experimental Psychology, the Division of Developmental Psychology and the Division of Educational Psychology of the American Psychological Association, and is a Fellow of the American Psychological Society.

Neil Brewer is Professor of Psychology at Flinders University, Adelaide, Australia. He researches eyewitness memory and identification, especially the relations between confidence and both recognition and recall accuracy. Recent publications appear in the *Journal of Experimental Psychology: General, Journal of Experimental Psychology: Applied, Journal of Personality & Social Psychology, Journal of Applied Psychology*, and *Law & Human Behavior*. He is an elected member of the Academy of Social Sciences in Australia, and an editorial board member of five of the major international journals in his field. He regularly provides invited addresses for conferences of judges and magistrates throughout Australia.

Barry S. Cooper is Director of Research and Development for The Forensic Alliance. A former senior psychologist for the Correctional Service of Canada, he is currently employed as a psychologist for the Forensic Psychiatric Services Commission in British Columbia, working at the Forensic Psychiatric Hospital and the Surrey Forensic Clinic. His research and clinical forensic interests include investigative interviewing, credibility/malingering assessment, forensic (e.g., risk) assessment, psychopathy and eyewitness memory in victims and offenders of crime. His private practice focuses on areas related to his research and clinical forensic expertise.

Samuel Demarchi is an Associate Professor at the University of Paris. He conducts empirical studies on investigative interviews, eyewitness recall and identification, and beliefs about eyewitnesses' memories and criminal investigations. His current research focuses on deception detection and the theoretical and applied aspects of memory, including the verbal recoding of visual memories (verbal overshadowing effect). In collaboration with Jacques Py, he has trained hundreds of French police officers to conduct optimal investigative interviews, including intensive cognitive interview courses, and effective line-ups.

Nadine Deslauriers-Varin is currently working as a Project Manager at the Centre for Research on Sexual Violence, School of Criminology, Simon Fraser University, BC, Canada. In collaboration with the Behavioral Analysis Service of the Sûreté du Québec (Quebec Police Force) and the School of Criminology, University of Montreal, she completed a Master's thesis investigating the factors leading to an offender's confessions during police interrogation, focusing on the strength of evidence. While still involved in research on police investigation, she is also working on her PhD, which explores innovations of *modus operandi* and offending patterns of high-risk sex offenders.

David Dixon is Dean of the Faculty of Law, University of New South Wales, Sydney, Australia. His books include *Law in Policing: Legal Regulation and Police Practices* and *Interrogating Images: Audio-visually Recorded Police Questioning of Suspects*. His research focuses on how regulation (legal and otherwise) affects policing practice and has included studies of comparative developments in criminal justice, drug policing and police reform, as well as interrogation.

Ronald P. Fisher is Professor of Psychology at Florida International University, Miami, USA, where he is the Director of the Legal Psychology programme. He is on the editorial boards of *Journal of Experimental Psychology: Applied* and *Legal and Criminological Psychology*. He is the co-developer of the Cognitive Interview (CI) procedure for enhancing witness memory, and has conducted training seminars on the CI with many police and other investigative agencies, including the FBI, British Police, NASA, the Israeli Air Force,

NTSB and NASA. He served on the Planning Committee and the Technical Working Group for the US Department of Justice to develop national guidelines on collecting eyewitness evidence. His research interests also examine the cognitive principles underlying detecting deception, and the relation between consistency of witness recollection and accuracy of testimony.

Hugues Hervé is a registered psychologist in British Columbia, Canada, specializing in forensic and medico-legal assessments and evaluations. A former psychologist for the Correctional Service of Canada and the Forensic Psychiatric Services Commission, he is currently a Partner and Director of Consulting Services for The Forensic Alliance. Committed to the investigation, application and dissemination of sound clinical forensic practice, he is actively involved in providing consulting, training and research services to various professionals, groups and organizations on such topics as effective interviewing, credibility/malingering assessments, risk assessments, eyewitness memory and psychopathology.

Robyn E. Holliday is Senior Lecturer in the Forensic Section of the School of Psychology, University of Leicester, England. She holds BSocSci (Hon.) and PhD degrees in experimental and developmental psychology from the University of Newcastle, Australia. She has published regularly in *Child Development, Cognitive Development, Memory, Applied Cognitive Psychology, Developmental Review* and *Cognition*, and written several book chapters. Her current research programme centres on the processes underlying true and false memories across the lifespan, particularly of children and the elderly; child and elderly eyewitness testimony, including identification abilities, and forensic interview protocols such as the Cognitive Interview. She is currently writing a book on child forensic psychology. She is a member of the British Psychological Society, Association for Psychological Science, American Psychological Association, European Association of Psychology and Law, American Psychology-Law Society for Research in Memory and Cognition, and the Experimental Psychology Society. She is a Chartered Scientist and a Chartered Forensic Psychologist and Member of the British Psychological Society Division of Forensic Psychology.

Carwyn Hughes is a Detective Inspector with the Sussex Police, England. He graduated in 1988 with a BA in History from Swansea University before joining the Royal Hong Kong Police, where he served as an inspector on uniformed operations, the drugs squad and the Criminal Investigation Department (CID). In 1997 he joined the Sussex Police and in 2002 became the Force Identification Officer initiating his interest in issues around identification evidence. In 2005 he graduated from Portsmouth University with a master's degree in Police Science and Management, gaining a distinction for his dissertation on identification procedures. He currently serves as a Detective Inspector in Brighton CID.

Joyce E. Humphries is Research Associate at the University of Leicester. Eyewitness memory is her major research interest, in particular, investigating factors that may influence eyewitness identification performance across the lifespan. Specifically, her research focuses on eyewitness identification procedures and cognitive and social processes that may influence developmental differences in eyewitness identification performance. While her main interest is eyewitness identification, she is currently investigating interviewing procedures that may improve the performance of older adult witnesses. She has presented papers at a number of national and international conferences on the subject of developmental differences in eyewitness identification accuracy.

Peter J. van Koppen is a psychologist and is Professor of Law and Psychology at the Faculties of Law, Maastricht University and Free University Amsterdam. He received a JD in 1984 from Erasmus University, Rotterdam. He is president of the European Association for Psychology and Law and co-editor of *Psychology, Crime, and Law.* He has published a large number of books and articles in the broad field of psychology and law, and specializes in the area of the evaluation of evidence by police officers and officers of the court.

Margaret Bull Kovera is Professor of Psychology at John Jay College of Criminal Justice, City University of New York, USA. She is a Fellow of the American Psychological Association, the American Psychology-Law Society (APLS) and the Society for the Psychological Study of Social Issues, and is the past-president of APLS. She received the Saleem Shah Award for Early Career Achievement in Psychology and Law and the APLS Outstanding Teacher and Mentor in Psychology and Law Award. For over a decade she has had continuous funding from the National Science Foundation for her research on jury decision-making and eyewitness identification.

Damien B. Maguire practised as a barrister at the Victorian Bar for over 30 years specializing in appearance and advice work in major criminal trials and associated proceedings such as matters involving corporate regulation, disciplinary proceedings and subpoena litigation. In early 2005 he was appointed to the independent statutory position of Chief Examiner for the State of Victoria, a position involving the control of and responsibility for the use of coercive powers introduced to assist investigating police in the fight against organized crime. In exercising his independent powers he is directly involved in the examination of witnesses required to attend for coercive questioning.

Gregory Mitchell holds a PhD in psychology and a JD from the University of California, Berkeley. He is the Daniel Caplin Professor of Law and the E. James Kelly, Jr. Class of 1965 Research Professor at the University of Virginia. His current research focuses on the application of social science to the law, employment discrimination, rational choice models of legal behaviour and popular conceptions of justice.

Stephen Moston is a Senior Lecturer in Forensic Psychology, James Cook University, Australia. He is Head of Department and coordinator of the post-graduate professional training programs in Forensic Psychology at that university. He was a former member of the Association of Chief Police Officers Investigative Interviewing Strategic Steering Group. He has conducted several major studies on police interviewing styles and suspect behaviour in England and Australia for the UK Home Office and the Royal Commission on Criminal Justice. His current research interests include evaluating police interviewing styles and tactics, public perceptions of police interviewing, and denial strategies by suspects.

Rod Munro is the Identification Head of Profession within Devon and Cornwall Constabulary having more than nine years' service dedicated to this area of police business. He was a co-founder and past chair of a national image database for video identification procedures, a board member of the National Video Identification Strategy and was heavily involved in the development of identification procedures nationally. He is a National Policing Improvement Agency registered lecturer in identification law and procedure and has addressed a number of national and international conferences and seminars.

James Ost is Senior Lecturer in the Department of Psychology, University of Portsmouth. His research focuses on the social nature of remembering. He has published papers on a variety of forensic issues, including the way in which the social dynamics of therapy sometimes mirror those in police interrogations, how false reports (or false memories) of childhood events arise, how multiple witnesses can influence the testimony of a sole witness, how exposure to media reports can lead to false reports of non-witnessed events, and how an interviewer's behaviour can impact on the quality of children's testimony in forensic interviews.

John Pearse (BSc (Hons), PhD, C. Psychol, AFBPsS, FRSM) is the managing director of Forensic Navigation Services Ltd., an independent company that combines forensic consultancy and investigation with psychological training and empirical research. He has been conducting and publishing research in the area of police interviewing and related issues since 1991. For three decades he served as a detective in London and was engaged in the fight against organized crime at a senior level. His work in specialist roles included armed robbery, criminal intelligence, hostage and kidnap negotiation, and he concluded his service as a senior officer in the terrorist arena with a number of high-profile and innovative terrorist prosecutions. He recently undertook a confidential national review of police interviewing with terrorist suspects.

Steven D. Penrod joined the John Jay College of Criminal Justice faculty as Distinguished Professor of Psychology in 2001. He earned his JD from Harvard Law School and his PhD in psychology from Harvard University and previously served as Professor of Psychology at Wisconsin and Nebraska and Professor of Law at Minnesota and Nebraska. He has published over 100 scientific articles on eyewitness reliability and jury decision-making and is a co-author of books on juries and on eyewitnesses. His research has encompassed factors that reduce eyewitness reliability, procedures that may enhance eyewitness performance and the relationship between confidence and accuracy.

Jacques Py is Professor of Social Psychology at the University of Toulouse, France. His work focuses on eyewitness testimony in particular situations where eyewitnesses have to recall testimony. He has aimed to adapt the Cognitive Interview to Napoleonic criminal proceedings, to develop with Samuel Demarchi a technique to improve the description of people and to assess how French police officers conduct line-ups. He is Chief Editor of *European Review of Applied Psychology* and past president of the French Psychological Society (Société Française de Psychologie).

Valerie F. Reyna is Professor of Human Development and Psychology at Cornell University, USA, and a co-director of the Center for Behavioral Economics and Decision Research. She holds a PhD in experimental psychology from Rockefeller University, and publishes regularly in such journals as *Psychological Review* and *Psychological Science*. Her research encompasses human judgement and decision-making, numeracy and quantitative reasoning, risk and uncertainty, medical decision-making, social judgement, and false memory. She is a developer of fuzzy-trace theory, a model of the relation between mental representations and decision-making that has been widely applied in law, medicine and public health. She is President-Elect of the Society for Judgment and Decision Making. She has been elected a Fellow of the American Association for the Advancement of Science. She is also a Fellow of the Division of Experimental Psychology, the Division of Developmental Psychology, the Division of Educational Psychology and the Division of Health Psychology of the American Psychological Association, and she is a Fellow of the American Psychological Society.

Jannie van der Sleen is a psychologist. She has owned Kinterview, a consulting agency on investigative interviewing, for seven years. Before that she worked at the Police Academy of the Netherlands for 15 years. She trains and coaches detectives on investigative interviewing of adult and child witnesses and vulnerable suspects. She also works as an expert court witness.

Geoffrey M. Stephenson is Emeritus Professor of Social Psychology at the University of Kent, England, having established the Psychology Department there in 1978. He promoted and conducted research and teaching in law and psychology, leading to the introduction of Kent's innovative MSc programme in Forensic Psychology. He has served on several ESRC/MRC research committees, including Law and Social Sciences. With extensive editorial and committee experience in the British Psychological Society he is also past President of the European Association of Experimental Social Psychology. He founded the *Journal of Community and Applied Social Psychology*, and remains its Consulting Editor. He is Programme Director of the MSc in Addiction Psychology and Counselling at South Bank University, London.

Michel St-Yves is a forensic psychologist with the Behavioural Analysis Service of the Sûreté du Québec, where he has served since 2002. As a critical incident specialist, he is actively involved in criminal investigations, both developing psychological profiles of suspects and preparing interrogations. He teaches at the École Nationale de Police du Québec and at the University of Montreal. His publications and papers focus on sexual assault, crisis negotiation and police interrogation. He is the author of *Psychologie des entrevues d'enquête: de la recherche à la recherche de la pratique* [The psychology of investigative interviews: from research to practice] (Éditions Yvon Blais, 2004), and *The Psychology of Criminal Investigations: The Search for the Truth* (Thomson Carswell, 2009).

Gary L. Wells gained his PhD from Ohio State University in 1977. He is Distinguished Professor at Iowa State University and also Director of Social Science at the Institute of Forensic Science and Public Policy in Greensboro, NC. He has authored over 170 articles and chapters and two books, much of which focuses on the reliability of eyewitness identification. He was a founding member of the Department of Justice Group which developed the first set of national guidelines in the USA for eyewitness evidence. He has worked with prosecutors, police and policy-makers across the USA to help reform the way police line-ups are conducted.

A. Daniel Yarmey received his BA (Hons), MA and PhD from the University of Western Ontario, Canada in experimental psychology (memory). He is a University Professor Emeritus in the Department of Psychology, University of Guelph where he teaches courses in Psychology and the Law, and Sport Psychology. He is the author of the *Psychology of Eyewitness Testimony and Understanding Police and Police Work: Psychosocial Issues*. He has been a consultant and expert witness in Canada and the USA on issues related to eyewitness and earwitness identification.

John C. Yuille is Professor Emeritus, University of British Columbia, Canada, and a registered psychologist with a private forensic practice. He has conducted research with children and adults for over 40 years. His research has included the areas of human memory, interviewing, credibility assessment and psychopathy. He regularly provides training to law enforcement, lawyers, child protection workers and judges on interviewing and credibility assessment. He has served as an expert witness in criminal, family and civil courts for over 30 years. He is the Chief Executive Officer of The Forensic Alliance.

Rachel Zajac is a Lecturer in Psychology at the University of Otago, New Zealand. She earned her PhD in 2002 from the University of Otago while training as a clinical psychologist. Her research interests encompass investigative interviewing, eyewitness identification, and external influences on memory. She lectures in forensic, developmental and clinical psychology. She is frequently called on to advise social workers, police, legal practitioners and healthcare providers on methods to interview children and adults about events in their past. Her research has been used in police and judicial education programmes in the UK and Australia, and in the US Supreme Court as scientific evidence.

Preface

Tom Williamson was to be the lead editor of this Handbook. To those who knew Tom, his premature death from lung cancer at the age of 59 was devastating. This tragic event occurred before any of the chapters had been written. Indeed, when I contacted the contributors, some of them could not recall that Tom had even invited them to write a chapter. Nevertheless, they produced excellent chapters that you will enjoy reading.

When conceiving of this Handbook, Tom invited me to assist him (given his view of my experience of co-editing books, especially for the international publisher Wiley). He also invited Tim Valentine to be the co-editor for the four chapters involving gathering information from eyewitnesses. When Tom was informed that he had a particularly aggressive form of cancer and that his health could deteriorate rapidly, he asked me to be prepared to take over as lead editor. Sadly, all too quickly I had to do this. I would like to thank all the contributors, and especially those who initially had no idea that they were on Tom's list, for their forbearance during the time it has taken to bring this Handbook to publication and for their willingness to respond constructively to our editorial guidance concerning the production of chapters that can be understood by a multidisciplinary (including policing) readership. Tom would very much have appreciated their efforts.

Tom Williamson was born on 11 June 1947 in a rural part of Scotland, the son of a dairyman. At the age of 17 he left Scotland for London, where he joined the Metropolitan Police Force, one of the largest police organizations in the world, as a cadet. After only a few years his abilities were noticed and he became a member of the anti-corruption branch set up by the head of the London Police.

In 1979 he was awarded a police-funded scholarship to study full-time for a BA in Psychology and he graduated in 1982.

He was regularly promoted and in 1989 reached the rank of Commander. He was one of the *first* (and of the *few*) to conduct research on the actual police interviewing of suspects (which in England since 1986 has to be tape-recorded), which resulted in the early 1990s in several groundbreaking, high-quality publications in research journals, and in the award in 1990 of a doctorate while he was still serving as a police officer. At the same time, he set up a committee of police and academic researchers whose task it was to pave the way for the move from *interrogating* suspects to seek confessions, to *interviewing* them to gather information.

I was honoured to be a member of that committee which prepared the ground for a working party of police officers to recommend in 1992 the PEACE approach to interviewing, which in 1992 was adopted by the Association of Chief Police Officers in England and Wales.

Some years later Tom was invited to a meeting in London to receive a national policing prize in recognition of what he had achieved in interviewing, and he generously asked me to accompany him (so typical of him).

In the early 1990s Tom took up the position of Commander of the London police training college at Hendon, where in the 1980s I had run a training evaluation and research project for several years. In the mid-1990s Tom came to see me when I was Head of the Department of Psychology at the University of Portsmouth to ask my advice on how he might go about arranging for the intensive two-year training and assessments that recruits to the London Police receive in law, social science, and the like might form part of undergraduate study towards a degree.

I advised him of some questions to ask the London universities (my own university being over 100 kilometres from London). A couple of months later Tom contacted me to say that the London Police wished to set up such an arrangement with my university.

In order to develop this I urged my university to set up a new Institute, which rapidly grew under the able directorship of Steve Savage. When Tom reached retirement age in 2001, having been Deputy Chief of the Nottinghamshire Police Force since 1995, he became a part-time member of the Portsmouth University Institute, which subsequently became the largest academic department in the university.

Tom's emphasis on what he called ethical policing derived in part from his years of being in charge of Britain's largest group of murder investigators. His obituary in the *The Guardian* stated that Tom was 'an operational detective par excellence'. His beliefs came from direct policing experience, but he used research and academia to support those beliefs.

Tom's 1993 research journal article, entitled 'From interrogation to investigative interviewing', is an example of how his vision set the scene for what is now referred to as Investigative Interviewing, which involves trying to find out what happened as opposed to trying to obtain a confession.

My last long conversation with Tom took place during a flight from Paris to East Midlands Airport on our way back from a five-day conference organized by the Gendarmerie Nationale under the auspices of the AGIS initiative of the European Commission, which provides funding to police organizations to hold international, research-oriented meetings on important policing topics. At this meeting Tom and I (plus the other few representatives from the UK) were pleased to learn that some other European police organizations were actively considering adopting the PEACE approach (the 'English approach', as some called it), as had Norway fairly recently. However, we were saddened that some eastern European countries (now free from communism) seemed to be adopting a coercive approach, which can result, for example, in reactance from guilty suspects. During this conversation Tom brought up the topic of who first used the term Investigative Interviewing. I said that I thought he had. He replied that he thought I had. Then we thought that it might have been Eric Shepherd – the late 1980s–early 1990s seemed so long ago, and so much had happened since then in England and Wales regarding police interviewing that it was hard to recall what precisely had taken place in those early, difficult days.

Around the time that Tom died, New Zealand decided to adopt the PEACE approach and in the last couple of years that country has invested much in training and retraining its police officers. Some police organizations in Germany are also very interested in the PEACE approach.

I decided that I would write this preface while actively continuing with what Tom had started. I am at a desk in an apartment at a residential police training academy in Germany, having been invited to present a lecture at the annual conference of the *Deutsche Gesselschaft für Kriminalistik* on the topic of 'Investigative Interviewing: The PEACE Model', during which I have been asked to explain why this massive change in police training occurred in England and Wales, describe how research, concepts and theory from psychology underpin the PEACE approach/philosophy, and give an account of our recent research findings from the analysis of recorded interviews with suspects of whether police officers are able to adopt this approach. This is the very kind of presentation that Tom should have been giving.

It is comforting to know that although Tom is no longer with us, his pioneering work continues to spread its crucial effect around the world.

Ray Bull
14 October 2008

Chapter One

The Psychology of Suspects' Decision-Making during Interrogation

Michel St-Yves

Behavioral Analysis Service
Sûreté du Québec (Quebec Police Force)
École nationale de police du Québec (Quebec National Police Academy)
School of Criminology
University of Montreal, Quebec

and

Nadine Deslauriers-Varin

School of Criminology
Simon Fraser University, British Columbia

Introduction

A number of studies carried out in the social sciences show that human behaviour can be significantly influenced by a multitude of factors. Publicity is a good example. To influence people's consumer practices, advertisement agencies will study the name of a product, a slogan, etc. to make sure that the consumer will choose this product rather than another one. This works very well and is influential, as shown in numerous research studies on the subject (see Gouldner, 1960; Cialdini, Vincent, Lewis, Catalan, Wheeler & Darby, 1975; Ury, 1991).

The parallel with police interrogation is fairly easy to make. With different strategies, the investigator tries to influence the suspect's decision, first to get the suspect to collaborate and then to confess, in spite of the stakes involved and the consequences related to a confession.

Handbook of Psychology of Investigative Interviewing: Current Developments and Future Directions
Edited by Ray Bull, Tim Valentine and Tom Williamson
© 2009 John Wiley & Sons, Ltd.

In this chapter, we shall describe the major factors – individual, criminal, contextual – that can influence a suspect's decision whether or not to confess to his or her crime. We shall examine more closely the influence of contextual factors, since recent research suggests that these are the most influential regarding the decision-making process. Amongst those contextual factors are the caution (the right to remain silent and to have an attorney), the perception of the strength of the available evidence and the interrogation/interview techniques. We shall conclude with a reflection on some of the interrogation methods currently used in North America, particularly on their effectiveness and on the controversy related to the use of such techniques.

The decision-making process

Every person interrogated by the police for a crime they have committed will find themselves in a very complex decision-making process: Should I talk or remain silent? Tell the truth or lie? Will a confession help or harm my defence? This decision-making process, which begins even before the interrogation, will be influenced by a variety of factors. Some authors have contended that the decision to confess or not is taken as soon as or before the interrogation begins and that persuasive methods have little influence on the decision, with some even concluding that such methods are pretty much useless, or at least not essential to obtain a confession (Irving & McKenzie, 1989; Moston, Stephenson & Williamson, 1992; Baldwin, 1993; Evans, 1993; Pearse & Gudjonsson, 1996; Pearse, Gudjonsson, Clare & Rutter, 1998; Bull, 2006).

Inbau, Reid, Buckley & Jayne (2001) contend that the vast majority of suspects initially intend to deny their involvement in the crime but, during the interrogation, thanks to the techniques used by the investigators, a high percentage of them change their mind and confess. In a recent study, we found that 25% of convicted people admitted that they changed their initial position during the interrogation. However, among these, almost half (46%) said they initially intended to confess but later changed their mind (Deslauriers-Varin & St-Yves, 2006). This shows that the decision-making process can be influenced either way. Deslauriers-Varin (2006) also noted that 43.5% of people who confessed their crime to the police said that they were ready to do so at the beginning of the interrogation. As for the others who confessed, 31.5% clearly stated that they were not ready to do so at the beginning of the interrogation. Why did they change their mind? Was it the influence of their attorney? The quality of the evidence? The attitude of the investigator?

Influencing factors on the decision-making process

In the following section, we describe the major factors that are likely to influence the decision to confess or not to the police. The few studies that have been carried out regarding factors associated with confessions can be classified in three categories: (i) individual factors; (ii) criminal factors; (iii) contextual factors (Gudjonsson, 2003; Kassin & Gudjonsson, 2004; St-Yves & Landry, 2004). First, we briefly describe individual and criminal factors, and then focus on contextual factors, given that these are the only factors on which police officers can have an influence during the interrogation.

Individual factors

A number of individual factors have been examined in relation to confessing during police interrogations. Although most studies carried out on the factors influencing the decision-making process of a confession obtain contradictory results, it is possible to establish general trends.

Age.   Suspects under the age of 21 confess more often than do older suspects (Baldwin & McConville, 1980; Softley, 1980; Pearse *et al.*, 1998; Phillips & Brown, 1998). This may be explained by the fact that the younger ones do not understand their rights as well as older suspects and thus are less likely to invoke them (Baldwin & McConville, 1980). Other studies emphasize the significant influence that the pressure associated with the interrogation can have on young suspects. Being less mature, they probably have more difficulties facing such a situation and understanding all its implications (Singh & Gudjonsson, 1992). However, when included in a logistic regression model, age of suspect does not seem to have a significant impact on their decision-making process (Pearse *et al.*, 1998; Deslauriers-Varin, 2006). Also, some studies have not found a significant relationship between age of suspect and tendency to confess (Neubauer, 1974; Mitchell, 1983; Leo, 1996; St-Yves, 2002).

Ethnic origin.   Caucasian suspects are, according to some studies, more inclined to confess than are other ethnic groups living in the same country (Leo, 1996; Phillips & Brown, 1998).The difference between Caucasians and other ethnic groups seems even more significant for sexual crimes (St-Yves, 2002; 2006b). Two factors could explain such differences: (i) cultural and religious differences; and (ii) in most studies the police interviewers were predominately white. However, other studies have not shown a significant relationship between ethnic origin and confession rates (Wald *et al.*, 1967; Pearse *et al.*, 1998). Phillips & Brown (1998) have suggested that the relationship between ethnic group and confession may be modulated by other factors such as age, criminal background and strength of evidence.

Feeling guilty.   According to Berggren (1975), confessing can provide suspects with sense of liberation which has a cathartic effect. Indeed, studies have found that feeling guilty leads to confessing during police interrogation (Gudjonsson & Petursson, 1991; Gudjonsson, 1992; Sigurdsson & Gudjonsson,

1994; Gudjonsson & Sigurdsson, 1999; St-Yves, 2002; Gudjonsson *et al.*, 2004a; 2004b). According to the final prediction model of a recent study, from all the individual factors included, only feelings of guilt significantly predicted confession during a police interrogation (Deslauriers-Varin, 2006). According to the same study, suspects reporting feelings of guilt regarding the crime were 50% more likely to confess than those not reporting such feelings. The first explanatory models of confession have in fact emphasized the role of the feelings of guilt in the decision-making process of confession, arguing that the internal pressures often pushed the suspect to confess to ease their guilt (Horowitz, 1956; Reik, 1973; Gudjonsson, 1992). This significant relationship between feelings of guilt and confession probably explains why some police officers use tactics such as appealing to the suspect's conscience and offering him or her moral justifications and excuses (Leo, 1996). Indeed, shouldn't we consider the feeling of guilt as a contextual rather than an individual factor?

Personality profile.   Extroverts, such as the antisocial and narcissistic, are less likely to collaborate and tend to resist more during police interrogation than do introverts (Gudjonsson & Petursson, 1991; Gudjonsson & Sigurdsson, 1999; Bernard & Proulx, 2002; St-Yves, 2002; 2004c). This could be explained by the notion that introvert personality profiles are more likely to experience remorse and feelings of guilt with regard to their crime (St-Yves, 2004d). In addition, people with an extrovert personality profile do not seem to confess their crime for the same reasons that introverts do. The former group, having none or little remorse, have a greater tendency to give way to external pressure – interrogation techniques and strength of the evidence – while the latter are more likely to give way to internal pressure, especially guilt and remorse (Eysenck & Gudjonsson, 1989; Gudjonsson & Sigurdsson, 1999; St-Yves, 2002; 2004b).

Criminal background.   Some authors have suggested that people without a prior criminal background are more inclined to confess their crime than those who have been arrested in the past (Neubauer, 1974; Pearse *et al.*, 1998). Leo (1996) explains this relationship by suggesting that people more familiar with the police environment and interrogation techniques are more inclined to invoke their legal rights and, therefore, not to collaborate with the police. On the other hand, some researchers found a positive relationship between having a criminal background and the rate of confession (Baldwin & McConville, 1980; Mitchell, 1983), while yet others did not find any significant relationship (Moston *et al.*, 1992; Phillips & Brown, 1998; St-Yves, 2002; Deslauriers-Varin, 2006; Deslauriers-Varin *et al.*, 2009). A study by Moston and colleagues (1992) demonstrated that the connection between criminal background and confession might be modulated by the quality of evidence possessed by the police at interrogation. When evidence was strong, suspects without a criminal background were more likely to confess their crime (78% vs. 59%) than were those with criminal backgrounds.

Criminal factors

Two criminal factors especially have attracted researchers' attention: the nature and the seriousness of the crime.

Nature of crime. Some authors have noted a difference in the rate of confession depending on the type of crime, especially when comparing non-violent and violent crimes. Neubauer (1974) observed that those who committed a non-violent crime were twice as likely to confess than those who committed a violent crime (56% vs. 32%). For some, the most difficult type of crime to confess to is sexual crime (Holmberg & Christianson, 2002; St-Yves, 2002; 2006b). This could be explained by the negative perception (e.g., shame, rejection, humiliation) associated with this type of crime. However, other studies have found no significant relationship between the type of crime and confession rate (Moston *et al.*, 1992; Deslauriers-Varin, 2006, Deslauriers-Varin *et al.*, 2009). Moston *et al.* (1992) contended that prior research looking at the possible link between the type of crime committed and confession and finding a significant connection used inappropriate methodology. They argued that prior studies had not taken into account the possible interactions between the type of crime committed and situational factors, such as access to legal advice and the quality and/or strength of evidence.

Seriousness of crime. It would be logical to think that the more serious the crime, the fewer people will confess because they fear the consequences; more serious crime usually leading to heavier penalties. That is the finding of empirical studies that have examined police interrogations held in various police departments (Neubauer, 1974; Moston *et al.*, 1992; Phillips & Brown, 1998; St-Yves, 2002). However, Moston *et al.* (1992) stress that the influence of other relevant variables, such as the more frequent use of an attorney in cases of serious crime, should not be ignored.

In the studies mentioned above, the majority of the individual and criminological factors have not received unanimous support regarding their role in the confession process during police interrogation. Confessing is a complex process which cannot be explained by one factor alone but, rather, by a series of factors that interact. To date, only a few studies have analysed or considered these interactions (Deslauriers-Varin *et al.*, 2009). Studies need to carry out multivariate, rather than bivariate, statistical analyses to check not only the unique effect of each variable but also their interaction with the other factors included in the model, thus helping to get an overall picture of the direct and indirect relationships explaining the decision-making process of confession of a crime.

Contextual factors

Recent studies show that contextual factors have most impact in the confession process of a suspect (Deslauriers-Varin & St-Yves, 2006; Deslauriers-Varin *et al.*, 2009; St-Yves & Tanguay, 2009). The main contextual factors are: the quality/strength of the evidence (real or perceived); access to legal advice; and strategies and techniques of interrogation.

Quality/strength of the evidence.   Even if the decision-making process of the confession is often affected by a combination of factors (Gudjonsson, 2003; St-Yves, 2004a), the suspect's perception of the strength of the evidence against him or her is a determining factor in the process of confession. Two-thirds of suspects (66.7%) admitted their crime when the evidence against them appeared strong to them, compared to a third (36.4%) when the strength of the evidence seemed modest, and one in ten (9.9%) when there was little or no evidence (Williamson, 1990). Gudjonsson *et al.* observed that nearly 70% of people interrogated by police admitted that they would not have confessed if they had not been suspected by police. Of those, between 55% and 60% said that they confessed because they were convinced that police had enough evidence against them (Gudjonsson & Petursson, 1991; Gudjonsson & Bownes, 1992; Sigurdsson & Gudjonsson, 1994). In a study of adult offenders sentenced to a federal term (two years or more), we observed that the rate of confession almost doubled (from 31.4% to 55.6%) when the evidence was perceived by the suspect as being relatively strong (Deslauriers-Varin, 2006; Deslauriers-Varin & St-Yves, 2006). In a logistic regression model, the suspects perceiving the strength of the evidence against them as good were three time more likely to confess during police interrogation (Deslauriers-Varin *et al.*, 2009). The explanation is simple: in the face of over-whelming evidence, denial is useless. For the suspect, there are only two possible choices: to remain silent or to give a version that will give him or her an opportunity to explain (while minimizing) his behaviour and/or 'save face'.

Access to legal advice.   The official caution can influence the decision to confess or not to the police. In Canada, the caution is made to any person in custody, arrested or not, and interrogated for a crime he or she is likely to be implicated in. And contrary to the practice in the USA and the UK, Canadian law does not recognize the moral necessity for the attorney to be present in the interrogation room; it only recognizes the right to inform the suspect of his or her right to remain silent and to contact an attorney immediately, usually by telephone. However, in accordance with the law on judicial procedures for teenagers, there is an exception when the person interrogated is aged between 12 and 18. However, it is left to the discretion of the police officer whether to allow the attorney to be present during the interrogation. In such a case, the attorney would become a witness and could be summoned as such if the statement is disputed and a *voir dire* becomes necessary. Beyond the caution, police officers will generally insist that the suspect contacts an attorney and will make sure that this strictly confidential conversation is entirely satisfactory to the suspect. Usually, the attorney will recommend that his/her client remains silent during the police interrogation. Sometimes, the attorney will even describe to the client the usual process of police interrogation and the most frequent strategies used by police officers to persuade suspects to confess.

If the perception of the strength of the evidence is a major determining factor in the decision to confess, availing oneself of the right to contact an attorney seems to be the factor that might best explain why some suspects do not confess or refuse to cooperate with the police (Moston, Stephenson & Williamson, 1992; Leo, 1996; Phillips & Brown, 1998; Deslauriers-Varin *et al.*, 2009). Moston *et al.* (1992) found in their study that one suspect in two (50%) who did not consult an attorney confessed compared to 30% of those who did. Pearse *et al.* (1998) and Phillips & Brown (1998) found that suspects who used their legal right to contact an attorney were four times less likely to confess to the police. The results recently obtained in a predictive model of confession make it possible to quantify the actual impact of this factor: access to legal advice reduced by 83% the odds of confessing (Deslauriers-Varin, 2006). This seems to confirm the perception of some police officers, who believe that suspects' access to an attorney is an impediment to their cooperation (Leiken, 1970; Walsh, 1982). However, Moston *et al.* (1992) observed that those choosing to remain silent are more likely to be sentenced than those who deny their crime during interrogation. Thus, remaining silent is not always an advantage.

Interrogation strategies and techniques.   The literature promoting various interrogation techniques is abundant. Kalbfleisch (1994) reviewed more than 80 books on the subject, the majority of them from the USA. Most of these, written by experienced investigators (see Macdonald & Michaud, 1987; Zulawski & Wicklander, 1992; Walters, 1995; Inbau *et al.*, 2001; Gordon & Fleisher, 2002), aspire to give techniques to police officers to obtain confessions. The most popular interrogation technique, not without controversy, is the Reid technique (see www.reid.com). According to the Reid Institute, this method, developed in the 1950s and first published in the 1960s, would be effective 80% of the time. However, Gudjonsson (2003) doubts this high success rate. In fact, confession rates found in North American studies, where most of the investigators were trained in the Reid (or related) technique, normally range between 42% and 57% (Neubauer, 1974; Leo, 1996; Cassell & Hayman, 1998; St-Yves & Lavallée, 2002; Deslauriers-Varin & St-Yves, 2006). Moreover, the mean confession rate (50%) has been relatively stable for the last 40 years (Gudjonsson, 2003).

The actual effectiveness of various interrogation techniques is difficult to measure. In a North American study, Leo (1996) demonstrated that the quantity and the nature of strategies used by police officers during interrogation influenced the rate of confession. Other than the use of a variety of interrogation strategies, appealing to the suspect's conscience is the technique that seems to have the greater influence on the confession process (Leo, 1996). Other strategies, such as identification of the contradictions in the suspect's denial and statement, using praise and flattery, then allowing the suspect to ease his guilt and justify himself, while giving him moral justifications or psychological excuses, have also shown their effectiveness (Leo, 1996). This is not surprising since those methods are inspired by factors – especially contextual ones – that favour confession.

Everyone interrogated by police for a crime that they have actually committed lives with fear with regard to the consequences of their actions. These stakes can become major obstacles that can hinder the confession process. The role of the police officer will thus be to overcome these obstacles by stressing the main facilitating factors, such as the quality/strength of the evidence (which police officers do not always have) and internal pressures (guilt, remorse). Despite all the efforts to obtain a confession and in spite of (sometimes) overpowering evidence, some people continue to deny or do not confess. The major reason is probably fear of the consequences. Two major types of consequences inhibit confession: real consequences and personal consequences (Gudjonsson & Petursson, 1991; Gudjonsson & Bownes, 1992; Sigurdsson & Gudjonsson, 1994). These inhibiting factors can obstruct the confession process and help explain why, even though they have remorse and think that police have enough or strong evidence against them, suspects can still decide to deny their crime or to remain silent.

We call *real* consequences all concrete consequences that can happen or worry a suspect while being interrogated for a crime he or she has committed. Amongst the most usual real consequences, there is the fear of penal sanction (Gudjonsson, 2003). Among people with no prior involvement with the criminal justice system, there is the fear of getting a criminal record and, especially, facing the consequences of this, such as losing a job or having difficulty finding employment. The fear of legal sanctions is associated with loss of freedom (imprisonment) and, in certain countries, with the death penalty. By confessing their crime, certain suspects also fear the consequences they will have to undergo if their statement incriminates others. Such consequences can become more undesirable for the suspect than the penal sanction.

Amongst other probable consequences, there is the fear of losing loved ones (spouse, children, family, friends). This fear is greater for individuals suspected of a sexual crime, as well as the fear of losing their job, especially if the crime has been committed at the place of employment. There are also financial losses, in particular regarding arson or major fraud. These consequences are potentially real – this is the reason why they can inhibit the confession process – but they are never immediate. Suspects can hope that their spouse will understand, that the boss still needs them, that the judge will show clemency. Sometimes, while discussing these fears with the suspect, the investigator can moderate their inhibiting influence. However, the investigator cannot use promises or threats to reduce these inhibiting factors. The illusion of promises/advantages or threats raises reasonable doubt regarding the free and voluntary nature of the subsequent statement and the true culpability of the accused (see St-Yves, in press).

Personal consequences are often feared more than judicial consequences because they are immediate and touch on integrity and self-esteem. As soon as suspects confess, they lose dignity and respect, initially from the self and then from people whom they care about. This is particularly true with sexual crimes (Holmberg & Christianson, 2002). To mitigate the influence of these inhibitors, the investigator often uses valorization or focuses on certain defence mechanisms, such as minimization, projection and rationalization. However, sometimes the investigator becomes an inhibiting factor because of his or her attitude (St-Yves, 2004b; 2006a).

Some recent studies have shown the importance of the quality of the interviewer–interviewee relationship for the outcome of an investigative interview, including the one made with the suspect. The preliminary steps that we can find in most interrogations conducted in North America are used not only to evaluate the conscious state of mind of the subject ('operating mind'), in particular his aptitude to be interrogated by police, but also to establish a trustful relationship with the suspect thus facilitating his or her confession. Indeed, active listening, empathy, openness, respect and the desire to discover the truth, rather than to try at all costs to obtain a confession, are, we contend, the essential qualities for carrying out investigative interviews (Shepherd, 1991; Williamson, 1993; St-Yves, Tanguay & Crépault, 2004; St-Yves, 2006a).

Are all interrogation techniques and strategies acceptable?

Although strong evidence is a determining factor in the confession process, police officers often do not have strong enough evidence. Certain studies have revealed that technical evidence (fingerprints, DNA, etc.) is only available in 10% of cases (Bottomley & Coleman, 1980; Horvath & Meesig, 1996). Instead, much of the available evidence usually rests on statements, including that given by the suspect.

Is it acceptable to use strategies and ruses to obtain a confession? This question raises legal considerations (e.g., what is allowed by law in various countries?) and ethical considerations (i.e., what is morally acceptable?). This is a subjective question that cannot be disassociated from the cultural and judicial context in which the interrogation is conducted. In certain countries, torture is common and legal. Furthermore, the perception and tolerance that the population can have towards certain interrogation methods is probably closely associated with the nature of the crime. The context can also influence the way interrogations are conducted. The war on terrorism has militarized criminal justice systems and changed the rules: 'Suspects are interrogated by military in ways that would never be accepted by the ordinary courts with criminal suspects' (Williamson, 2006: 5).

In Canada and the USA, tribunals accept the use of certain strategies and persuasive methods (see *R v Oickle* [2000]). The Supreme Court of Canada offers support for the investigator's need to be less than truthful during an interrogation. It referenced the often cited decision of Justice Lamer, who wrote that a criminal investigation and the search for criminals is not a game that has to follow the Queensbury rules (introduced in the nineteenth century to govern the rules of boxing and make it safer):

> The investigation of crime and the detection of criminals is not a game to be governed by the Marquis of Queensbury rules. The authorities, in dealing with shrewd and often sophisticated criminals, must sometimes out of necessity resort to tricks or other forms of deceit and should not, through the rule, be hampered in their work. What should be repressed vigorously is conduct on their part that shocks the community. (*R v Rothman* [1981])

To free guilty suspects because there is insufficient evidence or because the confession is inadmissible in court may be shocking to the community. However, the former is the outcome in almost a third of investigations (Irving & McKenzie, 1989; Moston *et al.*, 1992; Leo, 1996).

The Reid technique has been criticized by many over the decades, especially because it is said to be responsible for false confessions which can lead to miscarriages of justice. However, in Canada, where most police departments use the Reid (or a related) technique, miscarriages of justice linked to interrogations are few. Furthermore, when they do happen, they are often linked to other factors such as misidentification, insufficient expertise and police misconduct. The rare recorded miscarriages seem to be attributed to long interrogations where the questions were repetitive and very suggestive. Most of the time, a confession is deemed inadmissible because it has been obtained in an illegal or unethical manner rather than because it is false (St-Yves, in press). Sometimes, however, the method of questioning can be too suggestive and can corrupt the truth and lead to false a confession. The lack of objectivity – commonly known as tunnel vision – and an unprofessional attitude are other factors that we often find when such mistakes occur (FPT Heads of Prosecutions Committee Working Group, 2004).

One of the best ways to control abuses and misconduct is, without doubt, the audiovisual recording of the interrogations and the sensitization of police officers to the potential risks – especially the risk of obtaining a false confession – associated with certain strategies and interrogation techniques; more specifically, when the person being interrogated is mentally vulnerable (mental health problems, limited intellectual ability) (see Kassin & Wrightsman, 1985; Gudjonsson, 2003).

In Canada, the audiovisual recording of interrogations is not limited to the suspect's final statement (recapitulation of the confession on video), but includes the whole interrogation, from the caution to the end of the interrogation. In addition, to preserve a verbatim record of the interrogation, the use of the audiovisual recording stimulates investigators to produce better quality interrogations while protecting them from unjustified accusations (Pitt, Spiers, Dietz & Dvoskin, 1999). The audiovisual recording provides an objective file the judge can use to decide on the free and voluntary character of a confession and the circumstances in which it was obtained, as well as its contents, instead of relying on the subjective and interested claims made by the protagonists. It thus acts as an excellent way of preventing miscarriages of justice. It also acts as the most faithful witness of the interrogation process (St-Yves, 2004c).

Conclusion

The decision-making process during police interrogations can be influenced by numerous factors. But it is the contextual factors that seem to have the most impact on the suspects' decision-making process and, moreover, on which police officers have a potential influence. Amongst these contextual factors, we find the caution (the right to remain silent and to have access to legal advice), the quality/strength of evidence and the strategies and interrogation techniques. It is those interrogation methods that cause much of the controversy, either because they appear coercive, raise doubts with regard to the 'voluntary' nature of the confession, or can lead to false confessions and, ultimately, to miscarriages of justice. However, in spite of the risk of miscarriages of justice associated with interviews with witnesses and victims, there is no apparent opposition to the interview methods used to facilitate the mnemonic recall of witnesses. However, training police officers on interrogation techniques and the risks that some of these present, as well as recording the entire interrogation process, are conditions that can considerably reduce the risks and doubts associated with police interrogation. Police training in investigative interviewing is essential to ensure that the techniques used are in conformity with the law and that they exert a positive influence on the result of the investigation. It is also through training that we can recommend rules (see St-Yves, 2006a) and ethical principles (see Home Office circular 22/1992), as well as a philosophy centred on the search for truth instead of the quest for confession. Nevertheless, it is often through confession that we can reconstruct part of this truth.

References

Baldwin, J. (1993). Police interviewing techniques. Establishing the truth or proof? *The British Journal of Criminology, 33*, 325–352.

Baldwin, J. & McConville, M. (1980). *Confessions in Crown Court trials*. Royal Commission on Criminal Procedure Research Study No. 5. London: HMSO.

Berggren, E. (1975). *The psychology of confessions*. Leiden: Brill.

Bernard, G. & Proulx, J. (2002). Caractéristiques du passage à l'acte de criminels violents états-limites et narcissiques. *Revue Canadienne de Criminologie*, Janvier, 51–75.

Bottomley, A. K. & Coleman, C. A. (1980). Police effectiveness and the public: The limitations of official crime rates. In R. V. G. Clarke & J. M. Hough (Eds.), *The Effectiveness of Policing*. Farnborough: Gower.

Bull, R. (2006). *Research on the police interviewing of suspects*. Paper presented at the Séminaire d'échanges de bonnes pratiques sur les auditions de police judiciaire. Paris, 23–26 January.

Cassell, P. G. & Hayman, B. S. (1998). Police interrogation in the 1990s: An empirical study on the effect of Miranda. In R. A. Leo & G. C. Thomas III (Eds.), *The Miranda debate, justice and policing*. Boston, MA: Northeastern University Press, 222–235.

Cialdini, R. B., Vincent, J. E., Lewis, S. K., Catalan, J., Wheeler, D. & Darby, B. L. (1975). Reciprocal concessions procedure for inducing compliance: the door-in-the-face technique. *Journal of Personality and Social Psychology, 31*, 206–215.

Deslauriers-Varin, N. (2006). Les facteurs déterminants dans le processus d'aveu chez les auteurs d'actes criminels. Master's thesis. Université de Montréal.

Deslauriers-Varin, N. & St-Yves, M. (2006). *An empirical investigation of offenders' decision to confess their crime during police interrogation*. Paper presented at the 2nd International Conference on Investigative Interviewing, Portsmouth, 5–7 July.

Deslauriers-Varin, N., St-Yves, M. & Lussier, P. (2009). Confessing their crime: Factors influencing the offender's decision to confess during police interrogation. Paper submitted.

Evans, R. (1993). *The conduct of police interviews with juveniles*. Royal Commission on Criminal Justice Research Report No. 8. London: HMSO.

Eysenck, H. J. & Gudjonsson, G. H. (1989). *The causes and cures of criminality*. New York and London: Plenum Press.

FPT Heads of Prosecutions Committee Working Group (2004). *Report on the Prevention of Miscarriages of Justice*. http://canada.justice.gc.ca/fr/dept/pub/hop/index.html, accessed 8 December 2006.

Gordon, N. J. & Fleisher, W. L. (2002). *Effective interviewing and interrogation techniques*, New York: Academic Press.

Gouldner, A. W. (1960). The norm of reciprocity: A preliminary statement. *American Sociological Review, 25*, 161–178.

Gudjonsson, G. H. (1992). *The psychology of interrogations, confessions and testimony*. Chichester: John Wiley & Sons.

Gudjonsson, G. H. (2003). *The psychology of interrogations and confessions. A handbook*. Chichester: John Wiley & Sons.

Gudjonsson, G. H. & Bownes, I. (1992). The reasons why suspects confess during custodial interrogation: data for Northern Ireland. *Medicine, Science and the Law, 32*, 204–212.

Gudjonsson, G. H. & Petursson, H. (1991). Custodial interrogation: Why do suspects confess and how does it relate to their crime, attitude and personality? *Personality and Individual Differences, 12*, 295–306.

Gudjonsson, G. H. & Sigurdsson, J. F. (1999). The Gudjonsson Confession Questionnaire – Revised (GCQ-R): Factor structure and its relationship with personality. *Personality and Individual Differences, 27*, 953–968.

Gudjonsson, G. H., Sigurdsson, J. F., Bragason, O. O., Einarsson, E. & Valdimarsdottir, E. B. (2004a). Confessions and denials and the relationship with personality. *Legal and Criminological Psychology, 9*, 121–133.

Gudjonsson, G. H., Sigurdsson, J. F. & Einarsson, E. (2004b). The role of personality in relation to confessions and denials. *Psychology, Crime & Law, 10*, 125–135.

Holmberg, U. & Christianson, S. A. (2002). Murderers' and sexual offenders' experiences of police interviews and their inclination to admit or deny crimes. *Behavioral Sciences and the Law, 20*, 31–45.

Home Office Circular 22/1992. *Principles of investigative interviewing.* London: Home Office.

Horowitz, M. W. (1956). The psychology of confession. *Journal of Criminal Law, Criminology and Police Science, 47*, 197–204.

Horvath, F. & Meesig, R. (1996). The criminal investigation process and the role of forensic evidence: A review of empirical findings. *Journal of Forensic Sciences, 40*, 963–969.

Inbau, F. E., Reid, J. E., Buckley, J. P. & Jayne, B. C. (2001). *Criminal interrogation and confessions,* 4th edition. Gaithersburg, MD: Aspen.

Irving, B. & McKenzie, I. K. (1989). *Police interrogation: The effects of the Police and Criminal Evidence Act.* London: HMSO.

Kalbfleisch, P. J. (1994). The language of detecting deceit. *Journal of Language and Social Psychology, 13*, 459–496.

Kassin, S. M. & Gudjonsson, G. H. (2004). The psychology of confessions: A review of the literature and issues. *Psychological Science in the Public Interest, 5*, 33–67.

Kassin, S. M. & Wrightsman, L. S. (1985). Confession evidence. In S. M. Kassin & L. S. Wrightsman (Eds.), *The Psychology of Evidence and Trial Procedures.* London: Sage, 67–94.

Leiken, L. S. (1970). Police interrogation in Colorado: The implementation of Miranda. *Denver Law Journal, 47*, 1–53.

Leo, R. A. (1996). Inside the interrogation room. *The Journal of Criminal Law and Criminology, 86*, 266–303.

Macdonald, J. & Michaud, D. (1987). *The confession. Interrogation and criminal profiles for police officers.* Denver, CO: Apache Press.

Mitchell, B. (1983). Confessions and police interrogation of suspects. *Criminal Law Review,* September, 596–604.

Moston, S., Stephenson, G. M. & Williamson, T. M. (1992). The effects of case characteristics on suspect behaviour during police questioning. *British Journal of Criminology, 32*, 23–40.

Neubauer, D. W. (1974). Confessions in Prairie City: Some causes and effects. *Journal of Criminal Law and Criminology, 65*, 103–112.

Pearse, J. & Gudjonsson, G. H. (1996). Police interviewing techniques at two South London police stations. *Psychology, Crime and Law, 3*, 63–74.

Pearse, J., Gudjonsson, G. H., Clare, I. C. H. & Rutter, S. (1998). Police interviewing and psychological vulnerabilities: predicting the likelihood of a confession. *Journal of Community and Applied Social Psychology, 8*, 1–21.

Phillips, C. & Brown, D. (1998). *Entry into the criminal justice system: A survey of police arrests and their outcomes*. London: Home Office.

Pitt, S. E., Spiers, E. M., Dietz, P. E. & Dvoskin, J.A. (1999). Preserving the integrity of the interview: The value of videotape. *Journal of Forensic Sciences, 44* (6), 1287–1291.

Reik, T. (1973). *Le besoin d'avouer: psychanalyse du crime et du châtiment.* Paris: Payot.

Shepherd, E. (1991). Ethical interviewing. *Policing, 7,* 42–60.

Sigurdsson, J. F. & Gudjonsson, G. H. (1994). Alcohol and drug intoxication during police interrogation and the reasons why suspects confess to the police. *Addiction, 89,* 985–997.

Singh K. K. & Gudjonsson G. H. (1992). The vulnerability of adolescent boys to interrogative pressure: an experimental study. *Journal of Forensic Psychiatry, 3,* 167–170.

Softley, P. (1980). *Police interrogation: An observational study in four police stations.* Home Office Research Study No. 61. London: HMSO.

St-Yves, M. (2002). Interrogatoire de police et crime sexuel: profil du suspect collabo-rateur. *Revue internationale de criminologie et de police technique et scientifique.* 81–96.

St-Yves, M. (2004a). La psychologie de l'aveu. In M. St-Yves & J. Landry (Eds.), *Psychologie des entrevues d'enquête, de la recherche à la pratique* (pp. 31–52). Cowansville, Québec: Yvon Blais.

St-Yves, M. (2004b). Les facteurs associés à la confession: la recherche empirique. In M. St-Yves & J. Landry (Eds.), *Psychologie des entrevues d'enquête, de la recherche à la pratique* (pp. 53–71). Cowansville, Québec: Yvon Blais.

St-Yves, M. (2004c). La psychologie du suspect. In M. St-Yves & J. Landry (Eds.), *Psychologie des entrevues d'enquête, de la recherche à la pratique* (pp. 73–84). Cowansville, Québec: Yvon Blais.

St-Yves, M. (2004d). L'aveu chez les auteurs de crimes sexuels. In M. St-Yves & J. Landry (Eds.), *Psychologie des entrevues d'enquête, de la recherche à la pratique* (pp. 85–103). Cowansville, Québec: Yvon Blais.

St-Yves, M. (2006a). The psychology of rapport: five basic rules. In T. Williamson, *Investigative interviewing: Rights, research, regulation* (pp. 87–106). Cullompton: Willan Publishing.

St-Yves, M. (2006b). Confessions by sex offenders. In T. Williamson, *Investigative interviewing: Rights, Research, Regulation* (pp. 107–122). Cullompton: Willan Publishing.

St-Yves, M. (in press). Police interrogation in Canada: From the quest for con-fession to the search for the truth. In B. Milne, S. Savage & T. Williamson, *International Developments in Investigative Interviewing,* Cullompton: Willan Publishing.

St-Yves, M. & Landry, J. (2004). La pratique de l'interrogatoire de police. In M. St-Yves & J. Landry (Eds.), *Psychologie des entrevues d'enquête: de la recherche à la pratique.* Cowansville, Québec: Yvon Blais.

St-Yves, M. & Lavallée, P. R. (2002). *L'interrogatoire vidéo: État de la situation à la Sûreté du Québec.* Direction conseil et développement en enquêtes criminelles. Sûreté du Québec. Document inédit.

St-Yves, M. & Tanguay, M. (2009). The psychology of interrogation: A quest for a confession or a quest for the truth? In M. St-Yves & M. Tanguay (Eds), *The psychology of criminal investigations: The search for the truth* (pp. 9–40). Toronto: Thomson Carswell.

St-Yves, M., Tanguay, M. & Crépault, D. (2004). La psychologie de la relation: cinq règles de base. In M. St-Yves & J. Landry (Eds.), *Psychologie des entrevues d'enquête: de la recherche à la pratique* (pp. 135–153). Cowansville, Québec: Yvon Blais.

Ury, W. (1991). *Getting past no: Negotiating with difficult people.* New York: Bantam Books.

Wald, M., Ayres, R., Hess, D. W., Schantz, M. & Whitebread, C. H. (1967). Interrogations in New Haven. The impacts of Miranda. *Yale Law Journal, 76,* 1519–1648.

Walsh, D. P. J. (1982). Arrest and interrogation: Northern Ireland 1981. *Journal of Law and Society, 9,* 37–62.

Walters, S. B. (1995). *Principles of kinesic interview and interrogation.* New York: CRC.

Williamson, T. M. (1990). *Strategic changes in police interrogation: an examination of police and suspect behaviour in the Metropolitan Police in order to determine the effects of new legislation, technology and organizational policies.* Unpublished PhD thesis, University of Kent.

Williamson, T. M. (1993). From interrogation to investigative interviewing: Strategic trends in police questioning. *Journal of Community and Social Psychology, 3,* 89–99.

Williamson, T. M. (2006). Investigative interviewing and human rights in the war on terrorism. T. Williamson (Ed.), *Investigative interviewing: Rights, research, regulation* (pp. 3–22). Cullompton: Willan Publishing.

Zulawski, D. & Wicklander, D. (1992). *Practical aspects of interview and interrogation.* New York: CRC.

Cases

R v Oickle [2000] 2 R.C.S.3.
R v Rothman [1981] 1 R.C.S. 640.

Chapter Two

A Typology of Denial Strategies by Suspects in Criminal Investigations

Stephen Moston

Department of Psychology, James Cook University

and

Geoffrey M. Stephenson

Department of Psychology, London South Bank University

In this chapter we propose a typology of denials made by suspects in police interviews. This is an important forensic topic, first, because police officers need to consider in advance of an interview the likely strategies that might be adopted by those who intend to deceive them concerning their involvement in a criminal offence. Can officers nullify such attempts before the suspect commits to such a strategy? How should they respond if such a denial is not averted? Secondly, and perhaps more important still, is the ability to distinguish between the denials of those intent on deceit and those who are genuinely innocent of any involvement. Should all denials be treated with scepticism? Or should all denials be taken at face value pending discovery of contradictory evidence? Should denials be welcomed on the grounds that evidence will subsequently be used to prove the intention to deceive? Or should denials best be circumvented by adroit questioning, in the hope that a confession will subsequently be elicited?

We shall see that experts are not at one on these issues (e.g. Gudjonsson, 2006) and, moreover, that there is a dearth of evidence about the form that denials take generally. Before examining the questions further, we shall describe

Handbook of Psychology of Investigative Interviewing: Current Developments and Future Directions
Edited by Ray Bull, Tim Valentine and Tom Williamson
© 2009 John Wiley & Sons, Ltd.

briefly what is known about the opposite stance taken by suspects: confession to the crime in connection with which they are being interviewed.

Confessions in the police station

Since the introduction of the Police and Criminal Evidence Act 1984 (PACE) in the United Kingdom there have been several major observational studies, with sample sizes in excess of 500 cases, on police interviewing styles and responses to accusations of criminal wrongdoing by suspects in criminal inquiries by police officers (e.g., Moston, Stephenson & Williamson, 1992; Baldwin, 1993; Moston & Stephenson, 1993; Bucke & Brown, 1997; Phillips & Brown, 1998; Bucke, Street & Brown, 2000). In addition, there have been several smaller-scale studies focusing on specific populations (e.g., juveniles; Evans, 1993) or focused research issues (e.g., the impact of psychological vulnerabilities on confessions; Pearse, Gudjonsson, Clare & Rutter, 1998).

In each of these studies the percentage of suspects who confessed during interviews has been reasonably consistent, ranging from a low of 55% (Moston *et al.*, 1992; Phillips & Brown, 1998; Bucke *et al.*, 2000) to a high of 62% (Baldwin, 1993), with other studies falling within this narrow range (e.g. Bucke & Brown, 1997: 58%; Pearse *et al.*, 1998: also 58%; Moston & Stephenson, 1993: 59%; Evans, 1993: also 59%).

Surprisingly, there have been few comparable studies in other countries. In the USA there have only been two comparable attempts to quantify confession rates. Cassell & Hayman (1996) reported that 42% of suspects made confessions or admissions, while Leo (1996) suggested the confession/admission rate reached 64%. In Australia, Dixon & Travis (2007) provide data on two separate samples of cases, with one sample giving a confession/admission rate of 76%, while in the second sample the rate was lower, at 46%.

International comparisons are fraught with difficulties, as the sample sizes are often relatively small (e.g., 87 cases in Dixon & Travis's second sample) and different sampling techniques are used (e.g., Cassell and Haymann's study used a non-random sample). We must also recognize that police officers in different jurisdictions may be more or less scrupulous about whom they accuse of a particular crime. A similar variation may also occur between different forces in the UK. Indeed, there have been well-documented cases of remarkably high clear-up rates in some forces, suggesting that crimes 'taken into consideration' (TICs), to which suspects have obligingly confessed, have boosted the percentage of successful prosecutions (Gill, 1987).

Denials in the police station

Most suspects who do not confess, in one way or another deny their culpability. Others may remain silent or otherwise evade answering directly, although in the UK the numbers so doing may have decreased since a revised caution was introduced warning of the dangers should their silence subsequently be used to indicate guilty concealment. Existing data on the percentage of suspects who deny are harder to interpret, with some studies either failing to mention the denial rate altogether, or collapsing data (including denials, evasion and use of the right to silence) into a single category, perhaps better described as a 'non-confession' rate. Such problems notwithstanding, studies suggest that in the UK between 35% (Moston & Stephenson, 1993) and 45% (Phillips & Brown, 1998) of suspects deny involvement or do not confess.

Data from pre-PACE studies in the UK show a similar pattern, with Softley, Brown, Forde, Mair & Moxon (1980) reporting a denial rate of 35%, and Irving (1980) a rate of 42%, suggesting that changes in police questioning practices following the introduction of PACE and the mandatory tape-recording of interviews had little impact on this particular metric of interviewing effectiveness.

Why do suspects confess?

Moston *et al.* (1992) analysed over 1,000 cases in the UK in which suspects were interviewed by police officers. In addition to collecting detailed records of the cases through a questionnaire attached to custody records, they also analysed over 500 taped records of interviews. Their research found clear links between three case characteristics (strength of evidence, offence severity and legal advice) and the outcome of interviews. It was suggested that police interviewing techniques played a relatively minor role in influencing confessions. There were two reasons for this conclusion.

First, most admissions were freely volunteered at the outset of interviews and those suspects who denied an accusation at the outset of an interview typically maintained this denial throughout, even in the face of seemingly incontrovertible proof of their guilt. A similar pattern of results was found by Baldwin (1993), with only nine suspects from a sample of 600 showing a response shift from denial to admission during the course of questioning.

The second and perhaps most surprising observation was that police interviewing skills were not greatly in evidence. Only a limited range of questioning techniques was employed, and interviewers often appeared to be more nervous than the suspects they were questioning. Many officers concluded interviews at the first sign of resistance from suspects, whilst others doggedly continued with repetitive, stereotyped questioning or assertions.

Such findings run contrary to the popular myth concerning police interviews with suspects. It is probably the case that most people believe that a typical interrogation begins with an initial denial from the suspect, but that by skilled questioning the interviewer reveals the inconsistencies in that person's statement or its conflict with other evidence. When confronted with the high-lighted contradictions, the suspect recants their denial and makes a full confession. Such a dazzling sequence does occur in rare instances, but it is probably not that common.

Directions in research on police interviewing

Much psychological research on the process of police interviews with suspects has focused on how the inappropriate use of interviewing tactics can result in false confessions from innocent suspects (e.g., Kassin & Gudjonsson, 2004; Kassin, 2005). The impact of the same interviewing tactics on the decision-making of guilty suspects has largely been neglected. One reason for this stands out above all others: a number of those who deny their involvement in criminal activity are likely to be telling the truth, with the consequence that routine employment of deception, 'minimization', threats, false promises and other devious practices may result in an unacceptable number of erroneous convictions; this is especially problematic given the weight that has normally been accorded to confession evidence. Interviewing (with the aim of securing a confession) can all too easily be used as a shortcut to a search for independent evidence. Police officers are not often in the position of having undeniable proof of guilt before suspects are interviewed. If they have such evidence, then a confession is not essential but merely convenient. In fact, by the same token, interviews will sometimes be used by police in order to eliminate from further inquiry those suspects against whom there is little evidence or about whom there is, rightly or wrongly, a presumption of innocence.

The current emphasis on instructions to police officers in the UK is to interview to establish 'the truth' and to make no prior assumptions regarding guilt or innocence. In principle, suspects are to be treated as witnesses, albeit potentially, but not necessarily, as witnesses to their own guilt. The truth or falsity of denials, whatever form these denials may take, will be evaluated according to their plausibility when considered in relation to other evidence. If rigorously followed, this ethical, ideal route to justice will ensure a minimum of false convictions. However, police time is not unlimited, and investigations to prove the truth of a confession obtained in response to skilled questioning will undoubtedly be more speedily concluded than those made without assistance from the suspect. Research into the veracity or evidence value of different categories of denial may be of considerable value to the effectiveness and overall integrity of police interviewing.

The emphasis on avoiding false confessions has such clear importance for civil liberties that the current emphasis on the need to avoid prior assumptions of guilt needs little justification. The complexity of establishing the effectiveness of specific interviewing tactics on suspects, be they guilty or innocent, undoubtedly exerts a powerful influence on research design. Farrington (1981: 100) offered the following reasons why it was almost impossible to identify the effects of varying interrogation styles on suspect behaviour because of variations in other variables.

The relationship between style of interrogation and likelihood of confessing could be investigated in real life in a correlational study. Such a study could show that one style was associated with a significantly higher likelihood of confessing than another. However, it would be impossible to attribute this difference to the style variable in such a study, because of all the uncontrolled variables. For example, one style might be preferred by certain police officers who were more effective in inducing confessions for some reason unconnected with style; or one style might be used with certain suspects who might be more likely to confess than others (again for reasons unconnected with style). Only an experiment can isolate the variable of style and demonstrate unambiguously that it influences confessing.

Experiments have indeed established that 'confessing' can be increased by interviewing tactics, although, unfortunately, at the risk of increasing the false confession rate. For example, subsequent experimental research on police interviewing has shown that certain well-used tactics, such as minimization (Kassin & McNall, 1991), can increase the number of people who will falsely confess to a range of minor transgressions they have not committed. While such research is interesting, it often neglects to consider the potential impact of such tactics on guilty suspects. Further, an unwritten assumption seems to be that guilty suspects are relatively homogeneous and that a given tactic will be equally effective no matter what variations in offence (e.g., property offences vs. person offences), suspect (e.g., presence or absence of prior criminal history), interviewer (e.g., male vs. female) or evidence (e.g., eyewitness vs. fingerprint evidence) might exist. This is an important oversight as such variables can have a powerful influence on the attitudes and assumptions of interviewing officers. For example, Stephenson & Moston (1993) found that prior criminal history and strength of evidence predicted whether or not suspects were assumed to be guilty prior to questioning in the police station. However, an experimental study by Weber (2007) involving retired police officers found that only strength of evidence, and not criminal history, predicted presumptions of guilt.

It follows that differing assumptions about guilt or innocence may have a bearing on the choice of interviewing strategy. Experimental research by Kassin, Goldstein & Savitsky (2003), using mock interrogators and suspects, has shown that the presumption of guilt has a strong influence on the types of questions interrogators choose, with presumed guilt prompting more aggressive interrogations, which constrained the responses of the suspects. Similarly, Weber (2007) found that presumption of guilt was linked to the selection of confession-oriented tactics in mock interview plans developed by (retired) police officers.

A similar argument can be advanced for understanding a suspect's strategy during an interview. Variations in offence, suspect, interviewer or evidence might also be expected to influence how a suspect responds to an accusation, not simply in terms of the decision to confess, deny or say nothing, but also in the way in which the suspect denies. Truthful denials are of equally compelling interest as false confessions. Moreover, it would obviously help the police officer's pursuit of the guilty to be able to distinguish between those who are falsely denying and those who are merely being truthful. As a first step in understanding denials as a species of behaviour by suspects, we offer in this chapter an analysis of denials obtained in earlier studies of interrogation outcomes.

Denial strategies

What are the most common ways in which suspects deny accusations and what are the characteristics and motives of the suspects who utilize each of these 'denial strategies'? A central theme in this chapter is the way in which police officers react to denials and the likely implications of each denial strategy on the perceived credibility of the suspect. By perceived credibility we refer to the officer's assumption that the suspect is telling the truth or lying. That is, a denial is either accepted as the statement of an innocent person or as a lie put forward by someone trying to evade prosecution. Of course, a suspect may genuinely have a different perception of the content or significance of their behaviour from that of the officer. In many instances a denial in the police interviewing suite is akin to the alcoholic's denial of his or her lack of control over drinking. In such an instance it can be said of the suspect's behaviour, as of the alcoholics, that 'Denial is not lying. It is actually a perceptual incapacity – the most primitive of the psychological defences' (Thombs, 1999: 69).

In the criminal case the misperception may have been at the time of the event, as of the dangerous driver who is convinced they looked carefully before pulling out into the path of another vehicle, or the violent offender who misreads as provocation the perfectly reasonable observations the victim made about his conduct. Equally, as occurs in some sexual offences, a belief in their essential innocence may be the product of false premises about what constitutes an offence, or even disbelief that they would be capable of perpetrating such harm to another. Shame and anger may certainly motivate the drinker labelled an alcoholic to reject the help offered, and those motivations may well motivate the suspect labelled a rapist, for example, to deny the accusation.

Thombs goes on to describe the dangers of directly confronting the alcoholic with the reality of their situation: 'The use of confrontative procedures to break down the denial may in many situations have the unintended effect of actually strengthening it' (*ibid.*: 70).

The 'truth' is an elusive and negotiable interpretation of events; the difficulties of assuming otherwise will be discussed later. For the moment we will assume that officers are naturally inclined to assume that telling the truth on the one hand, and lying on the other, are mutually distinct categories, regardless of the oversimplifications this distinction introduces and regardless of the fact that this assumption may well be tactically inept.

There is currently a fundamental difference in attitude between different police jurisdictions towards the desirability and significance of denials of involvement in an offence by suspects. In view of this it is surprising that very little is known about the ways in which suspects deny accusations. Some forces view denials as an important factor that is crucially important evidence for establishing guilt or innocence, depending on their plausibility in relation to the evidence. Others seem to assume that denials are invariably best treated as potentially supporting false alibis. Either way, it seems there would be merit in preparing for an interview in such a way as to anticipate the types of denials (or alibis) that both an innocent and a guilty suspect might put forward. For example, in Australia the New South Wales Police (2005) are taught to ask questions to elicit full denials before introducing evidence such as fingerprints (there are no data to confirm or refute the actual use of such tactics). A similar approach is used in The Netherlands (van der Sleen, 2006), where the emphasis is on getting the suspect to give a detailed statement that would prevent a guilty suspect from rejecting the implication of the evidence in the case, whilst allowing innocent suspects the opportunity to explain how they have come to be under suspicion. This approach to interviewing is very different from the approaches seen in countries such as the USA, where the ever-popular Reid technique holds that denials by the suspect are to be avoided (see Inbau, Reid, Buckley & Jayne, 2001) in the interests of securing a presumably truthful confession. In both approaches, however, it is apparent that an analysis of 'denial strategies', potentially characterized according to their use by deceptive or by honest (even if mistaken) suspects, would inform the investigation and, we would hope, facilitate procedural justice.

One study that has explored the different verbal (and nonverbal) strategies employed by truth-tellers and liars was conducted by Hartwig, Granhag & Strömwall (2007). In this study mock suspects, role playing either guilty or innocent suspects, were interviewed by trainee police officers. The study found that liars used a series of strategies to appear credible. These included appearing to be calm and relaxed; telling the truth as much as possible; firmly denying guilt; avoiding incriminating details by denying having seen key items; pretending to be innocent; and being nice and pleasant. In another experimental study by the same authors (Strömwall, Hartwig & Granhag, 2006), during mock interrogations truth-tellers and liars differed in terms of their denial strategy, with liars favouring a 'keep it simple strategy'.

In Hartwig *et al.* (2007), and in research by Vrij (2006), truth-tellers and liars were also found to exhibit different nonverbal behaviours. Such results indicate that deceptive suspects are likely to enter into interrogations with a diverse set of strategies which may well set them apart from those who are telling what they believe to be the truth. While the above studies featured mock suspects, there is no reason to believe that suspects in real cases would be any less proactive.

A typology of denial strategies

The following descriptions of denial strategies are derived from a diverse range of available sources, including over 100 tape-recordings of interviews from the UK, which were supplied to the authors by colleagues from a number of UK police services, sometimes as part of wider research studies on police interviewing; interview transcripts from Australia and the United States, also supplied to the authors by police officers; and court transcripts that were available in the public domain (mainly from the UK and Australia). The one common element in each case was that during an interview in a police station, the suspect denied committing an offence. As this was a diverse set of data no attempt to quantify the frequency of each strategy was attempted. Subsequent research using representative samples of cases would be required to address that issue accurately.

All records of interviews have been anonymized and the participants labelled as 'interviewer' and 'suspect' (except in public domain cases). The approach here is primarily descriptive, with an emphasis on illustrating the typical characteristics of a range of denial strategies. Inevitably, we cannot say with certainty to what extent strategies are characteristic of suspects with either deceptive or honest intent. We do not have details of the subsequent history of the cases, who was charged, prosecuted and found guilty, as against those whose cases were not pursued and who dropped out of the system at one or other stage, for whatever reasons. Such research is needed, and when conducted will be guided by the categorization of denial strategies outlined in this study. We shall, however, where it seems justified, comment on the plausibility of ascribing one or another strategy to deceptive or honest intent, and comment on the anticipated response of interviewers to employment of the strategies in varying circumstances.

Denial strategies can first be classified into one of two broad typologies: passive and active. A *passive denial* is one in which the suspect denies the accusation but does not provide any exculpatory detail. An *active denial* does include exculpatory detail.

Passive denials

Simple denial of charge.   The denial of charge, or a simple denial, is the most elementary way in which a person can challenge evidence or refute an allegation, as in:

Interviewer: You were then seen to put the items in your bag.
Suspect: No.

The suspect does not support the statement or offer an alternative version of events. Instead, he simply offers a short statement ('No', 'That's wrong',

'You're mistaken', 'I didn't do it, all right?' etc.) rejecting the interviewer's assertion. The simple denial is characterized by a lack of elaboration on the part of the suspect. No alternative explanation of the facts is offered, nor is there any attempt to challenge the evidence in a case (e.g., a witness statement). This particular strategy has been seen in several high-profiles cases, such as the serial murderer Harold Shipman.

Interviewer: The letters in the will were all typed on your Brother typewriter. Can you account for that?

Shipman: No.

...

Interviewer: Can I put it directly to you, doctor, that you forged; you produced the letters of this will from your typewriter in the hope of benefiting from Mrs Grundy's estate.

Shipman: Is that a question or a statement?

Interviewer: I put it to you that that is the case.

Shipman: That is not the case.

Interviewer: I put it to you that you are responsible, you are the author of the letters and you manufactured the will. You forged the signatures.

Shipman: And I am saying I didn't do it.

Another high-profile case to feature this defence was employed in the trial of the child murderer Roy Whiting. Timothy Langdale QC, prosecuting, questioned the likelihood of Whiting being the 'unfortunate victim of an extraordinary accident'. Specifically, he questioned how it was possible that hair from a victim could have dislodged from an exhibit package taken from the victim's home and then got into a bag containing a red sweatshirt belonging to Whiting, where it was subsequently found.

Langdale: The alternative is that barring that extraordinary accident it can only mean one thing. ... You were the man who kidnapped, you were the man who killed that child and you were the man who buried her body. That is the only other alternative, is it not?

Whiting: It was not me.

According to Inbau *et al.* (2001), the credibility of simple denials is undermined further when suspects use qualifications such as 'I honestly wouldn't do that' or 'I swear I didn't do this'. It has, however, to be recognized that evaluation of the plausibility of simple denials has to be considered in the light of good evidence to the contrary. Without such evidence it would certainly be rash always to interpret simple denials as evidence of dishonesty.

Regardless of evidence, many interviewers become hostile when confronted with such denials. This may be due, in part, to surprise. The interviewer, having entered the interview confident of the suspect's guilt, encounters a denial that goes against their expectations, and frustration may lead to annoyance. Denial in the face of evidence is especially likely to be interpreted by the interviewer as stubbornness, or on occasion as stupidity on the part of the suspect.

Bewilderment: denial of knowledge. Some suspects will claim that they 'don't know anything' about the offence under discussion and so they cannot answer any questions. This particular strategy has a long history, with the Gospel according to Mark (14: 66–8) featuring the following exchange.

> As Peter was in the courtyard below, one of the maids of the high priest came, and seeing Peter warming himself, she looked at him, and said, 'You were also with the Nazarene, Jesus!' But he denied it, saying, 'I neither know, nor understand what you are saying.'

On some occasions the apparently exasperated suspect may attempt to convey a feeling of indifference or boredom with the accusation and questioning process. Others may state that they are keen to help: 'If only I could.' This enthusiasm might be coupled with a thirst for information, with the suspect eager to hear all about the crime.

For the guilty suspect this strategy no doubt represents an attempt to mimic the reactions of an innocent person. Unfortunately, it is always going to be difficult to determine whether a person is being truthful or deceptive. Independent evidence is required, which the suspect, if innocent, may well offer to provide. As with some of the other strategies described here, the suspect is trying to opt out of questioning, and this may or may not be justified. Suspicions may rightly be entertained, however, if, as frequently happens, suspects preclude the possibility that they could answer questions about any aspect of the incident under investigation and are unable to give a verifiable alternative account.

This type of denial is especially likely to reduce the credibility of the suspect when there is some evidence to implicate them. Then, the complete absence of any knowledge of the relevant incident or event will be deemed deeply suspicious by the interviewer.

Denial of perception. On some occasions, particularly those in which several suspects are thought to have acted together, say in a theft or assault, the (guilty) suspects will try to give the impression that even though they were present at the incident (which is probably incontestable – a key determinant of this strategy), they were only on the periphery of events, and as for whatever it is that the police are interested in, didn't see it. Any event which might implicate them or their accomplices will have occurred while they were 'looking the other way' or were 'out of earshot'. As with some of the other challenges, the suspects are unlikely to deny that the event occurred, merely that they did not see it. This stratagem may also be characteristic of an onlooker who wishes to protect the perpetrator of the offence.

Either way, the clear intention here is to divert the interviewer from pressing the suspect to explain what happened. By claiming not to have seen anything the suspect avoids the risk of lying. Claiming to have missed the event, the suspect is attempting to opt out of the process of questioning. Each question put by the interviewer will be met with a uniform 'I don't know' response.

A variation on this strategy is for suspects to claim that they were too drunk (or drugged) to remember anything that occurred. As with the other form of this type of challenge, this is often an attempt to opt out of questioning. The suspect will probably accept any suggestions from the interviewer, including admitting that 'I may have done it – if only I could remember'. The interviewer needs to be wary in such cases of listing the evidence and accepting the suspect's simple acquiescence.

Guilty suspects who use this strategy have two possible motives. First, it serves as a prompt for the police interviewer to reveal any evidence that implicates them. This is always a useful strategy for suspects, who can then decide whether or not to make any admissions depending on the strength of evidence against them. Second, it is an attempt to justify a criminal act as a consequence of alcohol/drugs, not criminal intent, that is, the offence was almost an 'accident'.

Denial of motivation.   Some suspects challenge on the grounds that the offence details do not fit because they are, 'just not my style', as in, 'I've done karate. If I'd hit that person they'd never get up'. Similar types of appeal might also be heard in burglary cases: 'You know me. I only pinch what I can carry.'

A common theme here is that the suspect is appealing to the interviewer for understanding, asking to be believed. Crucially, in such instances, suspects do not say that they did not commit the action; rather, that it simply does not fit their usual pattern, it is not in their character, dubious though their character admittedly is. This may well be most commonly used by those with considerable previous experience of police questioning. The suspect cleverly avoids directly responding to the accusation with an outright denial, giving the interviewer the chance to draw the right conclusion.

A variation on this strategy involves suspects challenging the accusation on the grounds that they would not have committed the offence because it 'simply wasn't worth it'. For example, the amount of money that could have been taken would have been very small, or in the case of goods, they would not have been worth taking. On some occasions the suspect may make reference to the possible punitive consequences that could have arisen: 'It wouldn't be worth going to prison for the sake of a few quid.' There is a further variation on this strategy, outlined by Inbau *et al.* (2001) in their description of the 'specific denial' strategy of a suspect who says, 'I didn't shoot her with a Colt. 357.'

Active denials

Denial of offence.   Seemingly a common defence in cases in which children have alleged that they had been sexually abused has been the claim that it was 'All a figment of their imagination'. In fact, this challenge is common in many sexual offences, even those in which adults are the accusers. It is clearly an attempt to undermine the credibility of the witness.

Interviewers tend to counter this defence by asking something like 'So you're saying this girl made all this up?' This may force the suspect to attack the credibility of the witness, either directly and personally or in terms of broad generalizations, such as 'Kids always make up stuff like that, don't they?'

The other common response to the interviewer's question is 'No, I'm not saying that', thus inviting an accusation of being self-contradictory, but probably designed to play for time in order to keep their defensive options open. The attempt to force the suspect's hand by asking something along the lines of, 'Then what are you saying? Is she a liar or isn't she?' is unlikely to secure an admission and may play into the suspect's hands, if, as does happen, the interviewer asks the suspect to explain why that person might bear a grudge or have a reason to lie. Although the suspect's explanation for the accuser's lack of credibility may be at a general level, as with the example 'Kids always make up stuff like that', a specific explanation based on past exchanges between the suspect and accuser are more likely to impress. The latter is likely to be perceived as more credible.

Denial of interpretation.   Some suspects suggest that the police have mis-interpreted an innocent action. Although on many occasions this could well be the case, this strategy is rarely used in a way that conveys credibility. Suspects sometimes appear unsure of the motives for their own actions and fail to offer a coherent explanation of events. In the following example, following an assault, a person has been arrested while running from the police:

Interviewer: Why were you running?
Suspect: Well, everyone else started running and I thought they were running for a train or something, so I ran as well, then one of your lot grabbed me.

One obvious problem here is the 'or something' that is included in the explanation. The suspect may well be hedging, that is keeping their options open in order to avoid presenting a story that might conflict with the account of any others who may also have been arrested. On occasions, interviewers may find it almost impossible not to contain their disbelief when this strategy is used, as is illustrated in the following example.

Interviewer:	But why do you think that he [the witness] would want to accuse you of a serious offence?
Suspect:	I don't know.
Interviewer:	The way you say it that you was walking along the street, next thing you know you was grabbed by a bloke who's got a knife and you haven't a clue what's going on.
Suspect:	I just really don't know. I don't know. I was baffled at the time, like all I was worried about was getting away from the knife, you know what I mean?
Interviewer:	Seems very strange. ... but you see, it just leaves that big gaping doubt. Why would a man want to accuse you of something you hadn't done ...
Suspect:	I don't know.
Interviewer:	... when you've never seen him before in your life?
Suspect:	I don't know. Perhaps he mistook me for someone. I don't know.

This type of denial probably reduces the credibility of the speaker. The suspect's statement contains so many hedges and ambiguities that it appears that his recall of the incident is especially poor. In practice, this style of denial will probably be interpreted as a lie, but certainly not necessarily deservedly.

Denial of causation.   Some suspects try to challenge facts, such as being found in possession of stolen goods, by suggesting that they did not know that the items were stolen and that they had borrowed them from a friend (thereby shifting the blame onto others). The suspect is not challenging the evidence itself, since that is likely to be incontestable; instead, they are challenging the assumptions that can be drawn from it, and in particular that they are guilty of an offence.

The purpose of this challenge is to divert attention from the suspect by drawing attention to another potential suspect, who may or may not be specified. One aspect of this challenge is that the suspect will probably be reluctant to directly accuse another person; often they are merely trying to raise the possibility that another person was involved. This challenge often loses credibility when the interviewer directly asks the suspect if the second person is the person responsible for the offence, as in the following example.

Suspect:	I didn't steal the tapes; I just borrowed them from Andy's house.
Interviewer:	But I've just told you they were stolen, so are you saying that Andy stole them?
Suspect:	Well, no, I'm not saying that.

Another classic scenario here would be 'I didn't steal it. I bought it from a man in the pub'. This strategy is low in credibility simply because it is intended to be vague (the man in the pub never has a name!) and thus difficult to verify. This denial strategy is often used as a direct consequence of police interviewing practices which place the suspect in a situation involving two undesirable options: accept the evidence or implicate a friend. If the latter course is chosen, the interviewer may have problems in deciding which of the suspects is truthful and which is deceptive.

A variation on this strategy is to invoke the hand of God:. 'I don't know how they got there' is a good illustration of this in relation to stolen goods. Here, the suspect suggests that the evidence against them (stolen property found in their possession) had mysteriously appeared and that they were even more surprised to find it than the police. There is no attempt to attribute any cause to this minor miracle, the police will not be accused of fabricating evidence (although some interviewers may feel this is being implied), nor will another person be implicated. It is as if the hand of God somehow intervened in the matter and placed the items there.

The key aspect of this denial strategy is the lack of any speculation about how the items came to be in the suspect's possession because, again, the guilty suspect will be reluctant to be tied down to a single explanation of events which might be discredited.

Presumed guilty

Officers in many countries tend to work on the premise that a good outcome of an interrogation is a confession (Stephenson & Moston, 1993; Weber, 2007), interviewing competence often being defined by the numbers of confessions elicited (Blair, 2005). This approach sets the scene for the possibility of false confessions, in that officers may adopt questioning techniques that coerce the suspect into retracting their earlier statement. Although, traditionally, officers are likely to interpret the retraction as justifying coercive techniques, UK judges have more recently taken a very different view. Confession evidence alone is unlikely to be persuasive, and confessions made under any kind of duress run a real risk of not being admitted in evidence (Williamson, 2006).

The current emphasis on the avoidance of false confessions reflects the great emphasis on the role played by police questioning techniques, specifically the psychological ploys adopted to manipulate the suspect's decision-making. For example, police questioning techniques are thought to be largely responsible for eliciting both coerced-compliant and coerced-internalized false confessions (see Kassin & Gudjonsson, 2004). This view has not been helped by the limited literature on police interviews with suspects (e.g., Inbau *et al.*, 2001), which tends to concentrate on how to overcome denials and elicit confessions. This emphasis remains prevalent in the USA and no doubt many other jurisdictions (Buckley, 2006).

Psychological research on the statements of child victims of sexual abuse has led to the development of techniques for analysing the accuracy of statements, such as criteria-based content analysis (for a review, see Vrij, 2005). The underlying assumption of these techniques is that the statements of a truthful child and a deceptive child are inherently different. Similar assumptions underlie police training in the detection of lie signs (e.g., Walkley, 1987). Lie signs are specific statements that are believed to be indicative of guilt. For example, a verbal lie sign would be a statement such as 'I hope my mother drops dead if I'm lying' or 'I swear on my kid's life'. Such statements, it is argued (e.g., Inbau *et al.*, 2001), are typically used by guilty suspects who overstate their innocence. Certain phrases may suggest deception because of their inherent lack of credibility, but they could also come from suspects with poor memories, or who were possibly trying to protect another person. It will also become apparent that certain forms of denial are sometimes a direct result of particular police questioning techniques.

Implicit in the notion of overstated innocence is the idea that guilty suspects protest too strongly. This assumes that an innocent person will protest their innocence at an optimal level. Such ideas lack any empirical evidence and are essentially 'words of wisdom' passed on by experienced investigators. Given that police officers are notoriously poor at detecting deceit, such statements can only be treated as spurious suggestions that are probably best avoided.

There are, however, a number of encouraging research developments on the detection of deception that encourage the expectation that greater understanding of the behaviour of suspects in response to accusations, and in particular variation in denial strategies, may contribute to the scientific analysis of deception (e.g. Frank, Yarbrough & Ekman, 2006). We shall conclude, however, with a consideration of how in practice police officers respond to denials by suspects.

Handling denials

One of the most obvious stumbling blocks for police officers when questioning a suspect is handling their challenges or denials. For police officers, it can be quite disconcerting to find that suspects do not immediately accept the seemingly obvious, namely, that they must be guilty. Many suspects challenge the evidence or deny the allegation, no matter how incontrovertible or incontestable it seems to the investigating officer. Police interviewers often appear to attribute denials to the stupidity or stubbornness of the suspect. A denial is met with a degree of disbelief reflecting the view that the suspect was just too stupid to accept that the evidence was clear-cut. On other occasions a denial is dismissed on the grounds that 'We just didn't have enough evidence'. That is, the interviewer would undoubtedly have obtained an admission if only they had gathered that bit more evidence. Finally, some interviewers may feel that they talked the suspect into a denial. The interview may have gone badly, with the interviewer failing to sound convincing or giving a false impression of the (strong) evidence against the suspect.

This chapter has shown that there is a wide range of strategies that suspects use when denying an allegation. Some strategies involve explicit denials, whilst others are more evasive, with some suspects willing to provide detailed answers to questions, whilst others will confine their replies to short, dismissive statements. One obvious problem that can arise during questioning is that when probing for additional verifying information, interviewers give the impression that they do not believe anything that the suspect has said. This may forestall any subsequent responses. If this occurs, the interviewer might make the unfortunate mistake of assuming that the person must have been lying.

Although it would be wrong to say that some forms of challenge by suspects are more likely to involve deception than others, it may be that interviewers perceive certain forms of reply as less credible than others. As a future hypothesis, it may be that certain types of denials, used in particular circumstances, are relatively unusual and thus predictive of credibility. Denial strategy might form one component for a form of statement validity analysis for adult suspects and contribute to the refinement of systems of interviewing analysis (e.g. Frank *et al.*, 2006).

References

Baldwin, J. (1993). Police interview techniques: Establishing truth or proof? *British Journal of Criminology, 33*, 325–352.

Blair, J. P. (2005). What do we know about interrogation in the United States? *Journal of Police and Criminal Psychology, 20*(2), 44–57.

Bucke, T. & Brown, D. (1997). *In police custody: Police powers and suspects' rights under the revised PACE codes of practice. A research and statistics directorate report.* London: Home Office.

Bucke, T., Street, R. & Brown, D. (2000). *The right of silence: The impact of the Criminal Justice and Public Order Act 1994. A research, development and statistics directorate report.* London: Home Office.

Buckley J. P. (2006). The Reid Technique of interviewing and interrogation. In T. Williamson (Ed.), *Investigative interviewing: Research, rights, regulation.* Cullompton: Willan Publishing.

Cassell, P. G. & Hayman, B. S. (1996). Police interrogation in the 1990s: An empirical study of the effects of Miranda. *UVLA Law Review, 43*, 839–931.

Dixon, D. & Travis, G. (2007). *Interrogating images: Audio-visually recorded police questioning of suspects.* Sydney: Sydney Institute of Criminology.

Evans, R. (1993). *The conduct of police interviews with juveniles.* Royal Commission on Criminal Justice Research Study No. 8. London: HMSO.

Farrington D. P. (1981). Psychology and police interrogation. *British Journal of Law and Society, 8*, 97–107.

Frank, M. G., Yarbrough, J. D. & Ekman, P. (2006). Investigative interviewing and the detection of deception. In T. Williamson (Ed.), *Investigative interviewing: Rights, research, regulation.* Cullompton: Willan Publishing.

Gill, P. (1987). Clearing up crime: The big 'con'. *Journal of Law and Society, 14,* 254–265.

Gudjonsson G. H. (2006). The psychology of interrogations and confessions. In T. Williamson (Ed.), *Investigative interviewing: Rights, research, regulation,* Cullompton: Willan Publishing.

Hartwig, M., Granhag, P. A. & Strömwall, L. A. (2007). Guilty and innocent suspects' strategies during police interrogations. *Psychology, Crime and Law, 13,* 213–227.

Inbau, F. E., Reid, J. E., Buckley, J. P. & Jayne, B. C. (2001). *Criminal interrogations and confessions.* 4th edition. Gaithersburg, MD: Aspen.

Irving, B. (1980). *Police interrogation: A case study of current practice.* Royal Commission on Criminal Procedure Research Study No. 2. London: HMSO.

Kassin, S. M. (2005). On the psychology of confessions. *American Psychologist, 60,* 215–228.

Kassin, S. M. & Gudjonsson, G. H. (2004). The psychology of confessions: A review of the literature and issues. *Psychological Science, 5,* 33–67.

Kassin, S. M. & McNall, K. (1991). Police interrogations and confessions: Communicating promises and threats by pragmatic implication. *Law and Human Behavior, 15,* 233–251.

Kassin, S. M., Goldstein, C. J. & Savitsky, K. (2003). Behavioral confirmation in the interrogation room: On the dangers of presuming guilt. *Law and Human Behavior, 27,* 187–203.

Leo, R. A. (1996). Inside the interrogation room. *Journal of Criminal Law and Criminology, 86,* 266–303.

Moston, S. & Stephenson, G. (1993). *The questioning and interviewing of suspects outside the police station.* Royal Commission on Criminal Justice Research Study No. 22. London: HMSO.

Moston, S., Stephenson, G. M. & Williamson, T. M. (1992). The effects of case characteristics on suspect behaviour during police questioning. *British Journal of Criminology, 32,* 23–40.

New South Wales Police (2005). *Code of practice for custody, rights, investigation, management and evidence (CRIME).* Sydney: NSW Police.

Pearse, J., Gudjonsson, G. H., Clare, I. C. H. & Rutter, S. (1998). Police interviewing and psychological vulnerabilities: Predicting the likelihood of a confession. *Journal of Community and Applied Social Psychology, 8,* 1–21.

Phillips, C. & Brown, D. (1998). *Entry into the criminal justice system: A survey of police arrests and their outcomes.* Home Office Research Study No. 185. London: HMSO.

Sleen, J. van der (2006). *A structured model for investigative interviewing of suspects.* Paper presented at 2nd International Investigative Interviewing Conference, University of Portsmouth, 6 July.

Softley, P., Brown, D., Forde, B., Mair, G. & Moxon, D. (1980). *Police interrogation: An observational study in four police stations.* Home Office Research Study No. 61. London: HMSO.

Stephenson, G. M. & Moston, S. (1993). Attitudes and assumptions of police officers when questioning criminal suspects. In E. Shepherd (Ed.), *Aspects of interviewing.* Issues in Criminological and Legal Psychology No. 18. Leicester: British Psychological Society.

Strömwall, L. A., Hartwig, M. & Granhag, P. A. (2006). To act truthfully: Nonverbal behaviour and strategies during a police interrogation. *Psychology, Crime and Law, 12,* 207–219.

Thombs, D. L. (1999). *Introduction to addictive behaviours.* London: Guilford Press.

Vrij, A. (2005). Criteria-based content analysis: A qualitative review of the first 37 studies. *Psychology, Public Policy, and Law, 11,* 3–41.

Vrij, A. (2006). Challenging interviewees during interviews: the potential effects on lie detection. *Psychology, Crime and Law, 12,* 193–206.

Walkley, J. (1987). *Police interrogation: A handbook for investigators.* London: Police Review Publishing Company.

Weber, Y. (2007). The effects of suspect history and strength of evidence on police interviewing styles. Master's thesis. Queensland: Department of Psychology, James Cook University.

Williamson, T. (2006). Towards greater professionalism: minimizing miscarriages of justice. In T. Williamson (Ed.), *Investigative interviewing: Research, rights, regulation.* Cullompton: Willan Publishing.

Statutes

Police and Criminal Evidence Act 1984

Chapter Three

A Structured Model for Investigative Interviewing of Suspects

Jannie van der Sleen

Kinterview, consulting agency on investigative interviewing

When interviewing a suspect the primary objective is to obtain a truthful statement while also ensuring that the suspect does not make a (partly) false confession. Numerous psychological studies have been conducted in recent years on the factors involved in this process.

Gudjonsson & Petursson (1991) conducted a self-report study in which suspects were asked about the circumstances that led them to confess. The study was repeated in Northern Ireland (Gudjonsson & Bownes, 1992) and Iceland (Sigurdsson & Gudjonsson, 1994; Gudjonsson & Sigurdsson, 1999). The researchers concluded that in most situations confessions were prompted by three types of facilitating factors:

- External pressure to confess: By this the researchers mean coercive interviewing techniques used by the police, police behaviour during the interview and the suspect's fear of being incarcerated.
- Internal pressure to confess: This occurs if the suspect feels guilty about the crime she or he has committed and wishes to relieve the sense of guilt by confessing to the crime.
- The suspect's perception of proof: Suspects believe that there is no point in denying their involvement because the police will ultimately be able to prove it.

Handbook of Psychology of Investigative Interviewing: Current Developments and Future Directions
Edited by Ray Bull, Tim Valentine and Tom Williamson
© 2009 John Wiley & Sons, Ltd.

The researchers involved in both studies found that the main factor (60%) that led suspects to confess was the strength of their belief in the evidence against them. It is interesting that this clearly has more to do with the suspect's *perception* of the evidence than with the objective evidence the police have against the suspect.

Another result that emerged from these self-report studies was that offenders' views and attitudes about their confession were related to the reasons they gave for giving it. Confessions that resulted primarily from external pressure were associated with the greatest amount of dissatisfaction and regret. The subjects in this group considered in retrospect that they had confessed far too readily and had not fully appreciated the consequences of their confession. They subsequently began to have bitter regrets about having made the confession. In contrast, the stronger the perceived proof and internal pressure to confess at the time of the police interrogation, the more satisfied the offenders remained about having confessed.

Bull & Milne (2004) reported that Soukara, Bull & Vrij (2002) studied the changes from denial to confession in real-life police interviews. They found that such changes were associated with:

- appropriate disclosure of evidence and the emphasizing of contradictions;
- repetitive questioning and the challenging of the suspect's account; and
- the interviewer demonstrating concern.

An information-gathering approach involves asking open questions and then pursuing a line of questioning based on the answers, while an accusatory approach involves levelling an accusation right from the start of the interview ('You took the wallet, didn't you?'). Vrij, Mann & Fisher (2006) found that information-gathering interviews were cognitively more challenging for the interviewees (i.e., had a higher cognitive load). Furthermore, information-gathering interviews also prompted more verbal and nonverbal cues to deceit (Vrij, 2006; Vrij, Mann & Fisher, 2006).

In light of his research, Vrij (2004) suggests several ways of increasing cognitive load during an interview. He recommends asking follow-up questions to get suspects to elaborate on what they said earlier. The follow-up questions are likely to go beyond the story that the suspect has prepared. Suspects who are lying will know that refusing to answer these questions is not (or is no longer) an option. Vrij also recommends asking time-related questions. If a suspect is using a script during the interview (which means that they are describing an incident that actually happened but not at the time they say it did, in which case the time of the incident is the only thing the suspect is lying about), questions that relate to the time of the incident increase the suspect's cognitive load. Vrij also recommends getting the suspect to repeat what they said earlier and to describe what happened in reverse order, or combining these two options and getting the suspect to repeat what they said earlier in reverse order. Vrij recommends that the interviewer can also instruct the suspect to maintain eye contact. A final recommendation involves the so-called strategic use of evidence (SUE), which means that the evidence against the suspect is not disclosed until a later stage in the interview. The interviewers ask information-gathering questions based on the evidence before disclosing the evidence to the suspect. A study of SUE by Hartwig, Granhag, Strömwall & Kronkvist (2006) compared interviews conducted by police officers trained in SUE techniques with interviews conducted by officers who were not trained in the techniques. The researchers found that suspects who were lying made statements that were more inconsistent with the evidence when interviewed by officers trained in SUE techniques. As a result, more of the SUE-trained interviewers (85.4%) were able to detect deceit than untrained interviewers (56.1%). A subsequent study (Hartwig, Granhag & Strömwall, 2007) revealed that SUE makes it easier to identify a guilty suspect without the suspect realizing that this is the case. It also makes it easier to identify innocent suspects, but in this case the innocent suspect is aware that the interviewer perceives him or her as innocent. The researchers believe that this is helpful in the interview process. Gaining further evidence that a suspect is guilty can be important in obtaining a truthful statement, but recognizing that a suspect is innocent is equally important in that it reduces the risk of a false confession being made in response to increasing pressure, because the innocent suspect's verbal and nonverbal behaviour is erroneously interpreted as an admission of guilt.

In the past false confessions have resulted in miscarriages of justice. In England the Guildford Four and the Birmingham Six are the two most famous cases in which this occurred. In the Netherlands this happened in the Schiedam Park murder case (Posthumus, 2005) and most probably in the Ina Post case (Israëls, 2004; Gosewehr & Timmerman, 2007) and in the Putten murder case (Blaauw, 2000). In Norway a 20-year-old youth falsely confessed to murdering his cousin (Gudjonsson, 2003). Several elements in the interviewer's attitude or behaviour have since been identified as factors that increase the risk of a false confession (Blaauw, 2000; Gudjonsson, 2003; Lassiter, 2004):

- Right from the start of the interview the interviewer is firmly convinced that the suspect is guilty. Once people form an initial belief or expectation, they unwittingly search for, interpret and create subsequent information in ways that confirm their beliefs, while overlooking contradictory data: confirmation bias and belief perseverance (Nisbett & Ross, 1980; Trope & Liberman, 1996; Nickerson, 1998; Lassiter, 2004). If an interviewer assumes from the outset that the suspect is guilty, he or she will inevitably interpret the suspect's behaviour and statements in that light, and will become increasingly convinced that the suspect is guilty. The interviewer's sole objective is to get the suspect to confess because this is consistent with the interviewer's conviction, which the interviewer believes to be the truth.

- Giving suspects positive feedback when they provide the information the interviewer wants and negative feedback when they provide information that the interviewer does not want. This risk factor stems from the interviewer's firm belief that the suspect is guilty of the crime being investigated. If the suspect makes statements that tend towards an admission of guilt, the interviewer reacts positively by saying things such as 'You see. You *do* know what happened'; 'At last, we're heading in the right direction. That way you'll be able to go home sooner'; 'Now we'll be able to wind this up in no time'. If the suspect makes statements that deny any involvement, this elicits a negative reaction, such as 'What a loser you are to sit there and lie like that'; 'If you had any guts, you'd say it like it was'; 'You'll be here all night at this rate'. Positive and negative feedback can also be expressed in the form of (not) allowing the suspect, for example, to have a break for refreshments.
- Getting the suspect to speculate and to make hypothetical statements: 'Suppose you had done it. How would you have gone about it?' Getting the suspect to explain how they would have committed the crime and directing their answers leads to the gradual piecing together of a story that appears to be a confession and may lead some suspects to believe in the story.
- Suggesting that there is enough evidence to prove that the suspect committed the crime, but that he or she may simply have forgotten that they did.
- Confronting the suspect with nonexistent evidence.
- Continuing to question the subject despite the fact that everything has already been discussed, so the interview essentially involves repeating what has been discussed earlier and trying to persuade the suspect to confess.

A structured model for investigative interviewing of suspects

At the beginning of the 1990s the Police Academy in The Netherlands developed a model that could be used to structure the questioning of suspects. The model has since been repeatedly revised and improved in light of new findings (Amelsvoort, Rispens & Grolman, 2007).

The approach proposed by the model is based on the following principles:

- Minimizing resistance. The interview is conducted in a way that elicits the least possible resistance on the part of the suspect. This reduces the suspect's reluctance to tell the truth. The suspect is confronted with increasingly incriminating evidence during the course of the interview. The disclosure of the evidence is carefully planned.

- The interviewer asks questions that relate to the evidence without disclosing the evidence to the suspect. Before confronting the suspect with the evidence, the interviewer validates the evidence by asking questions that enable him or her to explore and rule out possible alternative explanations that the suspect might otherwise resort to.
- If, after being confronted with the evidence, the suspect alters his or her statement to account for the evidence and therefore brings the statement more into line with the evidence, the interviewer responds in a mildly positive manner, and certainly not in a negative manner.

In order to be able to apply the model the following conditions must be met:

- There must be enough possible evidence against the suspect to draw up a questioning plan.
- The suspect must be willing and able to discuss the incident. It is not possible to use this approach if the suspect exercises the right to remain silent or is only prepared to discuss with the interviewer things that do not relate to the incident. It is also impossible to use this approach – or any other form of interview for that matter – if the suspect is psychotic or distraught, for example.

The preparation of a questioning plan

The interviewer draws up a list of all the possible evidence against the suspect. The source or traceable origin of each piece of evidence is also noted. A single piece of evidence may have several sources. For example, two witnesses who know the suspect personally may both have seen him or her at the crime scene.

The interviewer decides which pieces of evidence they wish to discuss during the interview. The interviewer then considers the ways in which the suspect might explain the evidence, regardless of whether the explanations given by the suspect are true or fabricated.

Example.   A man is suspected of committing a burglary at 10 Bishops Close during the night of Sunday, 2/Monday, 3 December. The suspect does not live near the house that was burgled – he lives 3 kilometres away. The suspect has been convicted of burglary on three previous occasions. A witness, a neighbour of the person who lives at 10 Bishops Close, saw the suspect's car parked in an isolated spot at 2 o'clock in the morning on the night in question and made a note of the vehicle registration number, because he thought it looked suspicious.

The suspect might give any one of the following explanations for the fact that his car was seen near Bishops Close. These explanations might be true or false.

- The suspect was there with his car.
- The suspect lent his car to someone else on the night in question.
- The suspect sold his car shortly before the night in question.
- Someone else used the suspect's car that night without the suspect noticing.
- The witness noted the vehicle registration number incorrectly. The suspect's car was nowhere near Bishops Close on the night in question.

The suspect might give any one of the following explanations for the fact that he was seen near 10 Bishops Close on the night in question. These explanations might be true or false.

- The suspect was there to commit a burglary.
- The suspect was there with someone else. It was the other person who burgled 10 Bishops Close.
- The suspect was visiting someone in the neighbourhood.
- The suspect had some other legitimate reason for being there (he was driving past and simply pulled over for a cigarette, or stopped to urinate, etc.).

Having considered the possible explanations, the interviewer then thinks up questions that can be asked to verify each of the pieces of evidence. These information-gathering questions must be open questions. The interviewer starts by asking general open questions and leads on to more specific open questions, using the so-called funnel model. While gathering information to verify the evidence it is important to ask open questions that do not provide the suspect with any information about what the interviewer knows or suspects.

Example. A question such as 'Were you in or near Bishops Close last weekend?' provides the suspect with far more information about what the interviewer knows or suspects than if the interviewer simply asks the suspect, 'What did you do last weekend?'

When asking information-gathering questions it is important to ensure that the questions do not focus exclusively on precisely what the interviewer wants to know. To start with, the questions need to be broader and more general and they must also specifically address things that are irrelevant or less relevant. If the person who committed the burglary is likely to have lost something at the crime scene, such as a cigarette lighter, when asking information-gathering questions it is better to start by asking about other items the person might have had with him, such as cigarettes, a pen or a wallet, rather than simply asking questions about the lighter. Where possible this helps to throw the suspect off guard so the suspect does not know where the interviewer is heading or what information the interviewer may have.

Besides asking questions that relate to the evidence, the interviewer can also ask questions that relate to the source of a piece of evidence. For example, this may be important if the suspect knows a witness who has provided a certain piece of evidence. Then, besides asking questions that relate to the evidence provided by the witness, it is also advisable to question the suspect about the source of the evidence to establish the suspect's impression of the source. If, in answer to the information-gathering questions, the suspect describes the witness as a reliable person and says that he has nothing against the witness, it will be more difficult for the suspect to claim that the witness is unreliable when subsequently confronted with the witness's information.

Example.   A man is found dead near a bar. The barman has stated that the victim and the suspect both frequently drank in the bar and that on the evening in question he saw the two men arguing there. He could tell that they were arguing from their gestures and because they were swearing at each other. They were shouting so loudly he could hear them above the music – this was partly because they were standing reasonably close to him.

In this case the barman is the source of this important piece of evidence. Once the interviewer has established that the suspect regularly frequents the bar, the interviewer can then ask the suspect the following questions:

- Who do you meet in the bar?
- Who else do you know who go there regularly?
- Who do you know who works there?
- What kind of work do they do there?
- What do you think of A, B, C and D? (The interviewer can inquire about the suspect's impression of the friendliness, honesty, reliability and work ethic of all of the people the suspect has named.) What kind of relationship do you have with A, B, C and D?

If the suspect describes the barman as a likeable, reliable fellow, or if he says that while he knows the barman he does not have a relationship with him (either positive or negative), it will be more difficult for the suspect to claim at a later stage that the barman is a fantasist or a liar who has a grudge against him and wants to do him harm.

When formulating information-gathering questions it is important to specify what the questions are meant to establish. To maintain a sense of clarity and structure for the interviewer and the suspect alike, each information-gathering question should have just one objective.

Example.   The suspect's car was parked outside 10 Bishops Close at 2 o'clock in the morning on the night of Sunday, 2/Monday, 3 December. Given that this is the case, the object of individual information-gathering questions is to establish that:

- The suspect was the only person who used the car on that night.
- The suspect's car was parked outside 10 Bishops Close on that night.
- The suspect's car was parked outside 10 Bishops Close at 2 o'clock in the morning on that night.

The next step in the preparation of the question plan is to decide what to do if the suspect's answers to the information-gathering questions are inconsistent with the evidence. Having asked the suspect as many information-gathering questions as possible, one possibility is to confront the suspect with the evidence immediately. It is also possible to confront the suspect with the evidence at a later stage. To proceed with either of these courses the suspect must have been asked enough information-gathering questions about the evidence to be able to confront the suspect with the evidence. At the same time, it is also important to consider whether, when it comes to increasing the pressure on the suspect, it is appropriate to confront the suspect with the evidence at that stage. For example, being confronted with a piece of evidence that places the suspect at the scene of the crime will put far more pressure on him or her than being confronted with a piece of evidence that places the suspect somewhere near the scene of the crime. Because the model is based on the principle that pressure should be built up gradually during the course of the interview in order to minimize resistance, it is important to ensure that, if possible, the build-up of pressure is sufficiently gradual in terms of the level of challenge in the successive confrontations.

Besides increasing the level of challenge in successive confrontations, the confrontations also need to be more specifically related to the crime and more frequent during the course of the interview. In other words, the confrontations need continually to home in on the crime, which makes them more incriminating for the suspect, as well as being made at shorter intervals during the course of the interview and, if necessary, one after another.

Not all information-gathering questions will lead to a confrontation, simply because no confrontation is possible at that point. If the interviewer has asked one or more information-gathering questions to establish whether the suspect or someone other than the suspect used the suspect's car on the night in question, the interviewer cannot subsequently confront the suspect if the interviewer does not have any evidence that the suspect was the only person to use the car that night. If, during the interview, the suspect states that he lent the car to an acquaintance that night, it will be necessary to check to verify the suspect's statement. If the investigation reveals that what the suspect has said is not true, the suspect may be confronted with that evidence in a later interview.

Once the preparation phase is complete, the interviewer will have a question plan that specifies which pieces of evidence are to be discussed with the suspect in what order and at what point in the interview. The plan will also indicate whether and, if so, at what point in the interview the suspect is to be confronted with the evidence in question.

An example of part of a question plan relating to the use of a car by a person suspected of burglary can be found at the end of this chapter.

The conducting of the interview

The interviewer does not have to know the question plan by heart and there is no reason why the interviewer should not take the question plan into the interrogation room. There is no need to be secretive about this. The interviewer can simply explain to the suspect that there are lots of questions he or she wishes to ask and that he or she has brought along certain documents to ensure that everything is covered that needs to be covered. This will usually make a positive impression on the suspect. However, given that the interviewer has drawn up the question plan and in doing so has carefully considered the questions that need to be asked during the course of the interview, the interviewer will usually know most of the plan by heart.

Effective use of the question plan during the interview requires skill on the part of the interviewer. It is not advisable to stick so closely to the plan that the interviewer simply fires off one question after another. The interviewer has to be sufficiently flexible so that at a relational level the interchange with the suspect is conducted as a 'normal' conversation. Sometimes it may be necessary for the interviewer to pursue a line of questioning that is not anticipated in the question plan. The plan simply serves as a (main) guideline during the interview.

During the interview the interviewer asks the suspect the information-gathering questions in the order in which they have been prepared. Once the interviewer has asked the suspect all of the information-gathering questions that relate to a certain piece of evidence, the interviewer summarizes what the suspect has said and checks that he or she has understood the suspect correctly. In summarizing what the suspect has said, the interviewer needs to ensure that his or her summary is as complete as possible and that it includes both relevant and irrelevant points.

Example.   A person suspected of robbing the Fortis Bank in King Street has stated that he has three bank accounts – one with the Fortis Bank, one with the Postbank and one with ABN Amro. In response to questioning he has said that he visited the Fortis Bank last month, he has not been to ABN Amro for years and that he runs his account with the Postbank via the internet. He has also said when he last visited the Fortis Bank and ABN Amro.

The interviewer should summarize this information as follows:

'So, if I understand you rightly, your account with the Postbank is via the internet. You last visited the Fortis Bank in King Street on Friday of last week when you withdrew money, but prior to that you had not been there for several months. You have not been to ABN Amro for years and no longer use your account with the bank. Is that right?'

The interviewer should *not* summarize this information as follows:

> 'So, if I understand you rightly, you last visited the Fortis Bank on Friday of last week. Is that right?'

If the answers to the information-gathering questions achieve the objectives established at the outset, the interviewer can proceed to ask the next set of information-gathering questions. This will be the case if the statement made by the suspect is consistent with the evidence. If not, the interviewer may choose to confront the suspect with the evidence (this will depend on action outlined in the question plan).

When confronting the suspect with a piece of evidence the interviewer should be brief, clear and neutral. When confronted with evidence that conflicts with his or her statement, the suspect will experience a certain amount of internal pressure to explain the inconsistency between his or her story and the evidence. If, when confronting the suspect with a piece of evidence, the interviewer talks for too long so the confrontation takes the form of a monologue, there is a risk that the internal pressure that the suspect is experiencing will diminish. There is no need for the suspect to say anything while the interviewer is speaking. This is why a confrontation needs to be brief. I t also needs to be clear. If it is vague, the suspect will be able to ask questions. If, for example, the interviewer says, 'Someone saw you there' the suspect can ask, 'Where did they see me?' or 'Really? Who saw me?' 'Really? When?' This will lessen the impact of the confrontation. If the interviewer fails to remain neutral and presents the confrontation in the form of an attack, it is easier for the suspect to respond to the tenor of the attack rather than the content of the confrontation. If the interviewer says, 'You're lying through your teeth', the suspect can respond by saying 'You think so? Well, work it out for yourself. That's my last word on the subject.' If the confrontation is formulated in a neutral manner the suspect has little choice but to respond to the content of the confrontation and to explain any inconsistencies.

Example of a confrontation formulated in the right way

Interviewer: So, on Sunday, 2 December you drove to your friends' house in X [another town]. You stayed there on Sunday night and drove back again late in the day on Monday, 3 December. Is that right? [summary]

Suspect: Yes.

Interviewer: So, how was it that a witness who lives in Bishops Close saw your car parked outside his house during the night of Sunday, 2/Monday, 3 December and made a note of your vehicle registration number?'

If, after being confronted with the evidence, a suspect stands by his or her original statement, which is inconsistent with the evidence, there is no point in the interviewer getting caught up in a 'yes you did'/'no I didn't' discussion with the suspect. It is better for the interviewer simply to proceed to the next step in the question plan.

If, after being confronted with the evidence, the suspect comes up with an entirely new explanation for the evidence, the interviewer can then pursue a line of questioning based on the new explanation so that the suspect's statement can be investigated.

If, after being confronted with the evidence, the suspect alters his or her statement to make it consistent with the evidence, the interviewer should not respond in a negative manner. For example, the interviewer should not say 'At last! Why on earth did you leave it so long? You could have said that right from the start!' If the interviewer reacts like this, the suspect will have little incentive to change any inaccuracies in what he or she said earlier as the suspect will feel that if he or she does, it will simply be met with negative feedback. It is better for the interviewer to be mildly positive: 'It's good that you've cleared that up.' The suspect will then realize that the interviewer will not object if he or she alters a statement made earlier. The suspect may then find it easier to alter the statement. It is not advisable for the interviewer to reward the suspect for altering the story to make it consistent with the evidence. If the interviewer does, the risk of exerting undue influence will be too high, especially if the suspect has a tendency to be compliant (Gudjonsson, 2003).

Once the suspect has altered his or her statement to make it consistent with the evidence, the interviewer can pursue a line of questioning based on the suspect's revised statement. Obviously it is not enough for the suspect simply to say, 'Yes, that's right. The fact is, I was there.' The interviewer must then ask the suspect to provide a more detailed explanation and – if possible and appropriate – in the form of free recall. 'OK. You say the truth is you were there. It's good that you've cleared that up. Now tell me precisely what happened.' The interviewer must then ask the suspect a series of open questions about his or her revised statement. The revised statement can subsequently be compared with the facts revealed by the investigation.

The limitations of the model

If all the evidence is provided by a single source, as is often the case in a sexual abuse case, for example, there will not be enough information to draw up a useful question plan. If, for example, a child has alleged that her father sexually abused her and all the evidence is based only on this child's statement, it is not possible to formulate effective information-gathering questions. Having said that, when preparing for the interview the source of the evidence (in this case, the child) can be discussed with the suspect.

Getting the suspect to repeat what he said earlier and getting the suspect to repeat what he said in reverse order are not part of this model.

Bull & Milne (2004) reported a study conducted by Soukara, Bull & Vrij which revealed that suspects were more likely to change their confession if the interviewer showed concern. A study conducted by Kebbell, Hurren & Mazerolle (2006) suggested that suspected sex offenders should be approached in an open-minded manner that displays humanity rather than dominance to maximize the likelihood of a confession. These aspects are not explicitly addressed in the model outlined above. The model simply focuses on the content of the interview and does not offer any guidelines on how to approach and treat individual suspects.

What are the advantages of using this model?

When a suspect is interviewed in accordance with the structured model, rather than experiencing external pressure (in the form of coercive interviewing techniques, promises, raised voices, etc.), the suspect experiences internal pressure. If in answer to information-gathering questions the suspect makes a statement that is inconsistent with a piece of evidence, the suspect is subsequently confronted with the evidence in a neutral way. The suspect then experiences increasing internal pressure as a result of the fact the he or she can see the inconsistencies between the statement and the evidence and feels obliged to provide an explanation.

Asking questions related to the evidence before confronting the suspect with the evidence affects the suspect's perception of proof. In ensuring that the evidence is verified to start with, the interviewer effectively increases the strength of the suspect's belief in the evidence against him or her. If the suspect has already answered a series of information-gathering questions, he or she is likely to find it far more difficult to come up with yet another explanation than if he or she were presented with the evidence before being asked a series of information-gathering questions. For example, if an interviewer tells a suspect that his or her fingerprints have been found at the scene of the crime without first asking a series of information-gathering questions, it will be fairly easy for the suspect to say that he or she had a legitimate reason for being at the crime scene. If the interviewer has already ruled out this possibility before telling the suspect about the fingerprints, it will be far more difficult for the suspect to provide a convincing explanation of how the fingerprints came to be at the crime scene.

The information-gathering approach postulated by the model imposes a high cognitive load on the suspect – certainly if the subject committed the crime – and this may well result in more verbal and nonverbal cues to deceit.

Several of the tips that Vrij (2004) gives for increasing the cognitive load on a suspect are included in the model or can be incorporated in the questioning plan: while gathering information the interviewer can ask the suspect a series of follow-up questions. Time-related questions can also be incorporated in the question plan.

The approach suggested by the model includes strategic use of evidence (SUE). This should enable the interviewer to identify guilty suspects *and* innocent suspects more rapidly. In answer to information-gathering questions innocent suspects will provide an explanation that is consistent with and accounts for the evidence.

Because the interviewer is forced to consider possible alternative explanations for the evidence against the suspect while preparing for the interview, the interviewer is less likely to assume automatically that the suspect committed the crime. The interviewer is forced to examine the evidence from different points of view and to consider possible explanations from the outset.

Rather than simply seeking to obtain a confession, the interviewer has to focus on asking questions and confronting the suspect with the evidence in the right way. Attempting to persuade the suspect that he or she must – or had better – confess, because there is already ample evidence to prove that he or she did it is no longer the main focus of the interview.

Because the interviewer is working with a prepared question plan, it is clear when the interview can be brought to a close. Once the interviewer has asked all the questions, the interview is complete. This helps to ensure that the interview does not degenerate into an endless discussion of points that have already been discussed which is really a thinly disguised attempt to convince the suspect that it would be better to confess.

In summary: the structured approach proposed by the model includes several elements which research has suggested to be helpful in extracting truthful statements from guilty suspects. At the same time, it also helps to minimize risk factors in the interviewer's behaviour that might otherwise prompt an innocent suspect to make a false confession.

Finally, a quote from an interview with a man who was convicted of murdering his girlfriend. During the investigation he was interviewed in accordance with the structured method. He describes his experience as follows (*Recherche Magazine*, 2002):

> ... I got caught out by my own statements, but I can't say they tricked me. They played it very smart ... They asked me so many questions that I couldn't keep my story straight. They were very skilful. They obviously thought it out very carefully. They proceeded correctly in every respect. They could have arrested me earlier, but they used the time to prepare everything. Ninety per cent of my fellow detainees have lots of complaints about the way they were treated. But I have to say I was always treated impeccably. The police were never aggressive.

References

Amelsvoort, A. van, Rispens, I. & Grolman, H. (2007). *Handleiding verhoor.* 's-Gravenhage: Reed Business Information bv.

Blaauw, J. A. (2000). *De puttense moordzaak.* Baarn: Uitgeverij De Fontein bv.

Bull, R. & Milne, R. (2004). Attempts to improve the police interviewing of suspects. In G. D. Lassiter (Ed.), *Interrogations, confessions, and entrapment* (pp. 181–196). New York: Kluwer.

Gosewehr, D. & Timmerman, H. (2007). *Wanneer de waarheid … Het ware verhaal over Ina Post.* Amsterdam: Rozenberg Publishers.

Gudjonsson, G. H. (2003). *The psychology of interrogations and confessions.* Chichester: Wiley.

Gudjonsson, G. H. & Bownes, I. (1992). The reasons why suspects confess during custodial interrogation: Data for Northern Ireland. *Medicine, Science and the Law, 32,* 204–212.

Gudjonsson, G. H. & Petursson, H. (1991). Custodial interrogation: Why do suspects confess and how does it relate to their crime, attitude and personality? *Personality and Individual Differences, 12,* 295–306.

Gudjonsson, G. H. & Sigurdsson, J. F. (1999). The Gudjonsson Confession Questionnaire-Revised (GCQ-R): Factor structure and its relationship with personality. *Personality and Individual Differences, 27,* 953–968.

Hartwig, M., Granhag, P. A., Strömwall, L. A. & Kronkvist, O. (2006). Strategic use of evidence during police interviews: When training to detect deception works. *Law and Human Behavior, 30,* 603–619.

Hartwig, M., Granhag, P. A. & Strömwall, L. A. (2007). Guilty and innocent suspects' strategies during police interrogations. *Psychology, Crime & Law, 13,* 213–227.

Israëls, H. (2004). *De bekentenissen van Ina Post.* Alphen aan den Rijn, Kluwer.

Kebbell, M., Hurren, E. & Mazerolle, P. (2006). An investigation into the effective and ethical interviewing of suspected sex offenders. *Trends & Issues in Crime and Criminal Justice,* no. 327.

Lassiter, D. (2004). *Interrogations, confessions, and entrapment.* New York: Kluwer Academic/Plenum Publishers.

Nickerson, R. S. (1998). Confirmation bias: A ubiquitious phenomenon in many guises. *Review of General Psychology, 2,* 175–220.

Nisbett, R. & Ross, L. (1980). *Human inference: Strategies and shortcomings of social judgment.* Englewood Cliffs, NJ: Prentice-Hall.

Posthumus, F. (2005). *Evaluatieonderzoek in de Schiedammer Parkmoord. Rapportage in opdracht van het College van procureurs-generaal.* Amsterdam.

Sigurdsson, I. & Gudjonsson, G. H. (1994). Alcohol and drug intoxication during police interrogation and the reasons why suspects confess to the police. *Addiction, 89,* 985–997.

Soukara, S., Bull, R. & Vrij, A. (2002). Police detectives' aims regarding their interviews with suspects: Any changes at the turn of the miliennium? *International Journal of Police Science and Management, 4,* 110–114.

Trope, Y. & Liberman, A. (1996). Social hypothesis testing: Cognitive and motivational mechanisms. In E. Higgins & A. Kruglanski (Eds.), *Social psychology: Handbook of basic principles.* New York: Guilford Press.

Vrij, A. (2004). Why professionals fail to catch liars and how they can improve. *Legal and Criminological Psychology, 9,* 159–181.

Vrij, A. (2006). Challenging interviewees during interviews: The potential effects on lie detection. *Psychology, Crime & Law, 12,* 193–206.

Vrij, A., Mann, S. & Fisher, R. (2006). Information-gathering vs. accusatory interview style: Individual differences in respondents' experiences. *Personality and Individual Differences, 41,* 589–599.

Part of a questioning plan regarding the use of a car during a burglary

No.	Evidence	Objective	Information-gathering questions	+/-	Summary	Confrontation	+/-	Confirmation	Further questioning or investigation
7	Howard drives the red Rover owned by his mother (vehicle registration number DP-KH-28). Source(s): Entry in our information system, Government Road Transport Agency and own observation	Establish that Howard drives his mother's red Rover (vehicle registration DP-KH-28).	How do you get about? What means of transport do you have? What else? Who does the car belong to? What colour is it? What is the vehicle registration of the car? What is the make? When do you use the car? When was the last time you used it? What do you use the car for? What agreements do you have with your mother as far as the car is concerned?	+ −	So you are able to use your mother's red Rover (vehicle registration DP-KH-28). Alternative	Confrontation 1: So how is it that there is an entry in our information system in which the police confirm that you were seen driving the red Rover owned by your mother (vehicle registration DP-KH-28)? Confrontation 2: So how is it that according to the Government Road Transport Agency your mother is the registered keeper of the red Rover with vehicle registration DP-KH-28 found near your home during the search?	+ −	That's clear	
8	X Source: None	Establish that Howard was the only person to use the red Rover for the last two days.	How long have you been driving the car? Who else uses the car? Anyone else? When was the last time you drove the car? Where do you keep the keys? Who else has a set of keys? When was the last time you used the car?	+	So you were the only person to use the red Rover for the last two days.	X No confrontation			

#									
9	The red Rover (DP-KH-28) was parked near Howard's home at 2 Mill Lane, Millwood this morning. Source: Report of the search and own observation	Establish that Howard parked the red Rover (DP-KH-28) near 2 Mill Lane, Millwood.	Where did you park the car the last time you used it? Where else do you park it? Where was the last place you parked it? Which street did you park it in? How far is that from your home? When was that? What time was it?	+ −	So you parked the red Rover outside/near number 2 Mill Lane in Millwood at …… on …… Alternative	+	So how is it that during our search we found the red Rover near your home at 2 Mill Lane?	+	Good. That's clear.
10	The red Rover was **locked** where it was parked. Source: Own observation	Establish that Howard locked the red Rover when he parked it near his home.	What did you do when you parked the car there? What else? How did you lock the car? How did you lock it? How many sets of keys are there?	+ −	So you locked the car where you parked it. Alternative	+	So how is it that we found the car locked during the search?	+	Great. That's clear
11	The keys of the Rover were found on the table in the living room during the search. Source: Report of the search	Establish that Howard left the keys on the table in the living room and that no one else used the keys.	What did you do with the keys after you locked the car? What do you usually do with the keys? What did you do with the keys after you entered the living room? Where did you leave the keys? Where were they lying precisely? Who touched the keys after that?	+ −	So you left the car keys on the table in the living room in the place where we found them during the search. Alternative	+	So how is it that we found the keys on the table in the living room during the search?	+	OK

No.	Evidence	Objective	Information-gathering questions	+/-	Summary	Confrontation	+/-	Confirmation	Further questioning or investigation
12	A red Rover with vehicle registration number DP-KH-2: was seen parked in Old Lane at 2.30 last Sunday morning. Source: Statement made by witness Tivey.	Establish that Howard parked his mother's red Rover in Old Lane, Millwood at 2.30 last Sunday morning.	Where were you coming from when you parked the car near your home? Where else did you go with the car? Where else did you park your car? Where else? Where was the car parked at 2.30 last Sunday morning?	+ −	So on Sunday night you drove the red Rover to ….. and you parked the Rover in Old Lane at 2.30 in the morning Alternative	So how is it that witness Tivey has stated that he saw a red Rover with vehicle registration DP-KH-2: parked in Old Lane at 2.30 last Sunday morning?	+	That's clear	
13	A man matching Howard's description was seen walking near the red Rover in Old Lane. Source: Statement made by witness Tivey.	Establish that Howard was walking in Old Lane at 2.30 in the morning last Sunday night.	Where did you walk last night? Which streets did you walk in? Where were you at around 2.30 in the morning? What time was it when you were walking in Old Lane?	+ −	So you were walking in Cock Street at 2.30 in the morning. Alternative	So how is it that witness Tivey has stated that he saw a man matching your description walking near the red Rover in Old Lane at 2.30 in the morning last Sunday night?	+	That's clear	

Source: Police Academy of the Netherlands.

Chapter Four

Finding False Confessions

Peter J. van Koppen

*Faculties of Law, Maastricht University
and Free University Amsterdam*

Confession made under torture

A confession is in many ways a religious experience. At the end of the Middle Ages everywhere in Europe a new system of evidence was introduced in which torture still had a place (the following is based on Langbein, 1977). The new rules replaced divine judgement with human judgement. It was understood, however, that assessing the evidence could only be trusted to humans if they were guided by strict rules. Thus, only a few types of evidence were allowed: (i) The court could convict on the statement of no fewer than two witnesses who actually saw the crime take place. (ii) If there were fewer than two witnesses, the suspect could only be convicted if he confessed. (iii) Indirect or circumstantial evidence alone, however convincing, could not secure a conviction.

So, two witnesses or a confession could constitute full proof, but because in many cases there were no eyewitnesses, the suspect's confession played a major role. If a suspect did not confess voluntarily, a confession could be extracted by force, using torture. Torture, however, could only be used in cases of the more serious crimes – crimes that carried the death penalty or some form of maiming. The rules did not apply to less serious crimes, the *delicta levia*. In these cases the court could convict on its belief, which in turn could be based on indirect, circumstantial evidence alone, so in these cases torture was no longer used.

Handbook of Psychology of Investigative Interviewing: Current Developments and Future Directions
Edited by Ray Bull, Tim Valentine and Tom Williamson
© 2009 John Wiley & Sons, Ltd.

The seriousness of the crime was not the only condition that had to be met before torture could be used. There should be at least 'half' proof. Such proof could be a single witness statement or serious circumstantial evidence. Of course, it was understood that everyone will confess to anything under severe torture. A confession obtained under torture, therefore, should at least demonstrate the suspect's intimate knowledge of the crime. The torturer was not allowed to ask leading questions or provide the suspect with detailed knowledge. The confession made under torture should be verified as far as possible against evidence from other sources. Even then a confession made under torture was not considered valid proof. This was the case only if the confession was repeated voluntarily in court. Of course, this could hardly be voluntary; suspects knew they would be returned to the torture chamber if they changed their story in court.

In this system there was little scope for a free evaluation of the evidence by the court. That did develop over time, but only indirectly. In the case of extenuating circumstances the court could ignore the mandatory sentence by rendering a *poeno extraordinario*. This could also be rendered if there was insufficient evidence against the suspect. A *poeno extraordinario* was always less than the mandatory sentence imposed in cases of complete evidence. Thus a system of evaluation of the proof by the court for serious crimes developed in line with that which already existed for *delicta levia*. This was enhanced by the substitution in more and more jurisdictions of lay judges with professional judges, to whom adjudication was entrusted. In this manner, the confession was no longer an essential part of the evidence and torture became obsolete, so that during the nineteenth century it was abolished formally everywhere in western Europe. 'Only when confession evidence was no longer necessary to convict the guilty could European law escape its centuries of dependence on judicial torture' (Langbein, 1983: 1555–1556).

Even though torture was abolished in the Netherlands in 1798 (art. 36 of the *Staatsregeling* [State Statute]), some of the other rules did not disappear. In the present Code of Criminal Procedure the evidence of a single witness remains insufficient for a conviction (art. 341, Code of Criminal Procedure). But in the case of confessions things have changed: a suspect cannot be convicted on the basis of his or her confession alone: further evidence is required. As a result, the importance of a confession formally was reduced to the same level as any witness statement. However, in practice things are different.

Confessions are considered a holy part of proof. Even in cases where there is an abundance of other evidence, police officers tend to interrogate suspects, not just to give them the opportunity to tell their story or their version of what happened, but also to get them to confess. An example is the case of Julien C (in the Netherlands the full names of suspects are not made public), who was accused of killing eight-year-old Jesse Dingemans. On 1 December 2006 a man entered a primary school, found Jesse alone in a classroom (Jesse was just collecting something) and slit his throat. There was an abundance of evidence against Julien – for instance, he was seen hiding his clothes which were soaked with Jesse's blood in the woods. Julien denied the killing, and accused three Eastern European men though his account was unbelievable. He was interviewed by the police during 13 lengthy interrogations. Julien was convicted by both the district court and the appellate court. He received a life sentence (Hof (Appelate Court)'s-Hertogenbosch, 26 February 2008, LJN-number BC 5105, see www.rechtspraak.nl).

If police officers feel the need to interrogate suspects like Julien in cases where there is overwhelming evidence, they surely will interrogate extensively in serious cases where the evidence against the suspect is not very strong. The police's need for a confession can as a result elicit false confessions.

In many cases it is hard to assess whether a confession is false or not. And that is the problem I want to discuss in this chapter: after a confession has been made, how do we identify a false one? Several approaches are possible: 1) assessing the psychological characteristics of the suspect; 2) assessing the characteristics of the (series of) interviews and circumstances of detention; 3) assessing the content of the confession. I shall conclude that in some cases, under some circumstances, a false confession can be distinguished from a true one. For that purpose, the content of the confession is more valuable than the other two approaches.

Psychological characteristics

Gudjonsson proposed that some personality traits make suspects susceptible to making a false confession: low IQ, lack of confidence in one's memory, psychological disturbance, suggestibility and compliance, and other related characteristics (Gudjonsson, 2003). In a long series of studies by Gudjonsson and others it was demonstrated that suspects with these traits more often make false confessions than others (see also Horselenberg, Merckelbach & Josephs, 2003).

That does not make personality characteristics the golden tool for identifying false confession: studies of false confessions are usually experimental, where the question is whether people with certain characteristics are more or less prone to making a false confession than others. In practice, however, the question is quite different: is this particular confession false? To answer that question, personality traits are not very useful. First, the problem in using personality traits to identify false confessions is that many suspects have a low IQ anyway, and the other characteristics mentioned above also apply to them. That means that, with little exaggeration, one can say that the base rate of personality characteristics of suspects are more or less the personality characteristics that make suspects prone to confess falsely. Deviations from a strong base rate, we know, are hard to predict.

Second, individual behaviour is not just the result of personality, but depends on interaction of personality with the situation (Bem & Funder, 1978; Mischel, 1977, 1979). That means that, for instance, with a gentle form of interrogation only impressionable suspects are susceptible to making a false confession, while a rough interrogation can make almost everybody confess almost anything. Third, even if a suspect is prone to making a false confession, he may have committed the crime and thus the confession may actually be true.

It seems fair to say that if a suspect has the personality characteristics mentioned above, knowing that does not help very much in distinguishing between true and false confessions. If, however, a suspect has the opposite characteristics – a high IQ, trust in his memory, sound faculties and is neither suggestible nor compliant – we may conclude that any confession made will not be the product of his personality. Thus, personality characteristics seem to be of some, but not great use in distinguishing between true and false confessions. However, that does not mean that they are not highly relevant to interrogations in another respect. So, police officers would be wise to interrogate carefully if they have reason to believe that a suspect has characteristics that make them susceptible to confess.

Situational characteristics

Should we then conclude that the nature of the interrogation is more relevant to identifying false confessions? That depends. Let us take extreme interrogations, those conducted under torture, or situations that come close to it. These are situations, we can assume, in which almost anyone will confess. If the police create a situation in which everybody or almost everybody confesses, the confession cannot distinguish between innocence and guilt, and thus would be meaningless as evidence (Wagenaar, Van Koppen & Crombag, 1993).

In the world of the regular police in Western society these kinds of interrogation situations are presumably rare. Nevertheless, there are all kinds of situations that may bring some or many suspects to make a false confession. For instance, in The Netherlands the court can order a suspect to be held in solitary confinement if free communication will hamper the police investigation. That means that a suspect is kept in his cell 23 hours a day, is not allowed to read newspapers or watch television, or communicate with anybody except his/her attorney and is then taken out of the cell to talk to two friendly police officers. It can be expected that any suspect will be happy to talk in these circumstances. Although we do not have solid experimental studies – ethical considerations prevent such studies – it can be expected that this situation will increase the probability that suspects will make a confession. And if the probability of a making a confession increases, so does the probability of making a false confession.

In this vein there are all kinds of police methods that may increase the probability of a false confession. But, again, that is not the question. We want to establish whether a particular confession is false or not. Even under duress a suspect may make a true confession. But at the same time, if we have a susceptible suspect who has been interrogated under circumstances that are known to increase the probability of making false confessions, there is good reason to scrutinize the confessions made, as in the following case.

Ceci n'est pas une confession*

Ofshe (1989), based on a case study, suggested that in order to make a false confession, the suspect is persuaded to do two things. First, the suspect has to accept that he committed the crime, even though he does not remember doing so. Second, the suspect has to be led to believe that there is good reason that he cannot remember anything about the crime (see also Ost, Costall & Bull, 2001).

A good example of Ofshe's contentions is the Sneek balcony murder. On 9 November 2004 Dennis, his girlfriend and his best friend Ronald went to spend the afternoon with Dennis's granny, who lived in a fourth floor apartment in Sneek. They all started drinking. In the afternoon Dennis and his girlfriend went their own way, but Ronald and granny continued drinking. At 6 pm granny fell from the balcony and later died in the hospital. At that time she had a very high blood alcohol level of 0.36%.

The question is, how did she fall? That is not decided very easily. There was a single witness who cycled past the apartment building minutes earlier. He says that he saw the old woman hanging over the balcony in a very hazardous way. The cyclist, though, did not take the trouble to stop and wait to see what would happen next. There was no one else who could in any way be called an eyewitness.

But something else happened. After granny fell, Ronald rushed downstairs and knelt next to her. A police officer, by then present at the scene, heard Ronald say: 'I pushed my friend Dennis over the balcony', or words to that effect. Other witnesses more or less said the same thing. Ronald was arrested and at the police station he maintained that the person who had fallen was his friend Dennis. His blood was tested and was found to contain 0.28% of alcohol. Later that evening Ronald was told that the deceased was not Dennis but his granny.

Ronald was pretty drunk. But after he sobered up, he was interrogated; in the coming days for some 15 hours in total. During these interrogations, he made a full confession. My colleague Marko Jelicic of Maastricht University tested Ronald and concluded that he is of fairly low intelligence, makes a lot of cognitive errors and distrusts his own memory, was suffering from psychological problems at the time of the interrogations, and is suggestible and compliant. He suggested that the court have experts take a closer look at the interrogations.

I served as an expert witness in this case. Ronald had certainly confessed, but in an odd manner. I base the following on studying the case file and on the tapes of the interrogations.

*After René Magritte, *La trahison des images*, 1928–29.

In its basic form, the interrogation went as follows. Two police officers kept on talking to Ronald to convince him that he had thrown granny over the balcony by accident. After they succeeded in that, they set about convincing Ronald that he had done it deliberately. In the third stage, they convinced Ronald that he had a motive: an argument about a library card. Ronald confessed to it all, but in a particular way. To everything he admitted to, he added a qualification. He seems highly compliant, when he says things like:

> Then I hope I've got it right this time ... pffft. (interrogation 10 November 2004 at 15h 11).

> I have been racking my brains about it all night. (interrogation 10 November 2004 at 15h 21).

The police officers encourage this:

Interrogator: You can deal with it better if you tell your story again and then again and then again.
Ronald: Of course, of course.
                  (interrogation 10 November 2004 at 16h 12).

But at the same time Ronald is in ignorance. He says things like:

Interrogator: Some people saw you there, didn't they?
Ronald: Yes, that is possible. Pffft, we didn't fight. That is almost impossible, it was a very sociable afternoon. ... I drank a lot, though, so I don't know any more.
                  (interrogation 10 November 2004 at 17h 12)

Interrogator: Did your attorney know you pushed granny over the railing?
Ronald: Uh ... no, because I myself don't know that.
                  (interrogation 11 November 2004 at 12h 18)

Interrogator: Do you know that for sure?
Ronald: No, I'm not sure. I can't remember that. I am sorry, I am very sorry. Really.
Interrogator: So in reality, you don't know?
Ronald: I really don't know. I'm sorry.
                  (interrogation 10 November 2004 at 18h 53)

Ronald: This says that I am responsible for the death of granny. But is that definite?
Interrogator: OK, so you aren't.
Ronald: Now, I really don't know.
Interrogator: How do you feel about it yourself?
Ronald: It can hardly be otherwise.
Interrogators: That is what we mean.
                  (interrogation 14 December 2004 at 14h 42)

For Ronald the interrogation is a form of reconstruction. Together with the interrogators he tries to reconstruct what might have happened when granny fell. The reconstruction is aided by some misleading techniques that seem obvious to anyone watching the videotapes of the interrogations, but seemingly not to the interrogators and Ronald.

First, Ronald is encouraged to guess all the time. The interrogators even use phrases like: 'You're getting warm. You are not completely there, but you are getting warm' (interrogation 13 November 2004 at 14h 50).

Second, the interrogators stress that Ronald can remember everything, but for some reason now has trouble in telling the whole story. When he knelt down next to the body of the dying granny, he knew:

Interrogator: That remark came from your subconscious at that moment.
                   There you were completely stressed and you did not have
                   the ability to think 'Hey, I am going to tell it differently from
                   how it really is'. … it came from your heart.
                   (interrogation 12 November 2004 at 10h 05).

Third, the interrogators apply the well known minimax strategy (*cf.* Vrij, 1998; Inbau, Reid, Buckley & Jayne, 2001) for example:

Ronald: I am still sure that I did not push granny on purpose. I wouldn't
                   dare.
Interrogator: No, not on purpose, but maybe by accident.
Ronald: It must have happened by accident. But I should have been
                   aware of that, shouldn't I?
Interrogator: You must be able to remember that – these kinds of things are
                   remembered.
Ronald: I don't know.
Interrogator: The consequences are so enormous, aren't they? For all parties
                   involved it is really sad.
                   (interrogation 10 November 2004 at 19h 09)

In this way, the interrogation is presented as a common enterprise to restore Ronald's memory:

Interrogator: You now know a lot more than you did yesterday. You are
                   doing very well.
                   (interrogation 10 November 2004 at 19h 56)

Interrogator: But from now on it is going to get better. Because now we are
                   working on a solution together, the three of us.
                   (interrogation 11 November 2004 at 11h 07).

Ronald: Well, I hope I am doing all this right.
Interrogator: What wouldn't you do right?
Ronald: Well, because I am so uncertain about what happened, because
                   I know so very little.
                   (interrogation 11 November 2004 at 11h 08)

Interrogator: You also want to know the truth, don't you?
Ronald: Yes, for sure, absolutely.
                   (interrogation 11 November 2004 at 14h12).

Ronald: The strange thing is that I myself hardly remember anything.
                   ... I've just lost whole pieces.
Interrogator: Then we must go deeper into everything and maybe things
                   will come back to you. I think that the prosecutor will
                   not be at all pleased this afternoon if someone says: 'I do not
                   know, I do not know, maybe I pushed her.' He wants a
                   clear story. If it is not for your benefit, it is for the victim's
                   family.
Ronald: I'm trying to cooperate fully.
Interrogator: You have certain responsibilities. If you were fucking around
                   with your drunk head on the [balcony] railing and dropped
                   [her] over it, then you are responsible.
                   (interrogation 12 November 2004, 9h 51)

Note that in this case there is no possibility of checking the information in the confession. There are no eyewitnesses, there is no trace evidence; even the manner in which granny fell from the balcony is unclear. The police made a full reconstruction of how granny might have fallen and established that, if she is 1.78 m tall, then she could have been pushed over; but if she was only 1.72 m, that would be impossible. The problem is that granny's height is unknown. The pathologist measured her at 1.79 m, but it is a known fact that people lying down are longer. Granny's passport states that she was 1.72 m and a doctor she visited a year earlier measured her as 1.69 m. Thus, all the information Ronald gave in his confession complies with how the police think everything happened and not necessarily with what really happened, because nobody knows.

What is more, Ronald does not know for a simple reason: he was too drunk to remember (*cf.* Van Oorsouw, Merckelbach, Ravelli, Nijman & Mekking-Pompen, 2004). The police convinced him about facts that are their reconstruction of events. Ronald consistently admitted to these facts but qualified this by saying that he cannot remember and the police officers have convinced him that this is what must have happened. His lack of memory is also evident from a letter Ronald wrote six months later, in which he apologized to granny's family. In the letter Ronald asserts that he is offering his sincere apologies because he 'must have killed' granny.

The Sneek balcony murder confession appears to be unproblematic at first sight for several reasons. First, the suspect apparently is telling a rather complete story. At a second look, the story is completely built on suggestions from the interrogating police officers. Second, there seems to be no strong interrogation or some form of duress for the suspect. In fact, real duress is not at all necessary to obtain a false confession. (See, for instance, some Dutch cases where we know a false confession was obtained, such as the Schiedam Park murder [Van Koppen, 2008] or the Putten murder case [Wagenaar & Crombag, 2005].)

In the Putten murder case two men were convicted of raping and murdering a young woman, Christel Ambrosius. Christel visited her grandmother who lived in a cottage on the edge of the woods on Sunday, 3 October 1995. As granny was out visiting friends when she arrived, Christel collected the back door key from the barn. Inside the house she was raped and murdered. Four men were arrested and subjected to lengthy interrogations. All four confessed, although one of them, Wilco Viets, did so as if he was recounting his dreams. Two suspects confessed to having stood outside, looking inside watching the other two committing the crimes. Wilco Viets and Herman Dubois confessed to the rape and murder and were convicted, even though semen found on Christel's leg of did not match that of any of the suspects. Also, the four confessions were different and incompatible and on many aspects did not fit the scene of the crime either. Years later Viets and Dubois were acquitted in a retrial. The other two have never been prosecuted.

The four men confessed to four separate pairs of police officers. The interrogations were taped, but the tapes were only used to write up the statement summary and then reused. As far as I can tell (I served as expert witness in the retrial of the case; see also Blaauw, 2002; Wagenaar & Crombag, 2005), the interrogations were not very harsh. The four suspects were brought to their confessions by interview tactics, of which six could be identified. First, the suspects were led to doubt their own memory. Second, they were encouraged to talk hypothetically about how the crime might have been committed. This was followed by discussions of how the crime was actually committed once the hypothetical situations had been sufficiently rehearsed. Third, the interrogators used tricks as, for instance, suggesting that traces found at the scene matched or would match the suspect. Fourth, as soon as some of the suspects made admissions, the other suspects were confronted with these statements. Fifth, the police officers gave away information. Finally, the suspects were encouraged to speculate about the crime. If their guesses were wrong, they were encouraged to go on; if they were right, the guess was recorded as the suspect's statement. To do all this, the police officers took their time; the suspect were interrogated for many hours. As far as is recorded, together they were interrogated on 200 different occasions, but probably more. The summaries of the known statements run to 812 pages.

The police tactics in the Putten murder case could be demonstrated using the summaries alone; undoubtedly, I could have said much more if there had been tapes of the interrogations. But even then, it could not have been expected that firm conclusions as to the veracity of the statements would have been possible. My analysis concluded that one should be very cautious with the confessions of the four suspects and even that there was support for the hypothesis that the confessions were false. At the same time, the hypothesis that these confessions were true could not be refuted from the statements alone. The fact that these statements were so different from what actually happened to Christel in her granny's house – as far as we can tell from the crime scene – and given the semen of an unknown man on Christel's body caused the court to acquit the two men in the retrial. The donor of the semen has still not been found.

To determine that the confessions were indeed false, a thorough analysis of the tapes of the interrogations and the rest of the case file would have been necessary. In the Steered balcony murder it could be demonstrated using the tapes how the suspect's statements were steered by the police officers' suggestions. In the Putten murder case there were no tapes to analyse. That made it much more difficult to draw firm conclusions. But it is not unusual for tapes of interrogations not to exist or not always be available. What are the possibilities then?

The content of the confession: on forms of knowledge

In many countries it is not customary to tape all suspect interrogations. In the Netherlands, for instance, taping interrogations was rare until recently. Now there are plans to videotape interrogations in all very serious cases, like murder and rape. The prosecution, the defence and the court used to rely entirely on the police report of the interrogations. The reports used to be, at best, a summary of all that was said, but often was no more than a summary of what the interrogators deemed relevant at the time of the interrogation.

Still, these police reports do allow for a check on the truthfulness of a confession. Let me give an example: the Schiedam Park murder (for a fuller description of this case, see Van Koppen, 2003; 2008). On 22 June 2000 two children, Nienke aged 10 years and her 11-year-old friend Maikel, were playing in the Beatrixpark in Schiedam, a town near Rotterdam. After a while, they thought it was time to go home for dinner. While going to retrieve their bicycles which they had left a little distance away, a young man grabbed them by their necks and walked them some 90 m into bushes. The attacker ordered the children to undress themselves, then he stabbed Maikel several times around his neck. Finally, he strangled both children using the shoelaces from the army boots Maikel was wearing. Maikel survived by playing dead; Nienke was killed.

After the assailant left, Maikel stepped out of the bushes, naked with the shoelace and boot still around his neck. He approached a man who was standing on a bridge near the bushes. That man stopped a passing cyclist, Kees Borsboom, who then called the police using his mobile phone.

In the two days following the murder Maikel was interviewed by the police in hospital, where he stayed for a few days because of his stab wounds. He told the police what had happened and also gave a description of the killer: a man aged between 20 and 35 years, 1.80 m tall, extremely pale, with acne and a scruffy face, the pustules on the attacker's face were scratched and were oozing blood and pus. As it later turned out, Maikel's statements were extremely accurate. The offender description was correct to the point of even describing the man's unusual features. Maikel was the only direct witness of the man taking the two children into the bushes or attempting to murder them.

Some weeks before the murder Kees Borsboom, the man who called the police, asked a boy in the same park whether he wanted to earn 25 guilders. Although the boy said 'no', Borsboom said: 'If you jerk me off, I'll give you 25 guilders.' The boy ran home. Some time after the murder the boy saw Borsboom again, went home and collected his father. His father, a police officer, identified himself to Borsboom and asked him what he had done to his son. Borsboom apologized immediately and told the police officer that he was in therapy for his behaviour and that he would never do it again. Nevertheless, he agreed to attend the police station a few days later. Before the meeting, the police officer entered Borsboom's name in the police computer and saw he was a witness in the Nienke murder case. From that moment on, Borsboom was the prime suspect. He was prosecuted and convicted both by the district court and the Court of Appeals. He was sentenced to 18 years in prison, followed by compulsory confinement in a forensic mental hospital; which in this case is effectively a whole-life sentence.

Borsboom did not fit the offender description given by Maikel at all and was, in fact, innocent. We know this because another man confessed to the murder some years later. He had intimate knowledge of the crime and his DNA matched samples from the scene of the crime. But let us return to Kees Borsboom.

During a weekend in September 2000 Borsboom made confessions. His interrogations were not recorded, nor was his attorney present, even though the attorney had asked to attend. The prosecutor refused. Borsboom later contended that the interrogations were made under duress. Of course, the two interrogating police officers denied this. Even at the time, there were indications that Borsboom was telling the truth. His confessions should have been suspected, not because Borsboom said they were false – a lot of suspects say so afterwards – but because his story was so different in so many details from Maikel's that the police should never have trusted his confessions. Please remember that Maikel was the only true eyewitness of the murder.

Let me give a few examples. 1) Maikel told the police that the killer grabbed them by the neck and said, 'Come on, come with me'. He had a knife in his hand all the time. Borsboom in his confession, however, said that to begin with the knife was in his hand, but put it in his pocket when he seized the children. 2) Maikel said that the killer ordered them to undress. Maikel had trouble taking off his army boots, so the killer started pulling them and jerking his clothes. Borsboom maintained that he did not touch the children while they were undressing until they were naked. 3) The killer was wearing a blue baseball cap. Borsboom said he was wearing no cap. In fact, none of the people who encountered him that day saw him with any hat. 4) The sequence in which the killer did everything in the bushes differs between Maikel's and Borsboom's versions.

Why, then, did the police not see all these discrepancies in Borsboom's confessions? There is a simple, though illogical, reason: they did not trust Maikel. Many in the team thought that Maikel might have killed Nienke. The police hired an educationalist, Ruud Bullens, to give guidance on the interviewing of Maikel and to serve the interests of Maikel during the interviews. Almost from the beginning, they did not trust Maikel much, even long before Borsboom had been arrested. The major reason for that seems to be that Maikel was much more intelligent than the police officers; they considered him to be a very odd boy. Also, Maikel had displayed behaviour that was considered odd: he did not yell at any point in time during the attack, even though a lot of people were passing by the bushes. More important, Bullens told the police that Maikel had 'a big secret', without specifying what that secret might be and without explaining – also afterwards – how he knew. The police suspected that Maikel had killed Nienke, stabbed and strangled himself and, moreover, concealed the knife, which has never been found. After Borsboom's arrest, the police tried to explain away the blatant differences between the confessions and the statements made by Maikel by rigorously interviewing Maikel again. The child did not give an inch, so the explanation had to be done by other means. This was done, again, using the statements of Bullens and a psychologist who reviewed the tapes of Maikel's interviews. Following their expert reports, it was concluded that the perception of Maikel has been so blurred by the high emotional tone of the situation, that his statements could not be trusted. So, the police, prosecution and courts did not trust his offender description and all the parts of his statements that contradicted the confession made by Borsboom.

Of course, there is no logic to this, but none of the trial participants seems to have bothered about this. Either Borsboom was the killer and Miakel was innocent and there is no reason to disbelieve him, or Borsboom is innocent, and only then is there reason to suspect Maikel and distrust him. Considering Borsboom guilty and distrusting Maikel at the same time – the police's choice – seems perverse.

Intimate knowledge of the crime is an important measure for the veracity of a confession. In fact, Dutch police officers learn during training that a suspect saying he committed a crime is of no interest. A suspect's account should conform to evidence the police have from other sources.

Testing a confession in this manner is less straightforward than it seems at first sight. First, if suspect's story is in line with evidence from other sources, that can only be seen as a sign of the veracity of the confession in combination with knowledge that the suspect did not get the information from other sources. So, we must know that police officers did not feed the relevant information to the suspect. A first step is that interrogations are tape-recorded. But then still we need to know that the police officers did not disclose intimate knowledge for instance when transporting the suspect from prison to the police station. Also, we need to establish the suspect did not get information from other sources, for instance because he was present at the scene of the crime, but not in the role of perpetrator, or the crime story was told to him later by the perpetrator.

In that sense, it is easier to establish that a confession is false. If a suspect does not have intimate knowledge of the crime at all or confesses to all kinds of wrong information, as Borsboom did for the killing of Nienke, the conclusion can be drawn that the confession is false.

In this vein Han Israëls proposed another form of knowledge that can be used to test the confession. He called this police knowledge (Israëls, 2004; Israëls & Van Koppen, 2006), using the Ina Post case to demonstrate how that works.

On the evening of 22 August 1986 the corpse of 89-year-old Ms. Kolstee was found in her apartment in Leidschendam, near The Hague. The police investigation soon turned to women who worked at a care institution for the elderly and who looked after Ms. Kolstee. She was not only murdered; cheques were stolen from her apartment, most of which were cashed. Some (but not all) of the carers were subjected to a writing test and only the handwriting of Ina Post vaguely resembled the handwriting on the cheques. She thus became the prime suspect. She had been interrogated in the apartment, helping the police to establish what might have been stolen. On 8 September, Post was arrested and on 11 September she confessed. There were no tape-recordings of the interrogations; that was unheard of in these days. In the police report Post is quoted as saying: 'In my previous statements I did not tell the truth. Now I am prepared to do so. … I needed the money, my accounts were in the red.' She told how she opened a cupboard looking for money. When Ms. Kolstee entered the room, Post hit her with her walking stick. Ms. Kolstee fell unconscious. 'I panicked', Ina Post claimed, and she strangled Ms. Kolstee with an electric cord.

The Ina Post case is special in that she was interrogated in the course of an ongoing police investigation. A lot was unknown to the police at that point. In fact, they were entertaining some strong misconceptions. These can be traced in Post's confessions, proving that what she confessed to could not have come from her own memory but could only have been suggested to her by the police. Let me give some examples.

Post confessed during the course of several interrogations, starting on the night of 11 September. That evening she told the custody officer in the police station that she wanted to be interrogated under hypnosis. He phoned the officer in charge of the investigation at home, who with another police officer returned to the police station. The other police officer drove past Ms. Kolstee's apartment to collect her mail. In the mail was a bank statement showing that all the cheques to that account were presented on 4 September (remember the murder took place on Friday, 22 August). So, the police assumed that all the cheques were cashed, starting on the Monday after the murder. That evening Post confessed that she cashed almost all the cheques during the week after the murder, between 1 and 4 September. Only later, when the police received the original cheques from the bank, did it turn out that the cheques were all cashed not at banks, but at a department store and not in the week after the murder, but the very next day, 23 August. What happened next? During the next interrogation Post confessed that she cashed the cheques on Saturday, 23 August at a department store in The Hague. So, we can be certain that Post only told the police she cashed the cheques in the week after the murder because she was following police suggestions.

The same can be seen in several other parts of her confessions. To give a second example, Ina Post confessed she stole several items, among which was a folder containing bank statements. That seemed intimate knowledge at the time, but we know now was based on police suggestion. What happened? Scene of crime detectives found the folder and examined it for traces. The interrogating police officers, however, were under the impression that it was missing. Thus Ina Post confessed that she had stolen it.

Let me give one other example. All the cheques were cashed at the department store's money counter for the maximum amount, except one. That one was used to buy something in the department store. Ina Post confessed to that, but her account was very odd. She confessed that she bought something costing 34 guilders – the amount written on the cheque – but did not know *what* she bought. This is alien to how people think: we usually remember what we have bought better than we can remember how much it costs.

Han Israëls defined such knowledge as police knowledge: the suspect confesses to something that can only be traced back to inaccurate suggestions made by the police. The police knowledge in Post's confessions proves that she got her knowledge of the crime from suggestions made by the police officers and not from her own memory.

Police knowledge thus can prove that the confession is false, or at least that a certain part of the confession is false. This poses the question of how much police knowledge is needed before we can conclude that the whole of the confession is false. In the same vein the question can be posed how much wrong intimate knowledge of the crime is necessary before we can conclude that the whole of the confession is false. I do not have a ready answer to that, but some elements seem relevant here. First, of course, it matters whether police knowledge or inaccurate intimate knowledge concerns central or peripheral elements of the crime. Second, some knowledge of that kind might be a much stronger indication of a false confession than other kinds of knowledge. A system comparable to what Olson & Wells (2004) proposed for alibis may be useful for confessions. Third, and last, it must be noted that using police knowledge and inaccurate intimate knowledge can logically prove that the confession is false.

Conclusions

Much knowledge has been gathered on false confessions and why suspects make them. Most of that knowledge, however, is concerned with what may predict or elicit a false confession. Forensic practice, however, requires different knowledge, namely how in retrospect a true confession can be distinguished from a false one. Less is known about how to overcome the problem. In this chapter I have argued that if much is known about the interrogations and the circumstances surrounding it (see the Sneek balcony murder case) definitive answers can be given to the veracity of the confession. If less is known, sometimes definitive answers can be given, as in the Schiedam Park murder. I have also argued that personality traits and the nature of the interrogations *per se* are not very useful, but also not entirely useless, in identifying false confessions.

Acknowledgement

I thank Menno Ezinga, Nicole Haas, Kim Megens and Roos Marijn Kok for their help in analysing the interrogations of the Sneek balcony murder. All quotes are from the formal police transcription of the interrogation and translated from the Dutch by the author.

References

Bem, D. J. & Funder, D. C. (1978). Predicting more of the people more of the time: Assessing the personality of situations. *Psychological Review, 85*, 485–501.

Blaauw, J. A. (2002). *De Puttense moordzaak: Reconstructie van een dubieus moor donderzoek [The Putten murder case: Reconstruction of a dubious murder inquiry]*, 3rd edition. Baarn: Fontein.

Gudjonsson, G. H. (2003). *The psychology of interrogations and confessions: A handbook*. Chichester: Wiley.

Horselenberg, R., Merckelbach, H. & Josephs, S. (2003). Individual differences and false confessions: A conceptual replication of Kassin and Kiechel (1996). *Psychology, Crime, and Law, 9*, 1–8.

Inbau, F. E., Reid, J. E., Buckley, J. P. & Jayne, B. C. (2001). *Criminal interrogation and confessions*, 4th edition. Gaithersburg, MD: Aspen.

Israëls, H. (2004). *De bekentenissen van Ina Post [The confessions by Ina Post]*. Alphen aan den Rijn: Kluwer.

Israëls, H. & Van Koppen, P. J. (2006). Daderkennis, politiekennis en sturend verhoren [Suspect knowledge, police knowledge and steering interrogations]. *Nederlands Tijdschrift voor Rechtsfilosofie en Rechtstheorie, 35*, 8–18.

Langbein, J. H. (1977). *Torture and the law of proof: Europe and England in the ancien régime*. Chicago: University of Chicago Press.

Langbein, J. H. (1983). Torture. In S. H. Kadish (Ed.), *Encyclopedia of crime and justice*. New York: Free Press.

Mischel, W. (1977). The interaction of person and situation. In D. Magnusson & N. S. Endler (Eds.), *Personality at the crossroads: Current issues in international psychology*. Hillsdale, NJ: Lawrence Erlbaum.

Mischel, W. (1979). On the interface of cognition and personality: Beyond the person–situation debate. *American Psychologist, 34*, 740–754.

Ofshe, R. J. (1989). Coerced confessions: The logic of seemingly irrational action. *Cultic Studies Journal, 6,* 1–15.

Olson, E. A. & Wells, G. L. (2004). What makes a good alibi? A proposed taxonomy. *Law and Human Behavior, 28,* 157–176.

Ost, J., Costall, A. & Bull, R. H. C. (2001). False confessions and false memories: A model for understanding retractors' experiences. *Journal of Forensic Psychiatry, 12,* 549–579.

Van Koppen, P. J. (2003). *De Schiedammer parkmoord: Een rechtspsychologische reconstructie [The Schiedam park murder: A legal psychological reconstruction].* Nijmegen: Ars Aequi Libri (met medewerking van Ch. Dudink, M. van der Graaf, M. de Haas, J. van Luik en V. Wijsman).

Van Koppen, P. J. (2008). Blundering justice: The Schiedam Park murder. In R. N. Kocsis (Ed.), *Serial murder and the psychology of violent crimes.* Totowa, NJ: Humana.

Van Oorsouw, K. I. M., Merckelbach, H., Ravelli, D. P., Nijman, H. L. I. & Mekking-Pompen, I. (2004). Alcoholic blackout for criminally relevant behavior. *Journal of the American Academy of Psychiatry and the Law, 32,* 364–371.

Vrij, A. (1998). Interviewing suspects. In A. Memon, A. Vrij & R. H. C. Bull (Eds.), *Psychology and law: Truthfulness, accuracy and credibility.* London: McGraw Hill.

Wagenaar, W. A. & Crombag, H. F. M. (2005). *The popular policeman and other cases: Psychological perspectives on legal evidence.* Amsterdam: Amsterdam University Press.

Wagenaar, W. A., Van Koppen, P. J. & Crombag, H. F. M. (1993). *Anchored narratives: The psychology of criminal evidence.* London: Harvester Wheatsheaf.

Cases

Hof (Appelate Court)'s-Hertogenbosch, 26 February 2008, LJN-number BC 5105 (see www.rechtspraak.nl).

Chapter Five

The Investigation of Terrorist Offences in the United Kingdom: The Context and Climate for Interviewing Officers

John Pearse

Managing Director of Forensic Navigation Services Ltd.

This chapter will reflect on how political and legal activity in the wake of the atrocities of September 2001 has impacted on police terrorist investigations and on the role of the police interviewer in particular. Specifically, it will examine fundamental differences between everyday criminal investigations and terrorist cases, recent legislative changes designed to limit the extent to which a detainee may exercise the right of silence, and finally provide an insight into the nature and type of tactics adopted by police in recent terrorist cases.

Introduction

The traumatic events in New York in September 2001 (9/11) served to propel terrorism to the forefront of everybody's mind; it was an outrage that precipitated a great deal of introspection not only at a personal level, but also at a national and political level. In the United Kingdom (UK) The Terrorism Act 2000 (TACT) had recently been enacted, replacing previous 'temporary' terrorist provisions. Though framed by the UK's experience of terrorism in Northern Ireland, the introduction of TACT was seen as a tacit acceptance of the need for permanent legislation to counter terrorist activity both within the UK and abroad. It replaced temporary legislation (Prevention of Terrorism [Temporary Provisions] Act) in force since November 1974 which had required

Handbook of Psychology of Investigative Interviewing: Current Developments and Future Directions
Edited by Ray Bull, Tim Valentine and Tom Williamson
© 2009 John Wiley & Sons, Ltd.

annual renewal by Parliament. The UK government's response in the face of this 'new' threat from global terrorists capable of executing a multifaceted attack unfettered by geographic location included additional terrorist legislation and an examination of the UK's response mechanisms and resilience to counter such terrorist activity within its own shores. The Anti-Terrorism Crime and Security Act 2001 (ATCS) was first signalled by the UK government as early as 3 October 2001. The fashion for legislation to be shaped by dramatic and tragic events, however, was not new; earlier examples appeared in the aftermath of the Birmingham bomb outrage in 1974 (ibid.), the Omagh tragedy in 1998, and more recently the Patriot Act 2001 in the United States (US) after 9/11. (For details of the ATCS act, see Walker, 2002.)

The substance and evolving framework of this counter-terrorism review is neatly captured in a discussion paper published by the Home Office (2004; see also the various reports on the operation of TACT by Lord Carlile and on proposals for changes to the laws against terrorism; www.homeoffice.gov.uk), which acknowledges the international dimension of the new suicide threat and the increased risks facing UK and US interests. It also confirmed that the terrorist groups used sophisticated new communication technology, were skilled in evading surveillance and had the ability to assume multiple identities and travel with some ease across borders. The unconventional, loose-knit structure of multiple terrorist groups gathered across the world, motivated by religious and cultural belief systems rather than any particular political ideology, was also identified as presenting considerable difficulties for the gathering and sharing of credible intelligence.

The successful prosecution of terrorist suspects according to the UK's established legal code remains one of the government's main objectives in the continuing fight against terrorism. However, in attempting to pursue such an objective, a number of practical and ethical issues emerged that conspired to frustrate. These included the reluctance of some foreign governments to allow their material to be used in an evidential format and the continuing difficulty experienced by the UK intelligence services in being able to release sensitive material that might meet the demands of the evidential threshold without endangering the original source or indeed the methodology concerned. Such a predicament was neatly encapsulated by the presence in the UK of a number of terrorist suspects of foreign nationality against whom charges could not be brought and who could not be deported to their country of origin for fear of possible human rights abuses. These individuals were detained without charge under Part 4 of the ATCS – a measure subsequently declared unlawful by the House of Lords in December 2004 ([2004] UKHL 56. The government has since repealed the Part 4 powers under the ATCS and replaced them with a system of control orders under the Prevention of Terrorism Act 2005 (see Walker, 2002).

The post-9/11 period also witnessed an increase in the number of terrorist atrocities around the world (e.g., Madrid, Bali, Saudi Arabia, Jakarta, Casablanca and Istanbul) and in the UK a number of high-profile, multi-agency counter-terrorist operations took place with New Scotland Yard's Counter Terrorism Command (CTC) assuming the investigative lead. Such operations included Operation Springbourne (commonly known as the 'Ricin Conspiracy'); the search and arrests at the Finsbury Park Mosque, in north London; prosecutions brought against those attempting to commit suicide attacks in London on 21 July 2005, and many others that are still to appear in court and are therefore *sub judice*. The international dimension also served to focus attention on the vagaries associated with so many different judicial systems and the compatibility, or lack of it, in relation to the exchange of evidence or the sharing of intelligence. However, amongst members of the UK security services and CT police there is a perception that the present legal system fails to recognize, or maximize, the opportunity to gather intelligence from persons detained for terrorist offences (see Report on the Operation in 2004 of the Terrorism Act 2000, p. 37, para. 136 et seq.).

Police interviewing of suspects remains one of the optimum scenarios for the gathering of evidence and intelligence and it may prove worthwhile to examine what we have learnt as a result of empirical research in the field of police interviewing before we consider the legal issues.

Police interviewing in the UK

In the UK, the interview process stands out as the only inquisitorial element within an adversarial system of justice. It is designed to allow the suspect an opportunity to refute any allegations, to provide his or her side of the story or to remain silent in the face of questioning and so limit the likelihood of self-incrimination. For the police it is an opportunity to investigate the credibility of an allegation and, where necessary, to challenge a detainee's version of events. The Police and Criminal Evidence Act 1984 (PACE) legislated that all police interviews with suspects had to be tape-recorded and by 1992 such technology had been deployed in all police stations in the UK. As well as providing a more transparent and accountable reference to assist the criminal justice process, the taping of interviews provided a reliable and accurate record of exactly what was taking place for research purposes.

The conduct of police interviewing was subject to a major overhaul after research conducted for the Royal Commission on Criminal Justice in 1993 (Home Office, Cmnd 2263) revealed a number of areas for improvement; in particular officers were found to be poorly prepared, lacking in confidence and often failed to grasp the core requirements of the prosecution case (see Baldwin, 1993). A national police interview training programme designed to remedy such deficiencies was implemented, and for the first time all police officers in England and Wales were provided with a clear structure to follow. The mnemonic PEACE (**P**lanning and preparation, **E**ngage and explain, **A**ccount, clarification and challenge, **C**losure and **E**valuation) was used to reinforce this new model, which was aimed at educating officers in the benefits of an information-gathering process, to provide them with a straightforward and adaptable mechanism, and to steer them away from seeking a confession *per se* towards a more ethical target of seeking the truth: a deliberate shift from interrogation to investigative interviewing (Williamson, 1993). This programme now represents the first level of interview training for all police officers.

Interestingly, a review of the quality of police station legal advice for the same Royal Commission identified similar problems and criticized the passive role adopted by many legal practitioners and the limited nature of the advice given (McConville & Hodgson, 1993). As a result the Law Society implemented a new training regime and all police station legal advisers who were not qualified solicitors were required to achieve accreditation within this new scheme (Law Society, 1994; Ede & Shepherd, 2000; this latter publication has been described as encouraging a more confrontational approach by police station legal advisers).

The availability of an accurate audio record of what took place in the police interview opened up for scientific research a dialogue that had previously taken place behind closed doors. Thus the role of the legal adviser, interpreter and the appropriate adult (AA), parties independent of the police whose role is to safeguard the welfare and rights of vulnerable individuals, were now also subject to scrutiny. Issues surrounding why people confess or chose to exercise their right of silence (RoS) also became subject to empirical investigation.

Research findings into why people confess

The research literature suggests that there are three important contextual factors associated with why a suspect would make an admission or a confession:

- access to legal advice;
- the strength of the evidence against the suspect; and
- the interviewing tactics adopted by the police.

(For an excellent review of this entire area of research, see Gudjonsson, 2003.)

There are also three overlapping facilitative (or internal) factors associated with the process of confession and admission:

- external pressure (persuasive interviewing tactics, fear of confinement, police behaviour);
- internal pressure (experiencing guilt and the need to confess);
- perception of proof (they believe there is no point in denial).

Intuitively, such factors make a great deal of sense.

The admission/confession rate in the UK ranges from 55% to 59%, although there is often great variation between stations. Suspects who choose to have access to legal advice are about four times less likely to make a confession or an admission compared to those without such advice (Pearse, Gudjonsson, Clare & Rutter, 1998). The presence of a legal adviser was found to have a significant influence on the extent to which a person will exercise their RoS. Moston, Stephenson & Williamson (1993) found great variation between stations, with 8% using the RoS in the Holborn area of London compared to 25% in Uxbridge. These researchers suggest that RoS was also associated with the seriousness of the offence and previous convictions. They also noted that RoS did not affect the decision to prosecute and that those using this tactic were more likely to be convicted than those who chose to deny the offence during the interview. In general terms, something like three-quarters of all suspects answered police questions, with the remainder failing to answer any question or being selective in relation to what they have to say. Such findings effectively extinguished one of the most enduring of police interviewing myths; that all suspects say nothing on the advice of their lawyer.

More recently, legislative changes introduced under sections 34–37 of the Criminal Justice and Public Order Act 1994 allow a judge and/or jury to draw adverse inferences from a suspect's silence during police questioning. Initial research concerning this additional power is in many respects equivocal. For example, nearly 40% of suspects exercising their RoS were given this 'special warning', yet relatively few gave a satisfactory account in response. On the other hand, the percentage of suspects refusing to answer some or all police questions fell from 23% to 16% and the proportion that gave a complete 'no comment' response fell from 10% to 6% (Bucke, Street & Brown, 2000).

The original intention behind this additional power was twofold: to discourage a suspect from fabricating a defence later and to encourage a suspect to disclose a genuine defence as early as possible in the process. More recently, the Home Office has been examining allegations that the opportunity to draw adverse inferences against a suspect's silence has effectively been undermined by the growing popularity amongst defence representatives to submit a prepared statement that allows their client to continue with a 'no comment' regime (internal correspondence between Home Office, Police, CPS and other agencies). In other words, where it is alleged that a suspect carried out a crime, the defence lawyer will collaborate with their client to create an often short and meaningless statement that simply refutes the allegation.

An important adjunct to the use of adverse inferences lies in the amount of pre-interview disclosure material supplied by the police. The Court of Appeal has held that if little or nothing of the case against a suspect is disclosed, so that a legal adviser cannot properly advise their client, this may be a good reason to advise the suspect to remain silent (see *R v Argent* [1997]; *R v Imran & Hussain* [1997]; *R v Noble* [1997] CLR 346). The onus is, therefore, on the investigating officer to disclose sufficient information to ensure that the suspect understands the nature and circumstances of their arrest. There is, however, no requirement for the police to present a *prima facie* case before questioning (*R v Imran & Hussein*; *R v Farrell* [2004]; and the House of Lords judgment in *Ward v Police Service of Northern Ireland* [2007], reported in *The Times*, 22 November 2007).

The second contextual factor – the strength of the evidence and, importantly, the suspect's perception of this state of affairs – was a very crucial determinant of behaviour. In the Moston, Stephenson & Williamson (1992) study when the evidence was weak, confessions occurred in less than 10% of cases and denials in 77%. Conversely, when the evidence was strong, the figures effectively reversed, with 67% confessions and 16% denials. In terms of the facilitative factors influencing a suspect what was important was when the suspect believed that there was no point in denying the offence because the police have sufficient evidence to eventually prove it. Such personal perceptions are exactly what a number of interrogation manuals recommend should be targeted and manipulated by interviewing officers. Such tactics stimulate a number of legal and ethical issues (for a comprehensive review see Gudjonsson, 2003; for detail of the specific tactics, see Inbau, Reid, Buckley & Jayne, 2001).

The third important contextual factor relates to the type and nature of tactics employed by the police. This overlaps with the internal facilitative factor of external pressure, which accommodates not only persuasive police tactics but also concern regarding police behaviour and fear of confinement. Research has identified a clear distinction between the type of tactics employed in general, run-of-the-mill cases and more serious cases (Pearse & Gudjonsson, 1999). In the former it would appear that the suspect has already made up his or her mind to confess or deny and is able to stick to that position regardless of external factors. Indeed, in such circumstances confessions are often made despite the tactics used, rather than because of them. In serious cases, such as murder, robbery, blackmail and rape, we are more likely to find coercive, manipulative and forceful tactics applied with more intensity and often over a much longer period of incarceration (*ibid.*; Pearse, 1997).

In 1997 the author examined a unique dataset of 20 very serious criminal cases where the suspects (both male and female) had been persuaded, on audio tape, to shift their position from denial to admission, despite the onerous consequences attached to an admission to such serious offences Pearse, 1997). However, finding examples of someone shifting their position from denial to admission during interview proved very difficult, as it is a quite rare occurrence. A detailed examination of what actually took place to achieve this shift revealed that the interviewing officers engaged in a combination of coercive and prolonged tactics that concentrated on exploiting many of the contextual factors and manipulating the internal factors identified above. Obvious differences with minor cases include duration (in minor cases average interview was 22 mins, range 2–109 mins, in serious cases 2 hrs 16 mins, range 24 mins–12 hrs 42 mins), as well as the overbearing nature of 'clusters of tactics'. Eight cases (40%) were ruled inadmissible at court although a legal adviser was present in five of those eight cases (63%) (Pearse, 1997).

In summary, whilst a number of factors were concerned with the decision-making process of suspects in relation to making a confession or denial, the main conclusion that can be drawn from the research 'is that the most frequent and important reason why suspects confess is the strength of their belief in the evidence against them' (Gudjonsson, 2003: 153).

Recent decades have also seen a growth in the availability of research conducted into the individual characteristics of persons detained by police who may be vulnerable to providing misleading information or who may be unable to appreciate the significance of their answers or the consequences attached to their predicament. The first empirical research in this area was for the 1993 Royal Commission. A number of relevant miscarriages of justice have been identified that suggest that the root causes will rarely be found in one place; rather it will be a combination of events and issues that together bring about such flawed prosecutions. Thus a suspect's psychological vulnerability (suggestibility, compliance and learning disability) may not be recognized or acted upon, their pre-existing mental illness or depression may not be acknowledged, and they could be subjected to lengthy periods of incarceration and extensive interviewing sessions by police. Environmental factors may also play a part brought about by continued isolation from peers, the alien and debilitating impact of detention, and sleep and food deprivation (Gudjonsson, Rutter, Clare & Pearse, 1993; see also Gudjonsson, 2003). In the terrorist arena a contemporaneous example has been created by the circumstances to be found at the Guantanamo Bay Detention Centre and Abu Ghraib Prison regime in Iraq (Pearse, 2006).

Legal perspective

Acts of terrorism are perceived as extreme examples of violence, perpetrated against often innocent individuals and special measures have to be introduced in order to combat this threat. The readiness of Parliament to bring forward new legislation supports such a contention. The same may also be said of the judiciary in the UK. Some legal authorities are of the view that

> there is a case for saying that terrorism, and legislation for the prevention of terrorism, should be regarded in a special way: the interference with a right or freedom may be more readily justified in the case of terrorism. (Rowe, 2000: 527–542)

Arguments in support of this stance can be found in the powers and duties of states to protect their citizens of the (European Convention on Human Rights, Article 2 – safeguarding the right to life), on moral grounds that condemn terrorism as an illegitimate form of violent expression, and finally that such acts are best understood as special forms of crime requiring a particular response to overcome the difficulties faced by the investigation and prosecution process. It has been argued 'That there is no greater challenge for a democracy than the response it makes to terrorism' (Home Office, 2004).

Evidence of legal recognition for the need to treat terrorist issues as special cases can be found in current terrorist legislation and legal judgments (Walker, 2002, who described TACT as 'the most extensive counter-terrorist code in western Europe'). For example, in the UK police powers to stop and search have been extended by section 44 of TACT. In March 2003, Brooke LJ and Mr Justice Maurice Kay said the use of the random stop and search powers and any resulting violation of human rights were justified because 'a threat greater than any that this country in general and its capital city in particular, have ever faced except in time of war' (2003 EWHC 2545) – a finding upheld by the House of Lords in March 2006. Terrorist suspects can, under some circumstances, be detained without access to a legal adviser for up to 48 hours and in other circumstances, a suspect may only consult a solicitor in the sight and hearing of a 'qualified' police officer (Schedule 8 (part I) of TACT paras 8 and 9 respectively).

The possession of articles for terrorist purposes, under section 57 of TACT, proved to be one of the fiercest debating points in the UK during the passage of the Act as it was interpreted as reversing the burden of proof from the prosecution to the defence. In giving judgment on this issue in the House of Lords, Lord Cooke was of the opinion that terrorism was to be treated as a special case and that it was not disproportionate to put burdens on the defendant in times of terrorism (Rowe, 2000: 529; see also the reverse burden provisions under section 18(2) of TACT). More recently Parliament has extended the detention period that suspects can be held without charge from 14 days to up to 28 days. This increase was granted after a major political debate in Parliament, which saw the government's original proposal for a period of 90 days' detention without charge defeated. The government continues to lay proposals before the House for additional periods of detention, the latest set at 42 days. Additional offences of encouraging and preparing or training for terrorism have been introduced (Terrorism Act 2006, sections 1, 5 and 6 respectively). Such an environment suggests that what takes place in the police interview scenario with terrorist suspects may also be at the boundaries of criminal law and practice, especially when compared with typical criminal cases.

In the UK, proposed changes to the terrorism legislation recently brought about considerable parliamentary and public debate and some indication of the logistics and scale of the tasks facing terrorist investigators was revealed by New Scotland Yard (http://www.homeoffice.gov.uk/Terrorism/ Terrorismandthelaw, letter from Assistant Commissioner Andy Hayman to the Home Secretary, Rt. Hon. Charles Clarke, 6 October 2005). This suggests that, unlike criminal cases, there is often a need to arrest terrorist suspects prematurely in order to protect the public and save lives. Such precipitous action may be based on sensitive intelligence and often before there has been time to gather sufficient evidence against the terrorist suspects that would allow the prosecution to consider there was a likelihood of conviction, unlike criminal arrests where the whole ethos behind the introduction of PACE was to provide police with sufficient powers to gather evidence prior to arrest and so reduce the period of detention.

Other obstacles encountered by the police included the extensive nature of the many enquiries undertaken in terrorist cases (identity fraud, telephone and other communication searches, hard drives and software to be interrogated – sometimes encrypted – international liaison, financial aspects) and the need for exhaustive forensic searches, some taking up to weeks to conclude. These were part of a number of the arguments put forward in order to extend the detention of terrorist suspects from 14 days to 90 days.

Unfortunately, there has been very little comprehensive research into terrorist cases in the UK and the exact dynamics within this particular interview scenario are not well known. The author was recently granted access to analyse a number of terrorist cases and to conduct face-to-face interviews with a broad range of serving CT officers which in turn led to the distribution of a questionnaire to serving officers within the CTC at New Scotland Yard. In this chapter, the main hypothesis under examination is that interviews with terrorist suspects will be treated by police in the same manner as serious criminal offences and that police officers will engage in a range of coercive and manipulative interviewing tactics in order influence the decision-making process of the suspect to obtain a confession or an admission.

Methodological considerations

This research was divided into three sections: an analysis of 30 CT cases; a survey of the views of a range of officers from senior investigators and managers to detective inspectors, sergeants and constables by undertaking personal interviews; and a customized questionnaire distributed randomly to investigating officers (detective sergeants and detective constables). There are restrictions on the amount of data that can be catered for within the confines of one chapter and I shall limit this review to important distinctions between criminal and terrorist cases, the impact of the 'special warning procedure' and the nature and type of interview tactics adopted by police.

In order for cases to qualify for this study the researcher needed to have access to the following items in each case:

* the audio-tapes of the terrorist interview;
* transcripts of all interviews;
* a copy of the suspect's custody record;
* sight of the initial Crown Prosecution Service (CPS) report or outline details of the case.

The CPS report was necessary in order to achieve some understanding of the nature of the allegations in each case, and access to the suspect's individual custody record provided an insight into any issues relevant to their detention, treatment or welfare. This might include medical observations – the result of examinations by doctors, information relating to his or her mental state and any condition related to the custodial environment.

The presence of both the audio-tape and the transcript of the interview provided the author with a contemporaneous insight into what actually took place, as well as an accurate reference document to annotate. This detailed methodology is far more extensive than many previous studies which relied solely on observational data or only one medium (e.g. transcripts) (see Pearse, 1997). In previous studies access to the audio tapes has proved invaluable in correcting a large number of sometimes very serious errors in the court transcripts – for example, a rape case with the person denying the offence: the transcript shows an admission, and then later admissions that should have been denials (*ibid.*: 181).

A total of 30 terrorist cases from the CTC at New Scotland Yard qualified for this study. Each case was studied in relation to the case details and the custody record checked for medical observations or indications of psychological vulnerability. The interview tapes were cross-referenced with the relevant transcripts and then divided into interview sessions for analysis. An interview session was defined as any period of continuous interviewing (i.e., with no breaks in excess of 60 minutes). In previous studies cases were often analysed according to the individual time of each tape, but this failed to capture the full extent and practicalities involved in the police interview. For example, it is not unusual to allow consultations with legal advisers to take place, or short adjournments for exhibits and refreshments. A total of 187 interview sessions were analysed. Thus with an appreciation of all relevant allegations and some knowledge of the individual suspect's detention experience, the author was in a position to begin to analyse each case.

Interview tactics and questionnaire distribution

The author has analysed many hundreds of police interviews and has developed a robust methodology for understanding and interpreting what takes place within this particular interaction. Essentially, the nature and type of tactics employed by the police can be captured within a specially designed coding frame predicated on a three dimensional typology: Delivery – Maximization – Manipulation (Pearse, 1997; see also Pearse, 2006. This extends the methodology to help understand the tactics employed at the Abu Ghraib and Guantanamo Bay detention centres).

Delivery is very much an overlapping category which is present throughout the process and is designed to capture 'what' type of questions are asked (closed, leading, open etc.); 'how' they are put (hushed, lowered tones, or harsh and aggressive) as well as any relevant contextual features (i.e. 'where' the questioning takes place – the custodial environment). It captures all the contextual features. Maximization is 'a hard-sell' technique in which the interrogator tries to scare and intimidate the suspect into confessing by making claims (false or otherwise) about evidence and exaggerating the seriousness and/or magnitude of the charges (Pearse, 2006: 76). This includes any tactic designed to increase a suspect's internal anxiety. Finally, manipulation relates to the more subtle and insidious form of questioning that attacks a suspect's perception of the crime or the consequences of his or her actions and will include manipulating details, or significant others, flattery, making unrealistic promises, as well as attacking a suspect's self-esteem or stature.

A total of 50 (71%) questionnaires were returned by CT officers out of 70 randomly distributed within the branch. The respondents were offered the traditional range of formats to answer questions, including 'yes' or 'no', or 'not selected'. Unfortunately, on occasions some respondents failed to make any selection. This has been recorded for statistical purposes as 'not selected' and will inevitably impact on the total responses per question and statistical findings. Many months of delay were experienced throughout the period of this research in accessing materials or personnel whenever a major case or investigation was under way. In a small number of cases (five) an isolated audio-tape could not be found, but in each instance the relevant transcript was available. To date three custody records cannot be located.

Findings and commentary

One of the first issues to arise from the face-to-face interviews with serving CT officers was the predicament that they were placed in when called upon to make an early arrest. The officers were asked:

> There is a suggestion that the strategic decision to arrests suspects prematurely (often to save life) impacts to the detriment of the detention and interviewing process. For example, by immediately imposing time pressure and without recourse to available and sufficient evidence, e.g. surveillance, forensic, computer access, financial and international inquiries. To what extent do you agree with this?

Forty-one officers (82%) 'agreed' or 'strongly agreed' with this proposition (Table 5.1).

In criminal arrests the ethos underpinning PACE was to provide police with sufficient powers to gather evidence prior to arrest and so reduce the period of detention. By contrast, there is often a need to arrest terrorist suspects early in order to protect the public and save lives. Such action may be based on sensitive intelligence and often before there has been time to gather sufficient evidence that would allow the prosecution to consider there was a likelihood

Table 5.1: Impact of early arrest on interview process

	Frequency *N = 50*	*Percentage*	*Cumulative*
Strongly disagree	5	10%	10%
Disagree	4	8%	18%
Agree	23	46%	64%
Strongly agree	18	36%	100%

of conviction (see the letter from Assistant Commissioner Andy Hayman to the Home Secretary, Rt. Hon. Charles Clarke, http://www.homeoffice.gov.uk/Terrorism/Terrorismandthelaw).

In this study such 'public safety' arrests precipitated a series of sterile and non-productive rounds of antecedent interviews, often preceded by vague disclosure notices, in turn prompting 'no comment' advice from resolute legal advisers: a cyclical impasse generating palpable levels of frustration and effectively undermining any opportunity for the officers to manage events, a situation best captured by one of the CT officers who, when placed in this dilemma, made the plea: 'Unless we get evidence soon, we may as well start telling jokes' (data obtained during debriefing sessions).

It was noticeable that over a third of all interview sessions (37%) took place within the first two days of detention, with a majority dominated by antecedent inquiries. Gareth Peirce, solicitor, in her evidence to the Home Affairs Select Committee (Terrorism Detention Powers, Fourth Report of Session 2005–06, Vol. II, p. ev 13), was of the opinion that 90% of interviews follow this pattern. The same activity also limits the opportunity to utilize the findings of relevant psychological studies that have identified the importance of the suspect's perception of events and in particular the nature, or their perception of the nature, of the evidence against them. According to the officers, the frequency of public safety arrests often places them in an untenable position and a negative mantra has evolved: why bother interviewing, [we have nothing to put to them and] the suspect is not going to say anything? One officer described the situation as similar to 'being stacked in a holding pattern over Heathrow – waiting for information, waiting for evidence to continue'.

In psychological terms, if we adopt the officers' perspective, they are already under pressure – required to interview international terrorist suspects in a very accountable environment – and they feel further exposed in public safety cases by the absence of credible evidence to allow a meaningful dialogue to take place. This heightened state of dependency and a negative frame of mind serve as a fertile combination to create an enduring self fulfilling prophecy.

Table 5.2 provides details of the extent of the use of various tactics by police officers during the 187 interview sessions. The most immediate finding is the limited use of many of the categories. 'Use of evidence' (95%) was the most popular tactic and covered the production of exhibits, photographs and other

Table 5.2: Extent of use of police interviewing tactics

Use N = 187 Tactics	Never Used	Infrequent Use	Average Use	Frequent Use	Very Frequent Use
Open question	0	3 (1.5%)	75 (40%)	104 (56%)	5 (2.5%)
Closed question	4 (2%)	54 (29%)	105 (56%)	21 (11%)	3 (2%)
Leading question	84 (45%)	73 (39%)	27 (14.5%)	2 (1%)	1 (0.5%)
Repeat question	159 (85%)	20 (11%)	8 (4%)	0	0
Multiple question	165 (88%)	14 (7.5%)	7 (4%)	1 (.5%)	0
Multiple officers	175 (94%)	7 (3.5%)	5 (2.5%)	0	0
Challenges	56 (30%)	42 (22.5%)	63 (34%)	19 (10%)	7 (3.5%)
Improper tactics	184 (98%)	3 (2%)	0	0	0
Manipulative tactics	150 (80.5%)	17 (9%)	19 (10%)	1 (.5%)	0
Minimization	170 (91%)	12 (6.5%)	5 (2.5%)	0	0
Maximization	123 (66%)	18 (9.5%)	39 (21%)	7 (3.5%)	0
Use of evidence	10 (5%)	23 (12%)	51 (27%)	63 (34%)	40 (22%)

materials, but it tended to occur in a rather sterile and perfunctory atmosphere. The limited use of 'challenges' is indicative of the polite and non-confrontational nature of these interactions, even though the use of silence by important suspects was prevalent. Given previous research from 1999 it was also surprising to find such limited use of maximization tactics (emphasizing the serious nature of offence), minimization (reducing suspect's perception of consequences) or manipulation (use of themes, flattery) (Pearse & Gudjonsson, 1999).

Such data are responsible for the summary that, in this study, interviews with terrorist suspects can best be described as 'Polite, non-threatening and often non-productive'.

Little use was made of the special warning procedure (sections 34–37 of the Criminal Justice and Public Order Act 1994; see Table 5.3). There were only three cases identified and they had no impact in the interview. No evidential use was made in the two cases that progressed to trial. Twenty-nine officers (58%) reported making use of the special warning procedure in previ-

Table 5.3:   Use and impact of a special warning (SW)

Use of SW N = 187	Frequency	Impact of SW in Interview	Impact of SW in Court
Yes	3 (2%)	0	0
No	184 (98%)	3	2*

* One case acquitted.

ous terrorist cases, but 24 (83%) claimed that it had no impact, and only one officer was aware of an example where an adverse inference was introduced at trial. It is of some concern that CT officers have very little faith in the probity of these valuable provisions.

This raises an interesting methodological question: how many warnings should have been given? Unfortunately, this is not a straightforward issue. In the first place the dataset is a biased selection – it contains only cases where people spoke and is therefore not representative. Secondly, if the suspect elects not to speak at the beginning of the interview but later does, can you assume that a SW should have been used immediately? It is obviously a question of judgement and one would need to be in possession of all the relevant facts and be alive to the many issues and context at that time. Perhaps a more productive approach would be to examine when a SW could and or should have been applied. With this criterion there was one case where a SW should have been given and a further three cases where one could have been applied.

What is more worrying is the officers' lack of faith in these provisions and it needs to be established whether there is any substance to their claim that adverse inferences are simply not used to their full potential by the prosecution. A recent Home Office review of this area called for improved training and the need for greater awareness throughout the prosecution process, but no solid research was undertaken to determine the extent of the problem (personal communication from the Home Office working party). The perception exists that the loss of an individual's right not to incriminate him- or herself was seen by the judiciary as an unacceptable erosion of individual freedom. Lord Carlile in his evidence to the Home Affairs Select Committee (14 February 2006) was dismissive of the value of the SW provision, which he labelled 'a fleabite' when set against the inherent danger of a client actually answering a police officer's questions in interview.

Discussion

The findings of this study (only briefly described here) indicate that the police interviewing of suspects in terrorist cases can best be described as polite, non-threatening and often non-productive. This research does not support the findings from the 1997 research in this field in relation to the type and nature of interview tactics used by police in England and Wales in serious criminal cases.

In order to make sense of these findings we need to examine not only the many contextual issues associated with this interaction but also, within the confines of police detention, the actual climate in which such interactions take place.

Contextual issues

There is clearly a multilayered dimension to the contextual issues relevant to the investigation of terrorist offences and it will only be possible in this chapter to outline briefly some of the many political, legal, psychological and organizational issues involved.

The UK prime minister's declaration that 'the rules of the game are changing' succinctly captures the declared intent and extent of the reform process that the government is prepared to consider in order to defeat the threat posed by terrorist activity to this country (Tony Blair, cited by John Piennar at http://newsvote.bbc.co.uk/mpapps/pagetools/print/news/bbc.co.uk/1/hi/uk-politics/47). Blair's reference to the 'rules of the game' is an unambiguous statement to give notice of the government's intention to review the balance between civil liberties and security and to bring about the necessary changes to ensure the protection of the very democracy that protects our liberty.

Further terrorist legislation has been announced that will usher in additional (and some retrospective) powers designed to create a more resolute environment against extremist elements and those engaged in preaching or justifying hatred and violence. The option to detain a person without charge for up to 28 days is likely to have a direct impact on the nature and dynamics of future police suspect interactions. It is perplexing that the period to detain terrorist suspects has increased from 7 to 14 days, and now up to 28 days' detention, yet there has been no empirical research to examine the likely impact of such a change on the overall process of investigation or to the psychological health and welfare of the suspect.

The legal context is, in some respects, similar to the political dimension in accommodating the extraordinary challenges posed by extremist activity: pushing at the boundaries of accepted practice, treating terrorist cases in a 'special way' and putting additional burdens on the defendant in a terrorist case that perhaps would not be permitted in conventional prosecutions. But perhaps just as relevant within the legal context of terrorist investigations is the operational relationship between PACE and TACT.

The principles underpinning PACE – fairness, openness and workability – are sustained in a major regard by the transparent and accountable nature of the investigation and prosecution process (Royal Commission on Criminal Procedure (1981). PACE has been referred to as the most accountable piece of criminal legislation in the world (Pearse, 1997: 8). Yet when PACE was first introduced in January 1986 there was concern over the increase in police powers of arrest and their access (on a judicial warrant) to property and items that had previously been beyond their reach. The balance to such powers was a strictly controlled and regulated framework which governed the detention and welfare of suspects and provided statutory judicial oversight at regular intervals and with established maximum periods of detention. The 1981 Philips Report which brought about PACE was predicated on the findings of a number of empirical studies in specific areas of legal and investigative practice; indeed, this was the first Royal Commission to engage such research studies. PACE was designed to provide police with authority to acquire sufficient evidence prior to arrest in order to facilitate a swift and efficient investigative process and so limit the period of incarceration suffered by a detainee. When terrorist suspects are arrested under TACT they are detained and interviewed within PACE.

According to the letter from New Scotland Yard to the Home Office, in a number of major cases the decision to arrest terrorist suspects does not bring with it the luxury of prior research and the availability of suitable evidence. A large number of arrests are made to preserve life and maintain public safety in an era where terrorist attacks are designed to cause mass casualties and without warning. This impasse and operational dilemma can now be understood in a systemic context where officers are presented with a number of suspects arrested under TACT whom they are required to interview under PACE with little or no credible evidence to put to each detainee. In some cases, they may not even know the true identity of those arrested.

In this study, it was possible (in a rather crude format) to examine this hypothesis and divide the cases into seven 'evidential' and 23 'public safety' arrests on information provided by the officers' concerned. (By design the major public safety arrests of the last few years could not be included in this sample as they failed to meet the criteria.) A number of distinctions emerged:

- All seven suspects in the 'evidential' group were charged with non-TACT offences; of these six pleaded guilty and one was found guilty.
- In interview the officers had sufficient evidence and exhibits at the outset.
- RoS was fully exercised in only one interview session out of 20.

It is appreciated that this is a relatively superficial and subjective examination of a complex subject (with a small and non-representative sample size), but the findings do support the general proposition. Eighty-two per cent of officers regarded public safety arrests as detrimental to the interview and detention process.

It was also clear that in the 'public safety' investigations the officers regularly engaged in general fact-finding and antecedent interviews simply to buy time whilst extensive forensic searches were undertaken or intelligence was gathered from partner agencies in the UK and abroad that might be disseminated for their use. The impact of this systemic failing is clearly evident in the minutiae of the interactions within this sample. There is clearly a need for more detailed research in this important area to examine the impact of 'intelligence' arrests on the investigative and prosecution process.

Having touched on the political, legal and systemic issues that provide some of the contextual framework for this study, it is important not to lose sight of the relevant psychological research.

There is no doubt that the introduction of audio-tapes to the police suspect interview spawned a noticeable increase in legal and investigative research that has substantially increased our knowledge and understanding of this complex social interaction. There is now a greater degree of confidence in analysing such interactions because research has identified relevant variables concerning the personal characteristics of the detainee and the psychological forces impacting on the interviewing officers; tactics and responses can be categorized and very lengthy interview sessions can now be broken down into a more manageable and visual format (Pearse *et al.*, 1999). The influence and effects of particular tactics and interviewing strategies designed to elicit a confession or admission are becoming well documented and a number of successful interview styles have been developed from this research. Crucially, an authoritative review of this entire research has concluded that the most frequent and important factor leading to a confession will be a suspect's knowledge of the evidence against them. Under such circumstances it is clearly regrettable that a substantial number of arrests in terrorist cases appear to take place before officers have access to such influential material.

In summary, there would appear to be the political will to provide the right legislative environment to combat the evolving terrorist threat, and there is a tacit recognition that conventional judicial boundaries may be challenged when terrorist prosecutions are brought, but the systemic issues appear more difficult to resolve. Currently, in major intelligence-led investigations against terrorist suspects police officers are expected to interview those detained without the benefit of sufficient evidence, a state of affairs that is wholly at odds with the published psychological research and one that is likely to seriously undermine the UK government's determination to successfully prosecute offenders.

The climate of terrorist interviews

In serious criminal cases police officers have sometimes in the past resorted to a combination of challenging and manipulative tactics but there is little evidence of that in this sample. In Table 5.2 'challenges' are 'never' or 'infrequently' used in more than half the interview sessions (52.5%). More surprising is the very limited use of the tactic of 'maximization'. This was 'never' or 'infrequently' used in three-quarters of the sessions. Maximization techniques can include emphasizing the serious nature of the allegation and their likely consequences, and are designed to increase the internal anxiety of the suspect.

One possible reason for the lack of a more robust approach to terrorist suspects may be found in the officers' concern about applying techniques that may later be considered to be oppressive and so undermine the fairness of the whole interview process. Some guidance is available from legal texts that suggest:

> Hostile and aggressive questioning which puts pressure on a defendant will not necessarily render the confession unreliable. The length of the interviews and the nature of the questioning are the important considerations. (*R v L* [1994], in Archbold, 2000: 1483)

As a guide to assessment in this study I was content to use the advice in the PACE Codes of Practice (p. 122) that one can expect to see 'particularly probing questions' in the interview.

Having listened to and studied 187 interview sessions, it was quite evident that the majority of officers were content to cross-examine a compliant suspect in relation to their knowledge and possible possession of countless exhibits, photographs and documents that had been recovered from various locations. Such activity was classified as a tactic – 'use of evidence' – but on many occasions concentration levels diminished, people switched off and an automated process was underway. There was little or no variation introduced by the officers, no checks or intrusive questions asked – no subtle references to test the depth and veracity of the information. It was often a support mechanism for the officers and a stress-free episode for the suspect. I found little evidence of any exposition of the many tactics and strategies advocated within the relevant police and psychological literature.

Another tendency was to engage in extended trawls for antecedent information, an apparently established tradition that often developed into an examination of political and religious belief systems and world affairs. In terrorist cases such information may be very relevant and considered important within the context of the wider prosecution issues, but in these examples there was no real urgency or consistency attached to the questioning. Officers were content to receive partial information from the suspects. Partial names, partial addresses and non-specific locations were not followed up by more detailed requests in a second phase of questioning. It was another automated process and I found little evidence of particularly probing questions.

The lack of robust questioning may be explained by the fact that this approach does not form part of the PEACE model and the findings may reflect, at least in part, the result of PEACE training and its underlying philosophy. What is of some concern, however, is the lack of intrusive questioning on the part of the officers and their ability to respond to a changing environment; they were too content to accept without reservation or to challenge superficial answers.

A suspect oscillating between speaking to the officer and asserting the right to silence was commonplace in individual cases. Given this level of occurrence it is somewhat surprising that a special warning was applied in only three sessions. This rather powerful piece of legislation, brought in to discourage a suspect from entering a bogus defence late in the day and to encourage a suspect to provide an explanation as soon as possible, could lead to an adverse inference being later drawn at court. At present CT officers clearly lack confidence in a valuable legal power.

Conclusion

This research has identified a number of important findings in relation to the effectiveness of police interviews with terrorist suspects that will advance our understanding of this important legal and social interaction and contribute to the limited psychological research literature available.

A number of contextual factors, often beyond the control of the interviewing officers, have been identified which conspire to prevent the opportunity for creating a fertile environment in which to make use of evidential material or to exploit opportunities to gather intelligence. In particular, the need to undertake 'premature' arrests in order to preserve public safety was identified as an important debilitating factor and within the interview scenario it was noted that there was an absence of particularly probing questioning regimes employed by the interviewing officers.

At present, the impact of the overall context surrounding the investigation of terrorist offences appears to cast an unhelpful shadow that has impacted on the climate within which the interviewing of terrorist suspects is taking place.

The extension of the detention period suggests that this is an opportune time to conduct further research in a number of crucial areas. These include:

- a comparative study to examine the qualitative and quantitative effect on the investigative and prosecution process brought about by the premature arrest of terrorist suspects in intelligence cases compared to evidential arrests;
- the need to examine the impact of extended detention times on the welfare and psychological wellbeing of detainees;
- an examination of the extent and impact of the use of the special warning provision in terrorist investigations and throughout the prosecution process.

References

Archbold: Criminal pleadings, evidence and practice: 2001 (2000). J. Richardson (Ed.). London: Sweet & Maxwell.

Baldwin, J. (1993). Police interviewing techniques. Establishing truth or proof ? *The British Journal of Criminology, 33,* 325–352.

Bucke, T., Street, R. & Brown, D. (2000). *The right of silence.* London: Home Office. Ede, R. & Shepherd, E. (2000). *Active defence,* 2nd edition. London: Law Society.

Gudjonsson, G. H. (2003). *The psychology of interrogations and confessions: A handbook.* Chichester: Wiley.

Gudjonsson, G. H., Rutter, S., Clare, I. C. H. & Pearse, J. (1993). *Persons at risk during interviews in police custody: The identification of vulnerabilities.* Research Study No. 12. London: HMSO.

Home Affairs Committee (2006). *Terrorism detention powers. Fourth Report of Session 2005–06.* London: HMSO.

Home Office (2004). *Counter-terrorism powers: Reconciling security and liberty in an open society: A discussion paper.* London: Home Office, Cm 6147.

Inbau, F. E., Reid, J. E., Buckley, J. P. & Jayne, B. C. (2001). *Criminal interrogation and confessions,* 4th edition. Gaithersberg, MD: Aspen.

Law Society (1994). *Advising a suspect in the police station: Guidelines for solicitors.* London: Law Society.

McConville, M. & Hodgson, J. (1993). *Custodial legal advice and the right of silence.* The Royal Commission on Criminal Justice, Research Study No. 16. London: HMSO.

Moston, S., Stephenson, G. M. & Williamson, T. M. (1992). The effects of case characteristics on suspects' behaviour during questioning. *British Journal of Criminology, 32,* 23–40

Moston, S., Stephenson, G. M. & Williamson, T. M. (1993). The incidence, antecedents and consequences of the use of the right to silence during police questioning. *Criminal Behaviour and Mental Health, 3*(1), 30–47.

Pearse, J. J. (1997). Police interviewing: an examination of some of the psychological, interrogative and background factors that are associated with a suspect's confession. Unpublished PhD thesis, University of London.

Pearse, J. (2006). The interrogation of terrorist suspects: The banality of torture. In T. Williamson (Ed.), *Investigative interviewing: Rights, research, regulation.* Cullompton: Willan Publishing.

Pearse, J. & Gudjonsson G. H. (1999). Measuring influential police interviewing tactics: A factor analytical approach. *Legal and Criminological Psychology, 4* (part 2), 221–238.

Pearse, J., Gudjonsson, G. H., Clare, I. C. H. & Rutter, S. (1998). Police interviewing and psychological vulnerabilities: predicting the likelihood of a confession. *Journal of Community and Applied Social Psychology, 8*(1), 1–21.

Report on the Operation in 2004 of the Terrorism Act 2000, p. 37, para. 136 et seq. Lord Carlile of Berriew QC. London: Home Office.

Rowe, J. J. (2000). The Terrorism Act 2000. *Criminal Law Review* (pp. 527–542). London: Sweet & Maxwell.

Royal Commission on Criminal Justice, Chairman Viscount W. G. Runciman (1993). Cmnd 2263. London: HMSO.

Royal Commission on Criminal Procedure (1981). Sir, C. Philips Cmnd 8092. London: HMSO.

Walker, C. (2002). *Blackstone's Guide to the anti-terrorism legislation.* Oxford: Oxford University Press.

Williamson, T. M. (1993). From interrogation to investigative interviewing. Strategic trends in police questioning. *Journal of Community and Applied Social Psychology*, 3, 89–99.

Cases

R v Argent [1997] 2 Cr App R 27

R v Farrell [2004] EWCA Crim 597

R (on the application of Gillan and another) v Metropolitan Police Commissioner and another [2003] EWHC 2545

R v Noble [1997] CLR 346

R v Imran & Hussain [1997] Crim LR 754 CA

R v L [1994] Crim. L.R. 839 CA

Ward v Police Service of Northern Ireland (2007)

Statutes
UK legislation

Anti-Terrorism Crime and Security Act 2001

Criminal Justice and Public Order Act 1994

Police and Criminal Evidence Act 1984

Prevention of Terrorism Act 2005

Prevention of Terrorism [Temporary Provisions] Act 1974

The Terrorism Act 2000

The Terrorism Act 2006

US legislation

Patriot Act 2001

Chapter Six

From Criminal Justice to Control Process: Interrogation in a Changing Context

David Dixon

Dean, Faculty of Law, University of New South Wales, Sydney

Introduction

The questioning of suspects takes place within a broader context of institutional practices, priorities and values. This chapter will indicate that this context is undergoing fundamental change in most Western democracies. What had been generally accepted as fundamental principles of criminal justice are being compromised, devalued and even abandoned in a shift towards what is better understood as a control process with very different values and priorities. These general trends will be illustrated by reference to examples of how some people thought to be connected to terrorist activities have been interviewed by Australian authorities, and the judicial consideration of the products of such questioning. The role of prosecutors and of government will also be considered.

Exponents of investigative interviewing need to be aware of these contextual changes. It will be argued that the current focus on interrogation of major suspects needs to be widened to take account of and make provision for the more common questioning of those on the margins.

Handbook of Psychology of Investigative Interviewing: Current Developments and Future Directions
Edited by Ray Bull, Tim Valentine and Tom Williamson
© 2009 John Wiley & Sons, Ltd.

From criminal justice ...

In the twentieth century, a paradigm of criminal justice matured in Anglophone jurisdictions in which the questioning of suspects had a specific place (Dixon, 2008). Suspects should be interviewed in a closely regulated period between being arrested and being charged with an offence. Such questioning should normally take place at a police station where police supervisors are responsible for ensuring access to various rights, notably of access to legal advice. The length of investigative detention was restricted by time limits (e.g. in England and Wales under the Police and Criminal Evidence Act 1984 , a maximum of 96 hours, although regulatory hurdles ensured that most suspects were charged or released within six hours). After being charged, a suspect could not be further interviewed about that offence. These were specific expressions of a criminal justice paradigm with deep roots in liberal democratic conceptions of relations between state and citizen.

For those of us who professionally grew up seeing these arrangements as normal, it is important to appreciate their relatively recent origins. Until the mid-nineteenth century, magistrates, not police, directed criminal investigations. Until the mid-twentieth century, the propriety of police questioning suspects between arrest and charge was unclear. For a long period, such questioning attracted judicial criticism. Until legislative interventions in many jurisdictions in the late twentieth century, the legality of investigative detention was contested (Dixon, 1997).

This confined and contested conception of interviewing's place was both product and part of a broader criminal justice paradigm. Key characteristics of this approach include:

- Individualism: the individual's responsibility for action is pivotal.
- Localism: criminal justice is aligned with jurisdictional boundaries.
- Rights: the individual is protected by rights which may be expressed in positive form and/or in a political understanding of the limits on state intervention into the liberty (and onto the property) of the individual.
- Process principles: to obtain a conviction, the prosecution must bear the burden of proving beyond reasonable doubt that the accused voluntarily and intentionally did (and often intended to cause the consequences of) an act which was prohibited at the time (i.e., no retrospectivity).
- Judicial independence: an individual is entitled to a fair hearing according to law before an unbiased judge and jury.
- Prosecutorial integrity: prosecutors have professional responsibility to act fairly and to be independent of government.
- Reactivity: completed actions and their results are the concerns of the criminal justice process.
- Desert: individuals are punished for what they have done.

... to control process

In the last decade, a new paradigm has taken shape which I call a 'control process', emphasizing that its concerns are neither exclusively about what is 'criminal' nor 'justice' in the senses commonly understood in the paradigm of criminal justice. The key characteristics of this paradigm are in stark contrast to those of criminal justice:

* Communalism and security of the group, rather than the rights of the individual, are paramount.
* Globalism: individuals may be penalized for acts committed and investigated in other jurisdictions.
* Proactivity and pre-emption: where possible, risks must be identified and preventive action taken against them. Going further, precaution requires action to be taken before risks even materialize.
* Incapacitation and prevention: punishment comes too late, so people must be stopped, including by incapacitative means such as custodial detention.
* Administrative action: alternatives to judicial processes are preferred.

(See Garland, 2001; Zedner, 2007; 2009; for a more positive view, see Dershowitz 2006.)

The central concepts of liberal democratic criminal justice are devalued in the new control process. The key concern is now the minimization of risk and the security of the group. The individual is no longer the focus of attention, and so there is less emphasis on the individual's rights and the need to prove the individual's guilt beyond reasonable doubt through a system of due process. Flexibility of process replaces certainty of rules and procedures as a virtue. 'Pre-emption', compliance and efficiency are more important than individual punishment or due process: preventive detention for potential sex offenders and others, anti-social behaviour orders, behaviour management contracts, non-association and space restriction order, and the use of bail conditions as a proactive crime control measure are just the more prominent examples. There is less interest in understanding crime's causation than in accepting crime as normal, a choice to be controlled and insured against, in which 'attempts to cure or punish appear less logical than do moves to manage crime and minimize its costs' (Zedner, 2005a: 284). The state's responsibility for crime control is 'contracted out to private providers wielding state franchises, delegated to individuals and communities, or completely over taken by the growing private security industry' (*ibid.*). Policing intervenes proactively, preventing and pre-empting problems rather than retrospectively solving them.

Simply to say that all this goes against basic principles is rather like complaining that a game of chess isn't being played according to the rules of draughts. The game has changed, allowing those in government to dismiss the standard civil libertarian response to new police powers as anachronistic and irrelevant. The contrast between criminal justice and control process is exaggerated here in order to clarify the difference. It has become trite to respond by pointing out that criminal justice has always included substantial preventive elements. The modern English policing tradition has a strong preventive commitment in the Peelite tradition. Preventive detention has been possible for those refused bail, the mentally ill, habitual offenders, those suffering from certain infectious diseases, illegal migrants, refugees, sex offenders and others. Similarly, deterrence is by nature forward-looking, but its activation depends on a crime having been committed. This illustrates the essential point that while criminal justice includes preventive and deterrent elements, these do not change the ideological core commitment to a reactive, individualistic process.

While these developments have been under way for some time, they accelerated quickly after 9/11. Parliaments are now in a constant cycle of extending anti-terrorism legislation in ways that routinely deviate from liberal democratic principles in the name of necessity. It must be acknowledged that the shift from criminal justice to control process did not happen suddenly on 9/11 any more than Islamic terrorism arrived on the world stage on that day. Rather, the response to terrorism must be seen as hastening changes which were already under way, notably in the other 'war' of our times, that on illegal drugs. The law enforcement response to illegal drugs, and the organized crime associated with their distribution, has entailed a long series of compromises and exceptions to basic principle, reducing and shifting the burden of proof from prosecution to defence and deploying incapacitative civil and criminal penalties. In addition, much of the groundwork for the new paradigm's emphasis on preventative intervention and detention was laid in responses to perceived threats from sexual predators and other dangerous risks.

However, the fundamental difference between criminal justice and control process is real and marked, and there is a shift from the former to the latter. These differences can be illustrated through analysis of the different role of interrogation in the two paradigms. In the criminal justice paradigm, police question a suspect between arrest and charge in order to obtain evidence about specific offences allegedly committed by the suspect which may subsequently be admissible in court. In the control process paradigm, the purpose of interrogation may be much broader: the focus is not the suspect's past actions but on what he or she knows about future actions by others. In response to 9/11, 'the interest of investigators has shifted from obtaining viable evidence for prosecution to obtaining credible information for preventing future acts of terrorism' (Strauss, 2003: 206). In this context, what counts as success may be much less than obtaining a confession:

> Interrogators find tiny bits of the truth, fragments of information, slivers of data. We enter a vast desert, hundreds of miles across, in which a few thousand puzzle pieces have been scattered. We spend weeks on a single prisoner, to extract only a single piece – if that. We collect, and then we pass the pieces on, hoping that someone above us can assemble them. (Mackey, 2004: xxv)

Controls on interrogation which are designed around the potential sanction of evidence being excluded as inadmissible are of limited value when producing admissible evidence is not the main objective. Criminal justice and control process are paradigms. They are neither clearly distinct nor sequential, with one simply replacing the other. Rather, it is exactly the discordant overlap which will emerge as a significant problem in some of the specific cases to be discussed below.

Torture and interrogation

Perhaps to the disappointment of some and the relief of others, this chapter is not primarily concerned with torture. While only a few years ago, torture was widely (although wrongly) regarded as an historical relic, its modern use has spawned a vast literature. The disclosure of (some of) what happened in Abu Ghraib and the global prison network of the USA's affiliates has been an extraordinary achievement by investigative journalists and human rights organizations. It provided the spur for many in the West to question and challenge the post-9/11 policies and actions of the USA and its allies. However, this concentration of attention appears problematic from two perspectives. First, some academic discussion of torture seems to share elements of the dark, obsessional, almost pornographic, interest displayed in some contemporary films and TV series. Secondly, and more relevant to this chapter's concerns, the focus on the negative means that we have been concerned with what must not be done rather than what can and should be done in questioning suspects. My own interest is in what should be permissible in the routine, everyday questioning of those thought to be on the fringes (or connected to the fringes) of the activities under investigation. For every high-profile suspect, there are hundreds of people whom the authorities detain and question in the process of accumulating the vast banks of information on which counter-terrorism depends.

The issue of torture – its morality, legality and effectiveness – has dominated debates about interrogation related to terrorism. This is inevitable: the fact that at the time of writing (2008) there continues to be serious talk about whether simulated drowning (known as water-boarding) should be regarded as torture is an indication of how far the compass has shifted in recent years. In 2008 President Bush vetoed a Bill which would have prohibited the CIA from using such interrogation methods such as water-boarding (New York Times, 2008). Meanwhile, Khalid Sheik Mohammed has been charged with murdering the 9/11 victims on the basis, *inter alia*, of confessions obtained by water-boarding. While it may have been necessary, the debate on torture and what should *not* be done in interrogation distracted attention from the practical question of what *should* be done. The answer to this question depends in part on the moral dilemmas founding the torture debate. But it also depends on what the interrogation is *for*. If it is part of a process which will or may lead to criminal law prosecution, the answer will be very different from if the interrogation is part of an intelligence-gathering exercise. Of course, in reality, this distinction is very difficult to maintain. As we shall see in the discussion of Australian cases, the overlap between criminal justice and control process has proved to be very problematic.

A good example of the problems is provided by a contribution to a conference on 'Law and Liberty in the War on Terror' by Neil James, who has operational, supervisory and training experience in interrogation. His paper provides a familiar critique of torture, focusing on instrumental issues of effectiveness and practicality. He seeks to distinguish torture from legitimate interrogation. Quoting from the Australian Defence Force's *Interrogators' Handbook* (of which he was the original author), James states:

> Among professional interrogators in countries abiding by the rule of law the common working definition of interrogation is 'the systematic extraction of information from an individual, either willing or unwilling, by the use of psychological attack only'. Thus, interrogation is essentially an intellectual process not a physical one. No physical or mental pain or severe suffering is involved. The subject is convinced to cooperate by reasoning and by overcoming their will to resist. (2007: 161)

Some may argue that the line between torture and interrogation is not as clear-cut as James suggests. However, this is not my concern here. Rather, my focus is on the acceptability of this form of interrogation in a criminal justice model. Any evidence lawyer's ears would have pricked up at this account of interrogation: unwilling extraction of information, psychological attack and overcoming of the will to resist provide ready ammunition for an argument that a confession was involuntary, so failing to get past the first requirement of evidential admissibility.

The problem is clarified when James goes further: 'measures or conditions of discomfort or annoyance designed to encourage cooperation are not unreasonable ... With obvious safeguards such conditioning may, for example, legally include the strictly controlled and temporary use of measures such as isolation, sensory deprivation or sleep deprivation' (*ibid.*: 162). While it may be the case that such treatment does not amount to a criminal offence, it certainly would render any confession thereby produced inadmissible under the current law of evidence in many countries.

James is concerned with more serious and difficult cases. My primary interest is rather different. An interrogation to discover a 'ticking bomb' will happen very rarely, if ever, despite the enormous attention this scenario has attracted. Stepping down the scale of seriousness, few interrogators will be called on to deal with the kind of suspect for whom even techniques such as sleep deprivation could be considered as appropriate. Just as has often been the case in policing more generally, there is an unfortunate concentration on everything except everyday and 'normal' practice. The vast majority of terrorism-related interrogations will continue to involve low-level people on the fringes. For them, length of detention will be the critical variable.

A now standard part of critiques of torture and related techniques is that other methods are more effective, even in questioning those allegedly involved in terrorism. In particular, it is argued that interviewers with appropriate language skills, cultural knowledge and training can build rapport with suspects and thereby produce results (Gelles, McFadden, Borum, R. & Vossekuil, B., 2006; Pearse, 2006). The problem is that such rapport is most unlikely to be established in the short periods allowed under standard criminal justice regimes. As Gelles *et al.* suggest, 'A rapport-building (or relationship-based) approach will yield the best results in an interview/interrogation that occurs over days/ weeks/months' (2006: 31). James confirms that the time available is crucial (*ibid.*: 161). In these approaches, it is taken for granted that the subject of interrogation must be detained for an extended period in order for interrogation to be successful. Yet this runs counter to one of the basic principles of criminal justice regimes such as PACE, which were constructed on an understanding that extended detention in itself could make confessions unreliable because people would say anything (even at long-term cost) to win a short-term reprieve from investigative detention.

If interrogation is intended to produce confessions and admissions which are acceptable to a criminal justice paradigm, lengthy pre-charge detention is unacceptable because it undermines the voluntariness which is a precondition of evidential admissibility. If interrogation is primarily intended to produce information and actionable intelligence rather than admissible evidence, then the concerns of criminal justice will not be paramount. In addition, problems for the authorities arise when the lengthy interrogation for intelligence is over. Are the subjects of interrogation to be detained indefinitely (or until the 'war on terror' is over, if there is a difference)? Are they simply to be released and placed under administrative control orders which limit their movements and contacts? Or should an attempt be made to create an *ersatz* criminal justice, dressing up a militaristic control process with some trappings of legality? These are, of course, the questions which the USA has been grappling with over the detainees at Guantanamo Bay.

Interrogating terrorism: three case studies

Much of the extensive post-9/11 literature on liberty vs. security and related changes in criminal justice has been general and abstract. This section seeks to provide a closer focus through brief analysis of three Australian cases involving alleged terrorist offences in which controversial interrogations have played crucial roles.

Jack Thomas

In 2003, Jack Thomas, an Australian citizen, was arrested and detained for five months in Pakistan. During this period, he was 'interrogated numerous times by Pakistani, American and Australian officials, often whilst blindfolded, hooded and shackled' (Lynch, 2006: 313). According to his account, which was accepted as truthful by an Australian court, he was assaulted, threatened with torture and with the rape of his wife, and offered inducements of favourable treatment in return for his cooperation.

In a final session in Pakistan, Thomas was interviewed by Australian Federal Police (AFP) agents. This took place in the same room as previous interviews with security and police officials, and the AFP interviewers had both attended some of the previous sessions. The purpose of this interview was 'to gather evidence in a form and by a process that would be admissible in an Australian court' (*ibid*.: 314). It was, in other words, an attempt to bridge the gap between control process and criminal justice, between a series of interviews conducted in a security facility in a foreign country and the proceedings of an Australian court. In this interview, the AFP agents attempted to meet criminal process requirements, explaining the right to remain silent and emphasizing that participation in the interview was voluntary. The relevant Australian law requires a suspect to be provided with access to legal advice: the AFP tried to arrange this, but Pakistani Inter-Service Intelligence officials refused (*ibid*.: 315). The Victorian Court of Appeal commented that the interview was 'conducted in what can be reasonably described as a conventional fashion' (*R v Thomas* [2006] at para. 51). Statements made by Thomas in this interview were subsequently presented as part of the case against him when (more than year later) he was arrested and charged in Australia with the offences of receiving funds from and providing support to a terrorist organization.

The crucial issue for the Australian courts was whether the final interview could be distinguished from what had preceded it so that the evidence produced could meet criminal justice standards – notably, the base requirement that a confession or admission must be made voluntarily. In a *voir dire*, the trial judge ruled that the admissions had been made voluntarily and Thomas was convicted and sentenced to five years' imprisonment. Narrow legalism, sympathy to police and prosecutors, and a narrow view of reality have often been characteristics of Australian criminal trial judges. The trial judge concluded that Thomas had a choice to answer questions or not, and exercised that choice. The pressure to answer came not from the interviewers 'either expressly or implicitly', but from Thomas's own assessment of the 'risk of indefinite detention in Pakistan or of removal to the United States or Cuba' (*DPP v Thomas* [2006] at para. 42). The judge found that this interview could be distinguished from the earlier interviews and the inducements offered in them: 'There was a clear bifurcation in purpose, function and form between the ASIO interviews and the AFP interview. Mr Thomas fully understood it' (*ibid*., at para. 50).

The Victorian Court of Appeal rejected this artificiality and restated the accepted common law principle that an earlier inducement (which may be a threat or promise – in lawyers' terminology, 'fear of prejudice or hope of advantage') – offered by a person in authority (such as the security interviewers) can continue to affect the suspect's voluntariness. The Court of Appeal's conclusion was the same as any common-sense understanding of the situation – the final interview could not be divorced from those preceding it ('same place, same AFP personnel, same topics' [2006 VSCA 165, at para. 84]).

> Obviously, the fact and circumstances of his detention, the various inducements held out and threats made to him, the prospect that he would remain detained indefinitely, can be seen to have operated upon the mind of the applicant when he decided to participate in the (final AFP) interview. Whist nothing occurred in the interview itself that could be seen to overbear the will of the applicant, there can be little doubt that he was, at that time, subject to externally-imposed pressure of a kind calculated to overbear his will and thereby restrict, in a practical sense, his available choices and the manner of their exercise. (*ibid.*, para. 92)

The AFP's attempt to lay a patina of criminal justice over a structure of control process was rejected. Notably, the failure to provide access to legal advice could not be excused simply because the refusal was by the local Pakistani authorities, not the Australian investigators. Their refusal meant that an interview conforming with Australian law could not be conducted in Pakistan (*ibid.*, para. 111).

For the future in a case like Thomas's, the alternatives for the authorities are clear. Either there must be a much greater distinction in time, place and personnel between interrogations carried out for different purposes, or prosecutions must be based on evidence other than confessions or admissions, or an alternative to criminal justice must be deployed. As we shall see, the Australian authorities are exploring all options. From this perspective, the trial judge's convolutions in Thomas's case are understandable: however flawed, they represented an attempt to maintain the relevance of a criminal justice paradigm.

Mohammed Haneef

Mohammed Haneef, an Indian doctor practising in Queensland, was detained following the London and Glasgow car bomb incidents in June 2007. These marked a significant shift in concern about terrorism. The previously accepted wisdom was that the threat of terrorism was associated with alienation and anomie in ethnic minorities, yet those allegedly associated with the London and Glasgow incidents were not unemployed inner-city youth, but doctors. The shift from risk to precaution (Zedner, 2005b; 2007) is illustrated by this. If members of a professional elite were engaged in terrorism, the attempt to identify auditable risk factors seems doomed: instead, the authorities respond as if risk is everywhere and that precautionary action is necessary.

Dr Haneef's alleged connection to the British incidents was that he was second cousin to a man who died from burns suffered in the Glasgow incident and a telephone SIM card purchased by Haneef had been found with the alleged car bombers' possessions. Suspicion was increased by his attempt to board a flight from Australia to India. With at least tacit encouragement from a government facing a general election which had previously exploited security scares for political advantage, sections of the media treated Haneef as a prize capture. It was alleged, for example, that he was planning to blow up an apartment block on Queensland's Gold Coast, a tourist area.

The 'case' against Haneef then spectacularly fell apart: his flight to India was to see his newborn child; the apartment bomb story was based on no more than a photograph of Haneef and his wife on a Gold Coast beach; the SIM card was found not, as initially reported, in the vehicle driven into Glasgow airport, but in Liverpool. (Haneef had passed it on when he left England so that the remaining credit would not be wasted.) As in Thomas's case, we see the courts applying the criminal justice principles; but these rub hard against exigencies of the new control process. When a magistrate took the brave and unusual step of ordering Haneef's release on bail, the Australian government intervened by withdrawing his immigration visa and converting investigative detention into pre-deportation detention. The 'orthodox process' of law was overtaken by administrative discretion (Lynch, 2007: 228). This was done in a way (citing the national interest) which sought (ultimately unsuccessfully) to prevent judicial scrutiny of the decision. Exposure of the weakness of the prosecution case and widespread public criticism of the police followed. While the Australian government continued to mutter darkly about Haneef's connections with terrorism, the Commonwealth Director of Public Prosecutions eventually dropped the charges against him. He was released and left for India to see his daughter for the first time (*ibid.*: 226–227). In a final humiliation for the government, the Federal Court, in a decision that was scathing about the Immigration Minister's behaviour, ruled that the visa cancellation was unlawful. At the time of writing, Haneef was considering returning to Australia to resume his medical career.

Interrogations conducted by Australia Federal Police agents with Haneef played a vital part in this reversal. Haneef was interviewed over several days. 'He was the first person to be detained under new anti-terrorism powers which enable Australian police to hold a suspect without charge for an extended period of time during which questioning up to a maximum of 24 hours may occur' (*ibid.*: 225). The interviews were lengthy but were carried out in accordance with criminal justice values and standards. The relevant legislation follows the standard practice of specifying a maximum period for active investigation to which is added 'time-outs' in which the detention clock is stopped while other investigations take place, and the suspects is allowed to rest and eat. The indeterminate length of detention under a 'time-out' system has been criticized. However, the problem of lengthy detention had rarely been so clearly demonstrated as in Haneef's case: he was detained for 12 days before being charged with providing 'support or resources' to an organization involved in terrorist activity (*ibid.*: 225–226). This was a much longer period than those responsible for drafting the legislation had thought would occur (*ibid.*: 228).

The interviewers were polite and respectful, if not very well prepared. We know this because Haneef's barrister, Stephen Keim, responded to the government, police and media misrepresentation of his client by releasing the transcript of the first of the recorded interviews to the press (see *The Hindu*'s website, www.hindu.com/nic/0058/haneef.htm). Apart from demonstrating Haneef's apparently full cooperation, the transcripts revealed that aspects of the prosecution case against Haneef were unfounded: he had, for example, a good reason for his supposedly suspicious attempted departure from Australia. It emerged that some of his actions were apparently inconsistent with guilt – for example, far from fleeing from investigators, he had made several attempts to contact the UK police (Lynch, 2007: 227). When the Immigration Minister proceeded to selectively release passages from the second interview in an attempt to justify his stance, while claiming that he was unable to release the full record on the basis that it might prejudice ongoing police investigations (*ibid.*), Haneef's lawyers again released the full transcript. Its anodyne contents deflated the government's attempts to justify Haneef's treatment. As in other contexts, a comprehensive record of interview (i.e., not just a recording of a rehashed confession) can provide suspect as well as police with valuable resources (Dixon, 2007).

Izhar Ul-Haque

In early 2003, Izhar Ul-Haque, an Australian citizen, spent three weeks at a camp in Pakistan run by Lashkar-e-Taiba, which would subsequently be proscribed under Australian law as a terrorist organization. Six months after his return, Ul-Haque was interrogated by Australian Security Intelligence Organization (ASIO) officers and subsequently was charged with an offence of training with a terrorist organization. The circumstances of Ul-Haque's interrogation emerged at his trial. In his ruling on a *voir dire* concerning the results of this interrogation, the trial judge was scathing about ASIO's conduct: not only refusing to admit the interview records into evidence, he concluded that the investigating officers had committed significant criminal and civil offences in their treatment of Ul-Haque. His judgment provides a vivid picture of the contrast between criminal justice and control process.

As noted above, in the criminal justice paradigm, interrogation is designed to produce information and, if appropriate, admissible evidence about an offence committed by an individual. In Ul-Haque's case, the function of the alleged offence was as a lever with which to put pressure on Ul-Haque to collect and provide information about a person suspected of more serious offences: the trial judge commented: 'It seems almost certain that the action taken against the accused by the authorities was instigated by his being connected with one Fadeen Lodhi.' (Lodhi was later convicted of terrorism offences.) Ul-Haque had a family connection with Lodhi: communication between the two following Ul-Haque's return from Pakistan was what 'excited the authorities and instigated the actions of the authorities that led to interviews here in question and his ultimately being charged' (*R v Ul-Haque* [2007] at para. 13). According to Ul-Haque, the officers told him that they did not wish to speak to him about his training in Pakistan: 'They said, "No, we know about that. We're not concerned with that"' (*ibid.*, para. 21). An officer told the court that his colleagues questioned Ul-Haque because 'we had an investigation underway and we had information which indicated (he) had information which could assist us in that investigation' (*ibid.*, para. 30). Ul-Haque claimed that an officer told him, 'we see you as a helper, as an informant and as a witness … I don't think you have done anything wrong' (*ibid.*, para. 78).

In November 2003, ASIO officers intercepted Ul-Haque at a railway station on his way home from university, where he was studying medicine. He was not formally arrested. The officers' and Ul-Haque's accounts of the initial confrontation differed somewhat, but the differences were not significant. It is clear that what occurred was a very familiar example of an order lightly camouflaged as a request: as Ul-Haque commented, 'the thought of choice never really occurred because I was under extreme pressure and stress' (*ibid.*, para. 21. On the relationship of 'consent' to the exercise of police powers, see Dixon, 1997: ch. 4). As the judge concluded, 'Although it is described as a request … his being told to accompany them to a nearby park was an instruction and was intended to be taken as such' (*R v Ul-Haque*, para. 27).

Sitting between two officers in the back of a car, he was taken to a public park and questioned about his knowledge of Lodhi. An ASIO officer told him that 'he was in substantial trouble and that his full cooperation with ASIO … would be required' (*ibid.*, para. 25). On the officers' own account, this included 'robust discussion and considerable prompting from the interviewing officers' (*ibid.*, para. 23). The interrogation was not contemporaneously recorded, and again the two sides' accounts differed in tone. They agreed that he was given a choice of cooperation or facing the consequences of failing to do so: in the officers' account, this meant continued investigation, while in Ul-Haque's it meant action against him unless he collected and provided information about Lodhi (*ibid.*, paras 20–1). To a young Muslim man aware of contemporary developments in the 'war on terror', the possible implications of the threat were very serious:

> when he said … 'we can do this the easy way or the hard way', I believed that unless I kept … answering their questions that they will use the hard way [which] to me meant … for example that I could either be deported, I could be arrested, I could be taken to a secret location for interrogation … and my family … would be taken into custody. (*ibid.*, para. 71)

The judge accepted Ul-Haque's account of his fears: 'the accused was given to understand that it was in his interests to co-operate, and there was an implicit threat that if he did not do so some adverse consequences might follow' (*ibid.*, para. 67).

Ul-Haque was then interviewed further in the car on the way to his parents' house, which was being searched by some 25 ASIO and police officers, and again on the way back to the railway station where Ul-Haque's car had been left. He then returned, accompanied by an agent, to his parents' house, where he was interviewed for a further 2 hours and 46 minutes, ending at 3.45 am. Later that day, and then again five days later, he was subjected to further questioning, on these occasions at a police station by Federal Police agents. Two weeks later (after numerous telephone contacts), the agents returned to Ul-Haque's house. The AFP's account was that they requested Ul-Haque to 'further assist the Federal Police by undertaking covert enquiries or acting as a witness'. Ul-Haque's account was that they threatened to prevent him from continuing to study medicine and 'make life difficult' for his family (*ibid.*, para. 110).

Many people will not be surprised at how ASIO treated Ul-Haque: this is how an intelligence agency may be expected to behave. The problem arose when an attempt was made to shift from control process to criminal justice by charging him. (The real motivation appears to have been to punish him for non-cooperation with ASIO rather than for his brief involvement with Lashkar-e-Taiba.) What might have been conventional security agency practice came under intense, critical scrutiny in a criminal court. The judge was merciless in his dissection of ASIO practice from a criminal justice perspective. The 'request' to go to the park was an unlawful arrest. Ul-Haque should have been informed of his rights, taken to a police station, detained according to regulations and had his interview recorded. The failure to specify his alleged offence and to tell him instead that 'he knew what he had done wrong' was 'reminiscent of Kafka' (*ibid.*, para. 31), while 'to conduct an extensive interview with the accused, keeping him incommunicado, under colour of the [search] warrant, was a gross breach of the powers given to the officers under the warrant' (*ibid.*, para. 44). The interviewers' 'prompting' of Ul-Haque was condemned as bad practice: according to the judge, 'the ASIO officers told him when they thought he was not telling the truth and told him, or suggested, what the truth was', which was a method not used by police because it is 'calculated to obtain what the suspect believes the interrogator wants to hear ... It is inevitable that the truth of what is said is likely – if not certainly – to be adversely affected' (paras. 46 and 102).

According to the judge, the ASIO officers' conduct did not merely affect the admissibility of evidence from the interviews with Ul-Haque: it included a string of criminal offences – false imprisonment, kidnapping and assault which were intentionally committed (*ibid.*, paras 59 and 61). These assessments were firmly located in a context of constitutional principle – the requirement of legal authorization for the executive to interfere with an individual's liberty (*ibid.*, para. 60). The conduct of the ASIO officers was

> grossly improper and constituted an unjustified and unlawful interference with the personal liberty of the accused (and) was a gross interference by the agents of the state with the accused's legal rights as a citizen, rights which he has whether he be suspected of criminal conduct or not and whether he is a Muslim or not. Furthermore, the conduct was deliberately engaged in for the purpose of overbearing the accused in the hope that he would co-operate. (*ibid.*, paras. 62 and 95)

It was made clear that ASIO was responsible for the individual officers' misconduct: 'The impropriety ... was grave. There is no suggestion that the officers acted contrary to ASIO protocols and good reason for thinking that they did not' (*ibid.*, para. 105).

As in Haneef's case, electronic recording assisted the defence. While the ASIO interrogations in the park, house and car were not contemporaneously recorded, that by the AFP at the police station was audio-visually recorded, allowing the judge to make an assessment of Ul-Haque's demeanour and manner of answering questions: 'The overwhelming impression that I got from watching the interview is that the accused was cowed' (*ibid.*, para. 73). This contributed to his assessment that the negative answers which Ul-Haque gave to the routine questions about threats, promises or inducements at the interview's close were made because 'he just decided he was going to be compliant and wanted the interview to end' (*ibid.*, para. 75). He regarded the questions designed to expose any threats, promises or inducements as 'an empty formality' (*ibid.*, para. 92). The judge recognized the strangeness of the legal fiction that any suspect whose will has been overwhelmed by threats, promises or inducements during an interview will be able to slough off their effects and to answer the concluding questions genuinely.

The three cases

These are very different cases: Thomas had, on his own account, been significantly involved with terrorist organizations and was a legitimate subject of investigation; Haneef's distant family connection appears to have been enough to excite Australian politicians making political capital out of a 'terrorist' drama and security agencies eager to show their worth; in the case of Ul-Haque, it appears that the investigation was conducted primarily to get Ul-Haque's cooperation in collecting and providing information about others and, when this cooperation was refused, punishing him by prosecution. What connects them for present purposes is their illustration of the uncomfortable relationship between criminal justice and control process paradigms and the central, controversial role played by interrogation.

The resources and limits of law

The criminal justice paradigm is not dead when there are responsible, independent professionals who take its principles and values seriously. Thomas's, Ul-Haque's and Haneef's lawyers provide an excellent example of the long tradition of lawyers who, refusing to be intimidated, rely on the basic principles of the rule of law and natural justice. Haneef's lawyers deserve particular comment: refusing to be swept along in the political and media hysteria about their client, they insisted on due process and took the fight to the authorities by releasing the interview records. The legal principles which provide the motivation for lawyers such as these are not complicated: a fair hearing according to law before an independent judge applying, in a criminal case, the principles of criminal justice outlined above.

As this statement indicates, judicial officers play a pivotal role. The justices of the Victorian Court of Appeal who heard Thomas's appeal, the Queensland magistrate who granted Haneef bail and the New South Wales judge in Ul-Haque's case can proudly take their places as members of a group identified by Dyzenhaus & Thwaites: '[t]here seems to be something like a judicial 'coalition of the willing' forming – judges prepared to uphold the rule of law in the face of executive claims about national security' (2007: 10). There is certainly evidence in the judgments quoted above of judges who are uneasy about current trends and who are prepared to challenge governments over aspects of them.

Some governments have expressed concern about the limitation or exclusion of legality from responses to terrorism. This frequently finds expression in calls for the rhetoric of war to be abandoned, and for countering terrorism to be seen as a task for law enforcement (Wilson, 2005). What 'law enforcement' means in this context is unsettled, with police and security overlapping, cooperating and occasionally squabbling.

However, law has familiar limits as a restraint on power. Court cases are expensive and slow. Lawyers acting for the prosecution too often resemble government agents rather than independent professionals. Too many of the heroic judicial affirmations of freedom have come from judges in dissenting judgments. Even if such judges carry the majority, courts can rarely have the final say: governments and parliaments can respond to judicial decisions which they do not like by undermining them by legislative action or by turning to administrative rather than judicial means of control. They are particularly able to do so in a jurisdiction like Australia's which has very limited constitutional protections of individual rights. For example, Thomas may not have been convicted, but he was made subject to an administrative control order (which the High Court found to be legal in *Thomas v Mowbray* [2007] HCA 33). Ironically, reliance on law may serve to push state action outside the reach of legal principle, as what was previously unacceptable is legalized. As Lynch concludes pessimistically, legal systems around the world are 'undergoing a rapid re-adjustment in order to respond to the post 9/11 world' (2007: 231–232).

Courts are increasingly attacked if they give any indication of being 'soft on terror' (Lynch, 2006). The judgments in the cases considered here attracted considerable criticism from popular media, although some of the quality press supported them. Of more concern is the official response: to date, there has been no recognition by the Australian government of the judicial critiques, far less any prosecution or disciplining of officers for demonstrated misconduct. Security authorities do not see acknowledgement of legality as an appropriate response to these court rulings. Finding ways around them seems more appealing: the Australian Federal Police Commissioner declared that 'Both in the UK and Australia we are testing the courts. We make no apologies for that … it's part of the work police do … and will help prevent a [terrorist] attack here' (The Australian, 2007). Action has been threatened against lawyers who challenge the authorities. For example, Stephen Keim, Haneef's barrister, had to defend himself against allegations that he had broken professional conduct rules in the way he released interview tapes to the media. The official response to the judge's criticisms in the Ul-Haque case was not to take action against the police and ASIO officers, but to launch an official complaint against the judge.

Conclusion

The vulnerability of the criminal justice paradigm to executive action and legislative change leads to a pessimistic conclusion. It is perhaps appropriate to end by referring to the cases of the two Australians who were held at Guantanamo Bay, Mamdouh Habib and David Hicks (Sales, 2007). Habib was released without charge, apparently because US authorities did not welcome the prospect of more public scrutiny of what happened to him in Egyptian jails during a lengthy stop-off on his rendered passage to Cuba. At the time of writing, Hicks is the only sometime detainee of Guantanamo Bay who has been 'convicted'. In a mere façade of legality, confessions produced by years of interrogation led to a plea of guilty to crimes which did not exist, in a court which was not a court, in a place which the US government had tried to isolate from international law. This guilty plea meant that neither his military 'commission' nor, *a fortiori*, a real court examined the means by which the confessions underlying it were obtained. At the time of writing, Hicks has just been released from the Australian jail where he spent the last few months of detention, apparently broken, not by torture, but by prolonged detention, often in isolation. Yet even in this case, the strength of legal principle became evident in the unlikely figure of Hicks's US army lawyer, Major Michael Mori, who, along with a team of other lawyers (Stafford Smith, 2007), fought for his client skilfully and at very considerable personal cost. Both Habib and Hicks are now subject to indefinite security surveillance and administrative control orders.

The legal and political issues discussed in this chapter may seem distant from the professional and technical concerns of investigative interviewing. This would not have been Tom Williamson's approach. What distinguished Tom's work was a commitment to investigative interviewing not just as a professional technique, but as an expression of adherence to human rights, legality, and justice (Williamson, 2006). In working through the implications for interrogation of the changing relationship between criminal justice and control process, Tom Williamson will continue to provide us with a fine example.

Vale Tom.

Acknowledgements

I am grateful to my colleagues Professor Jill Hunter and Associate Professor Andrew Lynch for their advice and assistance. My account of Thomas's case draws heavily on Dr Lynch's published research.

References

The Australian (2007). Keelty attacked for 'court testing'. *The Australian*, 17 December, p. 3.

Dershowitz, A. (2006). *Preemption*. New York: W. W. Norton.

Dixon, D. (1997). *Law in policing: Legal regulation and police practices*. Oxford: Clarendon.

Dixon, D. (2008). Authorise and regulate: a comparative perspective on the rise and fall of a regulatory strategy. In E. Cape & R. Young (Eds.), *Regulating policing* (pp. 21–44). Oxford: Hart.

Dixon, D. with Travis, G. (2007). *Interrogating images: Audio-visually recorded police questioning of suspects*. Sydney: Institute of Criminology.

Dyzenhaus, D. & Thwaites, R. (2007). Legality and emergency – the judiciary in a time of terror. In A. Lynch, E. Macdonald & G. Williams (Eds.), *Law and liberty in the war on terror* (pp. 9–27). Leichhardt: Federation.

Garland, D. (2001). *The culture of control*. Oxford: Oxford University Press.

Gelles, M. G., McFadden, R., Borum, R. & Vossekuil, B. (2006). Al-Qaeda-related subjects: a law enforcement perspective. In T. Williamson (Ed.), *Investigative interviewing* (pp. 23–41). Cullompton: Willan Publishing.

James, N. (2007). Torture: What is it, will it work and can be justified? In A. Lynch, E. Macdonald & G. Williams (Eds.), *Law and liberty in the war on terror* (pp. 155–164). Leichhardt: Federation.

Lynch, A. (2006). Maximising the drama: 'Jihad Jack', the Court of Appeal and the Australian media. *Adelaide Law Review*, 27: 311–334.

Lynch, A. (2007). Achieving security, respecting rights and maintaining the rule of law. In A. Lynch, E. Macdonald & G. Williams (Eds.), *Law and liberty in the war on terror* (pp. 222–233). Leichhardt: Federation.

Mackey, C. with Miller, G. (2004). *The interrogator's war*. London: John Murray.

New York Times (2008). 'Veto of Bill on CIA tactics affirms Bush's legacy'. *New York Times*, 9 March.

Pearse, J. J. (2006). The interrogation of terrorist suspects: The banality of torture. In T. Williamson (Ed.), *Investigative interviewing* (pp. 64–83). Cullompton: Willan Publishing.

Sales, L. (2007). *Detainee 002: The case of David Hicks*. Melbourne: Melbourne University Press.

Stafford Smith, C. (2007). *Eight o'clock ferry to the windward side: Seeking justice in Guantanamo Bay*. New York: Nation Books.

Strauss, M. (2003). Torture. *New York Law School Law Review*, *48*, 201–274.

Williamson, T. (2006). Investigative interviewing and human rights the war on terrorism. In T. Williamson (Ed.), *Investigative interviewing* (pp. 3–22). Cullompton: Willan Publishing.

Williamson, T. (Ed.) (2006). *Investigative interviewing*. Cullompton: Willan Publishing.

Wilson, R. A. (Ed.) (2005). *Human rights in the 'war on terror'*. Cambridge: Cambridge University Press.

Zedner, L. (2005a). *Criminal justice*. Oxford: Oxford University Press.

Zedner, L. (2005b). Securing liberty in the face of terror. *Journal of Law and Society*, *32*, 507–533.

Zedner, L. (2007). Pre-crime and post-criminology? *Theoretical Criminology*, *11*, 261–281.

Zedner, L. (2009). Fixing the future? Precaution and the pre-emptive turn in criminal justice. In S. Bronnit, B. McSherry & A. Norrie (Eds.), *Regulating deviance: The redirection of criminalization and the futures of criminal law*. Oxford: Hart.

Cases

DPP v Thomas [2006] VSC 243.

R v Thomas [2006] VSCA 165.

R v Ul-Haque [2007] NSWSC 1251.

Thomas v Mowbray [2007] HCA 33.

Statutes

Police and Criminal Evidence Act 1984

Chapter Seven

Major Crime (Investigative Powers) Act 2004: The Chief Examiner and Coercive Powers

Damien B. Maguire

Chief Examiner for the State of Victoria, Australia

Introduction

The topic of this chapter is the Major Crime (Investigative Powers) Act 2004, the Chief Examiner and Coercive Powers. In the course of the chapter I shall outline the circumstances in which this legislation came to be implemented, explain how the legislation operates and share my views as to what part the legal profession should play in representing witnesses in the 'coercive powers' examination hearing process.

The history of the creation of the statutory office of Chief Examiner

Appointment

On 25 January 2005 after some 30 years' practising as a barrister at the Victorian Bar in Australia I was appointed as the first Chief Examiner for the State of Victoria. The position of Chief Examiner is a creature of statute and is created by the Major Crime (Investigative Powers) Act 2004.

Handbook of Psychology of Investigative Interviewing: Current Developments and Future Directions
Edited by Ray Bull, Tim Valentine and Tom Williamson
© 2009 John Wiley & Sons, Ltd.

The circumstances in which the statutory office came into being

The office of Chief Examiner was created as part of a number of measures taken by the Victorian Government to deal with what had become known as the 'gangland wars' and serious issues as to police corruption.

The gangland wars

In the period between 1998 and 2004 21 killings were attributed to gangland wars, which were fought partly on the payback principle but mainly for control of the lucrative drug trade, particularly the trade in amphetamine, cocaine and ecstasy.

Some of the killings involved high-profile criminals. Without detailing the circumstances of each of these killings, reference to some will inform you as to why these events raised a great deal of public concern.

On 21 June 2003, Jason Moran was in a van with another man and a group of children at a football ground where a football clinic was taking place. Many other parents were present with their children. As Moran sat in the van the murderer appeared and fired into the vehicle killing Moran and his companion. Jason Moran with his father and brother Mark had played a major role in Melbourne's drug trade. His brother had also been murdered approximately three years earlier.

Moran made the mistake of thinking he was safe in his vehicle with his children amongst other parents and children.

On 25 October 2003 another man involved in the drug trade, Michael Marshal, was shot in front of his wife and five-year-old son outside his home.

On 23 March 2004 Andrew 'Benji' Veniamin was shot dead in the toilet at a pizza restaurant by a man called Mick Gatto, who was said to have been part of a group of men called the Carlton crew. Members of this group had been allegedly murdered by Veniamin. Gatto was tried on a charge of murdering Veniamin and was acquitted.

On 31 March 2004, the day after Veniamin's funeral, Lewis Moran (Mark and Jason's father) was shot dead in the late afternoon in a well-known inner suburban club with other persons present, and with trams, motor vehicles and pedestrians passing by.

It can be seen from the examples I have just given that even the normal conventions of the underworld were being flouted.

The Government and the police response

In the period particularly after the murder of Jason Moran there were strong calls from the community for the establishment of a Royal Commission and/ or the creation of a Crime Commission to seek to deal with the horrific number of murders which were taking place and with police corruption regarding drugs which was being exposed at or about the same time. There was also the issue of whether there was a link between the two.

The Victorian Government was consistently opposed to taking either of these courses. In the meantime Victoria Police were seeking to deal with these problems by establishing Special Task Forces to deal with the issue of police corruption and later with the gangland killings.

In the course of these investigations police made use of the coercive powers of the Australian Crime Commission, a federal body with limited powers to deal with state offences. Examination hearings were conducted under a drug-related Reference.

In the context of the use of the Australian Crime Commission's powers, the Chief Commissioner of Victoria Police asked the Government to give police the same powers. Although the Government was never going to give these powers directly to police, the Government did agree that police should have *access* to such powers, but with substantial constraints being imposed.

In May and June 2004 the Victorian premier announced a major crime legislative package, which included a commitment to provide new coercive questioning powers to enable police to investigate organized crime more effectively. The Government said that these powers were designed to assist police in breaking the 'code of silence' that often thwarted investigations into organized crime. At or about the same time another statutory office of Director Police Integrity was created to deal with police corruption.

The organized crime legislation was ultimately implemented in November 2004 and became operative from 1 July 2005. The Act which created the position of Chief Examiner and which sets out the procedures whereby coercive powers are utilized is the Major Crime (Investigative Powers) Act 2004.

The Major Crime (Investigative Powers) Act 2004: how it operates

Application by police for a coercive powers order

The Victoria Police are empowered by this legislation to apply to a single judge of the Supreme Court of Victoria for the issuing of what is known as a coercive powers order. Obtaining such an order is the start of a process which leads to police obtaining indirect access to a witness.

An application to the Supreme Court made by a member of Victoria Police must be sanctioned by the approval of the Chief Commissioner of Police or his or her delegate. In order for the application to succeed the applicant police officer must convince the Supreme Court Justice that he or she suspects on reasonable grounds that an organized crime offence has been, is being or is likely to be committed. The application must relate to an existing investigation. It cannot be made to support a search for intelligence. It is quite different from how the Australian Crime Commission operates, which is on the basis of what is known as a Reference which is generally not concerned with a particular investigation.

That term 'organised crime offence' is defined in the legislation as follows:

'Organised crime offence' means an indictable offence against the law of Victoria, irrespective of when the offence is suspected to have been committed, that is punishable by level 5 imprisonment (10 years maximum) or more and that –

(a)   involves two or more offenders; and
(b)   involves substantial planning and organisation; and
(c)   forms part of systemic and continuing criminal activity; and
(d)   has a purpose of obtaining profit, gain, power or influence.

There are a number of other matters which are required to be satisfied before a coercive powers order will be made, including the public interest; however, I shall leave these to another day.

If the Supreme Court agrees to make an order it will relate to the particular organized crime offence and may be allowed to operate for a period of up to 12 months. Conditions as to the use of the order may also be imposed.

The involvement of the Chief Examiner

When a coercive powers order is made, police may then apply to the Supreme Court or to the Chief Examiner for the issuing of the summons or the making of a custody order in relation to a person who is in custody. Usually these applications are made to the Chief Examiner. Without going into the fine detail, the Chief Examiner will issue a summons or make a custody order if certain legislative criteria are satisfied. Normally, such applications will involve witnesses chosen by police investigators. However, the Chief Examiner does have independent discretion in this regard.

After service of the summons or the execution of a custody order the examination hearing will, in due course, take place.

The legislation requires that the Chief Examiner will generally conduct the examination by personally interrogating the witness. However, if circumstances require, the examination may be conducted by the Chief Examiner using counsel assisting or some other appropriate person, perhaps with some specialized knowledge, to examine the witness.

Investigating police are involved in the examination by instructing the Chief Examiner in conference and providing materials which are relevant to the examination. This assistance will continue during the examination hearing.

The examination hearing

The examination hearing is inquisitorial and must be held in private, with the Chief Examiner having the power to give directions as to who may be present during an examination or part of an examination and as to the prohibition on publication or communication of evidence given during the examination.

The most significant matter applying in examination hearings is the abrogation of the privilege against self-incrimination. There are, however, limitations on how evidence obtained at examination can be used in later court proceedings.

Legal professional privilege does, however, apply. Therefore, unless a witness can rely on legal professional privilege, he or she must answer a question or produce a document or other thing when called upon to do so. (There is no right to silence.)

If a witness refuses or fails to take the oath or to make an affirmation or refuses to answer questions, he or she may be charged with contempt, they may be arrested and referred to the Supreme Court, and in addition the witness may be charged with a criminal offence which under the Act carries a penalty of up to five years' imprisonment upon conviction. Further, if the witness gives false or misleading evidence, the witness may be charged with an offence under the Act which carries the same penalty.

The witness at an examination hearing is entitled to be legally represented. However, because of the inquisitorial nature of the proceedings, the role of the legal practitioner is limited. I shall deal with this issue in more detail shortly.

Another important matter is that the Chief Examiner must ensure at the beginning of the examination that the proceedings are being video-recorded.

Obviously, there are many more details as to the legislation, the examination process and the function of the Chief Examiner which I could go into. However, I think that what I have already described gives the necessary background for there to be understanding of the context in which the examination process takes place.

The right to legal representation and the role of the legal practitioner in the examination hearing

The Act provides that a witness giving evidence at an examination 'may be represented by a legal practitioner' (section 34(1)). In my view this subsection is in its terms permissive and facultative so that the Chief Examiner would, in the normal course of events, be required to allow a witness to be legally represented if the witness wished it (see *Ward v Williams* [1955] at 505).

Further, it has been recognized that it is in the public interest that persons be legally represented because it assists and enhances the administration of justice (*Grant v Downs* [1976] at 685 per Stephen, Mason and Murphy JJ).

There are a number of other provisions in the Act relevant to the issue of legal representation.

Further provisions relevant to legal representation

Section 30 concerns the conduct of the examination and subsection (1) provides that: 'The Chief Examiner is not bound by the rules of evidence in conducting an examination and may regulate the conduct of proceedings as he or she thinks fit.'

Section 36(1) entitles a legal practitioner representing a witness to take part in the examination hearing subject to the discretion of the Chief Examiner as to what he or she thinks is appropriate or relevant to the investigation of the organized crime offence.

The power given to the Chief Examiner in these sections plainly means that an Examiner has a wide discretion as to how the examination hearing is to be conducted; that discretion will include regulating the part a legal practitioner should play in the examination hearing process.

There are a number of other sections which deal with other aspects of the role of legal practitioners.

Section 33(1) grants protection to a legal practitioner appearing for a witness in an examination hearing and impliedly reinforces the fact that a witness may be legally represented.

Section 35(2) gives a legal practitioner representing a witness a right to be present at an examination even though the Chief Examiner has not made a specific direction allowing such attendance under section 35(1). This right is, however, conditioned by the right of the Chief Examiner to regulate his or her own proceedings (see *Hogan v Australian Crime Commission* (2005) FCA 913. (2005) 154 ACrim.R336).

It is in my view clear that the law is that a witness is entitled to be legally represented at the coercive powers examination hearing.

The role of the legal practitioner

I now turn to consider the role that a legal practitioner will play in an examination hearing conducted before the Chief Examiner.

In conducting an examination under the Act the Chief Examiner is obliged to act according to the rules of natural justice; those rules must apply to a consideration of what role a legal representative should play in the examination hearing.

The relevant rules of natural justice may vary dependent in part on the nature of the inquiry, the legislation under which the person acts and the purpose of the examination hearing or process (see *National Companies and Securities Commission v News Corporation Ltd* [1984]).

Therefore, in considering how the rules of natural justice apply to the role of the Chief Examiner and legal representation, it is appropriate to examine the role of the Chief Examiner, the legislation and the purpose of the examination hearing process.

The examination of a witness under the Act takes place under the authority given by the coercive powers order to investigate an organized crime offence.

A witness who is examined must answer questions under penalty of imprison-ment and is expressly prohibited from relying on the privilege against self-incrimination.

The examination powers that a Chief Examiner utilizes in the examination hearing require that the hearing not be frustrated in its investigative purpose and that the process proceeds with expedition. It is in the context of these requirements that the application of the rules of natural justice must be bal-anced. In the result, in my opinion, the role to be exercised by a legal practi-tioner in the examination hearing will be restricted and the function he or she will perform will be totally different from the role played by counsel, for example, in a criminal trial.

In deciding what the actuality of the limited role is I have been greatly assisted by reference to High Court authority and legislation, which prescribes what the role of a legal representative will be in very similar coercive powers examination hearings.

The Corporations Act 2001 Part 5.9 legislates in relation to the mandatory examination of a person as to the affairs of a corporation.

Section 597(16) sets out the role of the legal practitioner in an examination hearing under that Act. This provision is in the following terms:

> A person ordered to attend before the Court or another court for examination under this Division may, at his or her own expense, employ a solicitor, or a solicitor and counsel, and the solicitor or counsel, as the case may be, may put to the person such questions as the Court, or the other court, as the case may be, considers just for the purpose of enabling the person to explain or qualify any answers or evidence given by the person.

It can be seen, therefore, that a legal practitioner appearing on a com-pulsory examination in relation to a corporations matter is restricted to a limited role, subject to the Court considering it to be just 'for the purpose of enabling the person to explain or qualify any answers or evidence given by the person'. The right afforded by this legislation is essentially allowing the legal practitioner to re-examine the witness after the examination process is completed.

The provisions of section 597(16) reflect and adopt the view taken by the High Court in relation to earlier similar legislation in the case of *NCSC v News Corporation*. In that case the Commission sought to restrict the role that the legal representatives of News Corporation would play in the Commission's investigation. The majority of the High Court upheld the right of the Commission to restrict the role of the legal practitioners in the context of an investigation where the Commission was not engaged in making findings. The High Court found that there was compliance with the rules of natural justice in the context of the investigative procedure being undertaken.

In my opinion, the purpose for which a compulsory examination is con-ducted under the Corporations Act and its legislative predecessors and proce-dures are very similar to the purposes and procedures applicable to examinations under the 2004 Act. Both involve compulsory examinations by way of an administrative inquiry which has been established by the executive arm of government and which are not judicial in character. Both seek to obtain information only and do not involve the making of findings against those who are the subject of the examination.

In these circumstances therefore, based on an application of the law, it is appropriate that the Chief Examiner conduct examination hearings in the same manner as compulsory examinations are conducted under the Corporations Act. The conduct of an investigation/examination hearing in such a manner is fair and complies with the rules of natural justice; nothing more is required to satisfy the requirements. Therefore, the Chief Examiner conducts examination hearings in the following manner in relation to legal representation.

- In the normal course of events the Chief Examiner will allow a witness to be legally represented.
- In some circumstances the exclusion of a particular legal practitioner employed by the witness from the examination hearing may be required. This requirement may arise in circumstances where the presence of a particular lawyer may prejudice the investigation. The Chief Examiner may prevent a particular lawyer from appearing by exercising the general power he or she has to regulate the conduct of the examination hearing (see *Hogan v Australian Crime Commission*).
- The legal practitioner acting for the witness would have only a limited part to play in the examination process as I have explained, and normally would not be able to raise objection.
- If the witness reasonably seeks legal advice during the examination hearing, then the examination hearing will be interrupted so that the legal practitioner can advise the witness.
- At the conclusion of the examination the legal practitioner acting for the witness may question his or her client in relation to issues which seek to explain away or qualify matters which have arisen during the examination of the witness. This procedure will be essentially a process of re-examination.
- No submissions will be allowed to be made by the legal practitioner acting for the witness at the conclusion of the examination.

Relevant matters of law of which a legal practitioner should be aware when representing a witness on an examination hearing

Despite the limited role that a legal practitioner plays in the examination process, there are many important matters that the legal practitioner should be aware of which must be the subject of advice to the client particularly in the period preceding the examination hearing. I propose to deal with some of these matters.

The first and most important matter is that if a witness is served with a witness summons, then the witness must attend at the examination hearing. Failure to do so will almost certainly involve the issuing of a warrant for the witness's arrest and charging of the witness with a criminal offence carrying a term of imprisonment of up to five years.

Where a client attends with the summons he or she will be likely to have in their possession a further document called a confidentiality notice. This is a document which the Chief Examiner or the Supreme Court must issue in certain circumstances; in other circumstances, there is discretion to be exercised as to whether or not a notice should issue. The service of this notice means that the person served must not, without reasonable excuse, tell anyone of the existence of the summons, the subject of the organized crime offence referred to in the summons (or order) or any official matter connected with the witness summons (or order) (see section 20 of the Act). The obtaining of legal advice would constitute a reasonable excuse and the term 'official matter' is defined in the Act.

The next important matter is that in the examination hearing the privilege against self-incrimination is abrogated (see section 39 of the Act).

However, the use of admissions made is restricted so that any answer given or document or other thing produced cannot be used in evidence against the person in a criminal proceeding or a proceeding for the imposition of a penalty. This means that the person must be in the position of an accused or a defendant in order to attract the benefit. It would not apply if the person were called as a witness.

It is, however, important to note that the Act does not limit any derivative use of information obtained during the examination hearing.

The legislation is obviously designed so that the witness is encouraged to give truthful and accurate evidence at an examination hearing. If a witness gives such evidence, it cannot be used against the person if he or she is charged and the person would not be at risk of being charged with an offence against the Act. In these circumstances it would seem to be good legal advice to tell the client to answer questions accurately and truthfully in an examination hearing.

Legal professional privilege does apply (see section 40 of the Act). However, subject to the privilege, it is an offence not to answer questions, to produce documents or other things when required to or to give false or misleading evidence. A refusal or failure to answer a question or to produce a document or other thing involves the commission of an indictable offence carrying a penalty of up to five years' imprisonment. It is also an indictable offence carrying the same term of imprisonment for a witness to give false and misleading evidence or to produce a document or thing that the person knows to be false and misleading in a material particular.

If an issue as to legal professional privilege arises at an examination hearing, the legal practitioner is likely to be called upon to make submissions on the issue. Different procedures apply in relation to whether the privilege issue arises first in respect of a question and second in relation to a document or thing.

Contempt

The Act provides that in certain circumstances the Chief Examiner may charge a person with contempt; if this occurs, then the witness is likely to be immediately arrested, charged and taken before the Supreme Court. The Supreme Court will then decide if an offence has been committed and what the appropriate penalty should be.

The contempt provisions are contained in section 49 the Act, and in subsection (1) the circumstances in which a contempt may take place are detailed. These circumstances are as follows:

(a) fails without reasonable excuse to produce any document or other thing the person is required by the witness summons to produce; or

(b) being called or examined as a witness at an examination, refuses to be sworn or to make an affirmation or without reasonable excuse refuses or fails to answer any question relevant to the subject matter of the examination; or

(c) engages in any other conduct that would, if the Chief Examiner were the Supreme Court, constitute a contempt of that Court.

The Supreme Court has jurisdiction to deal with the contempt charge under Order 75, Part 3 as contempt of an inferior court.

It is clearly important for a legal practitioner representing a witness to be familiar with the requirements of the legislation and to advise his or her client of possible results where there has been a failure to comply and it is also important to be aware of the contempt power which can be used under our Victorian legislation, but does not exist under the Australian Crime Commission Commonwealth legislation.

Examination to be held in private

The Act provides that an examination must be held in private and the Chief Examiner may give directions as to persons who may be present during the examination or part of the examination (see section 35 of the Act). Further, the Chief Examiner is required by law in some circumstances to restrict by direction the publication or communication of evidence given during an examination hearing, and in other circumstances he or she has discretion to or not to do so.

A breach of such a direction is a serious matter punishable by indictable charge carrying a term of imprisonment of up to five years. If you are representing a client at an examination hearing, you will likely be asked to make submissions as to whether or not such a direction must or should be given.

Conclusion

The Major Crime (Investigative Powers) Act is a unique piece of legislation. It puts in place a regime which allows the use of exceptional powers which, although based on the Australian Crime Commission legislation, differs in a number of important respects. It is likely that the Act will be utilized frequently by police in the future once the use of the powers becomes more familiar and widely known. In these circumstances the legal profession will also play an increasingly important role in the coercive powers examination hearings process.

Cases

Grant v Downs (1976) 135 CLR 674
Hogan v Australian Crime Commission [2005] FCA 913. (2005) 154 ACrim.R336
National Companies and Securities Commission v News Corporation Ltd (1984) 156 CLR 296
Ward v Williams (1955) 92 CLR 496

Statutes

Major Crime (Investigative Powers) Act 2004

Chapter Eight

The Relation between Consistency and Accuracy of Eyewitness Testimony: Legal versus Cognitive Explanations

Ronald P. Fisher

Florida International University

Neil Brewer

Flinders University

and

Gregory Mitchell

University of Virginia

Ten minutes after witnessing a bank robbery, Ms. Barnes is interviewed by the first police officer on the scene. She describes the robber as a white male, clean-shaven, medium height, husky, wearing sunglasses and a baseball hat. Three months later, Ms. Barnes is deposed by the defense attorney, and she is asked again to describe the robber. This time she reports some of the facts she had told the original police officer (white male, medium height, husky, wearing sunglasses), but she omits an earlier mentioned detail (wearing a baseball hat). More important, she now reports some new details that she had not described earlier (the robber wore a red shirt) and she contradicts a statement she had made initially (the robber has a beard). Months later the case goes to court, and Ms. Barnes takes the witness stand. Here, on cross-examination, the defense attorney focuses on the apparent inconsistencies in Ms. Barnes' two earlier descriptions. Specifically, the attorney draws attention

Handbook of Psychology of Investigative Interviewing: Current Developments and Future Directions
Edited by Ray Bull, Tim Valentine and Tom Williamson
© 2009 John Wiley & Sons, Ltd.

to two critical facts: first, Ms. Barnes contradicted herself across the two interviews ('clean-shaven' on initial police interview, 'bearded' in the deposition)
and second, she remembered a detail at the deposition (the red shirt), three
months after the crime, that she did not recall 10 minutes after the crime. 'So,
Ms. Barnes,' presses the defense attorney, 'were you wrong when you spoke
to the police officer and said the robber was clean-shaven, or were you wrong
in your deposition when you said the robber had a beard? Or, maybe you were
wrong both times?' Seeing that he has gained the upper hand, the attorney
presses on: 'Was your memory better 10 minutes after the crime, when you
did not recall the robber's shirt, or was it better three months after the crime,
when you reported that the robber had a red shirt?' Following Witness Barnes'
admission that her memory was better immediately after the crime, the defense
attorney tries to account for her newfound recollection, which seemingly violates everyone's intuitive beliefs that memory weakens with the passage of time.
The defense attorney might even plant a seed of doubt about the quality of
the police investigation by asking, 'Were you told by the police that the robber
had a red shirt?' Finally, in the concluding argument, the defense attorney
notes to the jury that Ms. Barnes' inconsistent recollections cast serious doubt
about the accuracy of her memory, and that the jury should question the credibility of her entire testimony.

Although the details of this account are fictitious, the series of events is
commonplace in a criminal investigation. Witnesses are likely to testify repeatedly during a criminal case. During these interviews, witnesses may contradict
themselves on specific statements or remember some details in later interviews
(police interviews, depositions, or in court testimony) that they did not recall
earlier. When this happens, their entire testimony is likely to be questioned.
We examine here these two critical issues: contradictions in witnesses' testimonies; and witnesses' later recollection of previously unreported facts (reminiscence). How predictive are contradictions and reminiscences of the overall
accuracy of a witness's testimony? How does the legal system account for these
phenomena, and how valid are their conclusions? We compare the legal analyses of these phenomena with analyses found within cognitive theory. Finally,
we describe several empirical studies that examine the relation between inconsistency and accuracy of eyewitness recollection under controlled laboratory
conditions, and in light of these findings we make recommendations for the
legal system.

The legal approach

Judges, litigators, and legal scholars deem witness consistency to be one of the
most important measures of witness credibility. Pattern jury instructions regularly used in federal and state courts in the USA direct jurors to consider
witness self-contradictions when deciding how much weight to give to a witness's trial testimony. A standard federal instruction on witness credibility

directs jurors to attend to whether 'the witness testified inconsistently while on the witness stand, or if the witness said or did something, or failed to say or do something, at any other time that is inconsistent with what the witness said while testifying' (Committee on Pattern Jury Instructions, Sixth Circuit Criminal Pattern Jury Instructions, No. 107, 2005). A standard state court instruction likewise informs jurors that '[y]ou may consider whether a witness made statements at this trial that are inconsistent with each other. You may also consider whether a witness made previous statements that are inconsistent with his or her testimony at trial' (Office of Court Administration Committee, New York Criminal Jury Instructions 2d, Credibility of Witnesses-Inconsistent Statements, 2007).

These instructions reflect a long-standing belief held by courts and commentators that 'a prior self-contradiction shows a defect either in the memory or in the honesty of the witness' (Wigmore, 1970: 993). The important empirical assumption is that specific contradictions indicate a general unreliability: 'upon perceiving that the witness has made an erroneous statement on one point, we are ready to infer that he is capable of making an error upon other points' (*ibid.*). Wigmore collected numerous American cases from the 1800s and 1900s in which courts endorsed this view, and belief in the correctness of this view remains strong. For instance, Uviller's (1993) survey of federal judges found that these judges believed internal inconsistency and external contradiction were the best measures of witness credibility. McCormick's influential treatise on evidence (as revised by Strong, 1999) states that 'the most widely used impeachment technique is proof that the witness made a pretrial statement inconsistent with her trial testimony' (Strong, 1999: 50–51). Others (e.g., Park, Leonard & Goldberg, 2004) agree with McCormick on the continuing popularity of this technique.

While courts and commentators advance the theory that inconsistency implies lack of credibility, litigators put the theory into practice rigorously. Attorneys and their assistants are trained to pore over witness statements to identify inconsistencies (Pozner & Dodd, 1993). Not only do they search through witnesses' previous statements to find inconsistencies, but they also question witnesses on the stand in such a way as to create such inconsistencies (e.g., Iannuzzi, 1999). Glissan (1991: 108) recommends: 'A true inconsistency can effectively destroy a witness, and sometimes a whole case … If you find a true inconsistency, or if you can manufacture one, then use the deposition of previous evidence to sheet it home.' Similarly, Bailey and Rothblatt (1971: 177) suggest, 'Capitalize on these conflicts. This is the most effective way of discrediting [the witness's] entire testimony.' These strategies are directed primarily toward contradictions, but similar recommendations exist to attack reminiscent statements. For instance, Mauet (1980) notes that a witness may be impeached if that witness recalls details that were omitted from earlier recall attempts. Others express the same concern: 'A witness' credibility can be attacked by showing that facts testified to [by the witness] were omitted from a [previous] document that they prepared, even though the document was prepared closer in time to the events in question' (Alavi & Ahmad, 2002: 18).

Instructing jurors to attend to inconsistencies should make these inconsistencies more salient. Is there any evidence, however, that jurors' decisions are actually influenced by inconsistencies? Two sources of evidence suggest that jurors, and many other participants in the legal system, are indeed influenced by inconsistent testimony. Brewer and colleagues surveyed a variety of people, including college students, police, prosecutors, and defense attorneys, about their beliefs of the diagnostic value of inconsistency on the credibility of a witness (Brewer, Potter, Fisher, Bond & Luszcz, 1999; Potter & Brewer, 1999). They found that inconsistencies within a witness's testimony were considered by all of these groups to be strongly indicative of inaccurate testimony. Additionally, experimental studies have examined the role of witness inconsistency on simulated juries (Lindsay, Lim, Marando & Cully, 1986; Berman, Narby & Cutler, 1995; Berman & Cutler, 1996; Brewer & Burke, 2002; Brewer & Hupfeld, 2004). In these studies, simulated juries, composed of college students and, sometimes, members of the general community, watched or heard an abbreviated version of a trial that contained inconsistencies in a prosecution witness's account. After the trial, mock-jurors made judgments on measures such as witness credibility or effectiveness, probability that the defendant committed the crime, and verdict. The majority – though not all – of these studies (e.g., Lindsay *et al.*, 1986; Brewer & Burke, 2002) have shown that testimonial inconsistencies harm witness credibility and, in turn, affect judgments about probability of guilt. In summary, much of the mock-juror research suggests that jurors' decisions are in line with attorneys' courtroom arguments and judges' instructions that inconsistencies cast doubt on the accuracy of witnesses' testimony.

Rationale of courtroom arguments and instructions

What is the underlying rationale guiding these courtroom arguments and jury instructions? We assume that jurors must rely on witness statements to determine what happened in the critical event, because they have no other relevant information about the event. Jurors most likely sense that witnesses' memories may be incomplete or inaccurate, and so look for clues to assess whether their recollections of the critical event are accurate and complete. What clues do jurors use to determine the quality of witnesses' testimony? One source of information is relevant world knowledge. Jurors may know, for instance, the amount of time required to travel from place X to place Y, and so they may be able to determine whether a witness's testimony is feasible. More likely, jurors will depend on behavioral cues related to the witness's description of the critical event. Does the witness seem to be confident about her story or is she unsure, as perhaps indicated by hesitations in her speech (Erickson, Lind, Johnson & O'Barr, 1978)? Does the witness describe the critical event in great detail, or does she provide only a few details (Wells & Leippe, 1981)? Does the witness provide the same details if she is asked repeatedly to describe the event, or does she change her story (Leippe, Manion & Romanczyk, 1992)?

We focus here on the clue of inconsistency, and specifically on contradictions and reminiscence. Different arguments underlie the assessment of contradictions and reminiscence, so we shall examine the two separately. When witnesses contradict themselves (e.g., saying on one occasion that the robber was clean-shaven and on another that he had a beard), it is obvious that at least one of these reports must be incorrect, as the robber cannot be both clean-shaven and bearded. When such inconsistencies occur, it is fair for the cross-examining attorney to ask if the witness was wrong earlier (when she said that the robber was clean-shaven) or if she is wrong now (when she says that the robber had a beard). Similarly, it is appropriate for judges to warn jurors about witnesses who make such contradictory statements, as at least a portion of their testimony must be incorrect. Having established that the witness's memory must be wrong about one aspect of the critical event (the robber's face), it seems reasonable to assume that the witness's memory about the entire event is not credible.

Reminiscence, recalling some details at a later time (e.g., at a deposition) that witnesses did not recall at a previous attempt (e.g., to the initial police investigator), seems to violate one of the intuitively obvious principles of memory, namely, that memory declines with the passage of time. Attorneys, therefore, argue that these counterintuitive events should occur rarely and, when they do occur, they should arouse suspicion. How else can we account for the witness's memory seemingly improving over time? At first glance, it is not unreasonable for attorneys to question the source of these new recollections. Perhaps the witness learned the additional facts from another witness, from the media, or even from the police investigators. If the witness really did learn about these newfound facts from a non-crime source, then the witness's reminiscent recollections do not necessarily reflect his memory of the crime itself, but what he was told about the crime from another source. Not surprisingly, the law looks askance at such extra-event witness knowledge and will often use the hearsay rule and personal knowledge rules to limit the ability of the witness to testify about facts learned after the event.

The preceding arguments are commonplace in the courtroom and seem reasonable. Are they correct, however, in their assumptions of how memory works? We examine these assumptions by seeing whether they predict the outcomes of controlled, laboratory experiments (see Fisher & Reardon, in press, for the advantages of using controlled, laboratory tests). Technically, we did not ask attorneys and judges to predict the outcomes of laboratory experiments. Instead, we examined their courtroom behaviors (attorneys' arguments and judges' instructions) and converted the apparent logic underlying these behaviors into specific predictions. That is, people who engage in the described courtroom behaviors should make the following predictions about the outcomes of controlled, laboratory experiments. We refer to the implicit theory that underlies these courtroom arguments and jury instructions as the

'Courtroom Theory' of memory. What, specifically, are the predictions of the Courtroom Theory?

1. Consistency of recollection is a direct indicator of the quality of a witness's memory. Therefore, factors that influence consistency of recollection should have the same effect on accuracy of recollection. Experimental factors that increase (decrease) consistency should increase (decrease) accuracy and vice versa. No experimental factors should dissociate (have different effects on) consistency and accuracy.
2. Contradictory statements should be inaccurate – at least as compared to consistent statements.
3. Witnesses who make many contradictory statements should be considerably less accurate overall (across their entire testimony) than witnesses who make few or no contradictory statements. Statistically, there should be a strong, negative correlation between amount of inconsistency in a witness's testimony and the overall accuracy of the witness's testimony.
4. Reminiscence should occur infrequently. Moreover, explaining reminiscence requires an extraordinary (non-cognitive) mechanism, such as police informing witnesses about crime details.
5. Reminiscent statements should be inaccurate – at least as compared to consistent statements.
6. Witnesses who make many reminiscent statements should be considerably less accurate overall (across their entire testimony) than witnesses who make few or no reminiscent statements. Statistically, there should be a strong, negative correlation between amount of reminiscence in a witness's testimony and the overall accuracy of the witness's testimony.

As opposed to the Courtroom Theory of memory, how would cognitive psychology account for these witness behaviors?

Cognitive Theory

Two principles of cognitive theory are responsible for the major distinctions between the predictions of the Courtroom Theory and Cognitive Theory: the importance of retrieval processes; and the independence of components. We describe these principles briefly.

Retrieval processes

Recollection reflects not only the contents of the memory store but also the process of retrieval (Tulving, 1983). If the retrieval processes applied on two occasions differ, the recollections will differ, even if the contents of memory do not change. The retrieval process is partially determined by the specific question that is asked. Thus, if the question that is posed to a witness changes from one interview to another, the witness's recollections may change. In general, the more different are the retrieval cues (questions) across interviews, the more dissimilar will be the recollections on the two interviews. Reminiscence may occur, therefore, if a retrieval cue is present on the second interview, but not on the first interview. The amount of reminiscence should reflect the amount of dissimilarity between the retrieval cues (questions) on two interviews.

Independence of components

Complex events are made up of many components, each of which is processed somewhat independently of the others (Fisher, Phillips & Krioukova, 2000; Mitchell, Haw & Fisher, 2003). Therefore, if a witness fails to recall one component of a crime, or even if she misperceives or mistakenly recalls one component of the crime, she may still perceive or correctly recall other components of the crime.

Based on these two principles, cognitive psychology predicts the following behaviours by witnesses who are interviewed repeatedly:

1. Some mental processes underpin measures of both consistency and accuracy. For instance, the quality of the memory trace should influence both consistency and accuracy. Better encoded events should be recalled more consistently and also more accurately than poorly encoded events. By comparison, other mental processes do not underpin both consistency and accuracy: Either they have opposite effects on consistency and accuracy or they influence one measure but not the other. For instance, the similarity of the retrieval cues used across two interviews should influence consistency of recollection, but not accuracy of recollection. We should, therefore, expect that some experimental manipulations will have similar effects on consistency and accuracy, whereas other manipulations will have different effects on consistency and accuracy (experimental dissociation).

2. As noted, better encoded events should be recalled more consistently and more accurately than poorly encoded events. We should also expect that encouraging witnesses to guess will lead to less consistent and less accurate responses than instructing witnesses to be certain before volunteering a response. Both of these propositions predict that consistent recollections will be more accurate than inconsistent recollections.

3. Each component of a complex event is processed independently of the other components. Therefore, accuracy of recalling some components of a complex event may not necessarily predict how accurately witnesses recall the other components. Witnesses who make many contradictory statements may be inaccurate on those specific statements; however, they may be accurate on the rest of their testimony. That is, the correlation between

amount of inconsistency and overall accuracy of a witness's testimony may be relatively weak.

4. Reminiscence should be a common experience. Furthermore, the amount of reminiscence should be explained easily by conventional cognitive theory, which relates reminiscence to changes in retrieval cues from one interview to another.

5. Reminiscent statements may or may not be accurate. Whether reminiscent responses are accurate or not depends on a variety of factors, such as the nature of the question that is asked: Open-ended questions or probes (e.g., Describe his face) should yield more accurate responses than closed questions (e.g., What color were his eyes?).

6. For the same reason as indicated in point 3 above (the independence of components), witnesses who make many reminiscent statements should not necessarily be inaccurate on the other (non-reminiscent) statements of their testimony. The correlation between amount of reminiscence and overall accuracy may be relatively weak.

Experimental testing

We report an overview of the results from 19 experiments to assess the predictions of the Courtroom and Cognitive theories. Each of the experiments conformed to the following general procedure. Witnesses (typically college students, but the same patterns of results also obtained for others) either watched a videotape of a simulated crime (robbery or homicide) or observed a live, innocuous event or a staged confrontation between two people. The witnesses were then tested formally (paper-and-pencil test) or, as in most experiments, participated in face-to-face interviews to assess their memories of the event. Most of the witnesses were tested twice. The tests or interviews occurred either shortly after observing the event (within 30 minutes) or after a delay of up to two weeks. The interview questions or probes were either open-ended (e.g., Describe the robber) or were closed. There were three kinds of closed questions: cued recall (e.g., What color were the robber's eyes?), multiple choice (What color was the robber's eyes: green, blue, black, or brown?) and True/False (The robber's eyes were green: true or false?). The witnesses were sometimes encouraged to be very certain before volunteering an answer, sometimes encouraged to guess, and sometimes not given any explicit instructions about certainty.

We compared the witness statements across the two interviews and categorized them as one of four types: Consistent (same answer at Time 1 and Time 2, e.g., *robber was a white male* at Time 1, and *robber was a white male* at Time 2), contradiction (contradictory answers at Time 1 (*clean-shaven*) and Time 2 (*bearded*)), reminiscent (no answer at Time 1, but witness provides an answer at Time 2 (*red shirt*), and forgotten (witness provides an answer at Time 1 (*baseball hat*) but does not answer at Time 2. We then calculated the accuracy of each of the four response categories (consistent, contradiction, reminiscent, and forgotten) in addition to the accuracy of the entire testimony. Accuracy was calculated by dividing the number of correct statements by the total number of statements. For instance, if a witness made eight correct statements out of ten total statements, then her accuracy rate was 0.8 (8/10).

The results of these experiments are organized around the predictions of the 'Courtroom' and 'Cognitive' Theories.

Experimental dissociations: common versus unique mental processes. Some experimental manipulations had the same effects on consistency and accuracy of testimony, whereas other manipulations had different effects on the two measures. When witnesses were instructed to be certain before volunteering answers, they were both more consistent and more accurate than when instructed to guess if unsure (Phillips, Fisher & Krioukova, 1999). Varying the format of the question (open-ended vs. closed) also had parallel effects on consistency and accuracy: Open-ended questions yielded more consistent responses and also more accurate answers than closed questions (Fisher & Patterson, 2004). Other manipulations, however, had different, and sometimes opposite, effects on consistency and accuracy of recollection. Specifically, witnesses were less consistent but more accurate when tested shortly after the critical event (within 30 minutes) than when tested after two weeks (Fisher, Schreiber, Burguera & Alvarez, 2003). That is, delaying the tests increased consistency but decreased accuracy. This experimental dissociation suggests that consistency and accuracy may reflect different underlying mechanisms (Tulving, 1985), in opposition to the Courtroom Theory.

Accuracy of contradictions. In all of our experiments, the accuracy rate of contradictory answers was low (Brock, Fisher & Cutler, 1999; Fisher & Patterson, 2004; Gilbert & Fisher, 2006;). For instance, in Gilbert & Fisher, the accuracy rate of contradictory statements was only 0.49; by comparison, the accuracy rate of consistent answers was almost perfect (0.95). Both the Courtroom and Cognitive theories correctly predicted the low accuracy of contradictory statements.

Contradiction as a predictor of overall accuracy. Although contradictory statements were considerably less accurate than consistent statements, witnesses who made many contradictory statements were *not* much less accurate overall (all of the statements in their entire testimony) than were witnesses who made only a few contradictory statements. Witnesses were scored in terms of the accuracy of their overall testimony and the proportion of all statements that were contradictory (typically, this proportion is relatively small, as witnesses who take their task seriously rarely make more than a few contradictions). Across the various conditions of the experiments, the correlations between the proportion of contradictory statements and the accuracy of the entire testimony was relatively low (the Pearson correlation coefficient was generally between 0.00 and 0.35) (Fisher & Cutler, 1995; Brewer *et al.*, 1999; Fisher & Patterson, 2004; Gilbert & Fisher, 2006). The finding that contradictions are poor predictors of witnesses' overall testimonial accuracy is in direct violation of the 'Courtroom' theory.

Reminiscence: frequency and extraordinary explanations.   In our studies, and also those of other researchers (e.g., Scrivner & Safer, 1988), reminiscence was a common phenomenon (see Payne, 1987, for a review). In Gilbert & Fisher (2006), 98% of witnesses who were tested twice (189 of 192) made at least two reminiscent recollections, hardly a rare phenomenon, as suggested by the Courtroom Theory. Furthermore, the number of reminiscent statements a witness made was highly related to the dissimilarity of the questions (retrieval cues) that were asked on the two tests. When the retrieval cues changed from Test 1 to Test 2, witnesses made almost twice as many reminiscent statements (10.1) as when the same cues were given on the two tests (6.1). As this finding is compatible with the Cognitive Theory, one need not postulate extraordinary mechanisms to account for reminiscence, as the Courtroom Theory suggests.

Accuracy of reminiscence.   Reminiscent statements varied in accuracy across studies, from a low of 0.66 (Brock *et al.*, 1999) to a high of 0.87 (Gilbert & Fisher, 2006). That reminiscent statements can be very accurate violates the dire predictions of the Courtroom Theory, which assumes reflexively that reminiscence is problematic (see also LaRooy, Pipe & Murray, 2005).

Although reminiscent statements were often accurate, they were not as accurate as either consistent or forgotten statements. In Gilbert & Fisher (2006), for example, the accuracy rates for consistent, forgotten, and reminiscent, statements were, respectively, 0.95, 0.93, and 0.87 (see also Brock *et al.*, 1999; Fisher & Patterson, 2004, for similar patterns). Reminiscent statements, however, were much more accurate than were contradictions (0.49). At the very least, then, we should distinguish between different kinds of inconsistency and pay most attention to direct contradictions.

Reminiscence as a predictor of overall accuracy.   The prevalence of reminiscent statements was not predictive of overall accuracy. Witnesses who made more reminiscent statements were only minimally, and non-significantly, less accurate than witnesses who made fewer reminiscent statements. In Gilbert & Fisher (2006) the Pearson correlation coefficient between proportion of reminiscent statements and overall accuracy was −0.05. This correlation was uniformly low across the two tests: Proportion of reminiscent statements was non-significantly correlated with overall accuracy at Test 1 (0.03) and also at

Test 2 (−0.14). Similar patterns of non-significant correlations were also found in Fisher & Patterson (2006) and Gordon & Follmer (1994).

Relative to consistent recollections, which are by far the most common category of response, reminiscent responses are relatively infrequent (approximately 22% of all responses in Gilbert & Fisher, 2006) and contradictions are very rare (less than 1%). To increase the reliability of these infrequent events, we therefore combined contradictory and reminiscent statements into one score to determine if these 'troublesome' inconsistencies, when aggregated, were more predictive of overall accuracy. Specifically, we examined whether the amount of inconsistency was related to the accuracy of consistent items. The number of inconsistencies (contradictions and reminiscences) was not at all predictive of the accuracy of consistent items (correlation coefficient = −0.06). Even when we compared the most discrepant witnesses (those who made 12–18 inconsistencies) to the most consistent witnesses (0–6 inconsistencies), the accuracy rates of consistent items did not differ, 0.94 vs. 0.96, respectively. No matter how we scored the data, there was no evidence to support the Courtroom Theory that reminiscence is predictive of inaccuracy of the overall testimony.

Resolving a puzzle

There is an apparent conundrum here: Inconsistent statements – and especially contradictions – are less accurate than consistent statements, yet witnesses who make more inconsistent statements (whether contradictions, reminiscences, or a combination of the two) are not much less accurate than witnesses who are consistent. We believe that this conundrum can be explained by the idea that the various components of a complex event (e.g., crime) are processed independently of one another. That is, accuracy of memory for one component of a complex event tells us very little about accuracy of memory for other components of the event. Thus, if a specific statement (e.g., facial hair) is believed to be inaccurate because the witness contradicted himself, this tells us very little or nothing about the accuracy of the remainder of his testimony. To test this idea, we conducted several experiments in which witnesses attempted to describe the various components of complex events. We then measured the relationships between accuracy levels for each of these various components or dimensions. For example, Brewer *et al.* (1999) classified the testimony of witnesses to a bank robbery into five dimensions – offender description, offender actions, bystander description, bystander actions, and objects – but failed to detect any meaningful relationships between accuracy on one dimension and that on any other. Other studies have replicated this finding (e.g., Fisher *et al.*, 2000; Mitchell *et al.*, 2003). It is not surprising, therefore, that inaccurate recollection for a few, isolated parts of a crime (as inferred by contradictory statements) cannot predict the accuracy of the witness's overall testimony. That is, inconsistent recollection, and especially a contradiction, informs us about the *specific statement* that is reported inconsistently, but it tells us little or nothing about the accuracy of the *rest of the testimony.*

An alternative predictor of overall witness accuracy

We were reluctant to dismiss a traditional cue used by the legal system (inconsistency) without suggesting an alternative to assess accuracy of witness testimony. Therefore, we re-examined the data from our experiments to see if another cue was more predictive of testimonial accuracy. One cue that was highly predictive of recall accuracy was the format of the question (open-ended or closed). Invariably, responses to open-ended questions were considerably more accurate than were responses to closed questions. For instance, in Fisher & Patterson (2004), responses to free recall probes (Describe the robber) were almost perfectly accurate whether witnesses were tested after a few minutes (proportion correct = 0.97) or after two weeks (0.94). By comparison, responses to cued recall tests (e.g., What color was the robber's jacket?) were considerably less accurate both when tested after a few minutes (0.70) and after two weeks (0.54). Likewise, responses to multiple-choice recognition tests (e.g., What color was the robber's jacket: blue, white, green, red?) were also poor when tested after a few minutes (0.74) or when tested after two weeks (0.64). Furthermore, this marked superiority for responses to open-ended questions held for the most consistent witnesses as well as the least consistent witnesses. If this marked superiority of open-ended questions obtains reliably in future testing, the courts may wish to pay more attention to question format, which appears to be highly diagnostic of response accuracy and less attention to consistency of responding, which appears to be less diagnostic of response accuracy.

Conclusion

Focusing the courtroom drama on inconsistencies in a witness's testimony, rather than on more diagnostic cues of testimonial accuracy, encourages litigators to exploit witness uncertainties and encourages jurors to discount evidence for the wrong reasons. If the cross-examination strategy is effective and witnesses are impeached because of their inconsistent recollections, jurors will discount some witness testimony and base their decisions on less information. Reducing the amount of accurate information that jurors consider should give rise to less accurate decisions. In short, contrary to two centuries of accepted legal folklore, an inconsistent witness may not be an inaccurate witness. Furthermore, in cases where one side puts up most of the witnesses, impeaching witnesses will influence the two sides disproportionately, thereby skewing the evidence. Both of these ills – reducing the amount of valuable witness evidence and skewing the evidence provided to jurors – are likely to pervert justice.

Recommendations

Based on our findings, we make the following recommendations:

1.   If jurors are encouraged to use consistency of testimony as a guideline to assigning credibility to evidence, they should be strongly encouraged to think in terms of the credibility of *individual statements* and not in terms of the credibility of the witness as a whole. Inconsistency is diagnostic of error, but only at the level of the individual statement: inconsistent statements are unlikely to be correct. Jurors should not, however, extrapolate to the level of the witness, as witnesses who make inconsistent statements, on the whole, are not less accurate than witnesses who make only consistent statements. Judges should instruct jurors to think in terms of individual facts of the case, not in terms of witnesses. At the very least, jurors should not discredit witnesses reflexively simply because they have made inconsistent statements. Over-reliance on (in)consistency as a means to the truth falls prey to Ralph Waldo Emerson's insight: 'Foolish consistency is the hobgoblin of small minds.'
2.   Not all inconsistencies are equally diagnostic of error. Direct contradiction should certainly be used to discredit a particular statement. By contrast, reminiscent statements are considerably more accurate than contradictions, and in some conditions are almost as accurate as consistent statements. Reminiscent answers should therefore be considered only 'mildly' inconsistent. At the very least, one should consider other factors before rejecting reminiscent answers, for example, were the questions on the two interviews similar to each other? Were the questions open-ended or closed? Were the witnesses encouraged to volunteer uncertain answers?

Limitations

The conclusions we have put forward here are tentative at best, as the database to support the conclusions is not robust. First, there is a paucity of studies, and most of the research has been conducted in only two laboratories. We encourage other researchers to conduct empirical studies to expand the data base. Second, all of the research was conducted in controlled laboratory conditions with volunteer witnesses. The logistic and ethical limitations of conducting such research prevent us from examining memory under highly arousing conditions and with long intervals between either the critical event and the interviews, or one interview and another. Expanding the research to include more arousing events and testing over longer intervals will certainly strengthen the database. Thus far, our studies have examined only college-aged students as the witnesses (although note similar findings with children; Gordon & Follmer, 1994; LaRooy *et al.*, 2005). Once again, including a wider sample of witnesses should improve our ability to generalize the results. All of the participants in our studies were motivated to be truthful. As such, our conclusions are restricted to cooperative witnesses who are attempting to volunteer truthful information. We make no claims here about the testimony of deceptive witnesses (see Granhag, Stromwall & Jonsson, 2003, for some recent, interesting findings on the consistency of liars and truth-tellers). Finally, we did not cross-examine witnesses in any of our studies. Perhaps a strong cross-examination will reveal more differences between accurate and inaccurate witness recollections. We strongly encourage future researchers to shore up some of the limitations of our studies. We hope that we have at least stimulated the appetites of researchers and those within the legal community to examine more carefully the matter of inconsistency within witness testimony.

Acknowledgement

This chapter is dedicated to memory of Dr Tom Williamson, a true friend, colleague, and gentle man.

References

Alavi, A. & Ahmad, N. (2002). *Credibility and impeachment: Fundamentals of direct and cross-examination*. Paper presented at the University of Houston Law Foundation Continuing Legal Education Workshop, 1–29.

Bailey, F. L. & Rothblatt, H. B. (1971). *Successful techniques for criminal trials*. Rochester, NY: The Lawyers Co-op Publ. Co. & Bancroft-Whitney Co.

Berman, G. L. & Cutler, B. L. (1996). Effects of inconsistencies in eyewitness testimony on mock-juror decision making. *Journal of Applied Psychology, 81*, 170–177.

Berman, G. L., Narby, D. J. & Cutler, B. L. (1995). Effects of inconsistent eyewitness statements on mock-jurors' evaluations of eyewitnesses, perceptions of defendant culpability and verdicts. *Law and Human Behavior, 19*, 79–88.

Brewer, N. & Burke, A. (2002). Effects of testimonial inconsistencies and eyewitness confidence on mock-juror judgments. *Law and Human Behavior, 26*, 353–364.

Brewer, N. & Hupfeld, R. M. (2004). Effects of testimonial inconsistencies and witness group identity on mock-juror judgments. *Journal of Applied Social Psychology, 34*, 493–513.

Brewer, N., Potter, R., Fisher, R. P., Bond, N. & Luszcz, M. (1999). Beliefs and data on the relationship between consistency and accuracy of eyewitness testimony. *Applied Cognitive Psychology, 13*, 297–313.

Brock, P., Fisher, R. P. & Cutler, B. L. (1999). Examining the cognitive interview in a double-test paradigm. *Psychology, Crime and Law, 5*, 29–45.

Committee on Pattern Jury Instructions of the District Judges Association of the Sixth Circuit (2005). *Sixth Circuit Criminal Pattern Jury Instructions*. Cincinnati, OH: Judicial Council for the U.S. Court of Appeals for the Sixth Circuit.

Erickson, B., Lind, E. A., Johnson, B. C. & O'Barr, W. M. (1978). Speech style and impression formation in a court setting: The effects of 'powerful' and 'powerless' speech. *Journal of Experimental Social Psychology, 14*, 266–279.

Fisher, R. P. & Cutler, B. L. (1995). Relation between consistency and accuracy of eyewitness testimony. In G. M. Davies, S. Lloyd-Bostock, M. McMurran & C. Wilson (Eds.), *Psychology and law: Advances in research* (pp. 21–28). Berlin: DeGruyter.

Fisher, R. P. & Patterson, T. (2004). *The relationship between consistency and accuracy of eyewitness memory.* Paper presented at 45th annual meeting of the Psychnomic Society: Minneapolis.

Fisher, R. P. & Reardon, M. C. (in press). Eyewitness identification. In Carson, D., Milne, R., Pakes, F., Shalev, K. & Shawyer, A. (Eds.), *Applying psychology to criminal justice.* Chichester: John Wiley & Sons.

Fisher, R. P., Phillips, M. R. & Krioukova, M. (2000). *Independent recall of the various components of a complex event.* Paper presented at the 41st Annual Meeting of the Psychonomic Society, New Orleans, November.

Fisher, R. P., Schreiber, N., Burguera, M. & Alvarez, C. (2003). *Consistency of eyewitness recollection as an indicator of accuracy.* Poster presented at the 44th annual meeting of the Psychonomic Society: Vancouver, Canada.

Fisher, R. P., Patterson, T. & Hazel, J. (2006). Question format and response consistency as predictors of the accuracy of eyewitness testimony. In preparation. Miami, FL: Florida International University.

Gilbert, J. A. E. & Fisher, R. P. (2006). The effects of varied retrieval cues on reminiscence in eyewitness memory. *Applied Cognitive Psychology, 20*, 723–739.

Glissan, J. L. (1991). *Cross-examination: Practice and procedure.* Sydney: Butterworths.

Gordon, B. N. & Follmer, A. (1994). Developmental issues in judging the credibility of children's testimony. *Journal of Clinical Child Psychology, 23*, 283–294.

Granhag, P. A., Stromwall, L. A. & Jonsson, A-C. (2003). Partners in crime: How liars in collusion betray themselves. *Journal of Applied Social Psychology, 33*, 848–868.

Iannuzzi, J. N. (1999). *Handbook of cross-examination: The mosaic art*, 2nd edition. Englewood Cliffs, NJ: Prentice Hall.

La Rooy, D., Pipe, M. E. & Murray, J. E. (2005). Reminiscence and hypermnesia in children's eyewitness memory. *Journal of Experimental Child Psychology, 90*, 235–254.

Leippe, M. R., Manion, A. P. & Romanczyk, A. (1992). Eyewitness persuasion: How and how well do fact finders judge the accuracy of adults' and children's memory reports? *Journal of Personality and Social Psychology, 63*, 181–197.

Lindsay, R. C. L., Lim, R., Marando, L. & Cully, D. (1986). Mock-juror evaluations of eyewitness testimony: A test of metamemory hypotheses. *Journal of Applied Social Psychology, 16*, 447–459.

Mauet, T. (1980). *Fundamentals of trial techniques*, 4th edition. New York: Little, Brown & Co.

Mitchell, T., Haw, R. & Fisher, R. P. (2003). *Eyewitness accuracy: Can accuracy for one statement be predictive of more 'global' accuracy?* Paper presented at European Psych-Law Society. Edinburgh.

Office of Court Administration Committee on Criminal Jury Instructions (2007). *New York Criminal Jury Instructions*, 2d. New York: NYS Office of Court Administration.

Park, R. C., Leonard, D. P. & Goldberg, S. H. (2004). *Evidence law*, 2nd edition. St. Paul, MN: Thomson West.

Payne, D. G. (1987). Hypermnesia and reminiscence in recall: A historical and empirical review. *Psychological Bulletin, 101*, 5–27.

Phillips, M. R., Fisher, R. P. & Krioukova, M. (1999). *Metacognitive processes in eyewitness memory.* Paper presented at the 40th Annual Meeting of The Psychonomic Society, Los Angeles, November.

Potter, R. & Brewer, N. (1999). Perceptions of witness behaviour–accuracy relationships held by police, lawyers and jurors. *Psychiatry, Psychology and Law, 6*, 97–103.

Pozner, L. & Dodd, R. (1993). *Cross-examination: Science and techniques.* Charlottesville, VA: The Michie Company.

Scrivner, E. & Safer, M. A. (1988). Eyewitnesses show hypermnesia for details about a violent event. *Journal of Applied Psychology, 73*, 371–377.

Strong, J. W. (1999). *McCormick on evidence*, 5th edition. St. Paul, MN: West Group.

Tulving, E. (1983). *Elements of episodic memory.* New York: Oxford University Press.

Tulving, E. (1985). How many memory systems are there? *American Psychologist, 40*, 385–398.

Uviller, H. R. (1993). Credence, character, and the rules of evidence: Seeing through the liar's tale. *Duke Law Journal, 42*, 776–832.

Wells, G. L. & Leippe, M. R. (1981). How do triers of fact infer the accuracy of eyewitness identification? Using memory for detail can be misleading. *Journal of Applied Psychology, 66*, 682–687.

Wigmore, J. H. (1904; revised by J. H. Chadbourn, 1970). *Evidence in trials at common law*, Vol. 3A. Boston: Little, Brown & Co.

Chapter Nine

The Cognitive Interview: Research and Practice across the Lifespan

Robyn E. Holliday

University of Leicester

Charles J. Brainerd

Cornell University

Valerie F. Reyna

Cornell University

and

Joyce E. Humphries

University of Leicester

Introduction

There has been a dramatic increase in research on witness testimony in the last 25 years. Much of this research has been concerned with obtaining accurate testimony from vulnerable witnesses and victims of crime (Ceci & Bruck, 1995; Brainerd & Reyna, 2005). This chapter will focus on vulnerable witnesses – children under the age of 16 years, adults aged 65 years and over, and children and adults with intellectual impairments. In such cases, it is crucial that these witnesses are interviewed as sensitively as possible so that the information that is reported is accurate and reliable.

A number of factors determine the reliability of witness testimony. This chapter is concerned with one of those factors, investigative interviews. The manner in which a witness is interviewed is crucial for criminal investigations

Handbook of Psychology of Investigative Interviewing: Current Developments and Future Directions
Edited by Ray Bull, Tim Valentine and Tom Williamson
© 2009 John Wiley & Sons, Ltd.

and successful prosecutions. This chapter will focus on a set of forensic inter-viewing techniques which have been tested extensively, namely the original Cognitive Interview (CI) protocol (Geiselman, Fisher, Firstenberg, Hutton, Sullivan, Avetissian & Prosk, 1984) and its revision (Fisher & Geiselman, 1992). First, we shall describe the original CI and the theoretical principles on which the CI techniques are grounded. This will be followed by empirical research presented chronologically, beginning with young children through to old age. We then consider the viability of CI techniques with learning disabled children and adults, and cognitively impaired older adults. We shall conclude with a discussion of the state of play in CI research and practice in the twenty-first century – promising applications of CI research with suspects (Fisher & Perez, 2007; Fisher & Castano, 2008), and progress on the development of shortened Cognitive Interviews for use with children and older adults. CI research in which these vulnerable individuals have been used is presented in Table 9.2.

The Cognitive Interview

Forensic interview protocols characteristically adhere to remarkably similar structures. For example, all typically adopt a phased (funnel) approach begin-ning with rapport-building, truth and lies testing, free recall requests followed by a questioning phase in which open-ended questions are followed by specific questions, and closure (Fisher & Schreiber, 2007). A number of interview protocols are available, such as the guidance documents for the UK (Memorandum of Good Practice, 1992 – MOGP; Achieving Best Evidence, 2001 and, 2007 – ABE, both produced by the Home Office) and the Canadian Stepwise protocol developed by Yuille, Hunter, Joffe & Zaparniuk (1993). One of the best-known investigative interview protocols is the Cognitive Interview (CI). The CI is based on empirical research and principles from cognitive and social psychology (Fisher & Castano, 2008).

The original CI was developed to improve adult (of any age) eyewitness testimony (Geiselman *et al.*, 1984). It has provided the impetus for much research (see Geiselman & Fisher, 1997; Fisher, Brennan & McCauley, 2002, for reviews). There are three fundamental psychological principles and sub-principles on which the CI protocol is based. A core principle is memory/general cognition, which can be broken down into five sub-principles:

(a)   *Limited cognitive processing* resources (e.g., Baddeley, 1986), that is, there is a finite amount of cognitive resources available to process infor-mation. If several cognitive tasks are attempted concurrently, it is likely that the quality and quantity of a witness's narrative of an event will be affected negatively. Fisher *et al.* (2002) advise that interviewers record the interview and refrain from interrupting an interviewee during his or her recall narrative.

(b) *Witness compatible questioning* – witnesses possess unique mental repre-
     sentations of their experiences; hence the interviewer must adapt ques-
     tions accordingly. In Holliday's research (Holliday, 2003a, 2003b;
     Holliday & Albon, 2004), questions were entirely based on the informa-
     tion recalled by each child in his or her narrative recollection.
(c) *Context reinstatement* – mental reconstruction of a witness's physical,
     cognitive and emotional states of the to-be-remembered event will
     improve memory (i.e., encoding specificity; Tulving & Thomson, 1973).
(d) *Multisensory coding* – in addition to conceptual representations, witnessed
     events have sensory properties (Paivio, 1971) such as smell, sounds, visual
     details (Fisher *et al.*, 2002). An example of the implementation of (c)
     and (d) is taken from Holliday and colleagues' research (Holliday &
     Albon, 2004). Children were given these instructions: *Close your eyes.*
     Picture yourself back in the room where you watched the video. How were
     you feeling? What can you see in the room? What can you hear in the room?
     Who were you sitting next to (p. 269)?
(e) *Varied retrieval* – memories can be accessed and retrieved by a number
     of retrieval paths (Tulving, 1974; Anderson & Pichert, 1978). Varied
     retrieval reduces the likelihood that a witness will use prior knowledge
     and expectations to fill any gaps in their memory of the witnessed event.
     Varied retrieval is facilitated by the instruction to *change perspective*:
     Recall the event from the perspective of another participant or location
     in the same event: *You said that Billy opened his presents. Now, I'd like*
     you to be Billy. What did you do first? (p. 269), and *change order*: Recall
     the event again in a different order (e.g., backwards), *Now I want you to*
     tell me about the very last thing you remember in Billy's birthday video.
     What happened just before that? This prompt was repeated until a child
     could recall no further details or had reached the beginning of the to-
     be-remembered event.

A second core principle of the CI is *social dynamics*. Forensic interviews,
whether of co-operative witnesses or suspects, reflect an imbalance of social
status (e.g., a police officer and a child witness). Social dynamics comprises:
(a) *active witness participation* – an interviewer must emphasize to the interviewee that it is the interviewee who is the expert about what he or she has
witnessed; hence the interviewee should actively control the interview (transfer
of control), and (b) *development of rapport* – interviewers should spend time
in the establishment of rapport (Fisher *et al.*, 2002).

The third core principle of the CI is *communication*. The interviewer needs
to extract from the witness specific details about their experience. Likewise,
the interviewee must convey to the interviewer the specific details he or she
witnessed. Communication is facilitated by *promoting extensive, detailed*
responses (Fisher *et al.*, 2002). The *report everything* instruction – informing
the witness that he or she should report all information regardless of whether
he or she considers it relevant or not – promotes detailed responses. For

example, *I want you to tell me everything you can remember, every little detail you can remember* (Holliday & Albon, 2004). Second, an interviewer should be mindful that some information that a witness wishes to relate might be non-verbal. In such instances, *code-compatible output* should be implemented. Fisher *et al.* (2002) give this example: 'if an event was experienced tactilely (e.g., brushing against a fabric) then the witness might respond in a similar tactile mode, by touching various fabrics' (p. 268).

Empirical evaluation of CI protocols

Numerous laboratory studies of the original and enhanced CI have been conducted in the USA, UK, Australia and Germany since the first CI research was published in 1984 (Geiselman *et al.*, 1984). In an early test of the original CI, college students witnessed a staged argument in class and were interviewed two days later (*ibid.*). Findings supported the prediction that students who were given instructions in the application of the four CI mnemonics whilst recollecting the witnessed event would recall more correct details than those in a control condition. No significant increases were observed in the amount of incorrect or confabulated information reported.

More than 100 studies have evaluated CI protocols since its inception (Fisher & Castano, 2008). There is no doubt that CIs improve witnesses' correct recollections of events using a number of different populations such as those discussed in this chapter (children, elderly, learning-disabled), and in a number of languages (other than English) including German (Köhnken, Schimossek, Aschermann & Hofer, 1995), Portuguese (Stein & Memon, 2006) and Spanish (Hernández-Fernaud & Alonso-Quecuty, 1997; Campos & Alonso-Quecuty, 1999).

Some early studies reported increases in incorrect and confabulated details along with the improved correct details. Indeed, almost 10 years ago, Köhnken, Milne, Memon & Bull (1999) published a meta-analysis of 55 research studies in which recollections using CI protocols vs. control interviews were compared. The researchers reported that CIs tended to produce small but statistically significant increases in false information compared to control interviews. Given that the number of published studies has almost doubled since publication of Köhnken *et al.*'s paper a new meta-analysis would be timely (for reviews, see Geiselman & Fisher, 1997; Fisher *et al.*, 2002; Fisher & Schreiber, 2007).

Do the positive effects of a CI extend to child witnesses?

Researchers have reported mixed results as regards the effectiveness of the CI with children. In general, however, more correct details are remembered with

CIs than with control interviews across early to late childhood (e.g. Geiselman & Padilla, 1988; Saywitz, Geiselman & Bornstein, 1992; McCauley & Fisher, 1996; Granhag & Spjut, 2001; Milne & Bull, 2002; 2003; Akehurst, Milne & Köhnken, 2003; Holliday, 2003a, 2003b; Larsson, Granhag & Spjut, 2003). In Holliday's (2003a) study with 4–5 and 9–10-year-old children, for example, more correct person, action and object details were reported in developmentally modified CIs (MCI) (omitting the 'change perspective') than in MOGP interviews (Home Office, 1992). In two later studies, Holliday (2003b) replicated these findings with four- and eight-year-old children. Holliday (2003b) reported evidence of developmental differences in the type of details recollected with a MCI. The older children recalled more correct person, action, object and location details than the younger ones. Similarly, Milne & Bull (2003) reported that children aged eight and nine years recollected more correct person and action details in CIs (omitting CP) than in control interviews. On the other hand, Memon, Cronin, Eaves & Bull (1996) found no evidence that a full CI improved six and seven year olds' recollections of an eye examination. Likewise, Memon *et al.* reported no differences in children's correct recall when each of the CI mnemonics was compared with a 'try harder' instruction.

As noted in early evaluations of CI protocols with adult participants, some developmental researchers have reported increased incorrect and/or confabulated recollections, as well as increased correct recall, when evaluating CI techniques (McCauley & Fisher, 1995; Memon, Cronin *et al.*, 1996; Hayes & Delamothe, 1997; Memon, Wark, Bull & Köhnken, 1997), although other researchers have reported no such effects (Milne & Bull, 2002; Akehurst *et al.*, 2003; Holliday, 2003a; 2003b; Holliday & Albon, 2004). In the next section, we discuss some exciting new developments in misinformation research and the CI.

Can CI protocols reduce children's suggestibility?

Holliday and her colleagues raised this important question in the first of four studies with children (2003a, 2003b; Holliday & Albon, 2004). Given that children under six years of age are disproportionately affected by misinformation, it is important to determine whether interview protocols such as the CI can reduce the negative effects of misinformation on child witnesses. Ceci & Bruck (1993) argued that children's recollections of witnessed events can be affected by a number of cognitive (e.g., memory, attention) and social (e.g., compliance, demand) factors. Many laboratory studies have reported that children's memories are negatively impacted by misinformation, with very young children (aged three and four years) disproportionately affected (see Bruck & Ceci, 1999, for a review). Much of this evidence has been collected using 'standard' and 'modified' forced-choice (e.g., Ceci, Ross & Toglia,

1987; Holliday, Douglas & Hayes, 1999, Holliday & Hayes, 2001; Zaragoza, 1991) or yes/no recognition memory tests (e.g., Holliday & Hayes, 2000; for reviews see Holliday, Reyna & Hayes, 2002; Reyna, Holliday & Marche, 2002).

A small number of laboratory studies have examined whether CI instructions minimize the impact of misleading questions on school-aged child witnesses. For example, in Memon *et al.*'s (1996) study, eight- and nine-year-old children watched a short film. They returned 12 days later and were asked misleading and neutral questions either before or following an interview in which the *context reinstatement* and *report everything* instructions were used as memory prompts. Memon *et al.* reported, as they had hypothesized, no effect of interview type on responses to the pre-interview questions. For those children who were questioned post-interview, however, those given (prior) CI instructions gave more correct responses to misleading questions than those given a control interview (see also Milne & Bull, 2003). Hayes & Delamothe (1997) reported that the *context reinstatement* and *report everything* instructions had no effect on suggestibility in six and ten year olds when the misleading suggestions were presented *before* the CI instructions. Holliday (2003a) found that whilst a CI increased five and ten year olds' correct recall in comparison with a control interview, no evidence was found that the suggestibility effects obtained on forced-choice memory tests given *after* a CI were influenced by interview type. Clearly, one of the keys to these disparate results could be the timings of the misinformation and of the interview.

This point was taken up by Holliday (2003b) in two studies with five- and eight-year-old children. The two studies were identical, with the exception that the timings of the misinformation presentation and interview. In the first study, children were misled *after* interview; in the second study they were misled *before* interview. The results were straightforward: reporting of misinformation during interviews and on subsequent memory tests was reduced if the children were interviewed with a developmentally modified CI (omitted CP) *before* they were given a memory test. Holliday & Albon (2004) replicated these findings with four and five year olds. Importantly, their research established that just two CI instructions (*contest reinstatement* and *report everything*) in combination reduced children's reporting of misinformation during the interview and later memory tests. We shall return to this study below.

Do CIs enhance older witnesses' recollections?

Older adults represent a special group of witnesses. In many countries, growing numbers of older adults are remaining active in the community. Hence, it is likely that some will witness or be a victim of a crime. Moreover, physical and emotional abuse of the elderly is being reported with increasing frequency (Action on Elder Abuse, 2004) with those over the age of 75 years being particularly vulnerable. Obtaining reliable eyewitness testimony from older witnesses has now become a key concern to policy-makers and professionals, yet only a small number of laboratory studies have evaluated the reliability and accuracy of older adults' recollections in an eyewitness context. Findings from these studies reveal that memory recall is less complete and less accurate in comparison to young adults, whether the witnessed event is a slide show (Yarmey & Kent, 1980), a short film (List, 1986) or a staged event (Yarmey, 1993). Such age differences are reported when memory is tested immediately, minutes or days after the witnessed event (Brimacombe, Quinton, Nance & Garrioch, 1997; see Mueller-Johnson & Ceci, 2007, for an excellent review).

A handful of studies have evaluated the effectiveness of CI techniques with older adults. In an early study, young (18–35 years) and old (65–80 years) adults were shown a short film of a staged robbery (Mello & Fisher, 1996). Half an hour later, both groups were given a regular police interview, a full CI or a modified CI (omitted *change perspective*). An unexpected age pattern was found in that when given a full CI older adults provided more correct information than young adults. Research by McMahon (2000) evaluated whether a full CI would increase correct recall of a film of a simulated crime. Young (18–50 years) and old (60–88 years) adults were interviewed 30 minutes after viewing the film. As expected, the younger adults recollected more correct information than the older adults, *but only in the control interview* (see also Isingrini, Vazou & Leroy, 1995). In Rose, Bull & Vrij's (2003) study, young (18–31 years) and old (59–84 years) adults viewed a short film of a staged robbery. Thirty minutes later all participants were presented with line-up identification tasks. Whilst the older adults made more incorrect identifications than the young adults, no effects of mental or physical context reinstatement instructions on performance were found. In a second recent line-up study with young (16–30 years) and old (64–86 years) adults, Wilcock, Bull & Vrij (2007) reported that context reinstatement increased correct rejections in target absent line-ups but only in the old adults.

More recently, two studies by Wright and Holliday provided evidence that CI protocols can increase correct recollections in elderly witnesses. Wright & Holliday (2007a) evaluated older witnesses' recall of a short film using full CI, a MCI (omitting *change perspective* instruction) or a control interview. The full CI increased correct recall by 20% for young adults (aged 17–31 years), 27% for young-old adults (aged 60–74 years), and 18% for old-old adults (aged 75–95 years), while the MCI increased correct recall by 14% for young adults, 17% for young-old adults and 15% for old-old adults. In the second study, Wright & Holliday (2007b) compared the recollections of old adults (aged 75–96 years) who displayed evidence of cognitive impairments on the Mini-Mental State Examination (MMSE) (Folstein, Folstein & McHugh,

1975) with old adults without cognitive impairments on MMSE. Old adults with a low MMSE score recalled fewer correct details and were less accurate than those with high scores. Importantly, high and low MMSE old adult groups reported substantially more correct information about Action, Person, Object and Surrounding details with a MCI than with a control interview.

Do CI techniques improve intellectually disabled witnesses' recollections?

Individuals with intellectual disabilities (ID) are considered vulnerable witnesses. Research with these adults reports that they are slower than typically developed adults to encode, store and retrieve details of an event (Milne & Bull, 2001). Adults with IDs have been considered by courts to be unreliable witnesses (*ibid.*). Yet the information that ID adults do recollect is just as accurate as that of other adult witnesses. However, ID adults *do* report fewer details of a witnessed event than other adults (Perlman, Ericsson, Esses & Isaacs, 1994; Milne & Bull, 2001). Given that these witnesses have been found to be highly suggestible (Cardone & Dent, 1996; Milne, Clare & Bull, 1999), it is of major importance that ID adults, like other groups of vulnerable witnesses, be questioned appropriately and non-suggestively. Research has demonstrated that ID adults are particularly susceptible to the negative effects of social demand factors. Kebbell & Hatton (1999) reviewed the research literature and reported that ID adults are likely to say 'yes' to questions irrespective of the content of such questions. ID adults are more likely than other adults to fabricate and change answers in response to the interviewer' questions (Clare & Gudjonsson, 1993; Ternes & Yuille, 2008). They are also highly suggestible (Milne, Clare & Bull, 2002; Ternes & Yuille, 2008).

The body of research in which CI protocols have been evaluated with cognitively impaired adults is sparse. In the first such study, Brown & Geiselman (1990) reported that ID adults recalled fewer correct details than other adults. This effect did not vary by type of interview (whether CI or control). ID adults also reported more confabulated details during a CI than other adults. In Milne, Clare & Bull's (1999) study, adults with and without mild ID watched a short film of an accident and were interviewed the next day with either a CI or a structured (control) interview (Köhnken, 1993). An increase in correct details was found for those given a CI. However, ID adults given a CI reported more confabulated details than ID adults given a control interview (Milne & Bull, 2001). More recently, CI principles have been tested on elderly adults with dementia (Wright & Holliday, 2007b). Adults (75–96 years) with and without cognitive impairments were given a modified CI (omit CP), or a full CI, or a control interview following viewing a short film. Cognitive-impaired adults remembered fewer correct details than non-impaired adults. Nonetheless, both types of CIs enhanced recollections of both impaired and non-impaired elderly adults, although impaired participants had particular difficulties with the CP instruction. Clearly, more research is needed before firm conclusions can be drawn about the benefits (or not) of using CI protocols with these vulnerable individuals.

The research literature in which CI protocols have been evaluated with intellectually disabled (ID) children is extremely small. At the time of writing, all this work has been conducted in the UK by Milne and Bull. Several years ago, Milne & Bull (2001) pointed out in a review article that the recollections of ID children for events they have experienced or witnessed are typically less complete than those of children without ID (much like ID adults). Therefore, they argued (*ibid.*) that it is crucial that researchers evaluate protocols that have the potential to enhance witness testimony, such as the CI. Milne & Bull (1996) gave ID children a CI or a control interview similar to the MOGP interview (Home Office, 1992) following a witnessed event. Children given a CI recollected a greater number of correct details in comparison to children given a control interview. Significantly, a CI did not lead to increases in reporting of incorrect and confabulated details.

How effective are CI protocols in the field?

The revised CI has proved beneficial when evaluated with adult witnesses and victims of real crime. In the first study (Fisher, Geiselman & Amador, 1989), police detectives from the Metro-Dade Police Department, Miami conducted interviews before and after four hours' training in the revised CI protocols. Importantly, the amount of information obtained from witnesses by police after training increased substantially (47%). A second field study was conducted in the UK by George (1991, cited in George & Clifford, 1996). Police who had been trained in the CI protocols interviewed young adults after they had witnessed a staged argument. Recall of correct details was substantially higher in CIs than in control interviews, without a concomitant increase in reporting of incorrect information. Notably, the size of this recall advantage is remarkably similar to findings from laboratory studies (Fisher & Schreiber, 2007). More recently, Fisher & Castano (2008) reported that CI protocols have been used effectively in the USA in several police investigations, including child sexual abuse, kidnapping, a bombing and a murder enquiry. In the last case, a CI was used with a female who had witnessed a murder 33 years earlier when she was five years old.

Promising applications of the CI protocols

Do the advantages of a CI remain with a shortened version?

For practitioners, shortened interview protocols that facilitate accurate recollections are important given the potential problems surrounding interviewing vulnerable witnesses (limited attention span, shorter memory) and pressures on police and other professionals to obtain maximum information as soon as possible after a crime. Wright & Holliday (2005) conducted a study in which police officers from a number of constabularies in the UK responded to a questionnaire. Police who were reluctant to use CI techniques stated that such protocols are far too long and mentally demanding to be of practical use when interviewing elderly witnesses and victims. Davis, McMahon & Greenwood (2005) evaluated a shortened version of a CI (CRI and RE instructions). College students viewed a short film of a staged crime and were subsequently interviewed with a full CI, a short CI or a control interview. Importantly, correct recollection of the film details was higher in the full CI and the short CI (equally) than in a control interview condition. Dando, Wilcock & Milne (2009), using college students, investigated two variations of context reinstatement instructions: mental context reinstatement (MRI) as used in cognitive interviews, and a shortened form they called 'sketch rein-statement of context' (MRC). The sketch MRC condition produced more accurate recollections of a filmed crime than the MRI and control interview conditions.

Holliday & Albon (2004) conducted a comprehensive study that aimed to develop a developmentally appropriate shortened CI for young children which minimized suggestibility. The rationale behind this research was Holliday's (2003b) findings that a Modified CI (MCI) reduced children's acceptance and subsequent reporting of suggestions. Given the short attention span of very young children, a shortened version of the MCI would be particularly useful. Children viewed a short film followed by exposure to a number of misleading suggestions. Children were then administered one of six interview protocols:

- a control interview (structured interview; Köhnken, 1993);
- a full CI (FCI) containing the CRI, RE, CO and CP instructions;
- a Modified CI, which was identical to the FCI except CP was omitted;
- an Enhanced Rapport MCI (ERMCI), which was identical to the MCI except for an additional five minutes of rapport-building in which children described a favourite game;
- a RE and CO interview, which was the same as the MCI except that CRI was omitted;
- a RE and CRI interview which resembled the MCI except that CO was omitted.

These interview protocols are presented in Table 9.1.

In terms of the quality of communication (e.g. rapport-building, active listening) and questioning methods, SIs and CIs used in Holliday & Albon's (2004) research are identical – each interview protocol employs a phased

Table 9.1: Child interview protocols tested in Holliday & Albon's (2004) research

Cognitive interviews	Control interview
1. Rapport-building phase Chat about general interests the child (e.g., pets, football) Describe their favourite game[1] Explain aims/rules of interview [a]	1. Rapport-building phase Chat about General interests of the child (e.g. of pets, football) Explain aims/rules of interview [a]

2. Free recall phase
  a. Context reinstatement[1,2,3,5]
  b. Report everything[1,2,3,4,5]
  c. Change order[1,2,3,4]
  d. Change perspective[3]
  e. Free recall report request[a]
	2. Free recall phase
	
	Free recall report request[a]

3. Questioning phase Details reported in Free Recall Phase are used as the bases of open-ended and specific and questions in this phase.[a]	3. Questioning phase Details reported in Free Recall Phase are used as the bases of open-ended specific questions in this phase.[a]
4. Closure [a]	4. Closure[a]

Notes:
[a] All interviews.
1. Enhanced rapport CI. 2. MCI. 3. Full CI. 4. Report everything and change order interview.
5. Report everything and context reinstatement interview.

approach proceeding from free recall to open, to closed, to specific questions.

The CIs produced more correct recollections than a control interview. As has been reported previously, CIs enhanced children's recall of person, action and object information (cf. Milne & Bull, 2002; 2003; Holliday, 2003a, 2003b), without an accompanying increase in reporting of incorrect or confabulated details (cf. McCauley & Fisher, 1996; Granhag & Spjut, 2001; Holliday, 2003a; 2003b). The finding that young children's recall of person details can be improved with CI instructions is very important given that investigative interviews necessarily require accurate witness descriptions.

In earlier CI research, concerns were raised that the CO and CP mnemonics might encourage young children to confabulate (e.g. Ceci, Bruck & Battin, 2000; Memon & Köhnken, 1992; Saywitz *et al.*, 1992), although others (e.g. Milne & Bull, 2002; Holliday, 2003a; 2003b) have reported no increase in reporting of incorrect or confabulated details in young children. The CO mnemonic was included in MCI, FCI, Enhanced Rapport Modified Cognitive Interview (ERMCI), and RE and CO interviews because research has shown that children can manage this instruction when it is accompanied by frequent prompts (Milne & Bull, 2002; Holliday, 2003a; 2003b). Given the concerns that correct implementation of the CP instruction may be beyond the capabilities of very young children (Geiselman & Padilla, 1988; Newcombe & Huttenlocher, 1992), and that it is unpopular with police officers in England (Memon & Stevenage, 1996), this instruction was only included in a FCI with the specific aim of evaluating its effectiveness with young children. However, as reported by others (e.g. Milne & Bull, 2002; Holliday, 2003a; 2003b) children had little difficulty in using the CO mnemonic, demonstrating the positive effects of this instruction with young children if it is accompanied by frequent prompts. Under the CP instruction, children were more likely to report correct than incorrect or confabulated details (cf. Akehurst *et al.*, 2003).

Notably, Holliday & Albon's (2004) research showed that the RE and CRI instructions, when used together, reduced four- and five-year-old children's reporting of misleading suggestions both during an interview and on subsequent memory tests. Moreover, children who were given MCI, ERMCI, RE + CO and RE + CRI interviews, but not FCIs, recalled more correct information about the film, and their reports were more complete than children given a control interview (see also Milne & Bull, 2002). In other words, developmentally appropriate CIs enhanced reporting of correct information and ameliorated the adverse effects of misinformation to some degree with very young children. The finding that a shortened CI is effective with young children is important given the problems surrounding interviewing these witnesses (limited attention span, rapid forgetting) and the pressures on police and practitioners to obtain correct information as soon as possible after a crime. The implication of this research is that a developmentally appropriate interview comprising these two CI instructions would take approximately 70% of the time of a full CI.

Is a shorter CI viable with elderly witnesses?

Holliday and Humphries and their colleagues (Milne, Bull, Memon) are conducting research in which *individual* CI instructions are being evaluated with young-old (60–74 years) and old-old (75–100 years) witnesses in the context of a participant-experienced staged event. The research will determine whether or not a different set of instructions is beneficial for young-old and old-old adults. There is good reason to expect that older witnesses are, like other special populations, capable of recollecting details that are forensically relevant if they are interviewed using an interview protocol that is specifically designed for them.

The next step: CIs of suspects

More than 20 years have passed since the original CI was developed by Geiselman *et al.* (1984) and over 15 years ago Professor Ray Bull wrote to the UK government proposing research on this, but to no avail (personal communication, 10 April 2008). It is therefore now time to determine its effectiveness with crime suspects. In a recent article, Fisher & Perez (2007) noted that the dearth of studies with these individuals may be due to ethical restrictions and to the nature of the individuals themselves – they are suspects in a criminal investigation. How likely are they to want to be interviewed for a research study when they have been accused of a crime? Fisher & Perez proposed that suspects who are innocent, suspects who feel ashamed of their crime and suspects who agree to provide information in the hope of a lighter sentence might participate. Hence, they argue that the next step in CI research should concentrate on testing whether or not a CI is viable with *cooperative* suspects who are motivated to tell the truth. A second avenue of fruitful research to consider is in contexts other than a criminal investigation. As Fisher & Perez point out, there are many areas in which difficulties exist in gathering information – accident investigations of air, rail, car or the workplace, war crimes and business decisions, to name but a few. This exciting new area of CI research will challenge researchers for another 20 years at least.

Table 9.2: Published studies of CI protocols in which vulnerable individuals have been studied

Children and the Cognitive Interview

Study	Age-group	Interviews	Type of Event	Time of recall	Results
Geiselman & Padilla (1988)	7–12 years (N = 15)	STDI, FCI	Video-simulated liquor store robbery	3 days	FCI without increasing errors and confabulations produced 21% more correct items than the STDI.
Saywitz, Geiselman & Bornstein (1992)	7–8 years (N = 20) and 10–11 years (N = 20)	STDI, FCI	15-minute live event involving children's games	2 days	FCI increased correct recall, without increasing errors.
Memon Cronin, Eves & Bull (1993)	6–7 years (N = 31)	SI, FCI	School vision check	2 days	No advantage of a FCI was found.

Table 9.2: *Continued*

Children and the Cognitive Interview

Study	Age-group	Interviews	Type of Event	Time of recall	Results
McCauley & Fisher (1995)	7–8 years (N = 86)	STDI, revised CI	Live event – watch or participate in action/play session	3 hours and 2 weeks	CI increased correct and incorrect recall.
McCauley & Fisher (1996)	7–8 years (N = 18)	STDI, MCI RA + CRI	10-minute live event – watch or participate in action/play session	2 weeks	CI elicited nearly twice as many accurate details compared to the STDI. No difference in incorrect details recalled.
Memon Cronin, Eves & Bull (1996)	5–6 years (N = 17); 6–7 years (N = 19); 8–9 years (N = 31)	Try harder (control), CO, CP, CRI	10-minute live event – two strangers taking part in assembly	1 week	No difference between try harder and CI instructions in correct or incorrect details. Age effects: youngest group recalled fewer correct details than the other two groups, but did not produce more errors and were no less accurate.
Akehurst, Milne & Köhnken (1997)	8–9 years (N = 32); 11–12 years (N = 32)	SI, FCI	2-minute video of a staged robbery	4 hours or 6 days	FCI elicited more correct details without increasing incorrect or confabulated details. No effect of delay.
Memon, Wark, Holley, Bull & Köhnken (1997)	16–19 years (N = 66)	SI, RA + CRI, and UI (untrained interview)*	1-minute 5 seconds video of a crime	5 days	No difference between RA + CRI and SI in the amount of correct, incorrect and confabulated information recalled.
Granhag & Spjut (2001)	9–10 years (N = 32)	SI, STDI, MCI RA + CRI	15-minute film of a performance by a fakir who hurts himself		Correct details higher in MCI RA + CRI. No increase in incorrect details.

Table 9.2: *Continued*

Children and the Cognitive Interview

Study	Age-group	Interviews	Type of Event	Time of recall	Results
Milne & Bull (2002)	18–45 years (N = 34); 8–9 years (N = 44); 5–6 years (N = 47)	RA; CO; CP; CRI, CRI + RA & control- try again	3-minute videotape of a road accident	48 hours	Compared to the try again control the individual techniques (RA, CO, CP and CRI) did not elicit more recall.RA + CR elicited more recall compared to RA, CP, CO & try again instructions. No effects of interview on age.
Larsson, Granhag & Spjut (2003)	10–11 years (N = 49)	SI, MCI RA + CRI	15-minute film depicting a performance by a fakir who hurts himself	7 days vs. 6 months	Children's recalled significantly more correct details with MCI RA + CRI than SI at 7 days and 6 months.

SI = Structured Interview; STDI = Standard Police Interview; FCI = Full Cognitive Interview; MCI = Modified Cognitive Interview (Change perspective mnemonic omitted); MCI- RA + CRI = Modified Cognitive Interview (Change Perspective + Change Order Mnemonics omitted); UI = Untrained Interview = identical to SI (transfer of control + do not fabricate instructions are omitted).

Children, suggestibility and the CI

Study	Age-group	Interviews	Type of Event	Time of recall	Results
Memon, Holley, Wark, Bull & Köhnken (1996)	8–9 years (N = 113)	SI, MCI RA + CRI	5-minute video of a magic show	12 days	MCI RA + CRI elicited more correct details without increasing incorrect information. Children given prior CI instructions gave more correct responses to misleading questions than those given a SI.
Hayes & Delamothe (1997)	5–7 years (N = 64); 9–11 years (N = 64)	STDI, MCI RA + CRI	12-minute video of a staged robbery	3 days	MCI RA + CRI elicited more correct details than the STDI. No effect of interview on acceptance of misinformation.

Table 9.2: *Continued*

Children, suggestibility and the CI

Study	Age-group	Interviews	Type of Event	Time of recall	Results
Holliday (2003a)	4–5 years (N = 32); 9–10 years (N = 32)	MCI and Memorandum	5-minute video depicting a child's birthday party	24 hours	Children's recall was more complete and more correct details were recalled in the MCI. No effect of interview on children's recall of misinformation.
Holliday (2003b)	Exp. 1 4–5 years (N = 41); 8–9 years (N = 35)	SI and MCI	5-minute video of a child's birthday party	24 hours	Children's recall was more complete, and more correct details were recalled in the MCI than the SI.
	Exp. 2 4–5 years (N = 35); 8–9 years (N = 35)	SI & MCI	5-minute video of a child's birthday party	24 hours	No effect of interview on children's recall of misinformation. Children's recall was more complete, and more correct details recalled in the MCI than in the SI. Children given a MCI after post-event misinformation were less likely to report misinformation during MCIs and on recognition tests.
Milne & Bull (2003)	8–9 years (N = 84)	SI, MCI	9-minute video of a magic show	24 hours	MCI elicited more correct information without increasing incorrect information. Children interviewed with MCI were more resistant to suggestive questioning.
Holliday & Albon (2004)	4–5 years (N = 104)	SI, FCI, MCI, ERMCI, MCI RA + CRI, MCI RA + CO	5-minute video of a child's birthday party	24 hours	

SI = Structured Interview; STDI = Standard Police Interview; FCI = Full Cognitive Interview; MCI = modified Cognitive Interview (Change perspective mnemonic omitted); MCI RA + CRI = Modified Cognitive Interview (Change Perspective + Change Order Mnemonics omitted)

Table 9.2: *Continued*
Older adults and the CI

Study	Age-group	Interviews	Type of event	Time of recall	Results
Mellow & Fisher (1996)	18–35- years (N = 20); 65–80 years (N = 20)	STDI, FCI, MCI (older age group only).	4-minute videotaped simulated robbery	30 minutes	The FCI elicited more information than the STDI without a reduction in accuracy rate. FCI vs. MCI – (older adults only) no difference in correct responses, incorrect responses or accuracy rate.
McMahon (2000)	18–50 years (N = 20); 60–88 years (N = 20)	SI & FCI	6-minute 50-second videotaped simulated robbery	30 minutes	FCI vs. SI – no difference in correct, incorrect and confabulated information.
Searcy, Bartlett, Memon & Swanson (2001)	18–30- years (N = 45); 62–79 years (N = 49)	SI & MCI RA + CRI	20-minute live interaction non-crime event	1 month	MCI RA + CRI vs. SI no difference in the number and accuracy of details recalled. Younger adults recalled more correct information than older adults.
Rose, Bull & Vrij (2003)	18–31 years (N = 36); 59–84 years (N = 36)	Mental or physical CRI	2-minute videotaped simulated robbery. Line-up identification	30 minutes	No effects of mental or physical CRI. Age effects – older adults more incorrect identifications than younger adults.
Wilcock, Bull & Vrij (2007)	16–30 years (N = 49); 64–86 years (N = 47)	CRI by photos	1-minute 50-second videotaped simulated robbery. Line-up identification	30 minutes	CRI increased correct rejections in TA line-up only for older adults. Age effects – older adults more incorrect identifications than younger adults.
Wright & Holliday (2007a)	17–31 years (N = 51); 60–74- years (young-old (N = 52); 75–95 years (old-old N = 51)	SI, MCI, FCI	2 minutes 40 seconds videotaped simulated non-violent attempted car break-in	30 minutes	FCI elicited more accurate details than MCI which elicited more accurate details than the SI. Young adults were more accurate than young-old and old-old adults.

SI = Structured Interview; STDI = Standard Police Interview; FCI = Full Cognitive Interview; MCI = modified Cognitive Interview (Change perspective mnemonic omitted); MCI RA + CRI = Modified Cognitive Interview (Change Perspective + Change Order Mnemonics omitted); TA = target absent, TP = target present.

Table 9.2: *Continued*

Individuals with intellectual disabilities and the CI

Study	Age-group	Interviews	Type of Event	Time of recall	Results
			Children		
Milne & Bull (1996)	7–10 years with mild learning disabilities (N = 75)	SI, MCI (Suggestibility condition also included)	9-minute video recording of a magic show	24 hours	MCI elicited more correct details than SI. No differences in incorrect or confabulated details across interview type. Non-significant trend to resist misleading questions after a MCI.
			Adults		
Brown & Geiselman (1990)	Adults with mild learning disabilities (21–45 years; N = 22)	STDI, FCI	4-minute videotape depicting an off-licence robbery (from the point of view of a police officer). 1 week later shown 4-minute video depicting a bank robbery (from the point of view of a witness)	2 days (in each case)	FCI elicited more correct information (32%) compared to the STDI, with no corresponding increase in incorrect information. FCI did produce more confabulations than the STDI.
Milne, Clare & Bull (1999)	Adults (19–62 years; N = 38); Adults (19–59 years; N = 47) with mild learning disabilities (LD)	SI, FCI	3-minute videotape of road accident	24 hours	LD group reported significantly fewer correct details and reported more confabulated details than the control group. For both groups the FCI elicited more correct details than the SI, although for the LD group there was a corresponding increase in confabulated person information, accuracy rates across the two interviews were similar.

Table 9.2: *Continued*

Individuals with intellectual disabilities and the CI

Study	Age-group	Interviews	Type of Event	Time of recall	Results
Wright & Holliday (2007b)	75–95 years (N = 51); 75–95 years indicating cognitive impairment (N = 36)	SI, MCI, FCI	2-minute 40-second videotaped simulated non-violent attempted car break-in	30 minutes	Recall of correct information for both groups was greater with the MCI and FCI than with the SI, with no corresponding increase in incorrect or confabulated information.

SI = Structured Interview; FCI = Full Cognitive Interview; MCI = modified Cognitive Interview (Change perspective mnemonic omitted).

References

Action on Elder Abuse (2004). *Hidden voices: Older people's experience of abuse.* London: Help the Aged.

Akehurst, L., Milne, R. & Köhnken, G. (2003). The effects of children's age and delay on recall in a cognitive or structured interview. *Psychology, Crime & Law, 9,* 97–107.

Anderson, R. C. & Pichert, J. W. (1978). Recall of previously unrecallable information following a shift in perspective. *Verbal Learning and Verbal Behavior, 17,* 1–12.

Baddeley, A.D. (1986). *Working memory.* Oxford: Clarendon Press.

Brainerd, C. J. & Reyna, V. F. (2005). *The science of false memory.* New York: Oxford University Press.

Brimacombe, C. A., Quinton, N., Nance, N. & Garrioch, L. (1997). Is age irrelevant? Perceptions of young and old adult eyewitnesses. *Law and Human Behavior, 21,* 619–634.

Brown, C. L. & Geiselman, R. E. (1990). Eyewitness testimony of mentally retarded: effect of the cognitive interview. *Journal of Police and Criminal Psychology, 6,* 14–22.

Bruck, M. & Ceci, S. J. (1999). The suggestibility of children's memory. *Annual Review of Psychology, 50,* 419–439.

Campos, L. & Alonso-Quecuty, M.L. (1999). The cognitive interview: Much more than simply 'try again'. *Psychology, Crime & Law, 5,* 47–59.

Cardone, D. & Dent, H. (1996). Memory and interrogative suggestibility: The effects of modality of information presentation and retrieval conditions upon the suggestibility scores of people with learning disabilities. *Legal and Criminological Psychology, 1,* 165–177.

Ceci, S. J. & Bruck, M. (1993). Suggestibility of the child witness: An historical review and synthesis. *Psychological Bulletin, 113,* 403–439.

Ceci, S. J. & Bruck, M. (1995). *Jeopardy in the courtroom: A scientific analysis of children's testimony.* Washington, DC: American Psychological Association.

Ceci, S. J., Ross, D. F. & Toglia, M. P. (1987). Suggestibility of children's memory: Psycho-legal implications. *Journal of Experimental Psychology: General, 116,* 38–49.

Ceci, S. J., Bruck, M. & Battin, D. B. (2000). The suggestibility of children's testimony. In D. Bjorklund (Ed.). *False memory creation in children and adults: Theory, research, and implications.* Mahwah, NJ: Lawrence Erlbaum.

Clare, I. H. & Gudjonsson, G. H. (1993). Interrogative suggestibility, confabulation and acquiescence in people with mild learning disabilities (mental handicap): Implications for reliability during police interrogations. *British Journal of Psychology, 32,* 295–301.

Dando, C., Wilcock, R. & Milne, R. (2009). The Cognitive Interview: The efficacy of a modified mental reinstatement of context procedure for frontline police investigators. *Applied Cognitive Psychology. 23,* 138–147.

Davis, M. R., McMahon, M., & Greenwood, K. M. (2005). The efficacy of mnemonic components of the cognitive interview: Towards a shortened variant for time-critical investigations. *Applied Cognitive Psychology, 19,* 75–93.

Fisher, R. P. & Castano, N. (2008). Cognitive interview. In B. Cutler (Ed.), *Encyclopedia of psychology and law.* Thousand Oaks, CA: Sage.

Fisher, R. P. & Geiselman, R. E. (1992). *Memory-enhancing techniques for investigative interviewing: The Cognitive Interview.* Springfield, IL: Charles C. Thomas.

Fisher, R. P. & Perez, V. (2007). Memory-enhancing techniques for interviewing crime suspects. In S. Christianson (Ed.), *Offenders' memories of violent crimes* (pp. 329–354). Chichester: John Wiley & Sons.

Fisher, R. P. & Schreiber, N. (2007). Interviewing protocols to improve eyewitness memory. In M. Toglia, R. Lindsay, D. Ross, & J. Reed (Eds.), *The Handbook of eyewitness psychology. Volume 1, Memory for events* (pp. 53–80). Mahwah, NJ: Lawrence Erlbaum.

Fisher, R. P., Geiselman, R. E. & Amador, M. (1989). Field test of the cognitive interview: Enhancing the recollection of actual victims and witnesses of crime. *Journal of Applied Psychology, 74,* 722–727.

Fisher, R. P., Brennan, K. H. & McCauley, M. R. (2002). The cognitive interview method to enhance eyewitness recall. In M.L. Eisen, J.A. Quas, & G. S. Goodman (Eds.), *Memory and suggestibility in the forensic interview.* Mahwah, NJ: Lawrence Erlbaum.

Folstein, M. F., Folstein, S. E. & McHugh, P. R. (1975). Mini-mental state: A practical method for grading the cognitive state of patients for the clinician. *Journal of Psychiatric Research, 12,* 189–198.

Geiselman, R. E. & Fisher, R. P. (1997). Ten years of cognitive interviewing. In D. G. Payne & F. G. Conrad (Eds.), *Intersections in basic and applied memory research* (pp. 291–310). Mahwah, NJ: Lawrence Erlbaum.

Geiselman, R. E. & Padilla, J. (1988). Interviewing child witnesses with the Cognitive Interview. *Journal of Police Science & Administration, 16,* 236–242.

Geiselman, R. E., Fisher, R. P., Firstenberg, I., Hutton, L. A., Sullivan, S., Avetissian, I. & Prosk, A. (1984). Enhancement of eyewitness memory: An empirical evaluation of the cognitive interview. *Journal of Police Science and Administration, 12,* 74–80.

George, R. C. & Clifford, B. R. (1996). The Cognitive Interview – does it work? In S. Lloyd-Bostock & G. Davies (Eds.), *Psychology, law and criminal justice: International developments in research and practice* (pp. 146–154). Berlin: de Gruyter.

Granhag, P. A. & Spjut, E. (2001). Children's recall of the unfortunate fakir: A further test of the enhanced cognitive interview. In R. Roesch, R. R. Corrado, & R. Dempster (Eds.), *Psychology in the courts* (pp. 209–222). London: Routledge.

Hayes, B. K. & Delamothe, K. (1997). Cognitive interviewing procedures and suggestibility in children's recall. *Journal of Applied Psychology, 82*, 562–577.

Hernández-Fernaud, E. & Alonso-Quecuty, M. (1997). Cognitive Interview and lie detection: A new magnifying glass for Sherlock Holmes? *Applied and Cognitive Psychology, 11*, 55–68.

Holliday, R. E. (2003a). The effect of a prior Cognitive Interview on children's acceptance of misinformation. *Applied Cognitive Psychology, 17*, 443–457.

Holliday, R. E. (2003b). Reducing misinformation effects in children with Cognitive Interviews: dissociating recollection and familiarity. *Child Development, 74*, 728–751.

Holliday, R. E. & Albon, A. J. (2004). Minimizing misinformation effects in young children with cognitive interview mnemonics. *Applied Cognitive Psychology, 18*, 263–281.

Holliday, R. E. & Hayes, B. K. (2000). Dissociating automatic and intentional processes in children's eyewitness memory. *Journal of Experimental Child Psychology, 75*, 1–42.

Holliday, R. E. & Hayes, B. K. (2001). Automatic and intentional processes in children's eyewitness suggestibility. *Cognitive Development, 16*, 617–636.

Holliday, R. E. & Hayes, B. K. (2002). Automatic and intentional processes in children's recognition memory: The reversed misinformation effect. *Applied Cognitive Psychology, 16*, 1–16.

Holliday, R. E., Douglas, K. & Hayes, B. K. (1999). Children's eyewitness suggestibility: Memory trace strength revisited. *Cognitive Development, 14*, 443–462.

Holliday, R. E., Reyna, V. F. & Hayes, B. K. (2002). Memory processes underlying misinformation effects in child witnesses. *Developmental Review, 22*, 37–77.

Home Office and Department of Health (1992). *Memorandum of good practice on video-recorded interviews with child witnesses for criminal proceedings*. London: HMSO.

Home Office and Department of Health (2001). *Achieving best evidence in criminal proceedings*. London: HMSO.

Home Office and Department of Health (2007). *Achieving best evidence in criminal proceedings*. London: HMSO. http://www.cps.gov.uk/publications/docs/achieving best_evidence_final.pdf.

Isingrini, M., Vazou, F. & Leroy, P. (1995). Dissociation of implicit and explicit memory tests: Effect of age and divided attention on category exemplar generation and cued recall. *Memory & Cognition, 23*, 462–467.

Kebbell, M. & Hatton, C. (1999). People with mental retardation as witnesses in court: A review. *Mental Retardation, 37*, 179–187.

Köhnken, G. (1993). The structured interview: A step-by-step introduction. Unpublished manuscript.

Köhnken, G., Schimossek, E., Aschermann, E., & Hofer, E. (1995). The cognitive interview and the assessment of the credibility of adults' statements. *Journal of Applied Psychology, 80,* 671–684.

Larsson, A. S., Granhag, P. A. & Spjut, E. (2003). Children's recall and the Cognitive Interview: Do the positive effects hold over time? *Applied Cognitive Psychology, 17,* 203–214.

List, J. A. (1986). Age and schematic differences in the reliability of eyewitness testimony. *Developmental Psychology, 22,* 50–57.

McCauley, M. R. & Fisher, R. P. (1995). Facilitating children's eyewitness recall with the revised cognitive interview. *Journal of Applied Psychology, 80,* 510–516.

McCauley, M. R. & Fisher, R. P. (1996). Enhancing children's eyewitness testimony with the Cognitive Interview. In G. Davies, S. Lloyd-Bostock, M. McMurran, & J. C. Wilson (Eds), *Psychology, law, and criminal justice* (pp. 127–133). Berlin: de Gruyter.

McMahon, M. (2000). The effect of the Enhanced Cognitive Interview on recall and confidence in elderly adults. *Psychiatry, Psychology and Law, 7,* 9–32.

Mello, E. W. & Fisher, R. P. (1996). Enhancing older adult eyewitness memory with the Cognitive Interview. *Applied Cognitive Psychology, 10,* 403–417.

Memon, A. (1999). Interviewing witnesses: The cognitive interview. In A. Memon & R. Bull (Eds.), *Handbook of the psychology of interviewing* (pp. 343–355). Chichester: John Wiley & Sons.

Memon, A. & Köhnken, G. (1992). Helping witnesses to remember more: the Cognitive Interview. *Expert evidence: The International Digest of Human Behavior, Science and Law, 1,* 39–48.

Memon, A. & Stevenage, S. V. (1996). A consideration of individual differences and imagery ability amongst cognitive interviewees. Reply to Douglas on witness-memory. *Psycoloquy.* 96.7.24. witness-memory.10.memon.

Memon, A., Cronin, O., Eaves, R. & Bull, R. (1993). The Cognitive Interview and the child witness. In G. M. Stephenson, & N. K. Clark (Eds.), *Issues in criminology and legal psychology.* Volume 20. *Children, evidence & procedure.* Leicester: British Psychological Society.

Memon, A., Cronin, O., Eaves, R. & Bull, R. (1996). An empirical test of the mnemonic components of the cognitive interview. In G. M. Davies, S. Lloyd-Bostock, M. McMurran & J. C. Wilson (Eds.), *Psychology and law: Advances in research* (pp. 135–145). Berlin: de Gruyter.

Memon, A., Holley, A., Wark, L., Bull, R., & Köhnken, G. (1996). Reducing suggestibility in child witness interviews. *Applied Cognitive Psychology, 10,* 503–518.

Memon, A., Wark, L., Bull, R. & Köhnken, G. (1997). Isolating the effects of the cognitive interview techniques. *British Journal of Psychology, 88,* 179–197.

Milne, R. & Bull, R. (2001). Interviewing witnesses with learning disabilities for legal purposes. *British Journal of Learning Disabilities, 29,* 93–97.

Milne, R. & Bull, R. (2002). Back to basics: a componential analysis of the original cognitive interview mnemonics with three age groups. *Applied Cognitive Psychology, 16,* 743–753.

Milne, R. & Bull, R. (2003). Does the Cognitive Interview help children to resist the effects of suggestive questioning? *Legal & Criminological Psychology*, 8, 21–38.

Milne R., Clare, I. C. H. & Bull, R. (1999). Using the cognitive interview with adults with mild learning disabilities. *Psychology, Crime & Law*, 5, 81–101.

Milne, R., Clare, I. C. H. & Bull, R. (2002). Interrogative suggestibility among witnesses with mild intellectual disabilities: The use of an adaptation of the GSS. *Journal of Applied Research in Intellectual Disabilities*, 15, 8–17.

Mueller-Johnson, K. & Ceci, S. J. (2007). The elderly eyewitness: A review and prospectus. In M. P. Toglia, J. D. Read, D. F. Ross & R. C. L. Lindsay (Eds.), *Handbook of eyewitness psychology*, Volume 1 (pp. 577–603). Mahwah, NJ: Lawrence Erlbaum.

Newcombe, N. & Huttenlocher, J. (1992). Children's early ability to solve perspective-taking problems. *Developmental Psychology*, 28, 635–643.

Paivio, A. (1971). *Imagery and verbal processes*. New York: Holt, Rinehart & Winston.

Perlman, N., Ericson, K., Esses, V. & Isaacs, B. (1994). The developmentally handicapped witness: Competency as a function of question format. *Law and Human Behavior*, 18, 171–187.

Reyna, V. F., Holliday, R. E. & Marche, T. (2002). Explaining the development of false memories. *Developmental Review*, 22, 436–489.

Rose, R., Bull, R. & Vrij, A. (2003). Enhancing older witnesses' identification performance: Context reinstatement is not the answer. *The Canadian Journal of Police & Security Services*, 1, 173–184.

Saywitz, K. J., Geiselman, R. E. & Bornstein, G. K. (1992). Effects of cognitive interviewing and practice on children's recall performance. *Journal of Applied Psychology*, 77, 744–756.

Stein, L. & Memon, A. (2006) Testing the efficacy of the Cognitive Interview in a developing country. *Applied Cognitive Psychology*, 20, 597–605.

Ternes, M. & Yuille, J. C. (2008). Eyewitness memory and eyewitness identification performance in adults with intellectual disabilities. *Journal of Applied Research in Intellectual Disabilities*, 21, 519–531.

Tulving, E. (1974). Cue dependent forgetting. *American Scientist*, 62, 74–82.

Tulving, E. & Thomson, D. M. (1973). Encoding specificity and the retrieval processes in episodic memory. *Psychological Review*, 80, 352–373.

Wilcock, R., Bull, R. & Vrij, A. (2007). Are old witnesses always poorer witnesses? Identification accuracy, context reinstatement, own-age bias. *Psychology, Crime & Law*, 13, 305–316.

Wright, A. M. & Holliday, R. E. (2005). Police perceptions of older eyewitnesses. *Legal & Criminological Psychology*, 10, 211–223.

Wright, A. M. & Holliday, R. E. (2007a). Enhancing the recall of young, young-old and old-old adults with the cognitive interview and a modified version of the cognitive interview. *Applied Cognitive Psychology*, 21, 19–43.

Wright, A. M. & Holliday, R. E. (2007b). Interviewing cognitively impaired older adults: How useful is a cognitive interview? *Memory*, 15, 17–33.

Yarmey, A. D. (1993). Adult age and gender differences in eyewitness recall in field settings. *Journal of Applied Social Psychology*, 23, 1921–1932.

Yarmey, A. D. & Kent, J. (1980). Eyewitness identification by elderly and young adults. *Law and Human Behavior*, 4, 359–371.

Yuille J. C., Hunter, R., Joffe, R. & Zaparniuk, J. (1993). Interviewing children in sexual abuse cases. In G. S. Goodman & B. L. Bottoms (Eds.), *Child victims, child witnesses: Understanding and improving children's testimony* (pp. 95–115). New York: Guilford Press.

Zaragoza, M. S. (1991). Preschool children's susceptibility to memory impairment. In J. Doris (Ed.), *The suggestibility of children's recollections: Implications for eyewitness testimony* (pp. 27–39). Washington, DC: American Psychological Association.

Chapter Ten

Investigative Interviewing in the Courtroom: Child Witnesses under Cross-Examination

Rachel Zajac

Psychology Department
University of Otago, Dunedin, New Zealand

Concern has long been raised regarding children's ability to testify competently in what is essentially a legal system designed for adults. Historically, this controversy has centred on whether or not children possess the ability to recall and recount their past experiences accurately. It is now well documented, however, that the reliability of children's eyewitness testimony has more to do with the interviewer and interview conditions than with the individual child. Over the past 30 years, researchers have firmly established the interview conditions under which we can obtain the most complete and accurate accounts from children and, conversely, the conditions that promote inaccuracy (see Ceci & Bruck, 1993; Warren & McGough, 1996; Bruck & Ceci, 1999, for reviews).

In line with these research findings, numerous countries have adopted strict guidelines for interviewers who elicit children's eyewitness reports (e.g., Achieving Best Evidence in Criminal Proceedings: Guidance for Vulnerable or Intimidated Witnesses, Including Children; Home Office, 2002). In addition, many countries have reformed the law pertaining to child witnesses, allowing them to avoid aspects of the adversarial trial procedure that may impair their testimony. For example, videotaped evidential interviews, conducted by trained interviewers shortly after an allegation is made, can often be played in court in place of the child's direct evidence, thereby reducing both the effect of delay on children's testimony and the need for repeated interviewing (Myers, 1996;

Handbook of Psychology of Investigative Interviewing: Current Developments and Future Directions
Edited by Ray Bull, Tim Valentine and Tom Williamson
© 2009 John Wiley & Sons, Ltd.

Pipe & Henaghan, 1996). In addition, the widespread implementation of screens and closed-circuit television (CCTV) facilities has meant that many child complainants do not have to face the accused while testifying (Myers, 1996; Pipe & Henaghan, 1996; Saywitz, Goodman & Lyon, 2002). Research suggests that these reforms to policy and practice have enabled children to communicate more effectively in legal proceedings (Goodman, Tobey, Batterman-Faunce, Orcutt, Thomas, Shapiro & Sachsenmaier, 1998; Goodman, Quas, Bulkey & Shapiro, 1999).

Although the modifications described above have addressed many problematic aspects of the adversarial process, some have argued that they have not gone far enough. Specifically, almost all of the recent recommendations and law reforms have focused on the interviewers who solicit children's primary evidence; one crucial component of the adversarial process has been overlooked. Surprisingly, very little research has examined the effect of cross-examination on children's testimony.

What is cross-examination?

Cross-examination is the process by which opposing counsel scrutinizes a witness's evidence for inaccuracies or inconsistencies that may render it unreliable (Yarmey, 1979). Without cross-examination, evidence presented in the courtroom would go unchallenged. Cross-examination is considered by legal professionals to be a necessary and central aspect of any adversarial trial, but it is deemed to be a particularly valuable tool in cases that hinge on verbal testimony (Eichelbaum, 1989). In theory, cross-examination aims to facilitate accuracy. In fact, it has been described as 'the greatest legal engine ever invented for the discovery of truth' (Wigmore, 1974: 32). In practice, however, cross-examination is commonly used with the aim of discrediting the witness's testimony, regardless of its accuracy (Henderson, 2002).

Techniques that can be used to discredit witnesses are commonplace in legal textbooks (e.g., Stone, 1988; Glissan, 1991). For example, lawyers might press witnesses to contradict themselves or to enlarge a story until it is improbable or unbelievable. Textbooks also encourage lawyers to fire damaging facts at the witness during cross-examination, to attack the witness's credibility or credentials, and to ask questions in an illogical sequence in order to prevent the witness from becoming aware of the purpose of questioning (Glissan, 1991). It is certainly not uncommon for cross-examining lawyers to directly accuse witnesses of fabricating aspects of their testimony (Davies, Henderson & Seymour, 1997). Given these types of strategies, it is not surprising that witnesses have traditionally viewed cross-examination as a negative and aggressive procedure relative to the other components of the evidential process.

Potential problems for child witnesses under cross-examination

Recently, the question has arisen as to whether cross-examination is an appropriate questioning procedure for children. Particular concern has been raised regarding sexual abuse cases, in which corroborating evidence is rare (Golden, 2000), making cross-examination the only available legal avenue with which to resolve conflicting verbal evidence.

Why should we be concerned about child cross-examinations? The simple answer is that the typical child cross-examination has been described as 'a virtual *how not to* guide to investigative interviewing' (Henderson, 2002: 279). That is, the questioning style often used during cross-examination directly contravenes almost every principle that has been established for obtaining complete and accurate reports from child witnesses. On the basis of prior empirical research, at least three aspects of cross-examination are likely to pose problems for children. These are outlined below.

Problem 1: Leading and suggestive questions

Children are particularly susceptible to the effects of suggestion (for reviews, see Ceci & Bruck, 1993; Bruck & Ceci, 1999). For this reason, questions that assume disputed facts (e.g., 'How fast was the red car going?' when the colour of the car has not been ascertained), or suggest the desired response (e.g., 'Was the car going far too fast?'), or needlessly restrict the range of responses that children can provide (e.g., 'Was it a red car or a blue car?') are strongly discouraged when eliciting children's primary evidence. In stark contrast, not only are lawyers conducting cross-examination allowed to ask children these types of questions, leading and suggestive questions are encouraged in many legal textbooks (e.g., Eichelbaum, 1989; Glissan, 1991). The right to lead witnesses has been described as 'one of the great advantages of cross-examination' (Glissan, 1991: 105).

Given the clear discrepancy in the types of questions permitted during different phases of evidential questioning, it is not surprising that studies of trial transcripts have shown that leading and suggestive questions are far more likely to be posed during cross-examination than during direct examination or evidential interviews (Davies & Seymour, 1998; Zajac, Gross & Hayne, 2003). In fact, these types of questions tend to make up the bulk of the questions that are asked during cross-examination. In our study of transcripts involving child sexual abuse complainants between the ages of five and 13, over two-thirds of the questions that children were asked during cross-examination were either leading (e.g., 'You talked to her two times, didn't you?') or closed (e.g., 'Did you go straight home after that?' Zajac *et al.*, 2003).

Problem 2: Complex questions

Most current best practice standards for investigative interviews with children recommend that the questions posed are developmentally appropriate for the child's cognitive skill and linguistic competence. Despite these recommendations regarding primary evidence, research suggests that the questions asked during cross-examination often exceed children's developmental capabilities (Brennan & Brennan, 1988; Walker, 1993; Carter, Bottoms & Levine, 1996; Davies & Seymour, 1998; Cordon, Goodman & Anderson, 2003; Zajac *et al.*, 2003). As with leading and suggestive questions, complex questions are significantly more common during cross-examination than during other aspects of evidential questioning (Goodman *et al.*, 1992; Davies & Seymour, 1998; Zajac *et al.*, 2003).

Several aspects of the language used during child cross-examinations have raised concern among researchers. First, the vocabulary and syntax used to construct cross-examination questions has been shown to be highly complex across several studies (e.g., Brennan & Brennan, 1988; Flin, Bull, Boon & Knox, 1992; Goodman *et al.*, 1992; Walker, 1993; Davies & Seymour, 1998; Zajac *et al.*, 2003), many of which have directly compared the language used during cross-examination with that used during direct examination (Goodman *et al.*, 1992; Davies & Seymour, 1998; Zajac *et al.*, 2003). Problematic grammatical constructions that are common to cross-examination include multifaceted questions (e.g., 'So he picked you up and then the two of you went to the movies and then he dropped you at the bus stop – is that correct?'), questions phrased in the negative (e.g., 'Did you not leave the house at 3 pm?'), and questions that are inappropriately grammatically or semantically linked (e.g., 'But you realize, I suggest, that he was there, didn't you?' Davies & Seymour, 1998). These types of cross-examination questions are difficult for children to repeat verbatim, let alone fully comprehend (Brennan & Brennan, 1988). Second, many cross-examination questions require children to understand and employ complex relational concepts (e.g., height, weight, age, time, date and distance; Brennan & Brennan, 1988; Walker, 1993), or recount highly peripheral aspects of the alleged event (Glaser & Spencer, 1990). Finally, during cross-examination, the topic of questioning often changes abruptly. This is likely to confuse children (Cashmore, 1991; Saywitz, 1995), who expect conversations to flow in a logical sequence (Grice, 1975).

Empirical research indicates that the mismatch between cross-examination questions and children's abilities may prevent children from responding to questions in a truthful and meaningful way. For example, children often believe that they have understood a question when in fact they haven't (Markman, 1977; 1979; Singer & Flavell, 1981; Carter *et al.*, 1996). Furthermore, even when children are aware that they have not understood a question, they rarely ask interviewers for clarification (Markman, 1977; 1979; Saywitz & Snyder, 1993; Kebbell & Johnson, 2000). Children will even attempt to answer questions that do not make sense (e.g., 'Where do circles live?' Hughes & Grieve,

1980; Pratt, 1990; Waterman *et al.*, 2000), especially when questions require only a yes or no answer (e.g., 'Is a stone slower than an ear?' Waterman, Blades & Spencer, 2001). As such, children's willingness to provide an answer should not be taken as evidence that they have understood and correctly interpreted the question (Walker, 1993). Not surprisingly, children's accuracy is significantly compromised when responding to complex questions (Carter *et al.*, 1996).

Why do cross-examining lawyers ask children questions that exceed their linguistic and cognitive capabilities? There are two possible explanations, and they are not mutually exclusive. The first is that lawyers use complex language unwittingly (Henderson, 2002). It is possible, for example, that some poorly constructed questions or sudden changes in topic merely reflect the relatively spontaneous nature of cross-examination. Complex questions could also be accounted for by limited knowledge of what constitutes a developmentally appropriate question. This point pertains especially to the criminal defence lawyer who, in the context of representing adult defendants, may only occasionally be required to deal with a child witness.

On the other hand, it is possible that the use of complex questions may, in some situations, be intentional (Glaser & Spencer, 1990; Davies *et al.*, 1997). Davies & Seymour, for example, raise the possibility that 'some lawyers are using difficult questions in a deliberate attempt to confuse young complainants' (1998: 7). Support for this argument comes from the observation that legal textbooks encourage some practices (e.g., abrupt changes in the topic of questioning during cross-examination; Stone, 1988; Eichelbaum, 1989), but discourage them when instructing lawyers on how to question their own witnesses.

Problem 3: Challenges to credibility

Casting doubt on the witness's testimony is one of the defining characteristics of cross-examination. In doing so, cross-examining lawyers frequently put forward an alternative version of events, the plausibility of which the witness is pressured to acknowledge (Davies *et al.*, 1997). Unfortunately, all of what we know about interviewing children advises that interviewers utilize a neutral manner so as to avoid contaminating children's reports with their own beliefs or knowledge. Biased interviewing has been shown to exert a considerable negative influence on children's reports (Pettit, Fegan & Howie, 1990; Thompson, Clarke-Stewart & Lepore, 1997).

On what grounds do lawyers attempt to discredit children's testimony during cross-examination? Davies *et al.* (1997) interviewed 14 New Zealand defence lawyers and studied court transcripts of child cross-examinations, uncovering many common techniques used by lawyers to discredit children's evidence in alleged cases of sexual abuse. In 73% of the transcripts studied, children were accused, either directly or indirectly, of lying about the alleged abuse. Lawyers' justifications for these accusations included inconsistencies or delays in abuse disclosure, the child's previously happy relationship with the accused, ulterior motives, an inability to distinguish between real and imagined actions, and pressure from an adult to fabricate an allegation. Westcott & Page (2002) note that lawyers who cross-examine child complainants of sexual abuse often rely on commonly held, but empirically unsupported, notions about sexual assault (e.g., that genuine victims of abuse will make a disclosure immediately).

Not surprisingly, children who have testified in adversarial trials consistently report finding the confrontational nature of cross-examination highly distressing (Prior, Glaser & Lynch, 1997; Eastwood & Patton, 2002; Wade, 2002). Cross-examination and, in particular, the attitude and behaviour of the defence lawyer were the 'overwhelming area of concern' for child complainants in Eastwood & Patton's Australian study (2002: 59). Flin and colleagues (1992) noted many anecdotal reports of children being so distressed during cross-examination that they 'clam up' or refuse to speak. A child witness from Wade's (2002) study reported:

> They were pushing me to say the opposite thing. ... And they shouldn't really do that. They should, like, ask you to say what happened and then ask you questions. But they didn't. They kept ... pushing me to say summat else. And as soon as I got out I started crying 'cos they pushed me and they scared me. (Wade, 2002, p. 225)

It is important to note, however, that not all child cross-examinations are conducted in an aggressive manner. Ten of the 14 New Zealand defence lawyers surveyed by Davies *et al.* (1997) considered that the best manner in which to cross-examine a child complainant was to be non-threatening and gentle, at least initially. These authors suggest that a friendly, charming questioning manner can render a child more trusting, while preventing the lawyer from alienating the jury. Some have even proposed that children's evidence can be discredited *more* readily by interviewing in a supportive manner than it can be using aggression (Flin, 1993).

How do these problems impact on children's testimony?

Although many laboratory studies have considered the three problems outlined above in isolation, research evaluating their combined effect on children's courtroom evidence is limited. As the only empirical study that has examined how child witnesses respond to the questions that they are posed during cross-examination, our court transcript analysis suggests that children do not cope well with this questioning style. Specifically, despite the fact that defence lawyers asked a high proportion of complex and grammatically unsound questions, child complainants of sexual abuse rarely requested clarification. Children in this study were also highly likely to comply with leading questions. Most notably, under cross-examination, over 75% of children changed at least one aspect of their earlier testimony. On average, children made three of these changes, with one child making 16 changes during a relatively short questioning period. The changes that children made ranged from peripheral details of the alleged event(s) to entire allegation retractions (Zajac *et al.*, 2003).

Although these findings give cause for concern, using court transcript data only allowed us to evaluate the effect of cross-examination on children's testimony, as opposed to children's accuracy. Given that cross-examination is often promoted as a truth-finding mechanism, the issue of accuracy is a critical one.

Cross-examination and children's accuracy

One widespread assumption within the legal profession is that cross-examination will not pose any problem for a witness who is telling the truth. If this were the case, then the only children to change their stories during cross-examination would be children whose primary evidence contained errors. In this scenario, the changes that the children in our transcript study made during cross-examination would have increased their overall accuracy levels. However, given that cross-examination language exhibits several characteristics likely to dramatically reduce resistance to suggestion, there is another possibility: the changes that children make during cross-examination may have little to do with accuracy, and may have even rendered children's testimony *less* accurate. Laboratory research is the only avenue by which to comprehensively evaluate these possibilities.

The first laboratory-based study of cross-examination was conducted in 1988 by Turtle & Wells. In this study, eight- and 12-year-old children and adults watched a film clip of a simulated child abduction. The next day, they were asked 10 direct examination and 10 cross-examination questions about the film. Although participants in all age groups were less accurate in response to the cross-examination questions than the direct examination style questions, eight-year-old children's overall accuracy rate (41%) was significantly lower than that of the adults and the 12-year-olds (61% and 65%, respectively).

While Turtle & Wells' findings confirmed many researchers' suspicions about the effect of cross-examination on children's accuracy, two main problems restrict their forensic applicability. First, participants in this study were cross-examined just 24 hours after viewing the film; most child witnesses in real trials are cross-examined long after their allegation is made (Goodman *et al.*, 1992; Lash, 1995; Plotnikoff & Woolfson, 1995; Eastwood & Patton, 2002). Second, because little detail was provided regarding the types of questions that were asked, it is impossible to assess whether the cross-examination questions were an accurate reflection of courtroom questioning.

In order to address these issues, we used court transcripts to develop a standardized laboratory analogue of cross-examination, which we used to interview five- and six-year-olds about a staged event (Zajac & Hayne, 2003).

Children visited the local police station, where they participated in four unique activities (e.g., getting their fingerprints taken). Six weeks later, they were interviewed about the visit. This interview mimicked the process adopted in several countries (e.g., New Zealand, Australia and England) which allows direct evidence to be pre-recorded for presentation in court. The interview consisted of general, open-ended prompts (e.g., 'Tell me everything that you can remember'), as well as specific questions about two true activities (e.g., 'Did you see the police car?') and two false activities (e.g., 'Did you get to try on handcuffs?'). After a forensically relevant eight-month delay, children viewed their direct examination videotape and were then interviewed using the cross-examination analogue. The aim of this cross-examination interview was to talk children out of their responses to the specific questions posed during direct examination, regardless of response accuracy. The questions used to achieve this were modelled after the kinds of questions asked by defence lawyers in Zajac *et al.* (2003).

Several important findings emerged. As in the courtroom, a large proportion of children (85%) changed at least one of their direct examination responses under cross-examination. In fact, one third of children changed *all four* of their previous responses. Crucially, the changes that children made during cross-examination were by no means limited to correcting earlier mistakes. In fact, children in this study were just as likely to change a correct response as they were to change an incorrect one. Overall, cross-examination style questioning significantly decreased the accuracy of children's reports, to a point where accuracy scores during the cross-examination interview did not differ significantly from chance (50%). This finding held even when only considering the substantial number of children whose direct examination reports were 100% accurate.

When the study was repeated with a sample of nine- and ten-year-olds, some age differences in cross-examination performance were evident. The older children made fewer changes during cross-examination than the younger children, and were more likely to change an incorrect response than a correct one. Nonetheless, older children still changed 43% of their correct responses, leading to a considerable decrease in accuracy (Zajac & Hayne, 2006).

The findings from these three laboratory studies raise serious concerns about the suitability of the cross-examination process for children. Specifically, they suggest that not only might cross-examination be an ineffective method for ascertaining the truth, but in some cases it might even create the types of errors that it aims to uncover. The potential for trial outcome to be impaired in these cases is immense. Distressed and confused child victims of abuse who are subjected to rigorous cross-examination could end up retracting their allegations altogether. Alternatively, these children could be coerced into admitting that they have mistaken the identity of their abuser. Child witnesses for the defence could end up (falsely) implicating an accused person. Even seemingly inconsequential inconsistencies in a child's testimony may be seen by jury members as a sign of unreliability.

Our attention has now turned to examining the factors that influence children's responses to cross-examination questioning. Some of these are factors over which the justice system has little control, but which may help to identify children who may be particularly vulnerable to cross-examination; others are procedural factors that may help to shed some light on a way forward.

Individual differences in cross-examination performance

As mentioned at the beginning of this chapter, it is now widely acknowledged that children's eyewitness accuracy hinges primarily on the way in which they are questioned. However, even when external factors are held constant, children do not respond uniformly to forensic questioning (Bruck, Ceci & Melnyk, 1997). In light of this finding, a recent body of research has focused on factors within the individual that may influence the reliability and accuracy of children's reports.

Despite an increasing number of studies examining the individual differences that influence children's primary testimony (see Bruck & Melnyk, 2004, for a review and synthesis), little is known about how individual factors might affect children's responses to cross-examination. Preliminary research has been conducted by Zajac, Jury & O'Neill (in press), who examined the role of several psychosocial variables on five- and six-year-old children's performance under cross-examination. Although cross-examination compromised accuracy in the vast majority of participants, children with low self-esteem, self-confidence and assertiveness performed particularly poorly. Given that child abuse has been associated with low scores on these variables (Martin & Beezley, 1977; Oates, Forrest & Peacock, 1985; Kaufman & Cicchetti, 1989; Howing, Wodarski, Kurtz & Gaudin, 1990), our findings raise the concerning possibility that the same factors that may make children targets for abuse, or may be the consequences of abuse, could also make them particularly susceptible to the cross-examination process. Similar research examining the role of cognitive factors (e.g., IQ, memory and language ability) on children's responses to cross-examination is underway, but preliminary findings indicate that, within the normal range of functioning, these variables contribute little to cross-examination performance (O'Neill, Jury & Zajac, 2005).

The impact of delay

Even in countries making concerted efforts to expedite trials involving child complainants, cross-examination typically occurs long after an allegation has been made. In New Zealand, for example, child witnesses can expect to wait an average of eight months between making an allegation and appearing in court (Lash, 1995). Child witnesses testifying in other countries also encounter lengthy delays (Goodman *et al.*, 1992; Plotnikoff & Woolfson, 1995; Eastwood & Patton, 2002), with some as long as three years (Eastwood & Patton, 2002).

In an attempt to model the conditions in actual forensic settings, the cross-examination interview in our original analogue studies (Zajac & Hayne, 2003; 2006) occurred eight months after direct evidence was pre-recorded. In light of research showing that suggestibility increases with delay (e.g., Zaragoza & Lane, 1994), we hypothesized that eliminating the delay between direct examination and cross-examination might facilitate five- and six-year-old children's accuracy during cross-examination. To test this hypothesis, we employed the same basic paradigm, but cross-examined children either 1–3 days or eight months after their direct-examination interview. Despite highly accurate initial reports, children's performance during cross-examination was very poor, even when they were cross-examined shortly after the target event. In fact, children's cross-examination accuracy scores did not differ as a function of delay, suggesting that reducing the delay between the allegation and the trial or conducting pre-trial cross-examination may do little to facilitate children's performance. Furthermore, when the direct examination interview questions were repeated one week following cross-examination, children's accuracy returned to pre-cross-examination levels. These data suggest that children's poor cross-examination performance cannot be solely attributed to memory impairment, and that the changes that children make during cross-examination do not necessarily result in memory impairment (Righarts, Zajac & Hayne, 2009).

Of course, delays during criminal investigations are not restricted to those occurring between allegation and trial. Child victims of sexual abuse, for example, may not disclose until many months or even years after the abuse has occurred. It is possible that, by conducting our direct examination interviews very soon after the target event, we have effectively inoculated children against the impact of delay. Consequently, our findings using short delays between each phase of the experimental paradigm might well be considered a best-case scenario of children's cross-examination performance.

Preparing children for cross-examination

The finding that children's responses to cross-examination cannot be attributed to memory impairment suggests that pre-trial interventions for children may hold promise, to an extent that they would not if memory was the primary issue. In light of this possibility, our most recent research has been exploring potential interventions to facilitate children's accuracy during cross-examination questioning.

Many jurisdictions have implemented formal preparation programmes for children who are required to testify in court. These programmes generally involve familiarizing children with their role as a witness and with courtroom personnel and procedures. Although these programmes are not specifically designed to facilitate accuracy, it is anticipated that reducing distress and con-fusion associated with testifying will indirectly help children to provide complete and accurate testimony. While systematic research evaluating these programmes is scarce, existing evaluations suggest that the preparation sessions increase children's understanding of the trial process, reduce their anxiety about giving evidence and help them to testify with more confidence (Dezwirek-Sas, 1992; Davies *et al.*, 2004).

Further to familiarization programmes, some researchers have explored interventions aimed specifically at facilitating children's accuracy. Many of these interventions have been remarkably simple, such as telling children that interview questions might be difficult, or that saying 'I don't know' is prefer-able to guessing an answer. Although these interventions have met with at least some success (e.g., Warren, Hulse-Trotter & Tubbs, 1991), their efficacy does not necessarily generalize to cross-examination, during which leading and complex questions are often delivered in a highly persuasive manner.

What does a warning about cross-examination need to encompass? As described earlier, several aspects of the language used during cross-examination are likely to promote compliance. First, reliance on leading questions (e.g., 'Your mother was there at the time, wasn't she?') can suggest to children that the interviewer has firsthand knowledge of the event, a problem likely to be exacerbated by the fact that adults, especially parents and teachers, often know the answers to the questions that they ask children. Anecdotally, when we ask our child participants leading cross-examination questions, they frequently ask us whether we accompanied them on the memory event. Second, because children tend to assume that adults are genuine conversational partners (Grice, 1975), they are unlikely to anticipate that the questioning style used during cross-examination might be unsupportive. Specifically, children are unlikely to expect attacks on their credibility or understand that complex language struc-tures can be used as a means to confuse them. Finally, children are often reluctant to disagree with adults, particularly adults in positions of authority. Children's willingness to correct adults' incorrect statements is likely to decrease even further when interviewers adopt a confrontational approach.

Could a brief verbal warning targeting these three areas increase children's resistance to misleading cross-examination questions? If so, does it matter who delivers the warning? These questions formed the basis for a recent study that we conducted with five- and six-year-old and nine- and ten-year-old children (Righarts & Zajac, 2009). The study followed the same general paradigm used in our past research, but some children were given a brief verbal warning immediately prior to their cross-examination interview. This warning informed children that they would be asked some more questions about the police station, that the interviewer did not visit the police station and therefore did not know what happened there, that the questions might be tricky and that it was OK to disagree with the interviewer if she got things 'muddled'. The warning was either delivered by an unfamiliar experimenter or by the experi-menter conducting the cross-examination interview. Children in the control group were not given a warning. As in previous studies, children were highly accurate during the direct examination interview, but accuracy scores during cross-examination were significantly compromised. The warning did not facilitate children's cross-examination performance, regardless of who delivered it. It therefore appears that the brief interventions that have proved successful in child suggestibility research may be insufficient to buffer children from the negative effects of cross-examination (Righarts & Zajac, 2009).

Could a more comprehensive intervention be successful? Following the unsuccessful warning intervention, we turned our attention to developing a means of preparing children for cross-examination questioning. One or two days prior to the cross-examination interview, half of the five- to six-year-old and nine- to ten-year-old children in the sample were given practice at answering cross-examination-style questions about a short film (unrelated to the memory event), with feedback on their responses. The duration of the preparation session was approximately 20 minutes. Control children watched the film, but were not given the practice and feedback. During the subsequent cross-examination interview, the children who received preparation made fewer changes to their earlier responses and changed a smaller proportion of their correct responses relative to the control children. Furthermore, overall accuracy levels during the cross-examination interview were significantly higher in the preparation group than in the control group. In short, the intervention was successful (Righarts & Zajac, 2009).

While this research is in its very early stages, our preparation intervention appears to have several advantages. First, during the preparation session, children were asked questions that were entirely unrelated to their 'testimony', making allegations of coaching less feasible. Furthermore, the intervention was effective despite being delivered by an unfamiliar interviewer, as would be the case in real-life situations where court preparation would be conducted by an independent third party. Finally, for the nine- to ten-year-old children, the success of the intervention was unrelated to their performance during the preparation session. That is, for these older children, mere participation in the preparation session was sufficient to increase accuracy during cross-examination.

Naturally, there are aspects of the intervention that require more comprehensive investigation. For example, although the intervention did not reduce the number of prior mistakes that children corrected during cross-examination, the absolute number of errors that children made during direct examination was very small, making the statistical power to observe a significant difference relatively low. It is also important to bear in mind that the preparation session in this study was conducted just one or two days prior to the cross-examination interview. Because such short timeframes may not be practical in actual cases, further research is necessary to ascertain the role that the timing of the intervention plays in its effectiveness.

Most important to note is that while the intervention facilitated children's cross-examination performance, it did not eliminate the negative effects of this questioning style in either age group. That is, even children in the preparation condition made changes to their earlier testimony that decreased their overall accuracy levels. This finding is further testament to the robust nature of the cross-examination effect.

Postscript: Adults under cross-examination

While the consistent finding that cross-examination questioning decreases the accuracy of children's reports is concerning on its own, it also raises the question of whether cross-examination could affect adults' testimony in a similar way. Zajac & Cannan (2009) note several reasons to suspect that this may be the case. Anecdotally, for example, we know that children are not the only witnesses who find cross-examination confusing and stressful. Many adults, including police witnesses report the same types of concerns (Flin, 1993), and much has been written to assist adult witnesses to cope with challenging cross-examination questions (e.g., Brodsky, 2004). Second, as described below, laboratory research has demonstrated that adults' eyewitness reports are susceptible to the same kinds of contaminating influences as those of children.

Like children, adults are vulnerable to the way in which a question is worded. As questions move from open to closed to leading, adults' reports become less accurate (Poole & White, 1991), and when faced with a question requiring only a yes or no answer, adults too are more likely to answer 'yes' than 'no' (Kebbell *et al.*, 2001). Adults will also attempt to answer nonsensical questions (Pratt, 1990), especially when they require only a yes or no answer (Waterman *et al.*, 2001). Even subtle changes in the wording of a question (e.g., replacing *a* with *the*) can impair adults' accuracy (Loftus & Zanni, 1975). Like children, adults also find it more difficult to accurately answer linguistically complex questions relative to questions phrased in simple terms (Perry *et al.*, 1995; Kebbell & Johnson, 2000), and adults' susceptibility to misinformation increases with increased question complexity (Loftus & Greene, 1980).

Furthermore, adults are far from immune to social pressure during the course of an interview. Social psychologists have reported for decades that adults are vulnerable to persuasion (see, for example, studies on conformity, Asch, 1956; Cialdini, 1988; and on obedience, Milgram, 1963; 1974). Adults' suggestibility increases markedly when they are under pressure or in an intimidating environment (Hyman, Husband & Billings, 1995; Kassin & Kiechel, 1996; Loftus, 1997; Horselenberg, Merchelbach & Josephs, 2003; Redlich & Goodman, 2003). Like children, adults are more susceptible to leading questions when the interviewer is of higher status (Roper & Shewan, 2002). In fact, adults are more likely to comply with another adult who is dressed in uniform as opposed a shabby outfit, suggesting that the mere emblems of authority can elicit compliance (Bushman, 1984; 1988).

In addition to the empirical findings described above, we also know that many adult victims of crime exhibit specific vulnerability factors that could render them particularly susceptible to cross-examination questioning. These factors may include testifying about traumatic or highly sensitive events, older age, or learning or communication problems. Adults who have been sexually victimized are likely to be a particularly vulnerable group of witnesses (Frazier & Haney, 1996; Baker, 1999; Edward & MacLeod, 1999; Lees, 2002), as sexual assault has been linked with low self-esteem and low self-confidence, both of which are associated with vulnerability to suggestion (Gudjonsson & Singh, 1984; Singh & Gudjonnsson, 1984).

Not only are adult witnesses likely to exhibit factors that may increase their vulnerability to cross-examination questioning, the questioning itself is likely to be qualitatively and quantitatively different from that used to cross-examine children. For example, we know that, compared to children, adult witnesses are asked more cross-examination questions, a higher proportion of which are complex and credibility challenging (Zajac & Cannan, 2009). Furthermore, when cross-examining adults, lawyers are likely to use different reasons for challenging a witness's story. In cases of a sexual nature, for example, adult complainants are likely to be challenged on the issue of consent, which is clearly not a valid means of cross-examining child complainants. Cross-examination of adult rape complainants is notoriously aggressive (Gregory & Lees, 1996; Brereton, 1997; Lees, 2002).

Our preliminary research on the courtroom cross-examination of adult sexual abuse complainants has confirmed that adults are not immune to the effects of cross-examination on their testimony (Zajac & Cannan, 2009). Although the adult complainants in this study were more likely than child complainants to resist or give extra clarification in response to closed and leading questions, other aspects of their responses provided cause for concern. For example, like children, adults appeared reluctant to seek clarification from cross-examining lawyers, even when the questions posed were ambiguous, highly complex or did not make sense. Most concerning was the finding that adult complainants undergoing cross-examination made just as many changes to their earlier testimony as children did. As with children, many of these changes were elicited by questions that were leading or challenged credibility. In light of these findings, it is now imperative that laboratory research explores the effect of cross-examination-style questioning on adults' accuracy.

Concluding remarks

A number of recent studies have cast doubt on whether cross-examination is an effective means of obtaining accurate eyewitness reports. Bearing in mind that the ultimate goal of any legal investigation should be to ascertain the truth, it is particularly concerning that the types of questions typically employed during cross-examination have been shown to exert a negative effect on the accuracy of children's reports. While recognizing that cross-examination is a mainstay of adversarial trial procedure, further research is required to identify the factors that may reduce or exacerbate the negative effects of cross-examination on the testimony provided by both children and adults.

References

Asch, S. E. (1956). Studies of independence and conformity: A minority of one against a unanimous majority. *Psychological Monographs: General and Applied, 70,* 1–70.

Baker, D. (1999). Shredding the truth. *American Bar Association Journal, 8,* 40–44.

Brennan, M. & Brennan, R. E. (1988). *Strange language: Child victims under cross-examination,* 3rd edition. Wagga Wagga, NSW: CSU Literary Studies Network.

Brereton, D. (1997). How different are rape trials? A comparison of the cross-examination of complainants in rape and assault trails. *British Journal of Criminology, 37,* 242–261.

Brodsky, S. L. (2004). *Coping with cross-examination and other pathways to effective testimony.* Washington, DC: American Psychological Association.

Bruck, M. & Ceci, S. J. (1999). The suggestibility of children's memory. *Annual Review of Psychology, 50,* 419–439.

Bruck, M. & Melnyk, L. (2004). Individual differences in children's suggestibility: A review and synthesis. *Applied Cognitive Psychology, 18,* 947–996.

Bruck, M., Ceci, S. J. & Melnyk, L. (1997). External and internal variation in the creation of false reports in children. *Learning and Individual Differences, 9,* 289–316.

Bushman, B. J. (1984). Perceived symbols of authority and their influence on conformity. *Journal of Applied Social Psychology, 14,* 501–508.

Bushman, B. J. (1988). The effects of apparel on compliance: a field experiment with a female authority figure. *Personality and Social Psychology Bulletin, 14,* 459–467.

Carter, C. A., Bottoms, B. L. & Levine, M. (1996). Linguistic and socioemotional influences on the accuracy of children's reports. *Law and Human Behavior, 20,* 335–358.

Cashmore, J. (1991). Problems and solutions in lawyer–child communication. *Criminal Law Journal, 15,* 193–202.

Ceci, S. J. & Bruck, M. (1993). Suggestibility of the child witness: A historical review and synthesis. *Psychological Bulletin, 113,* 403–439.

Cialdini, R. B. (1988). *Influence: science and practice,* 2nd edition. Glenview, IL: Scott Foresman.

Cordon, I. M., Goodman, G. S. & Anderson, S. J. (2003). Children in court. In P. J. van Koppen & S. D. Penrod (Eds.), *Adversarial versus inquisitorial justice: Psychological perspectives on criminal justice systems* (pp. 167–199). New York: Kluwer Academic/Plenum Publishers.

Davies, E. & Seymour, F. W. (1997). Child witnesses in the criminal courts: Furthering New Zealand's commitment to the United Nations Convention on the Rights of the Child. *Psychiatry, Psychology and Law, 4,* 13–24.

Davies, E. & Seymour, F. W. (1998). Questioning child complainants of sexual abuse: Analysis of criminal court transcripts in New Zealand. *Psychiatry, Psychology and Law*, 5, 47–61.

Davies, E., Henderson, E. & Seymour, F. W. (1997). In the interests of justice? The cross-examination of child complainants of sexual abuse in criminal proceedings. *Psychiatry, Psychology and Law*, 4, 217–229.

Davies, E., Devere, H. & Verbitsky, J. (2004). Court education for young witnesses: Evaluation of the pilot service in Aotearoa, New Zealand. *Psychiatry, Psychology and Law*, 11, 226–235.

Dezwirek-Sas, L. (1992). Empowering child witnesses for sexual abuse prosecution, in H. Dent & R. Flin (Eds.), *Children as witnesses* (pp. 181–191). Chichester: John Wiley & Sons.

Eastwood, C. & Patton, W. (2002). *The experiences of child complainants of sexual abuse in the criminal justice system*. Report to the Criminology Research Council, Australia.

Edward, K. E. & MacLeod, M. D. (1999). The reality and myth of rape: Implications for the criminal justice system. *Expert Evidence*, 7, 37–58.

Eichelbaum, T. (1989). Cross-examination. In T. Eichelbaum, T. Arnold & D. Wilson (Eds.), *Mauet's fundamentals of trial techniques* (pp. 199–247). Auckland, New Zealand: Oxford University Press.

Flin, R. (1993). Hearing and testing children's evidence. In G. S. Goodman & B. Bottoms (Eds.), *Child victims, child witnesses: Understanding and improving testimony* (pp. 279–299). New York: Guilford Press.

Flin, R., Bull, R., Boon, J. & Knox, A. (1992). Children in the witness-box. In H. Dent & R. Flin (Eds.), *Children as witnesses* (pp. 167–181). Chichester: Wiley.

Frazier, P. A. & Haney, B. (1996). Sexual assault cases in the legal system: Police, prosecutor, and victim perspectives. *Law and Human Behavior*, 20, 607–628.

Glaser, D. & Spencer, J. R. (1990). Sentencing, children's evidence and children's trauma. *The Criminal Law Review*, 371–382.

Glissan, J. L. (1991). *Cross-examination practice and procedure: An Australian perspective*, 2nd edition. Sydney: Butterworths.

Golden, O. (2000). The federal response to child abuse and neglect. *American Psychologist*, 55, 1050–1053.

Goodman, G. S., Taub, E. P., Jones, D. H. P., England, P., Port, L. K., Rudy, L. & Prado, L. (1992). Testifying in criminal court: Emotional effects on child sexual assault victims. *Monographs of the Society for Research in Child Development*, 57, 5, Serial No. 229.

Goodman, G. S., Tobey, A. E., Batterman-Faunce, J. M., Orcutt, H., Thomas, S., Shapiro, C. & Sachsenmaier, T. (1998). Face-to-face confrontation: Effects of closed-circuit technology on children's eyewitness testimony and jurors' decisions. *Law and Human Behavior*, 22, 165–203.

Goodman, G. S., Quas, J. A., Bulkley, J. & Shapiro, C. (1999). Innovations for child witnesses: A national survey. *Psychology, Public Policy, and Law*, 5, 255–281.

Gregory, J. & Lees, S. (1996). Attrition in rape and sexual assault cases. *The British Journal of Criminology*, 36, 1–17.

Grice, H. P. (1975). Logic and conversation. In P. Cole & J. L. Morgan (Eds.), *Syntax and semantics.* Volume 3, *Speech acts* (pp. 41–58). New York: Academic Press.

Gudjonsson, G. H. & Singh, K. K. (1984). Interrogative suggestibility and delinquent boys: An empirical validation study. *Personality and Individual Differences, 5,* 425–430.

Henderson, E. (2002). Persuading and controlling: The theory of cross-examination in relation to children. In H. L. Westcott, G. M. Davies & R. Bull (Eds.), *Children's testimony: A handbook of psychological research and forensic practice* (pp. 279–294). Chichester: John Wiley & Sons.

Home Office (2002). *Achieving best evidence in criminal proceedings: Guidance for vulnerable or intimidated witnesses, including children.* London: Author.

Horselenberg, R., Merckelback, H. & Josephs, S. (2003). Individual differences and false confessions: A conceptual replication of Kassin and Kiechel (1996). *Psychology, Crime & Law, 9,* 1–8.

Howing, P. T., Wodarski, J. S., Kurtz, P. D. & Gaudin, J. R. Jr. (1990). The empirical base for the implementation of social skills training with maltreated children. *Social Work, 35,* 460–467.

Hughes, M. & Grieve, R. (1980). On asking children bizarre questions. *First Language, 1,* 149–160.

Hyman, E. E., Husband, T. H. & Billings, F. J. (1995). False memories of childhood experiences. *Applied Cognitive Psychology, 9,* 181–197.

Kassin, S. M. & Kiechel, K. L. (1996). The social psychology of false confessions: Compliance, internalization, and confabulation. *Psychological Science, 7,* 125–128.

Kaufman, J. & Cicchetti, D. (1989). Effects of maltreatment on school-age children's socioemotional development: Assessments in a day-camp setting. *Developmental Psychology, 25,* 516–524.

Kebbell, M. R. & Johnson, S. D. (2000). Lawyers' questioning: The effect of confusing questions on witness confidence and accuracy. *Law and Human Behavior, 24,* 629–641.

Kebbell, M. R., Hatton, C., Johnson, S. D. & O'Kelly, C. M. E. (2001). People with learning disabilities as witnesses in court: What questions should lawyers ask? *British Journal of Learning Disabilities, 29,* 98–102.

Lash, B. (1995). Time taken to process sexual offence cases through the courts. Unpublished manuscript, Wellington, New Zealand: Department of Justice.

Lees, S. (2002). *Carnal knowledge: Rape on trial.* London: The Women's Press.

Loftus, E. F. (1997). Memory for a past that never was. *Current Directions in Psychological Science, 6,* 60–65.

Loftus, E. F. & Greene, E. (1980). Warning: Even memory for faces may be contagious. *Law and Human Behavior, 4,* 323–334.

Loftus, E. F. & Zanni, G. (1975). Eyewitness testimony: The influence of the wording of a question. *Bulletin of the Psychonomic Society, 5,* 86–88.

Markman, E. M. (1977). Realizing that you don't understand: A preliminary investigation. *Child Development, 48,* 986–992.

Markman, E. M. (1979). Realizing that you don't understand: Elementary school children's awareness of inconsistencies. *Child Development, 50,* 643–655.

Martin, H. P. & Beezley, P. (1977). Behavioral observations of abused children. *Developmental Medicine and Child Neurology, 19,* 373–387.

Milgram, S. (1963). Behavioral study of obedience. *Journal of Abnormal and Social Psychology, 67,* 371–378.

Milgram, S. (1974). *Obedience to authority.* London: Tavistock.

Myers, J. E. B. (1996). A decade of international reform to accommodate child witnesses: Steps toward a child witness code. In B. L. Bottoms & G. S. Goodman (Eds.), *International perspectives on child abuse and children's testimony: psychological research and law* (pp. 221–244). Thousand Oaks, CA: Sage.

Oates, R. K., Forest, D. & Peacock, A. (1985). Self-esteem of abused children. *Child abuse and neglect, 9,* 159–163.

O'Neill, S., Jury, E. & Zajac, R. (2005). *Who is most at risk from the negative effects of cross-examination?* Part 1, *Cognitive factors.* Presentation to Society for Applied Research in Memory and Cognition, Wellington, New Zealand, January.

Perry, N. W., McAuliff, B. D., Tam, P., Claycomb, L., Dostal, C. & Flanagan, C. (1995). When lawyers question children: Is justice served? *Law and Human Behavior, 19,* 609–629.

Pettit, F., Fegan, M. & Howie, P. (1990). *Interviewer effects on children's testimony.* Paper presented at the International Congress on Child Abuse and Neglect, Hamburg, Germany.

Pipe, M. E. & Henaghan, M. (1996). Accommodating children's testimony: Legal reforms in New Zealand. In B. L. Bottoms & G. S. Goodman (Eds.), *International perspectives on child abuse and children's testimony: Psychological research and law* (pp. 145–167). Thousand Oaks, CA: Sage.

Plotnikoff, J. & Woolfson, R. (1995). *Prosecuting child abuse: An evaluation of the government's speedy progress policy.* London: Blackstone Press.

Poole, D. A. & White, L. T. (1991). Effects of question repetition on the eyewitness testimony of children and adults. *Developmental Psychology, 27,* 975–986.

Pratt, C. (1990). On asking children – and adults – bizarre questions. *First Language, 10,* 167–175.

Prior, V., Glaser, D. & Lynch, M. A. (1997). Responding to child sexual abuse: The criminal justice system. *Child Abuse Review, 6,* 128–140.

Redlich, A. D. & Goodman, G. S. (2003). Taking responsibility for an act not committed: The influence of age and suggestibility. *Law and Human Behavior, 27,* 141–156.

Righarts, S. & Zajac, R. (2009). The negative effect of cross-examination questioning on the accuracy of children's reports: Can we intervene? Manuscript in preparation.

Righarts, S., Zajac, R. & Hayne, H. (2009). Children's responses to cross-examination style questioning: suggestibility or compliance? Manuscript submitted for publication.

Roper, R. & Shewan, D. (2002). Compliance and eyewitness testimony: Do eyewitnesses comply with misleading 'expert pressure' during investigative interviewing? *Legal and Criminological Psychology, 7,* 155–163.

Saywitz, K. J. (1995). Improving children's testimony: The question, the answer and the environment. In M. S. Zaragoza, J. R. Graham, G. C. N. Hall, R. Hirschman & Y. S. Ben-Porath (Eds.), *Memory and testimony in the child witness* (pp. 113–140). Thousand Oaks, CA: Sage.

Saywitz, K. J. & Snyder, L. (1993). Improving children's testimony with preparation. In G. Goodman & B. Bottoms (Eds.), *Child victims, child witnesses: Understanding and improving testimony* (pp. 117–146). New York: Guilford Press.

Saywitz, K. J., Goodman, G. S. & Lyon, T. D. (2002). Interviewing children in and out of court: Current research and practice implications. In J. Myers, L. Berliner, J. Briere, C. T. Hendrix, C. Jenny & T. Reid (Eds.), *The APSAC handbook on child maltreatment*, 2nd edition (pp. 349–377). Thousand Oaks, CA: Sage.

Singer, J. B. & Flavell, J. H. (1981). Development of knowledge about communication: Children's evaluations of explicitly ambiguous messages. *Child Development*, 52, 1211–1215.

Singh, K. K. & Gudjonsson, G. H. (1984). Interrogative suggestibility, delayed memory and self-concept. *Personality and Individual Differences*, 5, 203–209.

Stone, M. (1988). *Cross-examination in criminal trials*. London: Butterworths.

Thompson, W. C., Clarke-Stewart, K. A. & Lepore, S. J. (1997). What did the janitor do? Suggestive interviewing and the accuracy of children's accounts. *Law and Human Behaviour*, 21, 405–426.

Turtle, J. W. & Wells, G. L. (1988). Children versus adults as eyewitnesses: Whose testimony holds up under cross-examination? In M. M. Gruneburg, P. E. Morris & R. N. Sykes (Eds.), *Practical aspects of memory*. Volume 1, *Current research and issues* (pp. 27–33). Chichester: John Wiley & Sons.

Wade, A. (2002). New measures and new challenges: Children's experiences of the court process. In H. L. Westcott, G. M. Davies & R. Bull (Eds.), *Children's testimony: A handbook of psychological research and forensic practice* (pp. 219–232). New York: John Wiley & Sons.

Walker, A. G. (1993). Questioning young children in court: a linguistic case study. *Law and Human Behavior*, 17, 59–81.

Warren, A., Hulse-Trotter, K. & Tubbs, E. C. (1991). Inducing resistance to suggestibility in children. *Law and Human Behavior*, 15, 273–285.

Warren, A. R. & McGough, L. S. (1996). Research on children's suggestibility: Implications for the investigative interview. In B. L. Bottoms & G. S. Goodman (Eds.), *International perspectives on child abuse and children's testimony: Psychological research and law* (pp. 12–44). Thousand Oaks, CA: Sage.

Waterman, A. H., Blades, M. & Spencer, C. (2000). Do children try to answer nonsensical questions? *British Journal of Developmental Psychology*, 18, 211–225.

Waterman, A. H., Blades, M. & Spencer, C. (2001). Interviewing children and adults: The effect of question format on the tendency to speculate. *Applied Cognitive Psychology*, 15, 521–531.

Westcott, H. L. & Page, M. (2002). Cross-examination, sexual abuse and child witness identity. *Child Abuse Review*, 11, 137–152.

Wigmore, J. H. (1974). *Evidence in trials at common law*. Boston, MA: Little, Brown & Co.

Yarmey, A. D. (1979). *The psychology of eyewitness testimony*. New York: Free Press.

Zajac, R. & Cannan, P. (2009). Cross-examination of sexual assault complainants: a developmental comparison. *Psychiatry, Psychology and Law*. 16, S36–54.

Zajac, R. & Hayne, H. (2003). I don't think that's what *really* happened: The effect of cross-examination on the accuracy of children's reports. *Journal of Experimental Psychology: Applied*, 9, 187–195.

Zajac, R. & Hayne, H. (2006). The negative effect of cross-examination style questioning on children's accuracy: Older children are not immune. *Applied Cognitive Psychology*, *20*, 3–16.

Zajac, R., Gross, J. & Hayne, H. (2003). Asked and answered: Questioning children in the courtroom. *Psychiatry, Psychology and Law*, *10*, 199–209.

Zajac, R., Jury, E. & O'Neill, S. (in press). The role of psychosocial factors in young children's responses to cross-examination style questioning. *Applied Cognitive Psychology*.

Zaragoza, M. S. & Lane, S. (1994). Source misattributions and the suggestibility of eyewitness memory. *Journal of Experimental Psychology: Learning, Memory, and Cognition*, *20*, 934–945.

Chapter Eleven

Recovered Memories

James Ost

Department of Psychology
University of Portsmouth

When she was 27, Alice, a successful businesswoman, embarked upon a course of hypnotherapy to help her overcome an eating disorder. The hypnotherapist told her, 'You will start to remember things – things that you won't want to remember but they still come flooding back.' After six or seven sessions of hypnotherapy, Alice indeed began to recover memories of being sexually abused by her uncle sixteen years previously. Whilst Alice claimed to have always been aware that something was not right in her life, she also claimed that, prior to the hypnotherapy, she had had no memory of any episodes of abuse. (Ost, 2000: 10–15)

In the last 20 years psychologists were involved in the 'memory wars', one of the most contentious debates to date – contentious enough that Pezdek & Banks (1996: xii) refer to it as close to a 'religious war' (see also Brown, Goldstein & Bjorklund, 2000; Ost, 2003). The question that has caused such a divide in professional opinion concerns the extent to which memories, such as those 'recovered' by Alice, reflect events that actually occurred. Partly due to the uncertainties surrounding cases like these, the statutes of limitations, previously barring such cases from being tried in court, were lifted in many states in the USA (there are no time restrictions to bringing such charges under UK law). These changes enabled individuals like Alice to sue or bring criminal charges against their parents or other alleged abusers where the only evidence was previously 'repressed' or 'dissociated' memories of childhood abuse that

Handbook of Psychology of Investigative Interviewing: Current Developments and Future Directions
Edited by Ray Bull, Tim Valentine and Tom Williamson
© 2009 John Wiley & Sons, Ltd.

the individual had allegedly 'recovered' in adulthood (Loftus & Ketcham, 1994; Underwager & Wakefield, 1998). One problem with allowing such testimony is that there is, in fact, no reliable evidence that individuals 'repress' or 'dissociate' memories of traumatic events, although they may choose not to *report* such events (see McNally, 2003; cf. Brown, Scheflin & Hammond, 1998). A further problem is that research has shown that it is possible for people to come to report compelling and vivid 'memories' of events that did not happen (Porter, Yuille & Lehman, 1999). This raises the serious possibility that at least some of these 'recovered memories' might, in fact, be iatrogenic products of the therapeutic process itself – hence the term 'false memories'.

Indeed, there have been a number of high-profile malpractice cases in the USA where patients have taken legal action against their former therapists, accusing them of implanting 'false' memories of abuse, sometimes winning considerable damage settlements (see Loftus, 1997a). Furthermore, in one case an accused father was allowed, as a third party, to bring malpractice charges against his daughter's former therapist and was awarded $500,000 in damages (see Johnston, 1997). In a recent case in England, the General Medical Council (GMC) disciplined a general practitioner for using inappropriate questions and suggestions to lead a 13-year-old patient to believe falsely that she had been sexually assaulted (Catchpole, 2003). These, and other cases like them, highlight the importance of raising awareness amongst practitioners and policy-makers of the issues surrounding such cases in order that potential miscarriages of justice are avoided and that genuine victims of abuse receive the support they need. However, the issues are far from straightforward.

One concern is that claims of childhood abuse are sometimes made following, or during, an individual's participation in so-called 'recovered memory therapy'. Recovered memory therapy, although contentious to some, is a blanket term covering any therapeutic treatment in which the prime goal is to uncover repressed, dissociated or otherwise unavailable 'memories' of trauma, in order to resolve present-day psychological problems (Lindsay & Read, 1994; 2001). Professional opinion, however, is sharply divided over the risks associated with such therapy. On the one hand, there are researchers who claim that certain traumatic experiences are permanently stored in one form or another, that it is possible to revive 'memories' of these long-forgotten events and that such 'memories' are generally accurate (see Cameron, 1996; Freyd, 1998; Salter, 1998). If this argument is wrong, then families can be torn apart and individuals falsely branded as paedophiles and, sometimes, wrongly incarcerated (see Pendergrast, 1996; Brand, 2007) on the basis of such 'recovered memories'. On the other hand, there are researchers who claim that some 'recovered memories' arise as a result of inappropriate and highly suggestive therapeutic techniques (Lindsay & Read, 1994; 2001; Brandon *et al.*, 1997; Hyman & Loftus, 1997; Tsai, Loftus & Polage, 2000; Lynn, Lock, Loftus, Krackow & Lilienfeld, 2003; see also Hyman, 2000). But if this claim is wrong, the results are equally tragic, not only in individual cases, but also at a wider level. As Conway (1997) states, one concern is that genuine victims of childhood sexual assault will be less willing to come forward if there is a risk that their testimony may be dismissed as a case of 'false memory'. Despite the polarized nature of the debate there is some evidence that a middle ground is emerging (Read, 1999; Shobe & Schooler, 2001; Ost, 2003) with researchers on both sides acknowledging the possibility that some long-delayed claims of childhood abuse are genuine, whilst some are not.

In the early days, psychologists and other professionals were ill-equipped to answer questions about the veracity of these claims as there was only a handful of directly relevant studies (Wright, Ost & French, 2006). The aim of this chapter is to provide an overview of the research conducted over the last 20 years that has enabled psychologists to begin answering these questions. The first section addresses the question of whether people can 'repress' and then 'recover' memories of trauma. The second section focuses on whether people can come to falsely believe, or falsely remember, traumatic events that did not happen.

Can people repress or suppress memories of trauma?

The work of Sigmund Freud is usually credited as the source of the idea that the mind is somehow capable of blocking out memories of threatening, emotional and traumatic events, banishing them to a dark recess of the mind. Freud's term 'repression' is commonly used to explain why trauma survivors might have no memory for the events that they allegedly experienced. Despite continued efforts to demonstrate that repression occurs (e.g. Erdelyi, 2006) there is no convincing evidence for its existence (Kihlstrom, 2002; Loftus & Guyer, 2002a; 2002b; Hayne, Garry & Loftus, 2006). A second mechanism, dissociative amnesia, is also often cited to explain why people might not remember traumatic events. Initially credited to Pierre Janet (who later retracted the idea), dissociative amnesia allegedly occurs when the traumatic nature of the event leads people's consciousness to 'split', keeping the memory of the trauma out of conscious awareness. Some argue that, in extreme cases, this can lead to Dissociative Identity Disorder (formerly Multiple Personality Disorder) where these 'splits' in consciousness develop into full-blown *alter*-personalities (see Mollon, 1996). In this situation the 'core' personality would have no memory for the traumatic events stored in the *alter*-personality. However, rigorous critiques point strongly to the iatrogenic character of the disorder (Merckelbach, Devilly & Rassin, 2002), as well as the culture-bound nature of dissociative amnesia (Pope, Poliakoff, Parker, Boynes & Hudson, 2007).

So, while the existence of these two mechanisms is controversial at best, they nevertheless continue to have considerable influence in explaining alleged memory loss in survivors of trauma (Brown *et al.*, 1998). Why is this? One possibility, as McNally (2003) argues, is that an *unwillingness* to report trauma has been confused with an *inability* to do so. We know that some individuals with documented histories of trauma sometimes do not *report*, even when directly questioned, that they remember those events years later (e.g. Goodman *et al.*, 2003). Yet research strongly suggests that not *disclosing*, due to embarrassment, lack of rapport with the interviewer, consciously trying not to think about the events or ordinary processes of forgetting (Goodman *et al.*, 2003; McNally, 2006), rather than an *inability to remember*, is the most parsimonious explanation of such cases (Kihlstrom, 2002; McNally, 2006; Porter & Peace, 2007). If the non-disclosure of known trauma victims can be accounted for in terms of relatively 'ordinary' explanations (e.g., childhood amnesia or an *unwillingness* to report), then there is simply no reason to posit the existence of 'extraordinary mechanisms' of memory loss, such as repression or dissociative amnesia.

One 'ordinary' mechanism that might account for the *non-reporting* of some traumatic episodes is *suppression*. Suppression, which refers to our natural tendency to try to avoid thinking about unpleasant events, has been studied extensively by psychologists (see Wegner & Schneider, 2003). A recent line of research has examined whether *suppressing* memories of events can indeed lead to them becoming less accessible. This research, and the problematic interpretations that have been made as a result, will now be critically evaluated.

In 2001, Anderson and Green published a paper in *Nature* in which they claimed to have found strong evidence that the brain can suppress unpleasant memories. In their study, participants were first asked to learn sets of word pairs (e.g. ordeal–roach), so that presenting the cue word (e.g. ordeal) would lead participants to respond with the target word (e.g. roach). Next, participants were presented with the cue word of each pair followed by a cue either to 'remember' or 'forget' the target word. This is referred to as the Think/ No Think (T/NT) paradigm. In the final stage, participants were presented with all the cue words and asked to recall all the target words. Anderson & Green (2001) found that participants recalled fewer of the target words that they had been instructed to forget than the target words that they had been instructed to remember. This, they argued, was evidence that people can learn to selectively 'block out' certain memories. In a follow-up study, published in *Science*, Anderson *et al.* (2004) repeated the experiment. This time, however, whilst participants were attempting to 'remember' or 'forget' target words (e.g. roach) the experimenters used *f*MRI to measure participants' blood flow to different parts of the brain. As a result of this new experiment, Anderson *et al.* claimed that they had discovered which areas of the brain were responsible for the suppression of unwanted material.

So had Anderson and colleagues finally found concrete evidence that the mind can block out horrific events? Whilst some journalists appeared convinced (one headline in the UK read 'Freud proved'), psychologists were more circumspect (Garry & Loftus, 2004; Hayne *et al.*, 2006; Wade, 2007). Garry & Loftus (2004) pointed out several limitations with Anderson *et al.*'s findings. First, there are numerous theoretical and methodological problems with brain imaging techniques. For example, do increases in 'metabolic' activity (e.g.

blood flow) to an area of the brain necessarily indicate an increase in 'cognitive' activity? Do decreases in metabolic activity indicate decreases in 'cognitive activity'? At what point, statistically, do we conclude that one part of the brain has become 'more' or 'less' active? By creating an 'average' brain scan from the scans of different participants, are we running the risk of masking important individual differences in brain structure? Can we be sure that the brain areas identified are *facilitating* the processes under investigation (e.g. suppression), or could they be *inhibiting* another response? Brain imaging research is still in its infancy and many of these questions are a long way from being resolved. Thus any data derived from brain imaging studies need to be treated with caution (for detailed critiques, see Kagan, 2007; Uttal, 2001; see also Vul, Harris, Winkielman & Pashler, in press).

Secondly, and irrespective of methodological issues to do with brain scans, the effects of the T/NT paradigm appear to be quite fragile. As Garry & Loftus (2004) noted, the degree of suppression in the Anderson *et al.* experiments was not particularly severe – instructing participants to 'forget' the target word (e.g. roach) led to a 10% reduction in recall. This meant that participants still recalled about 80% of the target words. Importantly, another group of psychologists have failed to replicate these findings in three separate experiments (Bulevich, Roediger, Balota & Butler, 2006; Wade, 2007). Such a fragile effect is not convincing evidence that human being can block, consciously or unconsciously, entire autobiographical episodes from their memory.

Finally, the nature of the stimulus material used in these studies of *suppression* does not allow us to generalize to the kinds of traumas which allegedly results in *repression* or *dissociation*. Freudian repression and dissociative amnesia allegedly result in the blocking from awareness of traumatic, threatening and emotional information. As Garry & Loftus (2004) argued, word pairs (ordeal–roach) hardly mirror the impact of this kind of material. This last criticism was recently addressed by Depue, Banich & Curran (2006) in a replication and extension of Anderson *et al.*'s work. They examined whether the suppression effects found for word pairs would be replicated for more emotional material. Thus, rather than using words as both targets and cues, Depue *et al.* used faces as cues and either emotionally neutral or negative words, or pictures, as targets. Participants first practised recalling 40 face–word or face–picture pairs until they could recall them with a high level of accuracy (97%). They then took part in an experimental phase where they were shown 32 of the face cues. Sixteen of these face cues were paired with an instruction to 'think about' the associated word or picture targets, whilst the other 16 were paired with an instruction to 'not think about' the associated word or picture targets. For half of the face cues, these 'think' or 'no think' instructions were repeated five times and for the other half they were repeated ten times.

Depue and colleagues found that participants who were instructed to 'think' about the targets ten times recalled more of those targets in a final test than participants who were given the 'no think' instructions. Importantly, the 'no think' instructions led participants to recall fewer word or picture targets compared to baseline word or picture targets for which they had been given no instructions. The emotional nature of the stimuli also seemed to magnify the effect. Participants recalled more of the emotional word or picture cues after ten 'think' instructions than they did of the neutral word or picture cues. Similarly, participants recalled fewer of the emotional, compared to neutral, word or picture cues after the 'no think' instructions. Thus, according to Depue and colleagues, there is a 'cognitive control' process in the brain that deals differently with emotional and non-emotional memories. When emotional material is repeatedly processed (or thought about) it becomes more accessible than neutral material, but when emotional material is repeatedly suppressed (not thought about) it becomes less accessible. In a follow-up *f*MRI study, the authors also found evidence of two neural mechanisms which appear to be implicated in the suppression process (Depue, Curran & Banich, 2007).

So does this body of research provide evidence that people can suppress (avoid thinking about) unpleasant or traumatic events? The stark answer is no. The stimuli used in the Depue *et al.* studies represent an important methodological improvement over those used by Anderson and colleagues but still do not provide a good analogue for the experiences of people who have been sexually abused. The more serious problem with this body of research, however, is that it is cited as supporting evidence for the notion that people repress (i.e. are *unable* to remember) traumatic events. This is evident in the opening lines of Depue *et al.* (2007). The authors state that whilst there is evidence that people actively try to suppress memories, 'others claim that memory repression or suppression is a clinical myth in search of scientific support' (*ibid.*: 215).

This sleight of hand, in which *suppression* and *repression* were conflated, is problematic – the two terms are not interchangeable. Suppression refers to cases where people actively try *not to think about* something, usually with very limited degrees of success (Anderson & Green, 2001; Depue *et al.*, 2007). We've all had the experience of cringing and trying to distract ourselves when a memory for an embarrassing event suddenly comes to mind. Most of us try, often with limited success, not to think about events that upset us and psychological research shows that it is not a particularly effective strategy. This is mainly because the rule ('I must try not to think about *X*') contains the thing one is trying to forget. Thus, most of us cannot help but picture a white bear when explicitly instructed not to (Wegner, Schneider, Knutson & McMahon, 1991). Thus it comes as little surprise that, even when explicitly instructed to 'forget', most participants in the Anderson studies showed only a 10% reduction in recall. These are typical findings in studies of *suppression. Repression*, however, is when an individual is allegedly *unable to remember* something because the mind has unconsciously blocked out any memory of the event. Years of psychological research have indicated that this is indeed a 'clinical myth' (Kihlstrom, 2002; Hayne *et al.*, 2006; see also Loftus & Guyer, 2002a; 2002b, for a discussion of the case of Jane Doe in which an allegedly 'repressed' memory was 'recovered' during a videotaped interview). If participants in the

Anderson or Depue research have difficulty in suppressing non-traumatic words and pictures, it suggests that consciously or unconsciously 'forgetting' traumatic autobiographical events would be a far more difficult task (see McNally, 2003: 152).

Unfortunately, media reports of the Anderson and Depue work have provided the 'take home' message that the latest advances in technology are showing that people can *block out* memories of traumatic events (Highfield, 2007; Mundell, 2007). Most non-psychologists are, understandably, not alert to the critical distinction between *suppression* and *repression*. This has meant that the research findings concerning the former were sometimes interpreted, or presented, as evidence of the latter. One result of such misinterpretation is that it bolsters the belief that individuals are capable of unconsciously forgetting traumatic events. Individuals (therapists and their clients) may begin searching for evidence of such memories with the *a priori*, but misguided, conviction that they must be there to be discovered. One self-help book, for example, paradoxically claimed that the absence of a memory of abuse was evidence that a person had been abused (Blume, 1990). As psychological research has shown, this runs the risk of creating false beliefs or memories of events that never occurred. How and why such false memories and beliefs arise is the focus of the next section of this chapter.

Four main 'false memory' methods

There are four main methods that psychologists have used to examine the circumstances under which individuals might come to report events, or details of events, that they did not experience:

- the DRM method;
- the misinformation method;
- the 'crashing memories' method;
- the parental misinformation method.

As will be seen, there are strengths and weaknesses with each method. This means that these methods do not speak equally to the question of whether an individual can come to report that they remember an entirely false, autobiographical, emotionally-charged childhood event (see Smeets, Merckelbach, Horselenberg & Jelicic, 2005; Pezdek & Lam, 2007; Wade *et al.*, 2007). There is also a further problematic distinction concerning whether these methods are tapping into, or changing, *memories* of past events, *beliefs* about past events, *confidence* about whether a past event occurred or not or simply *reports* about past events (Smeets *et al.*, 2005; see also Ost, 2003; Loftus & Bernstein, 2005). Furthermore, whilst it has been argued that a false *belief* is an important and necessary precursor to developing a false *memory* (Gudjonsson, 2003), it does not follow that a false belief will always *lead* to a false memory (Ost, 2003). Therefore, some caution is warranted in interpreting these findings as a whole. Nevertheless, all four methods are cited in the literature as providing evidence that 'false memories' can occur. With these important caveats in mind, each method will now be critically examined.

The DRM method

Roediger & McDermott (1995) adapted a method previously developed by Deese (1959), referred to as the DRM method. In a typical study, participants are asked to remember a list of words, such as mad, fear, hate, rage, temper, fury, ire, wrath, happy, fight, hatred, mean, calm, emotion, enrage. Some time later, participants are recalled for a 'surprise' memory test and are asked to indicate whether the word 'anger' was contained in the original list. Many of them frequently report remembering the critical non-presented word (e.g. 'anger') as having been present in the original list. Several studies have successfully replicated this effect using various different experimental manipulations (e.g., Gallo, Roberts & Seamon, 1997; Brainerd & Reyna, 1998; Smith & Hunt, 1998). Roediger & McDermott (1995: 803) claim that the results of these studies 'reveal a powerful illusion of memory: people remember events that never happened', although there appears to be some confusion about what the term 'event' actually refers to in psychological research (see Freyd & Gleaves, 1996, and the reply by Roediger & McDermott, 1996).

There also appear to be individual differences that leave certain participants more likely to succumb to the DRM effect. For example, Winograd, Peluso & Glover (1998) found that participants who scored higher on measures of dissociation (high scorers have a tendency to experience problems in the integration of thoughts and feelings) and of vividness of mental imagery (high scorers report having more vivid imaginative abilities) were more likely to claim to remember the critical non-presented words. However, as Freyd & Gleaves (1996) note, there are important differences between misremembering words that have not been presented in a list, and misremembering an otherwise happy childhood as being abusive. Similarly, Wilkinson & Hyman (1998) demonstrated that in laboratory experiments there are important differences between participants' performance on word list tasks and their performance on autobiographical memory tasks. They found that self-reported dissociative tendencies were related to errors on both the word list and autobiographical memory tasks, but that self-reported vividness of mental imagery was only related to errors on the word list (DRM) task. Wilkinson & Hyman (1998) argue that this is because remembering words and remembering autobiographical events rely on different underlying psychological processes. They argue that it is therefore unwise to assume that participants who are susceptible to the DRM are also more vulnerable to developing false autobiographical memories.

The misinformation method

The second method that psychologists have used examines whether subtle changes in the way in which questions are asked about an event can change what participants subsequently claim to remember about that event. The classic studies of the misinformation effect, conducted by Loftus and colleagues, examined whether misleading post-event information could alter eyewitnesses' memories of events they had recently witnessed (Loftus, 1979). In two studies by Loftus & Palmer (1974) participants were shown a film of an accident involving two cars. Participants were then questioned to find out how much they could remember about the event. The question 'About how fast were the cars going when they *smashed* into each other' elicited higher estimates of speed than questions in which the verbs *collided*, *bumped*, *contacted* or *hit* were used (see also Loftus, Miller & Burns, 1978). This is a robust and easily replicated effect, although there is still disagreement as to the mechanisms that cause the misinformation effect (e.g., Bekerian & Bowers, 1983; McCloskey & Zaragoza, 1985; Zaragoza, McCloskey & Jamis, 1987; Weingardt, Loftus & Lindsay, 1995). Nevertheless it seems that subtle changes in wording can lead participants to report non-existent *details* of events that they have experienced (see also Nourkova, Bernstein & Loftus, 2004). However, it is also possible that such subtle changes in wording can lead individuals to report that they remember *entire events* that they did not witness.

The 'crashing memories' method

Crombag, Wagenaar & van Koppen (1996) asked participants whether they remembered seeing a film of a plane crashing into a block of flats in Amsterdam. No film of the crash existed so we can be sure that any participants who claimed to have seen it must be mistaken. Nevertheless, 55–66% of the respondents to Crombag *et al.*'s questionnaire claimed to have seen such a film. Participants were so convinced that they had seen it that they were willing to give details, such as the angle at which the plane hit the building, how long before fire broke out and how long it was before the emergency services arrived. Crombag *et al.* (1996) suggest that perhaps the vivid and emotionally-charged nature of the event led people to think about the event, picture it in their heads and then subsequently come to confuse the resulting imaginings as being real memories. This is referred to as a 'source monitoring' error and occurs when we misremember the source of information (Johnson, Hashtroudi & Lindsay, 1993).

Ost, Vrij, Costall & Bull (2002) replicated this effect using a different event – the car crash in Paris in which Diana, Princess of Wales, Dodi Fayed and the driver, Henri Paul, were killed. Whilst no film of the crash has ever been broadcast, there had been reports in the press that Diana's car was being pursued by paparazzi on motorbikes who were allegedly filming the chase. Ost *et al.* (2002) therefore asked participants whether they had seen the paparazzis' video recording of the moment of the crash on television. Whilst it has never been established whether such a film exists, it has certainly never been shown on television. Nevertheless, 44% of Ost *et al.*'s participants claimed to have seen it. Furthermore, many participants even went as far as to say on which television channel they had seen it. Ost *et al.* found that participants who scored higher on a measure of 'eagerness to please' (the self-monitoring scale; Snyder, 1974) were more like to claim to have seen the film than participants who scored lower on this measure.

In a replication of the Crombag *et al.* study, Granhag, Strömwall & Billings (2003) asked participants whether they had seen a (nonexistent) film of the sinking of the Estonia ferry. Again they found that 52% of their participants claimed to have seen the film. Granhag *et al.* (2003) were interested in whether these false reports were susceptible to social influence. Thus, in a novel twist, they had a confederate present when the participants completed the question-naire. This confederate either claimed to have seen the nonexistent film or claimed not to have seen it. Granhag *et al.* found that participants either increased, or decreased, their levels of false reporting in line with the social influence exerted by the confederate. When the confederate claimed to have seen the film, the number of participants also claiming to have seen it increased, and vice versa (see Ost, Hogbin & Granhag, 2006, for a replication).

The 'crashing memory' effect appears to be robust, with between 36% and 66% of participants in any given study claiming to have seen the nonexistent video footage (Jelicic, Smeets, Peters, Candel & Merckelbach, 2006; Wilson & French, 2006; but see Jelicic, Smeets, Candel, van Suijdam & Merckelbach, 2006). These rates, however, can be reduced by phrasing the misleading ques-tion in an unambiguous rather than ambiguous manner (i.e., asking about 'a' film, rather than 'the' film; Smeets *et al.*, 2006).

Parental misinformation method

The studies mentioned above show that some individuals will, when misled by subtle changes in wording, or by a confederate, come to report that they remember events, or details of events, that they did not witness. However, it is difficult to generalize these findings to cases of allegedly false or recovered memories of childhood events. The events in the Crombag *et al.*, Ost *et al.* and Granhag *et al.* studies were all relatively recent and had occurred whilst the participants in their studies were adults. In contrast, most delayed claims of childhood abuse concern events that, by definition, occurred many years beforehand (see Pendergrast, 1996). Can individuals be misled to report false events from their childhood?

Loftus & Coan (cited in Loftus & Pickrell, 1995) describe a study in which a 14-year-old boy, Chris, was asked to recall details over five days regarding four events involving family members. One of the events was false and other three were true (as verified by the family). Chris was interviewed in the pres-ence of a sibling (a confederate of the investigators) about these events. The sibling provided verbal corroboration that all the events (including the false event) had taken place. Over time Chris began to report more about the four events, even rating the false event (becoming lost in a shopping mall as a child) as more likely to have occurred than all but one of the three true events.

Loftus & Pickrell (1995) replicated this effect with a larger sample of undergraduate students. In this study participants were asked to complete a booklet concerning four events, the third of which was false (becoming lost in a shopping mall). Parents who confirmed that their child had never become lost in a shopping mall as a child also provided details of the three real events. Participants were interviewed three times over three weeks and also asked, between interviews, to write down in their booklets anything that came to mind about the events. Loftus & Pickrell (1995) found that after three weeks six out of 24 participants (25%) erroneously believed *part or all* of the false event. However, as Pezdek, Finger & Hodge (1997) argue, becoming lost in a shopping mall is a fairly common occurrence for which many people would have a 'script' (or 'schema'). Pezdek *et al.* contend that it would be relatively easy for an individual to create a convincing report of an event like this, although as Loftus (1997b: 180) argues, the important point is not that participants might be able to construct a general narrative of such an event, but that they report specific details suggested by the experimenter. In these studies participants 'were not asked about ANY experience of being lost. They were asked to remember being lost around the age of five, in a particular location, with particular people present, being frightened, and ultimately being rescued by an elderly person' (*ibid.*) In fact, Pezdek *et al.* (1997) demonstrated that an event that was lower in plausibility and for which participants were less likely to have 'script-relevant' knowledge (in this case receiving an enema as a child) was less likely to be implanted (although see Scoboria, Mazzoni, Kirsch & Relyea, 2004, for a discussion of plausibility).

Hyman, Husband & Billings (1995) attempted to address the criticisms of Pezdek *et al.* (1997) by suggesting to their participants that they had experienced more unusual events. Following the methodology devised by Loftus & Pickrell (1995) they asked their participants to try to remember three events (two of which had occurred and one of which had not). Hyman *et al.* conducted two studies in which they suggested that their participants had experienced one of the following false events when they were children:

- an overnight hospitalization with a suspected ear infection (study 1);
- a birthday party with a visit by a clown and pizza (study 1)
- spilling a punch bowl at a wedding (study 2);
- evacuating a grocery store when the sprinklers went off (study 2);
- releasing the handbrake of a car in a car park and colliding with something (study 2).

Their participants were interviewed three times over a three-week period and after each interview participants were asked to think about the events and try to remember more details before the next session. By the third and final interview 89–95% of the 'real' events were recalled along with 25% of the 'false' events (see also Hyman & Loftus, 1997). Thus, participants can be misled to report more unusual events from their childhood. However, critics argue that reporting that you remember spilling a punchbowl at a wedding does not compare to reporting that you remember being abused as a child – the latter is a much more negative, traumatic and emotionally-charged event. Nevertheless, one study has examined whether it is possible to mislead participants to report that they falsely remember negative, traumatic and emotionally-charged events from their childhood.

Porter *et al.* (1999), using a similar methodology to Loftus & Pickrell (1995) and Hyman *et al.* (1995), suggested to participants that they had experienced serious negative events as children, such as:

- a major medical procedure;
- getting lost;
- being seriously harmed by another child;
- a serious animal attack.

Porter *et al.* also verbally encouraged their participants to remember the events ('most people are able to retrieve lost memories if they try hard enough', Porter *et al.*, 1999: 522), as well as asking them to think about this for five minutes every night between interviews. By the third and final interview, Porter *et al.* found that 54% of participants reported a 'full' or a 'partial' false memory. In the final interview, Porter *et al.* (1999) also asked participants to deliberately fabricate an account of an event that did not occur. All three types of memory report (real, false and fabricated) were rated using a technique called the Memory Assessment Procedure (MAP) to investigate possible qualitative differences between them. Porter *et al.* found that real and fabricated memories were rated as more vivid, more coherent and were given higher confidence ratings than false memories. Fabricated memories were also rated as more stressful and contained more details than both real and false memories (Porter *et al.*, 1999; see also Pezdek & Talyor, 2000; Davies, 2001; Heaps & Nash, 2001; Loftus & Bernstein, 2005). Taken together, these studies indicate that, when misled by information provided by siblings or parents, participants will report that they remember unusual, negative, emotionally-charged and traumatic childhood events.

In the studies described above, some kind of verbal instructions was used to encourage participants to try to remember the events (the only exception to this is Hyman *et al.*, 1995, experiment 1). However, the extent to which, in the case of false reports of childhood events, the behaviour of the interviewer influenced the manner of recall is unclear. For example, Loftus & Pickrell (1995: 722) noted that 'the interviewers maintained a pleasant and friendly manner whilst pressing for details'. In order to explore the possible role of social pressure in the development of false memories Ost, Foster, Costall &

Bull (2005) followed a similar methodology to these previous studies, but trained their interviewers to interview in an appropriate and non-pressuring manner. Participants were asked about both positive and negative false events, similar to those used in previous studies, for example:

- becoming lost;
- a trip to the hospital;
- a serious accident;
- an eventful birthday party;
- winning a contest.

Levels of social pressure in the interviews were monitored by the participants (who were asked to rate, amongst other details, how pressured they felt to remember the event(s)) and by independent judges (who rated videotapes of the interviews). Overall levels of social pressure reported by both participants and independent judges were low. Despite the low levels of social pressure, Ost *et al.* (2005) found that seven out of 31 participants produced a 'full' or 'partial' report of a childhood event that did not occur. This study suggests that even minimal social pressure and repeated interviewing are sufficient to lead some individuals to come to report events from their childhood that never occurred.

Methodological limitations of parental misinformation studies.   There are several criticisms of the above studies that limit their generalizability to cases of delayed reports of childhood trauma. As already noted, Pezdek *et al.* (1997) argue that most of the false events that participants are asked to recall are events for which participants are likely to have a 'script'; an event that is lower in plausibility and for which participants are less likely to have 'script-relevant' knowledge (such as childhood sexual abuse) is less likely to be falsely reported.

Pezdek *et al.* (1997) tested this hypothesis by suggesting to Jewish and Catholic participants that they had taken part in both a Catholic ritual (receiving Communion) and a Jewish ritual (Shabbot), neither of which had actually occurred. Pezdek *et al.* (1997) argue that the plausibility of having taken part in a Catholic ritual would be low for Jewish participants, that they would have less script-relevant knowledge to draw on, and vice versa. They found, in line with their predictions, that seven of the Catholic participants but none of the Jewish participants reported the false Catholic event and three Jewish participants and one Catholic participant reported the Jewish false event. This shows that participants were more likely to remember the plausible false event than the implausible false event (i.e. Jewish participants were more likely to remember the false Jewish ritual than the false Catholic ritual). In a second experiment, Pezdek *et al.* (1997) replicated the study by Loftus & Pickrell (1995) and extended it by suggesting to participants that they had (a) been lost in a shopping mall (a plausible event) and (b) that they had received an enema as a child (an implausible event). Pezdek *et al.* (1997) found that whilst three out of 20 participants falsely reported becoming lost in a shopping mall, none of the participants falsely reported receiving an enema. These experiments, therefore, suggest that the probability that participants can be misled to report false events from their childhood is likely to be a function of the plausibility of, or familiarity with, the event concerned (although see Scoboria *et al.*, 2004, for a discussion of the differences between plausibility and script consistency).

However, certain 'scripts' are more familiar in our culture than might at first be imagined. Lynn & Pezzo (1994; cited in Lynn & Kirsch, 1996) found that participants were able to construct very convincing narratives of having been abducted by aliens even when given relatively little warning or further information. Lynn & Kirsch (1996) argue that narratives of alien abduction are so common in our culture that individuals are likely to have access to 'script-relevant' knowledge (see also Arndt & Greenberg, 1996). Given the large number of self-help books, media programmes, news articles and the like dealing with abuse, it is not inconceivable that some individuals could construct a false narrative of having been abused.

A second, often cited limitation with parental misinformation studies is that the events participants are misled to report are not of an abusive or traumatic nature. However, Porter *et al.* (1999) showed that participants could be misled to report negatively charged and traumatic events, such as being victim to a serious animal attack. Although untestable in the laboratory, the possibility remains that participants in situations other than a psychology experiment could be misled to report abusive events that did not occur (see also Hyman & Loftus, 1997). In fact, evidence from retractors (individuals who have repudiated their earlier claims of abuse) suggests that this does occur (see de Rivera, 1998; Ost, Costall & Bull, 2001; 2002; Ost & Nunkoosing, in press). Sometimes they became so convinced of the truth of their false beliefs that they initiated legal proceedings against their alleged abusers (de Rivera, 1998; Ost *et al.*, 2001; 2002). Worryingly, retractors reported that they experienced levels of social pressure and inappropriate questioning techniques not dissimilar to those that can lead to false confessions in police interrogations (Wrightsman & Kassin, 1993; Kassin, 1997; Ost, *et al.*, 2001; Gudjonsson, 2003).

A third limitation with parental misinformation studies is that it is not clear what degree of social pressure is required in order to lead participants to make false claims about the past (Ost *et al.*, 2005). For example, as mentioned above, Loftus & Pickrell (1995: 722) note that their interviewer 'maintained a pleasant and friendly manner, whilst pressing for details' yet do not provide details of how participants were 'pressed for details'. Porter *et al.* (1999) also state that they employed a degree of verbal encouragement ('most people can remember details if they try really hard', p. 522). Malinoski & Lynn (1999) found that positive verbal encouragement led participants to report earlier (and more implausible) memories. Ost *et al.* (2005) found that, even when social pressure was kept to a minimum (by appropriately training interviewers not to pressure participants), a number of participants still reported false events from their childhood (see also Erdmann, Volbert & Böhm, 2004, for similar findings with child witnesses). The role of social pressure in the genesis and development of false reports of childhood events is an important avenue for future research (Ost *et al.* 2001; 2005).

A final limitation of the parental misinformation studies is that they rely on parents or siblings to verify that certain events did, or did not, occur to participants when they were children. This may be unwise. Whilst it is probable that parents will be able to remember events in the lives of their young children with more confidence than the children themselves (see Ost *et al.*, 2005), this in itself is no guarantee that they will remember them with great accuracy (Conte, 1999). Indeed, in Ost *et al.* (2005), a few participants stated outright that their parents must have misremembered events or confused the participant with another sibling. Indeed, there is literature to suggest that parents are not the best at remembering events from their children's past (Wenar, 1961; Wenar & Coulter, 1962; see also Halverson, 1988). The problem, then, is that there is no way of knowing the 'ground truth' (i.e., whether an event did, or did not, occur) with any great certainty (Goff & Roediger, 1998).

As a result, psychologists have developed novel methodologies that do not rely on obtaining information from outside sources. Garry, Manning, Loftus & Sherman (1996) devised one such methodology. They asked participants to complete a Life Events Inventory (LEI) which asked them to indicate the *likelihood* that a list of 40 events (e.g. 'got in trouble for calling 911'; 'broke a window with your hand') had happened to them before the age of ten. Participants were asked to provide a rating for each event on a scale from 1 ('definitely did not happen') to 8 ('definitely did happen'). Two weeks later participants were asked to imagine some of the events (including some that had been given a rating of 'definitely did not happen') and answer questions about them. These events were referred to as 'critical items'. Participants were then asked to complete the LEI again (on the pretext that the original had been lost). Garry *et al.* (1996) found that the *likelihood* ratings were more likely to change for critical items compared to those that had not been imagined. Garry *et al.* (1996) concluded that the mere act of imagining a false event increased participants' subjective confidence that it had occurred.

This is known as the *imagination inflation* effect and it appears to be robust. It occurs when participants are asked to imagine recent events (Goff & Roediger, 1998) as well as implausible and bizarre events (Mazzoni, Loftus & Kirsch, 2001; Thomas & Loftus, 2002; Pezdek, Blandon-Gitlin & Gabbay, 2006). For example, in a recent experiment, participants were asked to perform, or imagine performing, familiar ('check the Pepsi machine for change') or bizarre ('propose marriage to the Pepsi machine') actions during a campus walk. Two weeks later, some participants misremembered performing both familiar and unfamiliar actions that they had, in fact, only imagined themselves doing (Seamon, Philbin & Harrison, 2006). However, critics question whether the changes in likelihood ratings are because participants have developed genuine false beliefs or whether they are the result of regression towards the mean. This is a statistical artefact where extreme scores on a measure (i.e., 'definitely did not happen') are likely, by chance alone, to become less extreme (i.e., 'possibly might have happened') when that measure is taken a second time (Pezdek & Eddy, 2001; see reply by Garry, Sharman, Wade, Hunt & Smith, 2001).

A second innovative paradigm is called the *false feedback* method (Bernstein, Laney, Morris & Loftus, 2005; Laney, Morris, Bernstein, Wakefield & Loftus, 2008). In *false feedback* studies, participants are asked to complete a questionnaire about their food preferences. This questionnaire is then fed into a computer for analysis, but the results of the analysis are, in fact, bogus. When the results of the questionnaire are interpreted, the experimenter tells that participant that the computer analysis indicates that, as a child, the participant got sick after eating too much of a certain food (either eggs or dill pickles). Bernstein and colleagues found that participants who were given this false feedback were more confident that this event had indeed happened than control participants (Bernstein *et al.*, 2005).

Ongoing challenges in false memory research

Despite all the advances made in recent years there is still a number of lingering issues that need to be resolved. The first is that it difficult to be sure whether we are really implanting false *memories* in laboratory studies. The difficulty is that any number of intervening processes could produce the same output (in this case a claim to 'remember'). It could be due to a report bias – a tendency to say 'yes'. It could be due to increases in subjective confidence – being more confident that an event *could have* occurred. It could be due to holding a genuine belief that the event occurred in the absence of a clear memory of the event (Ost, 2003) or it could be due to having developed a clear, yet inaccurate, memory of the alleged event(s). There is certainly evidence that some individuals will embellish suggested false beliefs with details from their own autobiography (see Bernstein *et al.*, 2005). There is also evidence that participants develop fairly detailed false recollections of events that are suggested to them (Bernstein *et al.*, 2005; Ost, Granhag, Udell & Roos af Hjelmstäter, 2008). One current challenge, then, is to investigate which of these processes are responsible for a given output and the manner in which these processes are related – in other words, how a belief becomes a fully-fledged memory (Mazzoni & Kirsch, 2002; Scoboria, Mazzoni, Kirsch & Relyea, 2004; Ost *et al.*, 2008).

The second, related, concern centres on the likely consequence of false beliefs or memories (Smeets *et al.*, 2005). Whilst there is evidence that recovering abuse memories has serious and negative impacts on people's lives

(Loftus, 1997a), it is difficult to establish whether participants in psychological experiments continue to accept the truth of the implanted beliefs or memories once they have left the laboratory. As Smeets and colleagues point out, one measure of how much someone has truly accepted a suggestion is the extent to which they would be prepared to change their behaviour as a result of that suggestion. Recently, psychologists have begun to tackle this question. In Bernstein *et al.*'s (2005) false feedback study, participants were give a questionnaire about an imaginary barbecue which asked them to indicate which kinds of food they would be likely to eat. They found participants who believed the false feedback about becoming sick as a child after eating too many eggs or pickles indicated that they would be less likely to choose to eat those foods than those who did not believe the feedback. Thus, this experiment demonstrates that false feedback about the likelihood of past events can influence later behaviour but, importantly, only for those participants who *believe* the feedback. In a novel twist, Laney, Morris, Bernstein, Wakefield & Loftus (2008) found that the same kind of false feedback could be used to positive effect to convince participants that, as a child, they really enjoyed eating a healthy food – in this case, asparagus.

Finally, there are concerns over the definition of the subject matter. The research on false memory has grown almost exponentially over the past few years. Pezdek & Lam (2007) analysed the psychological literature and demonstrated that, although the number of studies referring to 'false memory' increased, the proportion of them dealing with memories of entire events (e.g., 'rich' false memories) has remained low (13%). The highest proportion of studies referred to as 'false memory' in fact deals with the DRM word list paradigm (42%) (see also DePrince, Allard, Oh & Freyd, 2004). Pezdek & Lam (2007) questioned whether these DRM experiments are really studies of 'false memory' in any meaningful sense or whether they should be referred to as 'memory flaws' (see Wade *et al.*, 2007, for a rebuttal).

Conclusion

The psychological research presented in this chapter has shown that, under certain circumstances outside of therapy (e.g. repeated suggestive interviewing in a psychological laboratory), people will come to report that they remember events that did not occur. Further research is needed to examine what it is about these people, or the circumstances in which they find themselves, that leads them to make false memory reports, which can be vivid and compelling, yet entirely inaccurate. Practitioners and policy-makers therefore need to be sensitive to these issues if we are to deal appropriately with cases like Alice's, to prevent future miscarriages of justice and to ensure that genuine victims of abuse receive the support they need.

Acknowledgements

My thanks to Kimberley Wade for constructive comments on a draft of this chapter, part of which was published as Ost, J. & Wade, K. (2007). Can we forget bad memories? *British False Memory Society Newsletter, 15,* 4–8.

References

Anderson, M. C. & Green, C. (2001). Suppressing unwanted memories by executive control. *Nature, 410,* 366–369.

Anderson, M. C., Ochsner, K. N., Kuhl, B., Cooper, J., Robertson, E., Gabrieli, S. W., Glover, G. H. & Gabrieli, J. D. E. (2004). Neural systems underlying the suppression of unwanted memories. *Science, 303,* 232–235.

Arndt, J. & Greenberg, J. (1996). Fantastic accounts can take many forms: False memory construction? Yes. Escape from self? We don't think so. *Psychological Inquiry, 7,* 127–132.

Bekerian, D. A. & Bowers, J. M. (1983). Eyewitness testimony: Were we misled? *Journal of Experimental Psychology: Learning, Memory, and Cognition, 9,* 139–145.

Bernstein, D. M., Laney, C., Morris, E. K. & Loftus, E. F. (2005). False memories about food can lead to food avoidance. *Social Cognition, 23,* 11–34.

Blume, E. (1990). *Secret survivors: Uncovering incest and its after-effects in women.* New York: John Wiley & Sons.

Brainerd, C. J. & Reyna, V. F. (1998). When things that were never experienced are easier to 'remember' than things that were. *Psychological Science, 9,* 484–489.

Brand, N. (Ed.) (2007). *Fractured families: The untold anguish of the falsely accused.* Bradford-on-Avon: BFMS.

Brandon, S., Boakes, J., Glaser, D., Green, R., MacKeith, J. & Whewell, P. (1997). Reported recovered memories of child sexual abuse: Recommendations for good practice and implications for training, continuing professional development and research. *Psychiatric Bulletin, 21,* 663–665.

Brown, D., Scheflin, A. W. & Hammond, D. C. (1998). *Memory, trauma treatment, and the law.* New York: W. W. Norton.

Brown, R., Goldstein, E. & Bjorklund, D. F. (2000). The history and zeitgeist of the repressed-false-memory debate: Scientific and sociological perspectives on sug-gestibility. In D. F. Bjorklund (Ed.), *False memory creation in children and adults* (pp. 1–30). Mahwah, NJ: Lawrence Erlbaum.

Bulevich, J. B., Roediger, H. L., Balota, D. A. & Butler, A. C. (2006). Failures to find suppression of episodic memories in the think/no-think paradigm. *Memory & Cognition, 34,* 1569–1577.

Cameron, C. (1996). Comparing amnesic and nonamnesic survivors of childhood sexual abuse: A longitudinal study. In K. Pezdek & W. P. Banks (Eds.), *The recovered memory/false memory debate* (pp. 41–68). San Diego: Academic Press.

Catchpole, Z. (2003). Doctor led his patient to make sex claims. *The Daily Mail,* 9 September.

Conte, J. R. (1999). Memory, research, and the law: Future directions. In L. M. Williams & V. L. Banyard (Eds.), *Trauma and memory* (pp. 77–92). Thousand Oaks, CA: Sage Publications.

Conway, M. A. (1997). *Recovered memories and false memories*. Oxford: Oxford University Press.

Crombag, H. F. M., Wagenaar, W. A. & van Koppen, P. J. (1996). Crashing memories and the problem of 'source monitoring'. *Applied Cognitive Psychology, 10,* 95–104.

Davies, G. M. (2001). Is it possible to discriminate between true and false memories? In G. M. Davies & T. Dalgleish (Eds.), *Recovered memories: Seeking the middle ground* (pp. 153–174). Chichester: John Wiley & Sons.

de Rivera, J. (1998). Relinquishing believed-in imaginings: Narratives of people who have repudiated false accusations. In J. de Rivera & T. R. Sarbin (Eds.), *Believed-in imaginings: The narrative reconstruction of reality* (pp. 169–188). Washington, DC: American Psychological Association.

Deese, J. (1959). On the prediction of occurrence of particular verbal intrusions in immediate recall. *Journal of Experimental Psychology, 58,* 17–22.

DePrince, A. P., Allard, C. B., Oh, H. & Freyd, J. J. (2004). What's in a name for memory errors? Implications and ethical issues arising from the use of the term 'false memory' for errors in memory for details. *Ethics & Behavior, 14,* 201–233.

Depue, B. E., Banich, M. T. & Curran, T. (2006). Suppression of emotional and nonemotional content in memory. Effects of repetition on cognitive control. *Psychological Science, 17,* 441–447.

Depue B. E, Curran T. & Banich M. T. (2007). Prefrontal regions orchestrate suppression of emotional memories via a two-phase process. *Science, 317,* 215–219.

Erdelyi, M. H. (2006). The unified theory of repression. *Behavioral and Brain Sciences, 29,* 499–551.

Erdmann, K., Volbert, R. & Böhm, C. (2004). Children report suggested events even when interviewed in a non-suggestive manner: what are its implications for credibility assessment? *Applied Cognitive Psychology, 18,* 589–611.

Freyd, J. J. (1998). Science in the memory debate. *Ethics & Behavior, 8,* 101–113.

Freyd, J. J. & Gleaves, D. H. (1996). 'Remembering' words not presented in lists: Relevance to the current recovered/false memory controversy. *Journal of Experimental Psychology: Learning, Memory, and Cognition, 22,* 811–813.

Gallo, D. A., Roberts, M. J. & Seamon, J. G. (1997). Remembering words not presented in lists: Can we avoid creating false memories? *Psychonomic Bulletin and Review, 4,* 271–276.

Garry, M. & Loftus, E. G. (2004). I am Freud's brain. *Skeptical Inquirer*, May/June, 16–18.

Garry, M., Manning, C. G., Loftus, E. F. & Sherman, S. J. (1996). Imagination inflation: Imagining a childhood event inflates confidence that it occurred. *Psychological Bulletin and Review, 3,* 208–214.

Garry, M., Sharman, S. J., Wade. K. A., Hunt, M. J. & Smith, P. J. (2001). Imagination inflation is a fact, not an artifact. *Memory and Cognition, 29,* 719–729.

Goff, L. M. & Roediger, H. L. (1998). Imagination inflation for action events: Repeated imaginings lead to illusory recollections. *Memory and Cognition, 26,* 20–33.

Goodman, G. S., Ghetti, S., Quas, J. A., Edelstein, R. S., Alexander, K. W., Redlich, A. D., Cordon, I. M. & Jones, D. P. H. (2003). A prospective study of memory for child sexual abuse: New findings relevant to the repressed-memory controversy. *Psychological Science, 14,* 113–118.

Granhag, P-A., Strömwall, L. & Billings, F. J. (2003). 'I'll never forget the sinking ferry': How social influence makes false memories surface. In M. Vanderhallen, G. Vervaeke, P. J. van Koppen & J. Goethals (Eds.), *Much ado about crime: Chapters on psychology and law* (pp. 129–140). Belgium: Uitgeverij Politeia.

Gudjonsson, G. H. (2003). *The psychology of interrogations and confessions.* Chichester: Wiley.

Halverson, C. F. (1988). Remembering your parents: Reflections on the retrospective method. *Journal of Personality, 56,* 435–443.

Hayne, H., Garry, M. & Loftus, E. F. (2006). On the continuing lack of evidence for repressed memories. *Behavioral and Brain Sciences, 29,* 521–522.

Heaps, C. M. & Nash, M. (2001). Comparing recollective experience in true and false autobiographical memories. *Journal of Experimental Psychology: Learning, memory, and cognition, 27,* 920–930.

Highfield, R. (2007). How to forget bad memories. *Daily Telegraph,* 13 July, p. 10.

Hyman, I. E. (2000). The memory wars. In U. Neisser & I. E. Hyman (Eds.), *Memory observed: Remembering in natural contexts,* 2nd edition (pp. 374–379). New York: Worth Publishers.

Hyman, I. E. & Loftus, E. F. (1997). Some people recover memories of childhood trauma that never really happened. In P. S. Applebaum, L. A. Uyehara & M. R. Elin (Eds.), *Trauma and memory: Clinical and legal controversies* (pp. 3–24). New York: Oxford University Press.

Hyman, I. E., Husband, T. H. & Billings, F. J. (1995). False memories of childhood experiences. *Applied Cognitive Psychology, 9,* 181–197.

Jelicic, M., Smeets, T., Candel, I., van Suijdam, M. & Merckelbach, H. (2006). No, I don't remember seeing video footage of the killing of Theo van Gogh! Misinformation manipulations do not always elicit false memories. In K. Nixon (Ed.), *Forensic recall and eyewitness testimony* (pp. 21–25). London: IA-IP Publishing.

Jelicic, M., Smeets, T., Peters, M. J. V., Candel, I., Horselenberg, R. & Merckelbach, H. (2006). Assassination of a controversial politician: Remembering details from another non-existent film. *Applied Cognitive Psychology, 20,* 591–596.

Johnson, M. K, Hashtroudi, S. & Lindsay, D. S. (1993). Source monitoring. *Psychological Bulletin, 114,* 3–28.

Johnston, M. (1997). *Spectral evidence.* Boulder, CO: Westview Press.

Kagan, J. (2007). A trio of concerns. *Perspectives on Psychological Science, 2,* 361–376.

Kassin, S. M. (1997). False memories turned against the self. *Psychological Inquiry, 8,* 300–302.

Kihlstrom, J. F. (2002). No need for repression. *Trends in Cognitive Sciences, 6,* 502.

Laney, C., Morris, E. K., Bernstein, D. M., Wakefield, B. M. & Loftus, E. F. (2008). Asparagus, a love story: Healthier eating could be just a false memory away. *Experimental Psychology, 55,* 291–300.

Lindsay, D. S. & Read, J. D. (1994). Psychotherapy and memories of childhood sexual abuse: A cognitive perspective. *Applied Cognitive Psychology, 8,* 281–338.

Lindsay, D. S. & Read, J. D. (2001). The recovered memories controversy: Where do we go from here? In G. M. Davies & T. Dalgleish (Eds.), *Recovered memories: Seeking the middle ground* (pp. 71–94). Chichester, UK: John Wiley & Sons.

Loftus, E. F. (1979). *Eyewitness testimony.* Cambridge, MA: Harvard University Press.

Loftus, E. F. (1997a). Repressed memory accusations: Devastated families and devastated patients. *Applied Cognitive Psychology, 11,* 25–30.

Loftus, E. F. (1997b). Dispatch from the (un)civil memory wars. In J. D. Read & D. S. Lindsay (Eds.), *Recollections of trauma: Scientific evidence and clinical practice* (pp. 171–194). New York: Plenum.

Loftus, E. F. & Bernstein, D. M. (2005). Rich false memories: The royal road to success. In A. F. Healy (Ed.), *Experimental cognitive psychology and its applications* (pp. 101–113). Washington DC: American Psychological Association Press.

Loftus, E. F. & Guyer, M. (2002a). Who abused Jane Doe? The hazards of the single case history (Part I). *Skeptical Inquirer, 26,* 24–32.

Loftus, E. F. & Guyer, M. J. (2002b). Who abused Jane Doe? (Part II). *Skeptical Inquirer, 26,* 37–40.

Loftus, E. F. & Ketcham, K. (1994). *The myth of repressed memory: False memories and allegations of sexual abuse.* New York: St. Martin's Press.

Loftus, E. F. & Palmer, J. C. (1974). Reconstruction of automobile destruction: An example of the interaction between language and memory. *Journal of Verbal Learning and Verbal Behavior, 13,* 585–589.

Loftus, E. F. & Pickrell, J. E. (1995). The formation of false memories. *Psychiatric Annals, 25,* 720–725.

Loftus, E. F., Miller, D. G. & Burns, H. J. (1978). Semantic integration of verbal information into a visual memory. *Journal of Experimental Psychology: Human Learning and Memory, 4,* 19–31.

Lynn, S. J. & Kirsch, I. I. (1996). Alleged alien abductions: False memories, hypnosis, and fantasy proneness. *Psychological Inquiry, 7,* 151–155.

Lynn, S. J., Lock, T. G., Loftus, E. F., Krackow, E. & Lilienfeld, S. O. (2003). The remembrance of things past: Problematic memory recovery techniques in psychotherapy. In S. O. Lilienfeld, S. J. Lynn & J. M. Lohr (Eds.), *Science and pseudoscience in clinical psychology* (pp. 205–239). New York: The Guilford Press.

Malinoski, P. T. & Lynn, S. J. (1999). The plasticity of early memory reports: Social pressure, hypnotizability, compliance, and interrogative suggestibility. *The International Journal of Clinical and Experimental Hypnosis, 47,* 320–345.

Mazzoni, G. & Kirsch, I. (2002). Autobiographical memories and beliefs: A preliminary metacognitive model. In T. Perfect & B. Schwartz (Eds.), *Applied metacognition* (pp. 121–145). Cambridge: Cambridge University Press.

Mazzoni, G. A. L., Loftus, E. F. & Kirsch, I. (2001). Changing beliefs about implausible autobiographical events: A little plausibility goes a long way. *Journal of Experimental Psychology: Applied, 7,* 51–59.

McCloskey, M. & Zaragoza, M. (1985). Misleading postevent information and memory for events: Arguments and evidence against memory impairment hypotheses. *Journal of Experimental Psychology: General, 114,* 1–16.

McNally, R. J. (2003). *Remembering trauma.* Cambridge, MA: Harvard University Press.

McNally, R. J. (2006). Cognitive abnormalities in post-traumatic stress disorder. *Trends in Cognitive Science, 10,* 271–277.

Merckelbach, H., Devilly, G. J. & Rassin, E. (2002). Alters in dissociative identity disorder: Metaphors or genuine entities? *Clinical Psychology Review, 22,* 481–497.

Mollon, P. (1996). *Multiple selves, multiple voices: Working with trauma, violation and dissociation.* Chichester: John Wiley & Sons.

Mundell, E. J. (2007). Brain may be able to suppress memories. *Washington Post,* 12 July. from http://www.washingtonpost.com/wp-dyn/content/article/2007/ 07/12/ AR2007071201202_2.html. Accessed 14 August 2007.

Nourkova, V., Bernstein, D. M. & Loftus, E. F. (2004). Altering traumatic memory. *Cognition & Emotion, 18,* 575–585.

Ost, J. (2000). Recovering memories: Convergent approaches toward an understanding of the false memory debate. Unpublished doctoral thesis. University of Portsmouth.

Ost, J. (2003). Essay review: Seeking the middle ground in the 'memory wars'. *British Journal of Psychology, 94,* 125–139.

Ost, J. & Nunkoosing, K. (in press). Reconstructing Bartlett and revisiting the 'false memory' controversy. In J. Haaken & P. Reavey (Eds.), *Memory matters: Understanding contexts for recollecting child sexual abuse.* London: Routledge.

Ost, J. & Wade, K. (2007). Can we forget bad memories? *British False Memory Society Newsletter, 15,* 4–8.

Ost, J., Costall, A. & Bull, R. (2001). False confessions and false memories? A model for understanding retractors' experiences? *The Journal of Forensic Psychiatry, 12,* 549–579.

Ost, J., Costall, A. & Bull, R. (2002). A perfect symmetry? A study of retractors' experiences of making and repudiating claims of early sexual abuse. *Psychology, Crime & Law, 8,* 155–181.

Ost, J., Vrij, A., Costall, A. & Bull, R. (2002). Crashing memories and reality monitoring: distinguishing between perceptions, imaginings and false memories. *Applied Cognitive Psychology, 16,* 125–134.

Ost, J., Foster, S., Costall, A. & Bull, R. (2005). False reports of childhood events in appropriate interviews. *Memory, 13,* 700–710.

Ost, J., Hogbin, I. & Granhag, P-A. (2006). Altering false reports via confederate influence. *Social Influence, 1,* 105–116.

Ost, J., Granhag, P-A., Udell, J. & Roos af Hjelmsäter, E. (2008). Familiarity breeds distortion: The effects of media exposure on false reports concerning the media coverage of the terrorist attacks in London on 7th July 2005. *Memory, 16,* 76–85.

Pendergrast, M. (1996). *Victims of memory: Incest accusations and shattered lives,* 2nd edition. Hinesburg, VT: Upper Access.

Pezdek, K. & Banks, W. P. (1996). Preface. In K. Pezdek & W. P. Banks (Eds.), *The recovered memory/false memory debate* (pp. xi–xv). San Diego: Academic Press.

Pezdek, K. & Eddy, R. M. (2001). Imagination inflation: A statistical artifact of regression toward the mean. *Memory and Cognition, 29,* 707–718.

Pezdek, K. & Lam, S. (2007). What research paradigms have cognitive psychologists used to study 'false memory,' and what are the implications of these choices? *Consciousness & Cognition, 16,* 2–17.

Pezdek, K. & Taylor, J. (2000). Discriminating between accounts of true and false events. In D. F. Bjorklund (Ed.), *False memory creation in children and adults: Theory, research, and implications* (pp. 69–91). Mahwah, NJ: Lawrence Erlbaum.

Pezdek, K., Finger, K. & Hodge, D. (1997). Planting false childhood memories: The role of event plausibility. *Psychological Science*, 8, 437–441.

Pezdek, K., Blandon-Gitlin, I. & Gabbay, P. (2006). Imagination and memory: Does imagining implausible events lead to false autobiographical memories? *Psychonomic Bulletin & Review*, 13, 764–769.

Pope, H. G. Jr., Poliakoff, M. B., Parker, M. P., Boynes, M. & Hudson, J. I. (2007). Is dissociative amnesia a culture-bound syndrome? Findings from a survey of historical literature. *Psychological Medicine*, 37, 225–233.

Porter, S. & Peace, K. (2007). The scars of memory: A prospective, longitudinal investigation of the consistency of traumatic and positive emotional memories in adulthood. *Psychological Science*, 18, 435–441.

Porter, S., Yuille, J. C. & Lehman, D. R. (1999). The nature of real, implanted, and fabricated memories for emotional childhood events: Implications for the recovered memory debate. *Law and Human Behavior*, 23, 517–537.

Read, J. D. (1999). The recovered/false memory debate: Three steps forward, two steps back? *Expert Evidence*, 7, 1–24.

Roediger, H. L. & McDermott, K. B. (1995). Creating false memories: Remembering words not presented in lists. *Journal of Experimental Psychology: Learning, Memory, and Cognition*, 21, 803–814.

Roediger, H. L. & McDermott, K. B. (1996). False perceptions of false memories. *Journal of Experimental Psychology: Learning, Memory, and Cognition*, 22, 814–816.

Salter, A. C. (1998). Confessions of a whistle-blower: Lessons learned. *Ethics & Behavior*, 8, 115–124.

Scoboria, A., Mazzoni, G., Kirsch, I. & Relyea, M. (2004). Plausibility and belief in autobiographical memory. *Applied Cognitive Psychology*, 18, 791–807.

Seamon, J. G., Philbin, M. M. & Harrison, L. G. (2006). Do you remember proposing marriage to the Pepsi machine? False recollections from a campus walk. *Psychonomic Bulletin & Review*, 13, 752–756.

Shobe, K. K. & Schooler, J. W. (2001). Discovering fact and fiction: Case-based analyses of authentic and fabricated discovered memories of abuse. In G. M. Davies & T. Dalgleish (Eds.), *Recovered memories: Seeking the middle ground* (pp. 95–151). Chichester: John Wiley & Sons.

Smeets, T., Merckelbach, H., Horselenberg, R. & Jelicic, M. (2005). Trying to recollect past events: Confidence, beliefs, and memories. *Clinical Psychology Review*, 25, 917–934.

Smeets, T., Jelicic, M., Peters, M. J. V., Candel, I., Horselenberg, R. & Merckelbach, H. (2006). 'Of course I remember seeing that film!' – How ambiguous questions generate crashing memories. *Applied Cognitive Psychology*, 20, 779–789.

Smith, R. E. & Hunt, R. R. (1998). Presentation modality affects false memory. *Psychonomic Bulletin and Review*, 5, 710–715.

Snyder, M. (1974). The self-monitoring of expressive behavior. *Journal of Personality and Social Psychology*, 30, 526–537.

Thomas, A. K. & Loftus, E. F. (2002). Creating bizarre false memories through imagination. *Memory and Cognition*, 30, 423–431.

Tsai, A., Loftus, E. F. & Polage, D. (2000). Current directions in false memory research. In D. F. Bjorklund (Ed.), *False memory creation in children and adults: Theory, research and implications* (pp. 31–44). Mahwah, NJ: Lawrence Erlbaum.

Underwager, R. & Wakefield, H. (1998). Recovered memories in the courtroom. In S. J. Lynn & K. M. McConkey (Eds.), *Truth in memory* (pp. 394–434). New York: Guilford Press.

Uttal, W. R. (2001). *The new phrenology: The limits of localizing cognitive processes in the brain.* Cambridge, MA: MIT Press.

Vul, E., Harris, C., Winkielman, P., Pashler, H. (in press). Puzzlingly high correlations in fMRI studies of emotion, personality, and social cognition. *Perspective on Psychological Science.*

Wade, K. A. (2007). What is known about recovered memories? *False Memory Syndrome Foundation Newsletter, 16,* Spring. http://www.fmsfonline.org/newsletters.html. Accessed 14 August 2007.

Wade, K. A., Sharman, S. J., Garry, M., Memon, A., Mazzoni G., Merckelbach, H. & Loftus, E. F. (2007). False claims about false memory research. *Consciousness & Cognition, 16,* 18–28.

Wegner, D. M. & Schneider, D. J. (2003). The white bear story. *Psychological Inquiry, 14,* 326–329.

Wegner, D. M., Schneider, D. J., Knutson, B. & McMahon, S. R. (1991). Polluting the stream of consciousness: The effect of thought suppression on the mind's environment. *Cognitive Therapy and Research, 15,* 141–152.

Weingardt, K. R., Loftus, E. F. & Lindsay, D. S. (1995). Misinformation revisited: New evidence on the suggestibility of memory. *Memory and Cognition, 23,* 72–82.

Wenar, C. (1961). The reliability of mothers' histories. *Child Development, 32,* 491–500.

Wenar, C. & Coulter, J. B. (1962). A reliability study of developmental histories. *Child Development, 33,* 453–462.

Wilkinson, C. & Hyman, I. E. (1998). Individual differences related to two types if memory errors: Word lists may not generalize to autobiographical memory. *Applied Cognitive Psychology, 12,* S29–S46.

Wilson, K. & French, C. C. (2006). The relationship between susceptibility to false memories, dissociativity, and paranormal belief and experience. *Personality and Individual Differences, 41,* 1493–1502.

Winograd, E., Peluso, J. P. & Glover, T. A. (1998). Individual differences in susceptibility to memory illusions. *Applied Cognitive Psychology, 12,* S5–S27.

Wright, D. B., Ost, J. & French, C. C. (2006). Ten years after: What we know now that we didn't know then about recovered and false memories. *The Psychologist, 19,* 352–355.

Wrightsman, L. S. & Kassin, S. M. (1993). *Confessions in the courtroom.* London: Sage.

Zaragoza, M. S., McCloskey, M. & Jamis, M. (1987). Misleading postevent information and recall of the original event: Further evidence against the memory impairment hypothesis. *Journal of Experimental Psychology: Learning, Memory, and Cognition, 13,* 36–44.

Chapter Twelve

Obtaining and Interpreting Eyewitness Identification Test Evidence: The Influence of Police–Witness Interactions

Neil Brewer

School of Psychology
Flinders University

and

Gary L. Wells

Department of Psychology
Iowa State University

Introduction

Eyewitnesses to a crime are frequently asked to view an identification parade to see if they can identify the offender. Conduct of a line-up involves police or line-up administrators in a number of important decisions, such as who to put in the line-up, the method of presentation of the line-up, and what to say to witnesses before and after the line-up. The identification test can be conceptualized as a variant on an interview between the police and the witness, involving important interactions between police (or other line-up administrators) and witnesses. These interactions can profoundly influence witness decisions and impact on the characteristics of any subsequent evidence they provide in the courts. We shall focus on (i) the expectations that police/administrators can engender in witnesses and how these can shape witness behaviour; (ii) the instructions that are provided to witnesses prior to viewing the line-up; (iii) possible ways in which administrators can interact with (and hence influence) witnesses in the conduct of line-ups; (iv) the soliciting of confidence

Handbook of Psychology of Investigative Interviewing: Current Developments and Future Directions
Edited by Ray Bull, Tim Valentine and Tom Williamson
© 2009 John Wiley & Sons, Ltd.

assessments from witnesses; (v) the interpretation of witness confidence assessments; and (vi) the influence of interactions that occur post-identification on witnesses' subsequent reports about the event and the identification test.

Eyewitnesses to crimes are frequently asked by police to view an identification parade or line-up to see if they can identify the offender who, of course, may or may not be the police suspect. It is now well documented that eyewitnesses are far from infallible when it comes to making an identification, with their performance characterized by both mistaken identifications of innocent suspects and failures to identify the offender when present in the line-up (e.g. Cutler & Penrod, 1995; Wells, Memon & Penrod, 2006; Innocence Project, 2009). In sum, eyewitness identification tests are far from a fool-proof way of pinpointing the offender.

It is also well established that the conduct of a line-up requires police or other line-up administrators to make a number of decisions that can have a far-reaching impact on the outcomes of the identification test. These decisions include deciding upon the membership of the line-up (e.g., how many members, how closely those members resemble the appearance or the description of the perpetrator), the method of presentation of the line-up (e.g., photo spread vs. live line-up vs. video line-up; simultaneous vs. sequential), how to record the line-up decision and any associated behaviours of the witness (e.g., witness confidence, decision latency), what to say to witnesses before they are shown the line-up and after they have made their decision (e.g., feedback about their decision). The research literature on these issues is extensive and offers valuable guidelines for the conduct of line-ups (e.g. Technical Working Group for Eyewitness Evidence, 1999; Brewer, Weber & Semmler, 2005; Wells *et al.*, 2006), but many of these issues are not the focus of this chapter.

In this chapter we conceptualize the identification test as a special form of interview between the police and the witness. We examine the important interactions that can occur between police (or other line-up administrators) and witnesses. We show how these interactions can exert a significant influence on witness decisions and behaviour and, in turn, shape the characteristics of any subsequent evidence they provide (e.g., in the courts).

Pre-identification test interactions

An identification test is seldom likely to take place immediately after a crime. Rather, a more likely scenario is that police will first identify witnesses to the crime and interview them about the participants and events associated with the crime. At a later date (in the UK after a delay likely to exceed one month; Pike, Brace & Kynan, 2002) when police have a suspect, they may ask a witness to attend an identification test. There is some empirical evidence, and there are sound theoretical grounds, for believing that interactions that occur prior to the identification test may shape the responding of the witness at the identification test.

Effects of providing a description on identification performance

It is possible that providing a verbal description to police at an interview may, under certain circumstances, impair subsequent performance on an identification test, an effect labelled the verbal overshadowing effect (Schooler & Engstler-Schooler, 1990). Although Meissner & Brigham's (2001) meta-analysis of verbal overshadowing studies revealed a small negative effect of providing a description on recognition, the findings are certainly not universally supportive. Further, while the effect has been detected in experiments in which the identification test closely followed the verbal description (e.g., ≤10 minutes) – conditions that are unlikely to prevail in real investigations – a mild facilitation effect has been detected when this interval was extended (ibid.). It is probably a fair assessment of the state of the scientific literature in this area to say that the findings are not decisive, the effect sizes appear not to be large and the key theoretical mechanisms underpinning the effects are by no means resolved. From a practical perspective, the possible existence of the verbal overshadowing effect can perhaps be ignored, as the occurrence of a police interview with a witness early in an investigation, and prior to any identification test, would seem to be inevitable. Should, however, future research reveal a facilitation effect to be robust under conditions paralleling those likely to be found in real investigations, it is possible that clarifying the mechanisms underlying such effects could assist in the refinement of interviewing techniques that might facilitate identification performance.

Another possible effect of a prior interview on identification performance has been described by Brewer (2006). It is possible that the performance of a witness during a police interview will shape the witness's impressions of the quality of his or her memory, with these impressions affecting the likelihood that she or he will make a choice at the identification test. For example, it seems intuitive that a witness who had great difficulty describing the offender at interview may doubt the quality of their memory and be less likely to choose from the line-up; the opposite might be expected for a witness for whom the description seemed particularly easy. Witnesses' inferences about the strength of their memory for the perpetrator might also be shaped by any post-interview feedback provided by police interviewers.

Interestingly, however, the basic recognition memory literature suggests the possibility of a different, and counter-intuitive, effect. Word-recognition research conducted within a signal detection framework indicates that people who are likely to believe that they have a strong memory for particular stimuli (because they have studied the stimulus items extensively) expect to be able to remember those stimuli and set a more demanding criterion for reporting their occurrence (Stretch & Wixted, 1998; Morrell, Gaitan & Wixted, 2002). Conversely, people who believe the opposite (i.e., a weak memory) relax their criterion and are more likely to report that they have seen a stimulus before

(Stretch & Wixted, 1998). Clear evidence for the influence of such witness metacognitions has not yet been published in the scientific literature. However, preliminary results from research currently underway in our laboratory reveal patterns consistent with the latter, counter-intuitive hypothesis.

Expectations of witnesses about the identification test

Most witnesses are likely to have limited experience with, or knowledge of, identification tests. Indeed their background probably derives mainly from viewing television programmes involving police and lawyers. Nevertheless, what witnesses almost certainly appreciate is that somewhere in the line-up is a police suspect. Thus, when witnesses are contacted and asked to attend an identification test, they are probably going to infer that the police investigation has led them to pinpoint a suspect. To the extent that a witness believes that the suspect is likely to be the offender, the witness may also reason that a sign of a capable witness will be the ability to pick the suspect from the line-up, thereby assisting in bringing that person to justice.

While we are not aware of any data that provide an unambiguous indication of witness beliefs on this issue, Memon, Gabbert & Hope (2004) reported that more than 90% of participant witnesses across multiple experiments indicated that they had assumed the perpetrator's presence in the line-up, despite having received line-up instructions explicitly warning them that the perpetrator may not be present. These estimates involved retrospective reports from witnesses who had just seen a line-up and may not, therefore, reflect witnesses' a priori expectations about the presence of the perpetrator. Unpublished data from our laboratory indicate that approximately 50% of university students (sampled when attending the laboratory to participate in other non-eyewitness studies) believe that more than 70% of 'real' police line-ups are likely to contain the perpetrator. Around 75% believe that at least 50% of line-ups are likely to contain the perpetrator.

Despite the limitations of such surveys, they reinforce the position that witnesses who attend an identification test are likely to entertain the belief that the perpetrator is in the line-up, a belief that is likely to bias the witness towards making a choice from the line-up. This bias can readily be enhanced if the police or line-up administrator provides, knowingly or unknowingly, additional cues to the witness. One example would be if the witness was contacted and told, 'We know who did it, but we need you to come view a line-up.' But, it does not have to be this blatant. For instance, the police might say, 'We have made great progress on the case and now we need to show you a line-up'. Even the phrase 'We would like you to come to the station and see if you can identify the perpetrator' implies to the witness that the perpetrator is in the line-up and that the only question is whether the witness is capable of picking him out. Interestingly, raising the expectation that the perpetrator will be in a later line-up need not come from a conversation about a line-up at all. For example, 'This guy has done this type of offence before and we need to get him off the streets' is the type of statement that communicates to the listener that the police know who did it. Hence, if a line-up is shown later, the witness is going to assume that the police have the villain in the line-up; otherwise, why are they showing the line-up?

Given the overwhelming evidence from laboratory and field studies of witnesses' propensity to misidentify innocent suspects, ensuring that witnesses about to attend a line-up are not biased towards making a positive identification becomes a crucial part of the interaction between the line-up administrator and the witness.

Police–witness interactions at the identification test: pre-decision influences

During the administration of the identification test, abundant opportunities exist for the line-up administrator to influence the decision-making of the witness and the judicial outcome of the test. Some of these opportunities occur prior to the witness actually making their decision about the line-up; others occur after the decision. Consequently, eyewitness researchers insist that certain procedures should be adopted to protect the witness from being influenced by the line-up administrator. At the pre-decision stage there are two important procedures to follow: one involves what is called double-blind line-up administration; the other involves the use of unbiased line-up instructions.

Double-blind administration

Double-blind administration means that the line-up administrator has no knowledge of which line-up member is suspected of being the perpetrator and which line-up members are merely fillers. Fillers are known-innocent members of the line-up who fit the same general description but clearly are not the perpetrator. The purpose of the fillers is to prevent the witness from knowing which person the police suspect and to make the witness rely on his or her memory instead. Obviously, if the line-up administrator somehow communicates to the eyewitness which line-up member is the suspect (and/or which are mere fillers), then the entire idea of using fillers is undermined. The use of a double-blind line-up administrator to prevent such communication for eyewitness line-ups was first proposed more than 20 years ago (Wells, 1988), but the idea of double-blind test administration is a long-established staple for human testing protocols in basic and applied science. The pharmaceutical industry, for example, is required to use double-blind testing for new drugs in which the medical testers of the patients cannot know whether the patient is in the placebo condition or the drug condition because the testers might fail to ask the placebo patients about side-effects or improvements, or the patients might infer from the testers' behaviours that they are in the placebo condition. The effect of experimenters' knowledge and expectations on the people they test has long been established scientifically (Harris & Rosenthal, 1985). Conducting a line-up is functionally analogous to conducting an experiment with human participants (Wells & Luus, 1990). How might a line-up administrator who knows who is the suspect and who are fillers influence the witness? The possibilities are almost endless, but the reader should keep in mind that we are not suggesting that these influences are intentional, nor are we suggesting that the line-up administrator or the witness is necessarily aware of these influences. Consider the dynamics of the administrator–witness interaction. The administrator is very aware that she or he has placed the suspect in position 3 and that positions 1, 2, 4, 5 and 6 are mere fillers who could not have committed the offence. The witness now looks at the line and says, 'Well ... number 2', then pauses. A natural and understandable reaction of the line-up administrator at that point might be, 'Now ... take your time, don't be too quick' or, 'Be sure that you look at all the pictures.' At that point, any witness with a modicum of intelligence realizes that number 2 is not the suspect and will move on to another photo. Suppose, on the other hand, the witness says, 'Well ... number 3'. To number 3 the reaction of the administrator is likely to be quite different – for example, 'Tell me about number 3.' It is not uncommon for eyewitnesses to waver between two or more line-up members. This conversational process shapes the witness's behaviour away from fillers and towards the suspect. Notice, however, that it is not the witness's memory that is guiding the process, but the beliefs of the line-up administrator.

There are various ways in which the double-blind administration could be put into practice, though essentially what is required is that the line-up administrator operates completely independently of the personnel responsible for line-up construction and is unable to cue the witness in any way. The latter is, of course, more readily achieved when the line-up presentation is computerized or otherwise automated, thereby removing any interaction between line-up administrator and witness during the conduct of the line-up. Criticisms sometimes levelled at a requirement for double-blind line-up administration include the associated increased resource demands and insufficient flexibility to accommodate the sometimes immediate and pressing needs of police seeking to conduct a line-up.

It is important to note that, even when double-blind line-up administration is used, opportunities for line-up administrator influence may still exist. Douglass, Smith & Fraser-Thill (2005) showed that a combination of sequential line-up administration (i.e., presenting line-up members one at a time) and multiple eyewitnesses can result in line-up administrator influence. Douglass *et al.* required participant line-up administrators to test, in succession, two witnesses. The line-up administered was a perpetrator-absent line-up. The first witness (a confederate) picked the fifth line-up member presented (an innocent foil), and did so either quickly and confidently or slowly and with low confidence. They found that the second witness, who had actually witnessed the crime and was genuinely attempting an identification, was more likely to replicate the first witness's choice if the latter had been slow and unconfident. Douglass *et al.* (2005) suggested that the unconfident confederate's behaviour may have suggested to the administrator that the identification task was a difficult one, leading the administrator to impart some subtle cues to the second witness to assist with their (difficult) decision.

The obvious practical implication of the Douglass *et al.* (2005) findings is that, when there is more than one witness to a crime involved in an identification test, the conduct of the test should be carried out by separate administrators who are not only blind to the suspect's identity but also to the outcome of any previous line-up conducted. In a series of studies currently underway in the first author's laboratory, the pattern of findings detected by Douglass *et al.* has not been replicated consistently. Nevertheless, this does not rule out the possibility that line-up administrator influence could not occur in double-blind line-ups under at least some conditions. Accordingly, until further research clarifies this issue, the above practical recommendation remains a sensible one.

One possible solution to both the resource issue (i.e., requiring an additional person to administer the line-up) and the problem of successive administration by the double-blind administrator is to computerize the line-up. In fact, many eyewitness research labs' eyewitnesses have used computers for many years to administer photographic line-ups for which, in effect, the computer administers the line-up, delivers instructions and collects the witness's responses. The American Judicature Society's Institute of Forensic Science and Public Policy in North Carolina headed the development of such a program (called the 'laptop line-up procedure'), which is being used in some police departments.

Unbiased line-up instructions

A highly influential interaction between the line-up administrator and the witness occurs at the time the line-up administrator instructs the witness just prior to viewing the line-up. Unbiased instructions explicitly advise the witness that the perpetrator may or may not be in the line-up. Biased instructions fail to include the second element of these instructions, namely, that the perpetrator may not be present. Given the expectations that witnesses are likely to bring to the identification test, it is possible that, for many witnesses, the delivery of unbiased instructions leads to the first inkling that, while there may be a police suspect in the line-up, the suspect may not be the perpetrator.

That this is likely to be the case is dramatically illustrated by the effects of varying the line-up instructions on witness choosing rates. Failure to warn a witness that the perpetrator may not be in the line-up significantly increases the likelihood that the witness will make a choice from a perpetrator-absent line-up (Malpass & Devine, 1981; Steblay, 1997; Brewer & Wells, 2006), thereby increasing the possibility of a damning misidentification of an innocent suspect. The impact of instructional bias on choosing is also apparent for target-present line-ups. Biased instructions produce fewer line-up rejections, with the increased choosing leading to a greater likelihood of target or foil identifications (Clark, 2005; Brewer & Wells, 2006). These patterns have been demonstrated for both adult and child witnesses (Keast, Brewer & Wells, 2007).

Biased instructions can be communicated in a variety of ways. Interestingly, the mere absence of a warning instruction that says that the perpetrator may or may not be in the line-up is itself generally considered by eyewitness scientists to be a biased instruction (although it is technically a bias resulting from non-instruction or the failure to instruct). In fact, most research studies compare the unbiased instruction to no instruction. But there are even higher levels of bias than simply not instructing the witness. One type of explicitly biased instruction places pressure on the witness to think that not choosing someone is a bad thing and that they are expected to identify someone. For example, 'I am going to show you a line-up. Choose the person whom you saw commit the offence.' This instruction can be construed by the witness as saying that neither the 'not sure' option nor the 'not there' option is acceptable. Or consider the instruction 'Are you able to tell me which of these is the guy you saw that night?' Notice how such an instruction not only implies that the witness is expected to choose someone, but also seems to imply to the witness that this is a test of whether the witness is able, in the sense of 'capable' or 'reliable'. In other words, if you cannot identify someone, then you are not able or not reliable, and hence a 'bad witness'. Obviously, any explicitly biased instructions like these have to be avoided because it is desirable for uncertain witnesses to say that they are unsure rather than guess, and it is desirable for witnesses to indicate that the perpetrator is not there if, in fact, that is the case.

From a line-up administrator's perspective, there is clearly some temptation to use biased instructions as this may well increase the likelihood that the police suspect is identified. However, the dramatic inflation of false identifications which has been so consistently demonstrated highlights the likely costs for the delivery of justice. In sum, witnesses should receive a very clear warning that the perpetrator may not be in the line-up.

Police–witness interactions at the identification test: the decision

While the following may seem so obvious as to be not worth saying, we emphasize the following crucial points. The faithful recording of each eyewitness's decision at the identification test constitutes an important part of the preservation of evidence. Quite simply, the line-up administrator should clearly record each witness's exact response. This recording should clearly distinguish between response options such as (a) the witness identified a particular line-up member; (b) the witness indicated that the perpetrator was not present in the line-up;

(c) the witness indicated that he or she was not sure enough to make an identification; (d) the witness indicated that it could be number 4 or number 6; or (e) the witness indicated that number 3 looks a lot like the perpetrator. Each of these response options has different implications for assessments of the likelihood that the police suspect in the line-up is or is not the perpetrator. Yet a failure to record the exact response of each witness may, for example, lead to some witnesses' decisions (e.g., responses (b) and (e)) not being preserved for tendering in any subsequent trial, or perhaps to a 'transformation' of the witnesses' responses between the identification test and the trial (e.g., response (c) may transform into response (a)). In sum, the failure to record carefully each witness's decision can have far-reaching practical implications for the overall nature and quality of evidence that may be tendered at trial.

Police–witness interactions at the identification test: post-decision influences

After the witness has indicated his or her identification decision (i.e., chosen a line-up member, indicated that the perpetrator is not present or perhaps that the witness is just not sure enough to make a decision), there are opportunities for a whole new set of interactions that are now known to be of considerable forensic relevance. Some of the most important of these are associated with soliciting an expression of confidence in the identification decision from the eyewitnesses. Here we consider issues such as why this type of information may prove to be important in any particular case, what it suggests about the likely accuracy of the identification decision, how it should be collected in order to maximize its informational value, and what use of this information should be made in the courtroom. We also look at how these interactions can influence other witness judgements about the witnessed event.

The relationship between identification confidence and accuracy

It is a common occurrence for people either to express spontaneously their confidence in the judgements that they have made or to be asked to do so. Although most people probably do not accept that judgemental confidence necessarily equates with judgemental accuracy, the existence of at least a reasonably close correspondence between confidence and accuracy is likely to align with people's intuitions. It is not surprising, therefore, that police, lawyers, judges and jurors are interested in knowing about witnesses' confidence in their identification decisions. Nor is it surprising to know that there is ample evidence demonstrating that these groups find an eyewitness's confidence persuasive with respect to the likely accuracy of his or her testimony

(Cutler, Penrod & Stuve, 1988; Lindsay, Wells & O'Connor, 1989; Potter & Brewer, 1999; Bradfield & Wells, 2000; Brewer & Burke, 2002).

If a witness's confidence in an identification decision is likely to be interpreted as a strong pointer to identification accuracy, it is important to consider whether this interpretation is justified. This issue has been a controversial one in the psychology–law field, with eyewitness researchers typically presenting quite a different perspective from that which characterizes many people in the criminal justice community. Specifically, many of the former group have maintained that confidence in an identification provides no useful guide to the accuracy of that identification. The focus here is not on the nature of these differences, although it is worth noting that the specific approach used to examine the relationship has made an important contribution to the different perspectives (see Brewer, 2006). Rather, we shall outline what we believe (based on current knowledge) to be some reasonable generalizations about the characteristics of the confidence–accuracy (CA) relationship for eyewitness identification, and spell out precisely what the implications are for the interpretation of witnesses' expressions of confidence by police investigators, lawyers, judges and jurors, and line-up administrators' interactions with witnesses.

Detailed examinations of the CA relationship (e.g., Sporer, Penrod, Read & Cutler, 1995; Juslin, Olsson & Winman, 1996; Lindsay, Read & Sharma, 1998; Wells & Bradfield, 1998; 1999; Brewer, 2006; Brewer & Wells, 2006; Keast, Brewer & Wells, 2007) suggest the following generalizations are appropriate. First, identification confidence expressed well after the identification (e.g., in court) should be considered uninformative (we return to consider this issue in detail in the next section of this chapter). Second, witnesses who express high confidence immediately after making the identification are by no means guaranteed to have made an accurate decision; the CA relation is likely to be characterized by some degree of overconfidence, though there may be exceptions. Third, for adult witnesses who made a positive identification, CA calibration data indicate that an immediately recorded confidence estimate does provide a guide to likely identification accuracy. This conclusion does not, however, hold for non-choosers; nor does it apply to identifications made by children, at least for those in the 10–12 year age range.

There are several important implications of these findings. First, the line-up administrator should record the witness's confidence assessment immediately after the identification and, as will become clear shortly, this assessment should be provided independently by the witness. Second, no matter how confident the witness may be in the identification decision, police investigators should not assume the identification is accurate. Rather, a very confident identification made by an adult (but not a child) witness should suggest to investigators that their suspect is at least a plausible one and a continued search for corroborating evidence is warranted. Further, a positive identification that is not made with high confidence should suggest to investigators that there is a very real possibility that their suspect is not the culprit. Third, although a line-up rejection provides a valuable pointer that the suspect does not match the witness's memory (Wells & Olson, 2002), the confidence expressed in a line-up rejection does not assist in determining whether the rejection is likely to be accurate. Similar interpretations of confidence recorded at the time of the identification should be made by lawyers, judges and jurors.

Post-identification influences on confidence

In the previous section we emphasized the importance of obtaining a confidence estimate from the witness immediately after the identification decision. Why is this important? Basically, the objective should be to obtain a confidence judgement that provides an independent assessment of the witness's memory strength rather than one that is shaped by social influences emanating from post-identification test interactions. We are not suggesting here that an immediately provided verbal confidence assessment guarantees a precise index of the witness's memory quality. Rather, we are acknowledging the now overwhelming body of evidence demonstrating the malleability of identification confidence and, hence, the potential unreliability of delayed post-identification confidence assessments.

After making an identification, a witness may receive feedback (explicit or implicit) from a number of sources. The line-up administrator might clearly indicate to the witness that he or she has picked the 'right guy' (e.g., 'That's our man', 'Good, you identified the suspect' or the simple statement/question 'Great! You would testify to that in court, right?'). Or, the administrator's facial expression or non-verbal demeanour following the witness's decision might be interpreted as confirming the choice. There are many non-verbal signs of acceptance, or positive reaction such as smiles, head nods and other spontaneous gestures.

Interestingly, disconfirming feedback following filler identifications is also considered a problem. Telling an eyewitness that she or he has identified a filler leads witnesses to 'back off' from their identification and claim that they were not as certain as they in fact were. But, research shows that filler identifications have diagnostic value because they are more frequent when the suspect is innocent than when the suspect is guilty (Wells & Lindsay, 1980; Clark & Wells, 2008). In effect, witnesses who identify a filler are saying that the person they identified looks more like the perpetrator than does the suspect. If they are fairly certain in this judgement, then it would make sense to ask them how certain they are before telling them that they identified a filler.

Confirming or disconfirming feedback might also emerge if the witness is placed in a situation where he or she discusses the identification test with another witness to the crime. Such feedback or cues from line-up administrators or co-witnesses are known to exert a powerful effect on witnesses' subsequent expressions of confidence in their identification decisions. Confirming feedback inflates witness confidence, whereas disconfirming feedback has the opposite effect (Luus & Wells, 1994; Wells & Bradfield, 1998; 1999; Bradfield, Wells & Olson, 2002; Wells, Olson & Charman, 2003; Hafstad, Memon & Logie, 2004). This pattern occurs both for positive identifications and for line-up rejections, and it occurs for witnesses' recollection of their confidence at the time of the identification and at the time they are asked about it (Semmler, Brewer & Wells 2004). The effect is not dependent on delivery by a 'live' administrator, occurring also when delivered by a computer or co-witness (Luus & Wells, 1994; Semmler *et al.*, 2004). Moreover, it has even been detected when the line-up administrator knew the suspect's identity but did not provide any verbal feedback, reinforcing the potential for influence via non-verbal cues (Garrioch & Brimacombe, 2001).

Given our earlier observations about the persuasiveness of confident witnesses and identifications, the implications of these confidence malleability findings are reasonably obvious. Witnesses who pick the police suspect and/or make the same choice as a co-witness may, as a result of cues provided by the line-up administrator or another witness, end up expressing confidence levels way above (or below) what they would have reported if there had been no interaction with the line-up administrator or co-witness. Imagine the likely difference in the impact on a jury if a witness reports that they are about 70% certain that they observed the defendant commit the crime vs. reporting absolute certainty in the identification. Clearly, this malleability of confidence judgements means that expressions of confidence obtained from witnesses in the courtroom are not only uninformative but also potentially highly misleading. Moreover, it means that witnesses should be asked to indicate their identification decision confidence immediately after making the decision and prior to any social interactions with line-up administrators or police, and that this confidence estimate should be recorded and be the confidence estimate that is tendered as evidence.

The consistent implementation of this practice for recording and tendering confidence evidence would represent a significant breakthrough. Nevertheless, we should highlight at least one caveat. Although there is now evidence that mock-jurors downgrade the credibility of witnesses who display confidence inflation (Bradfield & McQuiston, 2004), this is not a uniform reaction. Jones, Williams & Brewer (2008) found that while mock-jurors discredited witnesses who provided unconvincing reasons for their confidence inflation, they were less likely to do so when the witness was able to offer some plausible insight that apparently justified the inflation. This finding suggests that simply tendering as evidence a confidence estimate obtained at the time of the identification will not always be sufficient to combat the impact of confidence inflation.

Post-identification influences on other witness judgements

Another striking finding in the eyewitness identification literature is that post-identification feedback affects not only witnesses' recollections of how confident they were at the time of the identification but also their perceptions of both the witnessing and the identification test experience. For example, post-identification feedback results in witnesses 'inflating' their perceptions of the quality of their view of the event, the amount of attention they were paying at the time, and the ease and speed with which they had made the identification (Wells & Bradfield, 1998; 1999). Just as witness confidence shapes judgements of witness credibility, so too are these perceptions likely to shape jurors' evaluations of the extent to which the witness's identification should be relied upon. Accordingly, to ensure that what is essentially distorted evidence does not shape juror judgements, ways of recording such witness perceptions immediately after the identification test (e.g., via recording of the witness–line-up administrator interaction) need to be encouraged.

Putting these recommendations into practice

How do recommendations such as those we have outlined in this chapter get incorporated into practice? There is no magical formula. There are, however, a variety of possible approaches, any or all of which may be effective given the right timing. Clearly the DNA exoneration cases in the USA have been a catalyst for change in that country and elsewhere. In the USA, a number of these recommendations (e.g., providing unbiased instructions, obtaining a confidence measure directly after the identification) have already been embodied in the National Institute of Justice Guidelines for the Collection of Eyewitness Evidence (Technical Working Group for Eyewitness Evidence, 1999). Some of these recommendations (e.g., unbiased instructions) have been widely adopted by police jurisdictions in different parts of the world. Which recommendations are likely to be adopted, and why, is difficult to ascertain, particularly given the complexity of factors that drive organizational change.

One thing that the authors advocate, however, is working hard to promote the implications of scientific research to relevant practitioner groups such as police, lawyers and judges. Over many years Gary Wells has conducted scores of lectures, workshops, etc. for police, lawyers and judges in the USA. More recently, Neil Brewer has presented numerous lectures and workshops for judges and magistrates in most Australian legal jurisdictions. While none of this guarantees any policy or practical change, a common thread noted by both authors is that their audiences have engaged enthusiastically and intelligently in such discussions. Assuming that researchers are persistent in their influence attempts, such responses bode well for the likelihood of effecting change in identification test procedures.

Acknowledgement

Research supported by Australian Research Council Discovery Grant DP0556876.

References

Bradfield, A. & McQuiston, D. E. (2004). When does evidence of eyewitness confidence inflation affect judgments in a criminal trial? *Law and Human Behavior, 28,* 369–387.

Bradfield, A. L. & Wells, G. L. (2000). The perceived validity of eyewitness identification testimony: A test of the five Biggers criteria. *Law and Human Behavior, 24,* 581–594.

Bradfield, A. L., Wells, G. L. & Olson, E. A. (2002). The damaging effect of confirming feedback on the relation between eyewitness certainty and identification accuracy. *Journal of Applied Psychology, 87,* 112–120.

Brewer, N. (2006). Uses and abuses of eyewitness identification confidence. *Legal and Criminological Psychology, 11,* 3–4.

Brewer, N. & Burke, A. (2002). Effects of testimonial inconsistencies and eyewitness confidence on mock-juror judgments. *Law and Human Behavior, 26,* 353–364.

Brewer, N. & Wells, G. L. (2006). The confidence–accuracy relationship in eyewitness identification: Effects of line-up instructions, foil similarity and target-absent base rates. *Journal of Experimental Psychology: Applied, 12,* 11–30.

Brewer, N., Weber, N. & Semmler, C. (2005). Eyewitness identification. In N. Brewer & K. D. Williams (Eds.), *Psychology and law: An empirical perspective* (pp. 177–221). New York: Guilford Press.

Clark, S. E. (2005). A re-examination of the effects of biased line-up instructions in eyewitness identification. *Law and Human Behavior, 29,* 395–424.

Clark, S. E. & Wells, G. L. (2008). On the diagnosticity of multiple-witness identifications. *Law and Human Behavior, 32,* 406–422.

Cutler, B. L. & Penrod, S. D. (1995). *Mistaken identification: The eyewitness, psychology, and the law.* New York: Cambridge University Press.

Cutler, B. L., Penrod, S. D. & Stuve, T. E. (1988). Jury decision making in eyewitness identification cases. *Law and Human Behavior, 12,* 41–56.

Douglass, A. B., Smith, C. & Fraser-Thill, R. (2005). A problem with double-blind photospread procedures: Photospread administrators use one eyewitness's confidence to influence the identification of another witness. *Law and Human Behavior, 29,* 543–562.

Garrioch, L. & Brimacombe, C. (2001). Line-up administrators' expectations: Their impact on eyewitness confidence. *Law & Human Behavior, 25,* 299–314.

Hafstad, G. S., Memon, A. & Logie, R. (2004). Post-identification feedback, confidence and recollections of witnessing conditions in child witnesses. *Applied Cognitive Psychology, 18,* 901–912.

Harris, M. J. & Rosenthal, R. (1985). Mediation of interpersonal expectancy effects: 31 meta-analyses. *Psychological Bulletin, 97*, 363–386.

Innocence Project (2009). *Innocence project.* http://www.innocenceproject.org/about/index.php. Accessed 23 March 2009.

Jones, E. E., Williams, K. D. & Brewer, N. (2008). 'I had a confidence epiphany!': Obstacles to combating post-identification confidence inflation. *Law and Human Behavior, 32*, 164–176.

Juslin, P., Olsson, N. & Winman, A. (1996). Calibration and diagnosticity of confidence in eyewitness identification: Comments on what can be inferred from the low confidence-accuracy correlation. *Journal of Experimental Psychology: Learning, Memory, and Cognition, 22*, 1304–1316.

Keast, A., Brewer, N. & Wells, G. L. (2007). Children's metacognitive judgments in an eyewitness identification task. *Journal of Experimental Child Psychology, 97*, 286–314.

Lindsay, D. S., Read, J. D. & Sharma, K. (1998). Accuracy and confidence in person identification: The relationship is strong when witnessing conditions vary widely. *Psychological Science, 9*, 215–218.

Lindsay, R. C. L., Wells, G. L. & O'Connor, F. J. (1989). Mock-juror belief of accurate and inaccurate eyewitnesses. *Law and Human Behavior, 13*, 333–339.

Luus, C. & Wells, G. L. (1994). The malleability of eyewitness confidence: Co-witness and perseverance effects. *Journal of Applied Psychology, 79*, 714–723.

Malpass, R. S. & Devine, P. G. (1981). Eyewitness identification: Line-up instructions and the absence of the offender. *Journal of Applied Psychology, 66*, 482–489.

Meissner, C. A. & Brigham, J. C. (2001). A meta-analysis of the verbal overshadowing effect in face identification. *Applied Cognitive Psychology, 16*, 911–928.

Memon, A., Gabbert, F. & Hope, L. (2004). *The ageing eyewitness.* In J. Adler (Ed.), *Forensic psychology: Debates, concepts and practice.* Cullompton: Willan Publishing.

Morrell, H. E. R., Gaitan, S. & Wixted, J. T. (2002). On the nature of the decision axis in signal-detection-based models of recognition memory. *Journal of Experimental Psychology: Learning, Memory and Cognition, 28*, 1095–1110.

Pike, G., Brace, N. & Kynan, S. (2002). *The visual identification of suspects: Procedures and practice.* Briefing Note 2/02. London: Home Office.

Potter, R. & Brewer, N. (1999). Perceptions of witness behaviour–accuracy relationships held by police, lawyers and jurors. *Psychiatry, Psychology and Law, 6*, 97–103.

Schooler, J. W. & Engstler-Schooler, T. Y. (1990). Verbal overshadowing of visual memories: Some things are better left unsaid. *Cognitive Psychology, 22*, 36–71.

Semmler, C., Brewer, N. & Wells, G. L. (2004). Effects of postidentification feedback on eyewitness identification and nonidentification confidence. *Journal of Applied Psychology, 89*, 334–346.

Sporer, S. L., Penrod, S. D., Read, J. D. & Cutler, B. L. (1995). Choosing, confidence, and accuracy: A meta-analysis of the confidence-accuracy relation in eyewitness identification studies. *Psychological Bulletin, 118*, 315–327.

Steblay, N. M. (1997). Social influence in eyewitness recall: A meta-analytic review of line-up instruction effects. *Law & Human Behavior, 21*, 283–297.

Stretch, V. & Wixted, J. T. (1998). On the difference between strength-based and frequency-based mirror effects in recognition memory. *Journal of Experimental Psychology: Learning, Memory and Cognition, 24,* 1379–1396.

Technical Working Group for Eyewitness Evidence (1999). *Eyewitness evidence: A guide for law enforcement.* Washington, DC: US Department of Justice, Office of Justice Programs.

Wells, G. L. (1988). *Eyewitness identification: A system handbook.* Toronto: Carswell Legal Publications.

Wells, G. L. & Bradfield, A. L. (1998). 'Good, you identified the suspect': Feedback to eyewitnesses distorts their reports of the witnessing experience. *Journal of Applied Psychology, 83,* 360–376.

Wells, G. L. & Bradfield, A. L. (1999). Distortions in eyewitnesses' recollections: Can the postidentification-feedback effect be moderated? *Psychological Science, 10,* 138–144.

Wells, G. L. & Lindsay, R. C. L. (1980). On estimating the diagnosticity of eyewitness nonidentifications. *Psychological Bulletin, 88,* 776–784.

Wells, G. L. & Luus, E. (1990). Police line-ups as experiments: Social methodology as a framework for properly-conducted line-ups. *Personality and Social Psychology Bulletin, 16,* 106–117.

Wells, G. L. & Olson, E. A. (2002). Eyewitness identification: Information gain from incriminating and exonerating behaviors. *Journal of Experimental Psychology: Applied, 8,* 155–167.

Wells, G. L., Olson, E. A. & Charman, S. D. (2003). Distorted retrospective eyewitness reports as functions of feedback and delay. *Journal of Experimental Psychology: Applied, 9,* 42–52.

Wells, G. L., Memon, A. & Penrod, S. D. (2006). Eyewitness evidence: Improving its probative value. *Psychological Science in the Public Interest, 7,* 45–75.

Chapter Thirteen

Recent Developments in Eyewitness Identification Procedures in the United Kingdom

Tim Valentine

Goldsmiths, University of London

Carwyn Hughes

Sussex Police

and

Rod Munro

Devon and Cornwall Police

Introduction

In the initial stages of an investigation, the potential of eyewitness identification may be assessed from an interview with a witness. An initial interview will often involve taking a description of the perpetrator. In the absence of physical forensic evidence such as a DNA profile, investigators may rely on an eyewitness to provide the necessary identification. The interaction between the eyewitness and the police is critical to the reliability of identification evidence.

The frailty of eyewitness identification has long been recognized. In response to public concern about the reliability of eyewitness identification following several wrongful convictions in the early 1970s, the British government established an enquiry into eyewitness identification chaired by Lord

Handbook of Psychology of Investigative Interviewing: Current Developments and Future Directions
Edited by Ray Bull, Tim Valentine and Tom Williamson
© 2009 John Wiley & Sons, Ltd.

Devlin. More recently, over 230 people wrongfully convicted in the USA have been exonerated by DNA evidence that was not available at their original trial. Investigation of the causes of these wrongful convictions has shown that mistaken identification was a cause in three-quarters of the cases (Innocence Project, n.d.).

Devlin revisited

Devlin (1976) reported an analysis of the outcome of all cases from England and Wales which involved disputed identification in 1973. From an analysis of 2,116 live line-ups (known as identity parades in the UK), Devlin noted that the police suspect was identified in 45% of line-ups; no identification was made for 46% of line-ups; and a volunteer was identified in 9% of line-ups. Thus a known mistaken identification (of a volunteer) was made in almost one in ten line-ups.

Eyewitness identification is a very powerful form of evidence. Devlin (1976) reported that 90% of suspects who were identified in a line-up were prosecuted, and 82% of these prosecutions resulted in a conviction. In contrast, only 9% of those not identified were prosecuted on the basis of other evidence, and 86% of these cases resulted in conviction. Devlin reported separately cases involving disputed identification in which the *only evidence* consisted of identification by one or more eyewitnesses. Seventy-four per cent of such cases resulted in a conviction.

Devlin (1976) made the following recommendation:

> We do however wish to ensure that in ordinary cases prosecutions are not brought on eyewitness evidence only and that, if brought, they will fail. We think that they ought to fail, since in our opinion it is only in exceptional cases that identification evidence is by itself sufficiently reliable to exclude a reasonable doubt about guilt. (para. 8.4, p. 150)

It is instructive to compare this recommendation with a Court of Appeal judgment made almost 30 years later (*R v Mitchell*, 2005). The judgment concerned the issue of whether corroboration is required to convict on the basis of the opinion of a single expert, who concluded that his analysis of CCTV imagery provided very strong support for the contention that the appellant was the person in the CCTV image. Lord Justice Tuckey stated:

> as a matter of principle it is open to the jury to convict on the evidence of an expert qualified in facial mapping ... There is no need for some independent support for such evidence ... Were it otherwise it would not be possible to convict a defendant on the identification evidence of a single witness and we all know that this often happens. (para. 11)

Notwithstanding Devlin's recommendation, in 2005 convictions on the evidence of a single eyewitness occur 'often'.

Legal safeguards

A direct outcome of the Devlin inquiry was a landmark ruling in the Appeal Court in London (*R v Turnbull*, 1976) which established the principles a trial judge must use to caution the jury of the special need for caution in cases of disputed eyewitness identification.

The Turnbull guidelines

English case law is based on the premise that a distinction can be drawn between good and poor eyewitness identification evidence. When identity is disputed, a trial judge must advise the jury to consider carefully the circumstances of an identification. The requirements for a 'Turnbull warning' are summarized in the acronym ADVOKATE. The jury must be advised to consider the following: Amount of time for which the perpetrator was in view. Distance of the witness from the perpetrator. Visibility of the perpetrator. How good was the lighting? Obstruction to the witness' view? Known to the witness? Has the witness seen the suspect before? How often? Any reason to remember? If only seen occasionally before, did the witness have any reason to remember the suspect? Time delay between the incident and the formal identification procedure. Error. Is there any material discrepancy between the description given to the police at the time of the incident and the appearance of the suspect?

The Police and Criminal Evidence Act 1984

The Police and Criminal Evidence Act 1984 (PACE) established a code of practice (known as Code D) which governs the conduct of identification procedures in England and Wales. The current code came into effect in 2008 and covers a wide range of circumstances of which the major provisions are as follows. If identification is disputed, a video identification procedure containing moving images must be offered unless it is not practicable or a 'live' identification procedure is more suitable. Line-ups should consist of a minimum of eight foils and one suspect. The foils should, 'so far as possible resemble the suspect in age, general appearance and position in life'. Witnesses must be advised that the person they saw may not be present and must view the entire line-up at least twice. They are instructed that if they cannot make a positive identification, they should say so. The person who runs the procedure should not be involved in the investigation. The suspect has the right for his or her legal representative to be present when the witness views the line-up. The suspect's representative may make reasonable objections to the procedure (e.g. the selection of foils). If the objections cannot be resolved (e.g., by substituting a different foil) the reason for the objection must be recorded, together with a reason why it could not be resolved. If the witness has previously been shown photographs, details of the photographs shown should be recorded. Anything the witness says should be written down before he or she leaves the identification room.

Is PACE working?

There have been a number of studies of live line-ups conducted by the police under the PACE guidelines (Slater, 1994; Wright & McDaid, 1996; Valentine, Pickering, & Darling, 2003). In all three studies approximately 40% of witnesses identified the suspect, approximately 40% of witnesses did not make any identification and approximately 20% of witness identified a foil. With field data such as these it is impossible to know how many line-ups contained the actual perpetrator. However, we do know that at least 20% of witnesses made a mistaken identification of an innocent person. It is interesting to note that the rate of mistaken identification in these studies is higher than the rate noted by Devlin (20% vs. 9% respectively). At first sight this is a cause for concern. However, it could be argued that the increased rate in identification of foils reflects fairer construction of line-ups. Using foils that resemble the suspect may make it more likely that a witness will make a mistaken identification. Nevertheless, the data show that the instruction that 'the person seen may or may not be present' did not inhibit many unreliable witnesses from making an identification.

Archival data collected by the police from 1,776 identity parades showed that the suspect was identified in 48% of cases, but did not distinguish non-identifications from identification of a foil (Pike, Brace & Kyman, 2002). An archival analysis of 58 live line-ups conducted in US criminal cases found that the suspect was identified in 50% of cases, a foil was identified in 24% of cases and the witness was unable to make an identification or rejected the line-up in 26% of cases (Behrman & Davey, 2001). It should be noted that in the USA there is no minimum number of foils, although use of five is common.

Devlin (1976) did not identify any flaw in the procedure of the identity parade that substantially increases the risk of error. Instead, it was argued that the only way to reduce the risk of wrongful conviction was to increase the burden of proof. Devlin noted that this would make it more difficult to convict the guilty as well as the innocent and he recommended that this course should be followed with restraint. At the time when the Devlin Report was published the modern era of research on eyewitness testimony had barely begun. Devlin had the foresight to hear evidence from psychologists and is to be commended for appreciating the contribution that psychological science had to make.

Theoretical issues in eyewitness identification

Relative and absolute judgements

A persistent problem in understanding eyewitness identification is to explain why a sizeable minority of witnesses make mistaken identifications, despite appropriate warnings that the perpetrator may not be present in the line-up. Wells (1993) demonstrated that at least part of the problem may be attributable to witnesses who make a *relative* judgement rather than an *absolute* judgement. When confronted with a line-up a witness may only identify a person if their resemblance to the culprit exceeds some criterion of recollection (an absolute judgement). Alternatively, a witness may examine all the members of a line-up and identify the person who most closely resembles the perpetrator (a relative judgement). Wells (1993) and Clark & Davey (2005) have shown that a proportion of witnesses, who would be able to identify the culprit if present in a line-up, make a mistaken identification of a foil when asked to make an identification from a line-up that does not include the culprit even when the option not to identify anybody is explicitly available. These data suggest that relative identification decisions are a cause of mistaken identifications.

Sequential vs. simultaneous presentation

A method of sequential line-up presentation was developed to prevent witnesses from making a relative judgement. In a sequential presentation, photographs of faces are presented one at a time (Lindsay & Wells, 1985). The witness is not told how many faces will be presented, but must decide as each face is presented whether or not it is the culprit before the next face is presented. The line-up administrator should not know the identity of the suspect. Furthermore, witnesses must not be allowed a second choice or to see again a face previously presented (Lindsay, Lea & Fulford, 1991).

Sequential presentation has been found to reduce the number of mistaken identifications from culprit-absent line-ups, but it also reduces the number of correct identifications from culprit-present line-ups (Steblay, Dysart, Fulero & Lindsay, 2001). Meissner, Tredoux, Parker & Maclin (2005) found that sequential line-ups induce a more conservative response criterion, but do not affect discrimination accuracy. In short, both the guilty and the innocent are less likely to be identified from a sequential line-up. Use of sequential line-ups instructions in the context of video identification is discussed below.

Recollection and familiarity

It would be beneficial to have a better understanding of the conditions that encourage use of a relative judgement. One possibility is that witnesses may be prone to using relative judgements when the recognition task is difficult. Valentine, Darling & Memon (2007) found that witnesses were more likely to report using relative judgements when they saw culprit-absent line-ups than when they saw a culprit-present line-up. If a witness is able to recollect seeing a culprit at the crime scene, she or he can rely on an absolute decision. However, in the absence of recognizing the culprit, the witness may be tempted to rely on a feeling of familiarity (e.g. 'number 2 seems familiar'). Witnesses may be more likely to rely on a relative judgement when responding on the basis of familiarity alone, i.e., the witness may identify the person who feels most familiar. A feeling of subjective familiarity can arise from the perceived typicality of a face or similarity to previously seen faces, other than the culprit (Bartlett, Hurry & Thorley, 1984; Valentine, 1991).

The distinction between recollection and familiarity has been made in theoretical models of recognition memory (e.g. Mandler, 1980, Jacoby & Dallas, 1981; see Yonelinas, 2002, for a review). A similar distinction has been characterized as that between *remembering* and (just) *knowing* that a stimulus has been seen before (Tulving, 1985). There is empirical evidence that the distinction captures distinct ways of remembering (see Gardiner & Richardson-Klavehn, 2000 for a review). Applying this theoretical framework to eyewitness identification suggests that it may be beneficial in future research to explore use of instructions to witnesses that encourage a recollection judgement and discourages identification based on a feeling of familiarity.

Factors that affect eyewitness identification

Crime scene investigators take great care to avoid contaminating a crime scene by introducing new trace evidence. The memory of an eyewitness should be treated similarly, as part of the crime scene. Investigating officers should take care to ensure that they do not distort a witness's memory, but instead use a sensitive and fair procedure to obtain identification evidence of the highest quality. An investigating officer has control over many aspects of an eyewitness's interaction with the investigation. For example, an investigator may develop a strategy to interview a witness, decide which witnesses will be asked to make an identification, selecting an appropriate method, brief the witness and control the information provided to the witness after an identification procedure.

The selection and design of identification procedures can have a strong impact on the reliability of the eyewitness evidence obtained. A poorly designed procedure might distort a witness's memory, potentially leading to a mistaken identification of an innocent suspect or a missed opportunity to collect identification evidence against a guilty suspect. Psychological science can evaluate identification procedures. For example, the selection of foils for a line-up, the instructions given to witnesses and prior viewing of photographs have all been shown to have a marked effect on the reliability of eyewitness identification.

Selection of foils

The PACE code of practice specifies that the foils for line-ups must be selected to 'resemble the suspect'. This is known as a suspect-resemblance strategy. Luus & Wells (1991) argued that a better strategy is to select foils who match the witness's description of the culprit. It is reasonable to assume that the witness can remember the description that he or she gave to the police and may expect to identify somebody who matches their description. Therefore, the witness may be inclined to disregard any foils that do not match their description, or conversely pay special attention to anybody who is a better match to their description than the rest. Luus & Wells suggested that it does not introduce a bias against an innocent suspect if line-up members differ on a feature that was not mentioned in the original description. Differences in the facial features of line-up members will help a witness who has a reliable memory to distinguish the culprit from the foils. If the suspect is not the culprit, he or she is no more likely than anybody else to be mistakenly identified by a feature not mentioned in the description because the witness has not seen the suspect before. All persons in a fair line-up should match the witness's description of the culprit.

Sometimes a witness may not mention the sex or race of a person, or may neglect to say that somebody did not have a beard or was not wearing glasses. This may occur because the witness assumes a default value (Lindsay, Martin & Webber, 1994). When constructing a culprit-description line-up, account must be taken of default values. Alternatively, if a witness's description is very vague or if the suspect does not match the description, it may be necessary to resort to a suspect-resemblance strategy. The important principle is that the suspect should not stand out in the line-up.

Different foils may be required for a culprit-description line-up for each witness, because their descriptions of the culprit may differ. Therefore, use of culprit-description line-ups would require additional police resources. In the UK current practice requires only a single line-up to be used for all witnesses, although the position of the suspect may differ across different witnesses.

Empirical support for the superiority of a culprit-description line-up is mixed. Wells, Rydell & Seelau (1993) and Juslin, Olsson & Winman (1996) reported more correct identifications from culprit-description line-ups than from suspect-resemblance line-ups when the culprit was present in the line-up, and no significant difference in the number of mistaken identifications from culprit-absent line-ups. In contrast, Lindsay *et al.* (1994), and Tunnicliffe &

Clark (2000) did not find any statistically significant advantage for culprit-description line-ups over suspect-resemblance line-ups. Use of culprit-description line-ups in the context of video identification is discussed below.

Instructions to witnesses

A witness may believe that they have been invited to attempt an identification because the police have good reason to believe that the suspect is guilty. Therefore, a witness may assume that it will help the police if they identify the suspect. It is important that the instructions to the witness should emphasize the possibility that the offender may not be in the line-up. The PACE code of practice includes the instruction that the person whom the witness saw 'may or may not be present'. Furthermore, the witness must be instructed that 'If you cannot make a positive identification, you should say so'. Instructions that do not point out that the culprit may not be in the line-up are regarded as 'biased' (e.g., 'Can you identify the man who assaulted you?'). A meta-analysis of 18 studies showed that when biased instructions are given, witnesses are more likely to make an identification, whether it is correct or incorrect. Biased instructions increase the likelihood of an innocent suspect being identified from culprit-absent line-ups (Steblay, 1997).

Blind administration of line-ups

'Blind' is used in the sense that the line-up administer does not know (i.e. is blind to) the identity of the suspect. The procedure is often referred to as 'double-blind', meaning that both the witness and the line-up administrator are blind to the identity of the suspect. A double-blind procedure should be used to prevent any inadvertent influence on the witness. Such influence can be very subtle and entirely unconscious. For example, the administrator may look at the witness when the suspect's image is being viewed, or be more likely to accept a tentative identification only if it is of the suspect. Currently, the PACE code of practice does not require double-blind administration.

There is little direct evidence on the double-blind administration of line-ups. However, the effects of experimenter-induced influence are well established in a broader context in psychological science (Harris & Rosenthal, 1985). For this reason a double-blind procedure is an essential feature of clinical drug trials. The essential point to appreciate is that double-blind administration of identification procedures removes any possibility of that the witness may have been influenced. Therefore, double-blind administration protects the police from malicious accusation of bias and enhances the perceived integrity of the identification evidence. Widespread use of photographs for identification in the USA and of video in the UK greatly facilitates use of a double-blind identification procedure.

Number of foils

Video or live line-ups in England and Wales are required to have a minimum of eight foils. It is recommended by the US Department of Justice that photo line-ups have a minimum of five foils and live line-ups have a minimum of four foils (Technical Working Group on Eyewitness Identification, 1999). These guidelines raise the question of how many foils is optimal.

The similarity of foils to the culprit is more important than the absolute number of line-up members. A foil who is dissimilar to the culprit will be discounted by the witness. The ability to identify a target face from target-present and target-absent photo line-ups decreases with increasing size of the line-up (Meissner *et al.*, 2005). Thus the target person is most likely to be identified from a one-person line-up (a show-up or confrontation) and least likely to be identified from a 12-person line-up. This result is unsurprising because a line-up that offers more alternative responses provides a more difficult test of memory. It is only an identification of an *innocent suspect* that is a *forensically relevant* mistaken identification (i.e., likely to lead to a miscarriage of justice). In a one-person target-absent line-up all mistaken identifications will be of the innocent suspect. Fewer mistaken identifications are likely to be of an innocent suspect in a large target-absent line-up than in a small line-up. In summary, there is no clear empirical guide to the optimal size of a line-up, but if foils are appropriately chosen, a larger line-up is likely to pose a more challenging assessment of eyewitness memory.

Prior exposure to photographs

If the police have not identified a suspect, the witness may be shown photographs of people associated with similar offences (mugshots). This procedure differs from a line-up in that all the people are potential suspects. Therefore, any identification will lead to that person being investigated. Later in the investigation the police may want to collect formal identification evidence from a line-up, or may be required to do so by legislation. Would a subsequent line-up be biased against the suspect if the witness has previously seen their photograph in a mugshot album?

Deffenbacher, Bornstein & Penrod (2006) provide a systematic review of the effects of mugshot exposure. They found that prior viewing of a photograph of somebody who subsequently appeared in a line-up increased the probability of a mistaken identification from the line-up. This effect is due to transference of familiarity from the photograph which is mistakenly attributed to having being seen at the crime scene. The effect is stronger when few mugshots were viewed (8–15 or fewer) than when more mugshots have been viewed. The effect is particularly strong if the person was mistakenly identified as the perpetrator from the mugshot photographs. This is known as an effect of commitment to the earlier identification. There was no ill-effect of showing photographs if none of the people seen appeared in the subsequent line-up.

Video identification and its advantages

Since 2003 video technology has been used to replace virtually all live identity parades in England and Wales. A video line-up consists of 15-second clips showing the head and shoulders of each line-up member. First, they are looking at the camera and then rotate their head to show both profiles, before looking back at the camera. The images are captured under standardized conditions. Each line-up member is shown sequentially, with a digit in the top left corner of the screen to identify each individual.

Video offers a number of benefits compared to live line-ups:

1. Video can dramatically reduce the delay before an identification can be organized. A video line-up can be produced and transmitted via a secure network within two hours of request.
2. The administration of the video identification procedure can be arranged at the convenience of the witness rather than at the convenience of the suspect, because the suspect does not attend the video identification procedure. This results in fewer identification procedures being cancelled.
3. A large database of video clips (in excess of 20,000) is available, providing more foils for selection. This makes it easier to select foils that resemble the suspect in appearance.
4. Video is less threatening to victims, who no longer have to attend an identification suite where, for example, their attacker may be physically present.
5. Video equipment can be taken to a witness who is unable to attend the police station. For example, a victim of a violent attack may be able to view a video line-up from a hospital bed or a witness could view a line-up anywhere in the world.
6. The suspect no longer has the opportunity to change their appearance if their image was captured for the video identification when they were first detained.
7. A video line-up does not require the continuing co-operation of the suspect. Once the suspect's image has been captured for a video line-up, the suspect's co-operation with the procedure is no longer required.

Video identification has had a considerable impact on the investigative process due to development of legislation and technology. In certain instances when there is a suspect known to the police but who is unavailable, identification officers may hold an identification procedure in advance of any arrest using any suitable still or moving image of the suspect. This same principle of using historically held imagery may be applied to a person suspected of committing a crime many years ago and whose appearance has changed (*R v Folan*, 2003). Forensic advances in the use of DNA evidence and an ever-increasing database of suspect images means that this aspect of crime investigation is set to increase. Overall, the speed of process that video identification provides has, in many instances, hastened the outcome of an investigation where identification is deemed an issue. It is not unusual, particularly where serious crime is involved, for the identification procedure to be conducted whilst the suspect is in custody. A further feature of video technology is the ability to cover or replicate distinguishing features on the faces of the suspect and/or the foils (e.g. scars, tattoos etc.) to ensure a procedure complies with legislation. This issue is discussed in more detail below.

The increased use of eyewitness identification evidence

Devlin (1976) ascertained that 2,116 identity parades were held in England and Wales during 1973. PACE resulted in an increase in the use of identity parades, because it gave suspects the right to an identity parade if identification is disputed. Slater (1994) reported data from 24 of 52 UK police forces showing a sharp rise in the number of identity parades organized during the period 1990–93. In 1993 the 24 police forces who reported data organized 13,652 identity parades. The introduction of video together with further legislative changes, which has made it easier to organize identification procedures, has resulted in a further sharp increase in demand. The best estimate for 2006 suggests that the number of video identification procedures had reached a minimum of 80,000 annually. Paradoxically, the courts now rely more on eyewitness identification than they did in the 1970s when Devlin analysed eyewitness identification evidence.

Research on video identification

The format of presenting a line-up (photographs, video, live) and manipulation of the richness of cues available (e.g. stills, moving images, people walking) has a surprisingly small effect on identification accuracy. A possible reason is that the face is the most reliable way to recognize somebody and the face can be sufficiently well perceived from a good quality still photograph. Therefore, relying on cues such as gait, build or colour images would add little extra benefit. Reviewing the literature, Cutler, Berman, Penrod & Fisher concluded: 'With respect to current practices, the conservative conclusion is that, based on available research, there is no reason to believe that live line-ups, videotaped line-ups or photo arrays produce substantial differences in identification performance' (1994: 181).

Fairness of video line-ups

The research available suggests that video identification is likely to be no more or less sensitive than a live line-up. However, the number of video clips available in a database to construct video line-ups is much greater than the number of volunteers available to stand on a live line-up. Therefore, there is good reason to believe that in an operational context it should be possible to construct video line-ups that are fairer than live line-ups. Indeed, research has found that video line-ups from criminal cases were fairer to the suspects than conventional 'live' line-ups (Valentine & Heaton, 1999). Furthermore, video line-ups were equally fair to white European and African–Caribbean suspects (Valentine, Harris, Colom Piera & Darling, 2003). In these studies, participants ('mock witnesses') were given the first description of the offender provided by the original witness and were required to select the line-up member whom they thought was most likely to be the suspect. As a mock witness has not seen the perpetrator, the suspect should be chosen no more often than predicted by chance if the line-up is perfectly fair: 11% (one in nine) of choices should be of the suspect from line-ups containing eight foils. Valentine & Heaton (1999) found that the mock witnesses identified the suspect in live line-ups more frequently (25%) than by chance, but were not able to select the suspect from video line-ups (15%) significantly more often than chance. Valentine *et al.* (2003) found that video line-ups of African–Caribbeans and of white Europeans were equally fair, using equal numbers of mock witness from both ethnic backgrounds.

Perception of identification officers

Hughes (2005) examined the opinions of 30 experienced police identification officers of video identification procedures. Almost all identification officers regarded video identification as a better method than a live line-up. The point was made that it facilitated use of identification evidence for volume crime rather than just serious crime. Interestingly, 37% of identification officers thought identification evidence was wholly reliable. This figure increases to 51% if witness confidence is high and the procedure is held shortly after the crime. The majority of officers (66%) thought that video identification is fair to both suspect and witness; nobody thought it unfair to the suspect, but 33% thought it unfair to the witness. The concern was that aspects of the procedure made the task of identification too difficult. There was a clear view (90%) that more should be done to brief and support the witness prior to the procedure.

Evaluation of revised procedures for video line-ups

Valentine, Darling & Memon (2007) tested whether adopting the strict sequential presentation rules described above would enhance the reliability of video identification evidence. The strict sequential presentation procedure, by which the witness was instructed to make a response to each face as it was presented, was compared to the British procedure in which witnesses are told to watch the whole video twice before making a decision. The line-up administrator was blind to the position of the suspect in a nine-person line-up under both the 'strict sequential' and the 'existing' conditions. There was no reliable effect of the presentation procedure on the number of mistaken identifications from perpetrator-absent line-ups, but there were fewer correct identifications of the perpetrator when he was present in the line-up under the 'strict sequential' condition.

Darling, Valentine & Memon (2008) tested the use of a culprit-description strategy instead of suspect-resemblance strategy to select foils for a nine-person video line-up. It was established, from pairwise ratings of similarity provided by participants who did not take part in the main study, that the foils in the culprit-description line-ups were more dissimilar to each other than were the foils in the suspect resemblance line-ups. Nevertheless, there was no statistically significant difference in the rate of correct or mistaken identification between culprit-description and suspect-resemblance line-ups. The experiments reported by Valentine *et al.* (2007) and Darling *et al.* (2008) followed British police video identification procedures and used line-ups constructed from a police national database. These data explicitly compared procedures advocated in the research literature with existing procedures in an operational context in the UK. There was no evidence that either the sequential presentation instructions or the culprit-description strategy would improve the existing video identification procedures.

Suspects with distinguishing marks

How can a fair line-up be constructed if a suspect has a distinguishing mark, for example a tattoo, scar or distinctive mark on their face? A witness may have described a mark or tattoo and the suspect may have been arrested because they have a similar mark. Alternatively, the suspect may have a mark that was not described by a witness. If the suspect is the only person in the line-up with a scar or tattoo on his face, he will stand out in comparison to the foils, rendering the line-up unfair. In the UK the suspect's solicitor is likely to object to a line-up in which his or her client is the only person with a scar or tattoo.

There have been two solutions to this problem. Most frequently the area of the distinguishing feature is masked on the face of the suspect and the foils. For video identification the area is pixelated, using a mosaic of squares in a grid that have an average colour and luminance to occlude the area. This process can be automated in moving video so that the mosaic occludes the same area of the face as the view changes. The alternative strategy is to replicate the distinguishing mark on the faces of the foils. This process is time-consuming and expensive, so the mark is usually replicated only on full-face and profile views. Under these circumstances still images are shown to the witness instead of moving images.

Is it better to mask or replicate? The disadvantage of masking a distinguishing feature is that it changes the appearance of the suspect's face. A distinctive feature will be a salient cue to recognizing the face of a perpetrator (Winograd, 1981; Valentine, 1991). Therefore, a better strategy is to replicate the feature on the foils. If replication is used, the identical feature is normally replicated. However, this strategy means that the witness cannot use their knowledge of the distinguishing mark to recognize the perpetrator. A better approach would be to use the culprit-description strategy described above. The feature replicated on each face should be consistent with the witness's description, but the precise properties (location, size, colour or style) may vary across foils within the constraints set by the description. This variation would allow the witness to use recognition of a distinguishing mark to support recognition of the perpetrator. However, variation in the characteristics of the distinguishing mark would not introduce any bias against an innocent suspect whom the witness has not seen before.

As replication can only be implemented on still images, the question arises of whether use of still images rather than moving video would impair identification accuracy. The effectiveness of moving video and a single, still, full-face image was compared in an otherwise identical video identification procedure by Valentine *et al.* (2007) and Darling *et al.* (2008). No effect on identification of perpetrators from culprit-present line-ups was observed. A foil was less likely to be mistakenly identified from culprit-absent line-up when moving images were used in one experiment (Valentine *et al.*, 2007), but the effect was not replicated in a second experiment (Darling *et al.*, 2008). The data suggest that use of moving images has little if any reliable influence on the outcome of a line-up.

Eyewitness confidence and accuracy

It has been appreciated for a long time that a confident witness may be mistaken (Devlin, 1976). Indeed, a caution to this effect is included in the Turnbull judgement on eyewitness evidence. In recent years it has been demonstrated that the relationship between the confidence of an eyewitness and the accuracy of their identification is moderately strong for witnesses who identify somebody at a line-up. However, the relationship is weaker amongst witnesses who reject the line-up (Sporer, Penrod, Read & Cutler, 1995). Confidence is most closely associated with accuracy when measured immediately after an identification has been made (Cutler & Penrod, 1989), and critically before the witness acquires any further information about their identification. However, as the association between confidence and accuracy is far from perfect, confident but mistaken eyewitnesses will be encountered fairly frequently.

Malleability of witness confidence

A very important research finding is that witness confidence is changeable and is influenced by information that the witness acquires after attending an identification procedure. Receiving feedback that the person identified is the suspect, or that somebody else made the same identification, will increase the witness's confidence in their identification. Not only does confirming feedback tend to make the witness subsequently more confident in their identification, but it also tends to inflate estimates of a range of subsequent testimony, including how long the culprit was seen for, how close they were and how much attention the witness paid (Wells & Bradfield, 1998). Furthermore, confirming post-identification feedback tends to make eyewitnesses overconfident; that is, they now express more confidence in their identification than is warranted (Semmler, Brewer & Wells, 2004). By the time a witness gives evidence in court they are likely to have received confirming feedback. Therefore, the confidence a witness displays in court may well be determined by the feedback they have received in addition to their initial confidence at the identity procedure.

The confidence of real witnesses

Wright & Skagerberg (2007) took advantage of the practice of Sussex Police to routinely inform witnesses at a video line-up whether they had identified the suspect. After the witness had made an identification but before they received feedback each witness provided a rating on a 10-point scale for three questions, one each about their opportunity to view the culprit, the identification they had just made and how good they believed their general memory to be. After receiving feedback, each witness provided a rating on three questions, and again one question addressed each of the same three aspects. Witnesses evaluated the identification task as more difficult after feedback that their identification was mistaken, but witnesses who were told that they had identified the suspect evaluated the task as easier. Wright & Skegerberg (*ibid.*) make an important contribution by demonstrating that malleability of confidence previously observed in laboratory studies is also observed in real witnesses and victims of crime. There is no provision in the current PACE code of practice to record a statement of confidence, although anything the witness does say must be written down. In contrast, the US Department of Justice guide on eyewitness identification does recommend taking a clear statement of confidence immediately after the witness makes an identification and before any feedback is given (Technical Working Group for Eyewitness Identification, 1999).

The code of practice for England and Wales requires that witnesses are instructed: 'If you cannot make a positive identification, you should say so.' Hughes' (2005) survey showed that the meaning of the word 'positive' was ambiguous even amongst identification officers. Interpretation ranged from 'any identification' to 'a definite 100%' confidence. Only 7% of identification officers said that they ask the eyewitness about their confidence in their identification before they leave the ID suite. Ninety-three per cent of officers know the position of the suspect in the video line-up (i.e., the identification procedure is not run blind). The majority (70%) did not think that blind testing would enhance justice. Nineteen per cent of police forces have a policy of telling witnesses whether they identified the suspect. One reason given for this policy is to enhance witness care as most witnesses want to know if they have identified the suspect. Unfortunately, only 36% of respondents who inform the witness of the outcome of an identification procedure take a statement before providing the feedback. Making a written record of confidence before providing feedback is essential to preserve an accurate record of confidence at the time of identification. Prior to trial a witness is likely to receive or deduce feedback that will bolster their confidence.

Conclusions and recommendations

The evidence is very clear that mistaken identification is the leading cause of wrongful conviction. Furthermore, wrongful conviction is a major problem – there have now been more than 230 DNA exonerations in the USA. Whilst this evidence relates specifically to that country, there is good cause to believe that a similar problem exists in the UK. Approximately 20% of eyewitnesses in the UK make a known mistaken identification. However, a mistaken identification of a foil in a line-up will not lead to a wrongful conviction. It is the unknown mistaken identification of the police suspect that leads to a miscarriage of justice. The legal system in the UK is very different from that in the USA. Identification procedures in England and Wales are regulated by the code of practice (code D) required by the Police and Criminal Evidence Act. In addition, a special warning about the frailty of eyewitness identification must be given to the jury by the trial judge. Nevertheless, uncorroborated eyewitness identification evidence remains sufficient to secure a conviction in England and Wales.

The PACE code of practice does include a number of elements of best practice which are not often discussed in the research literature on eyewitness identification. The suspect's legal representative has the right to be present when a witness views a video or live line-up. If no representative is present, the procedure must be videotaped. This provision has the potential to be an effective protection of the suspect's rights and to discourage overtly leading behaviour. A further provision that allows the suspect or their legal representative the opportunity to object to line-up members provides a practical means to improve the selection of foils, which is likely to enhance the fairness of line-ups.

Although the PACE code of practice is extensive, there are a number of areas in which practice could be improved. As virtually all identification procedures are run on video double-blind testing, in which the line-up administrator does not know who the suspect is, can be easily implemented (see Valentine, 2006, for a practical suggestion of implementing this provision). Blind testing would enhance the integrity of identification procedures and safeguard the police against accusations of malpractice. The code of practice should be amended to include provision to take a clear statement of confidence immediately after any identification made. Feedback on the identification should not be given to the witness. However, it is important to explain carefully to the witness the reasons for not giving feedback. The final area for improvement is the issue of improving support for the witness. Attending an identification procedure can be a difficult and stressful experience. Guidance should be developed to ensure the experience is made as easy as possible for the witness. Provisions should include clear guidelines for briefing the witness about the procedure and checking their understanding of the process and procedure following the identification. Special care is needed for briefing children, elderly and vulnerable witnesses. The Scottish Executive has recently published guidance on the conduct of video identification with child witnesses, which includes information booklets for children and for parents and carers (Scottish Executive, 2005a; 2005b; 2005c).

References

Bartlett, J. C., Hurry, S. & Thorley, W. (1984). Typicality and familiarity of faces. *Memory & Cognition, 12*, 219–228.

Behrman, B. W. & Davey, S. L. (2001). Eyewitness identification in actual criminal cases: An archival analysis. *Law and Human Behavior, 25*, 475–491.

Clark, S. E. & Davey, S. L. (2005). The targets-to-foils shift in simultaneous and sequential line-ups. *Law and Human Behavior, 29*, 151–172.

Cutler, B. L. & Penrod, S. D. (1989). Forensically-relevant moderators of the relationship between eyewitness identification accuracy and confidence. *Journal of Applied Psychology, 74*, 650–652.

Cutler, B. L., Berman, G. L., Penrod, S. & Fisher, R. P. (1994). Conceptual, practical and empirical issues associated with eyewitness identification test media. In D. F. Ross, J. D. Read & M. P. Toglia (Eds.), *Adult eyewitness testimony: Current trends and developments* (pp.163–181). Cambridge: Cambridge University Press.

Darling, S., Valentine, T. & Memon, A. (2008). Selection of line-up foils in operational contexts. *Applied Cognitive Psychology, 22*, 159–169.

Deffenbacher, K. A., Bornstein, B. H. & Penrod, S. D (2006). Mugshot exposure effects: Retroactive interference, mugshot commitment, source confusion and unconscious transference. *Law and Human Behavior, 30*, 287–307.

Devlin, P. (1976). *Report to the Secretary of State for the Home Department of the Departmental Committee on evidence of identification in criminal cases.* London: Her Majesty's Stationery Office.

Gardiner. J. M. & Richardson-Klavehn, A. (2000). Remembering and knowing. In E. Tulving & F. I. M. Craik (Eds.), *Handbook of memory* (pp. 229–244). New York: Oxford University Press.

Harris, M. J. & Rosenthal, R. (1985). Mediation of interpersonal expectancy effects: 31 meta-analyses. *Psychological Bulletin, 97,* 363–386.

Hughes, C. (2005). Making the best use of video film identification parades and providing a fair and consistent approach to witnesses. Unpublished MSc thesis, University of Portsmouth.

Innocence Project (n.d.). http://www.innocenceproject.org/understand/Eyewitness-Misidentification.php. Accessed 7 January 2008.

Jacoby, L. L. & Dallas, M. (1981). On the relationship between autobiographical memory and perceptual learning. *Journal of Experimental Psychology: General, 110,* 306–340.

Juslin, P., Olsson, N. & Winman, A. (1996). Calibration and diagnosticity of confidence in eyewitness identification: comments on what can be inferred from the low confidence–accuracy correlation. *Journal of Experimental Psychology: Learning, Memory and Cognition, 22,* 1304–1316.

Lindsay, R. C. L. & Wells, G. L. (1985). Improving eyewitness identification from line-ups: Simultaneous versus sequential presentation. *Journal of Applied Psychology, 66,* 343–350.

Lindsay, R. C. L., Lea, J. A. & Fulford, J. A. (1991). Sequential line-up presentation: Technique matters. *Journal of Applied Psychology, 76,* 741–745.

Lindsay, R. C. L., Martin, R. & Webber, L. (1994). Default values in eyewitness descriptions: A problem for the match-to-description line-up foil selection strategy. *Law and Human Behavior, 18,* 527–541.

Luus, C. A. E. & Wells, G. L. (1991). Eyewitness identification and the selection of distracters for line-ups. *Law and Human Behavior, 15,* 43–57.

Mandler, G. (1980). Recognising: The judgement of previous occurrence. *Psychological Review, 87,* 252–271.

Meissner, C. A., Tredoux, C. G., Parker, J. F. & MacLin, O. (2005). Eyewitness decisions in simultaneous and sequential line-ups: A dual-process signal detection theory analysis. *Memory & Cognition, 33,* 783–792.

Pike, G., Brace, N. & Kyman, S. (2002). *The visual identification of suspects: Procedures and practice.* Briefing note 2/02, Policing and Reducing Crime Unit, Home Office Research Development and Statistics Directorate. http://www.homeoffice. gov.uk/rds/prgbriefpubs1.html. Accessed 7 January 2008.

Police and Criminal Evidence Act 1984. Sections 60(1)(a), s.60(1) and s.66(1)) codes of practice (2008). http://police.homeoffice.gov.uk/operational-policing/ powers-pace-codes/pace-code-intro/ Accessed 1 April 2008.

Scottish Executive (2005a). *Guidance on the conduct of identity parades with child witnesses.* http://www.scotland.gov.uk/ Publications/2005/10/14104449/44500. Accessed 1 April 2008.

Scottish Executive (2005b). *Video identification parades. A booklet for children and young people.* http://www.scotland.gov.uk/Publications/2005/10/14104300/ 43005. Accessed 1 April 2008.

Scottish Executive (2005c). *Your child is attending a video identification parade. A booklet for parents and carers.* http://www.scotland.gov.uk/Publications/ 2005/10/14104354/43549. Accessed 1 April 2008.

Semmler, C., Brewer, N. & Wells, G. L. (2004). Effects of postidentification feedback on eyewitness identification and nonidentification confidence. *Journal of Applied Psychology*, *89*, 334–346.

Slater, A. (1994) *Identification parades: A scientific evaluation*. London: Police Research Group (Police Research Award Scheme), Home Office: London.

Sporer, S., Penrod, S., Read, D. & Cutler, B. L. (1995) Choosing, confidence and accuracy: A meta-analysis of the confidence-accuracy relations in eyewitness identification studies, *Psychological Bulletin*, *118*, 315–327.

Steblay, N. M. (1997). Social influence in eyewitness recall: A meta-analytic review of line-up instruction effects. *Law and Human Behavior*, *21*, 283–297.

Steblay, N., Dysart, J., Fulero, S. & Lindsay, R. C. L. (2001). Eyewitness accuracy rates in sequential and simultaneous line-up presentations: A meta-analytic comparison. *Law and Human Behavior*, *25*, 459–473.

Technical Working Group for Eyewitness Identification (1999). *Eyewitness evidence: A guide for law enforcement*. Washington, DC: US Department of Justice. www. ncjrs.org/nij/eyewitness/tech_working_group.html. Accessed 11 December 2007.

Tulving, E. (1985). Memory and consciousness. *Canadian Psychologist*, *26*, 1–12.

Tunnicliffe, J. L. & Clark, S. E. (2000). Selecting foils for identification line-ups: Matching suspects or descriptions? *Law and Human Behavior*, *24*, 231–258.

Valentine, T. (1991). A unified account of the effects of distinctiveness, inversion and race in face recognition. *Quarterly Journal of Experimental Psychology*, *43A*, 161–204.

Valentine, T. (2006). Forensic facial identification. In A. Heaton-Armstrong, E. Shepherd, G. Gudjonsson, & D. Wolchover (Eds.), *Witness testimony; Psychological, investigative and evidential perspectives* (pp. 281–307). Oxford: Oxford University Press.

Valentine, T. & Heaton, P. (1999). An evaluation of the fairness of police line-ups and video identifications. *Applied Cognitive Psychology*, *13*, S59–S72.

Valentine, T., Harris, N., Colom Piera, A. & Darling, S. (2003). Are police video identifications fair to African-Caribbean suspects? *Applied Cognitive Psychology*, *17*, 459–476.

Valentine, T., Pickering, A. & Darling, S. (2003). Characteristics of eyewitness identification that predict the outcome of real line-ups. *Applied Cognitive Psychology*, *17*, 969–993.

Valentine, T., Darling, S. & Memon, A. (2007). Do strict rules and moving images increase the reliability of sequential identification procedures? *Applied Cognitive Psychology*, *21*, 933–949.

Wells, G. L. (1993). What do we know about eyewitness identification? *American Psychologist*, *48*, 553–571.

Wells G. L. & Bradfield, A. L. (1998). 'Good, you identified the suspect': Feedback to eyewitnesses distort their reports of the witnessing experience. *Journal of Applied Psychology*, *66*, 688–696.

Wells, G. L., Rydell, S. M. & Seelau, E. (1993). The selection of distracters for eyewitness line-ups. *Journal of Applied Psychology*, *78*, 835–844.

Winograd, E. (1981). Elaboration and distinctiveness in memory for faces. Journal of Experimental Psychology, *Human Learning and Memory*, *7*, 181–190.

Wright, D. B. & McDaid, A. T. (1996). Comparing system and estimator variables using data from real line-ups. *Applied Cognitive Psychology, 10*, 75–84.

Wright, D. B. & Skagerberg, E. M. (2007). Postidentification feedback affects real eyewitnesses. *Psychological Science, 18*, 172–178.

Yonelinas, A. P. (2002). The nature of recollection and familiarity: A review of 30 years of research. *Journal of Memory and Language, 46*, 441–517.

Cases

R v Folan (2003) EWCA Crim 908
R v. John Darren Mitchell (2005). EWCA Crim 731
R v Turnbull (1976) 3 All ER 549

Statutes

Police and Criminal Evidence Act 1984

Chapter Fourteen

A Method to Enhance Person Description: A Field Study

Samuel Demarchi

Laboratoire de Psychologie Sociale
Université Paris 8

and

Jacques Py

Université Toulouse 2

Verbal descriptions of perpetrators are important components of both the preliminary and the long-term investigation of a crime. Law enforcement officers generally attempt to obtain descriptions rather swiftly following the onset of the investigation, and those descriptions are given to officers for the identification of potential suspects in the vicinity of the crime. In addition, person descriptions provide a way of estimating the congruence between a witness's initial recall of the perpetrator and the physical appearance of the suspect who is eventually apprehended. As a result of the notion that a verbal description represents some memory characteristics, researchers have frequently encouraged its use when constructing line-ups for eyewitnesses (Wells, Small, Penrod, Malpass, Fulero & Brimacombe, 1998), when conducting subsequent tests of line-up fairness (Doob & Kirshenbaum, 1973; Wells & Bradfield, 1999; Py, Demarchi & Ginet, 2003) and when constructing a facial composite or sketch of the perpetrator's face (Green & Geiselman, 1989).

Handbook of Psychology of Investigative Interviewing: Current Developments and Future Directions
Edited by Ray Bull, Tim Valentine and Tom Williamson
© 2009 John Wiley & Sons, Ltd.

Contents for person description

Despite their importance in the investigative process, it has been extensively observed that perpetrator descriptions reported by witnesses were superficial. For example, Kuehn (1974) analysed 100 police reports based on the account of a single victim who was unacquainted with the suspect. The reports were taken from a random sample of criminal cases (homicides, rapes, aggravated assaults and armed robberies). Results showed that the majority of victims provided 7.2 physical characteristics. Several other archive-based studies corroborate Kuehn's findings on completeness of perpetrators' description (see Table 14.1). Note that all the descriptions included in those studies have been obtained using standard police interview protocols, which means that no standardized or specific methods, such as the Cognitive Interview (Geiselman, Fisher, Firstenberg, Hutton, Sullivan, Avetissian & Prosk, 1984) have been used to obtain descriptions.

Another aspect of person recall refers to the nature of information provided by witnesses, in particular their frequency of occurrence and their quality (or accuracy rate). Usually, descriptions contained more physical details than descriptions of clothing (Sporer, 1996; van Koppen & Lochun, 1997; Demarchi, 2003). Concerning physical information, witnesses report more general features (gender, height, build, age and ethnicity) than facial features (e.g. mouth, nose, eye or hair colour, etc.). The majority of facial descriptors referred to the upper half of the face, in particular the hair and, with lower frequency, eye colour. Other facial characteristics (e.g., chin or mouth) were rarely mentioned (Sporer, 1996; van Koppen & Lochun, 1997; Demarchi, 2003; Fahsing, Ask & Granhag, 2004).

From a qualitative point of view, witnesses are quite accurate in their descriptions. Yuille & Cutshall (1986) reported an average accuracy rate of

Table 14.1:   Completeness and accuracy of descriptions from archive studies

Studies	Completeness	Accuracy [a] (%)
Kuehn (1974)	7.2	–
Lindsay, Martin & Webber (1994)	3.9	–
Tollestrup, Turtle & Yuille (1994)	6.9	–
Sporer (1996)	9.7	–
van Koppen & Lochun (1997)	8.4	76
Demarchi (2003)	8.6	78
Fashing, Ask & Granhag (2004)	9.4	87

Notes

'–' = unavailable data.

a. Sum of correct descriptors reported by participants, divided by the sum of all descriptors reported, multiplied by 100.

Table 14.2: Occurrence and accuracy of descriptors from archive studies

Attributes	van Koppen & Lochun (1997) (N = 2,299)		Demarchi (2003) (N = 216)		Fahsing et al. (2004) (N = 250)	
	Occurrence (%)	Accuracy (%)	Occurrence (%)	Accuracy (%)	Occurrence (%)	Accuracy (%)
Gender	95	100	100	100	100	100
Height	70	97	83	58	91	78
Ethnicity	64	80	85	97	50	92
Build	48	51	65	74	84	90
Age	55	98	86	43	62	60
Hair	–	–	–	–	18	97
Hair colour	36	82	43	77	–	–
Hair length	–		51	84	–	–
Hair type	34	33	0	–	–	–
Face shape	12	100	0	–	10	85
Eye colour	5	75	11	78	4	100
Nose	3	37	2	–	–	–
Facial hair	10	3	0	–	2	100
Mouth	2	39	1	–	2	20
Accent	31	32	-	–	47	99

Note
'–' = unavailable or incalculable data.

75.6%. Results of others' studies are similar or slightly higher (Fashing *et al.*, 2004). More precisely, witnesses' descriptions of sex and ethnicity are almost always consistently accurate, whereas descriptors of facial and other character-istics are poorer or inconsistent across studies (see Table 14.2).

Thus, witnesses have a general impression of their assailants, but cannot recall discrete features (nose, mouth, etc.). In other words, eyewitnesses' verbal descriptions of criminals are usually too few in number and too vague to identify a specific suspect. Furthermore, the majority of information available for those in search of a perpetrator (e.g. age, build, height, hair, etc.) may be incorrect or can be easily altered (e.g. hair colour or length). This results in an inappropriate selection of likely suspects from a mugshot database because the algorithm may select suspects who match the vague description of the criminal, but not their actual appearance.

Results of laboratory studies dealing with various aspects of human memory offer another way to investigate the nature of person descriptions. The majority of descriptions provided contain approximately 10 features, with an overall accuracy rate greater than 70% (see Table 14.3). In a study of verbal recall,

Table 14.3: Completeness and accuracy of descriptions from laboratory studies

Studies	Completeness	Accuracy (%)
Wells, Rydell & Seelau (1993)	5.1	–
Lindsay, Martin & Webber (1994)	7.4	–
Finger & Pezdek (1999)[a]	11.6	90
Finger & Pezdek (1999)[b]	12.1	90
Finger & Pezdek (1999)[c]	15.2	85
Finger & Pezdek (1999)[d]	12.9	88
Geiselman *et al.* (2000)	5.3	87
Tunnicliff & Clark (2000)	6.3	–
Meissner, Brigham & Kelley (2001)	9.0	90
Meissner (2002)[e]	6.5	83
Meissner (2002)[f]	5.7	83
Meissner (2002)[f]	6.0	83
Meissner (2002)[g]	4.9	77
Brown & Lloyd-Jones (2003)	15.9	71
Pozzulo & Warren (2003)	9.9	87

Notes

'–' = unavailable data.

a. experiment 1, 10 min delayed recall. b. experiment 2, 1 hr delayed recall. c. experiment 3, 5 min delayed recall. d. experiment 3, 24 min delayed recall. e. experiment 1, 15 min delayed recall. f. experiment 2, 15 min delayed recall. g. experiment 2, 1 week delayed recall.

Lindsay, Martin & Webber (1994) observed that height was reported by 86% of their participants, followed by build (51%), gender (46%), age (45%), ethnicity (43%) and weight (22%). For facial features, upper features are reported more than lower, and in the following relative frequency order: hair, eyes, nose, face shape, eyebrows, chin, lips and mouth (Ellis, Shepherd & Davies, 1980; Laughery, Duval & Wogalter, 1986). It is worth noting that Davies, van der Willik & Morrison (2000) observed a similar order among participants who constructed a composite of a face: participants began their assigned task by selecting hair, and then applied a downward selection strategy. In addition, all of these results are compatible with face processing, in particular the prevalence of upper facial features (notably hair) in face perception and recognition (Tanaka & Farah, 1993). In fact, although descriptions reported by experiment participants are significantly more complete than those provided by real witnesses (Lindsay *et al.*, 1994), they remain insufficient in terms of the informative value which might help police officers to detect the criminal. Despite this, they contain more information about ethnicity, height, body build, hair length, colour and style, eyes, facial hair, complexion and shape.

How can person descriptions be improved?

Several methods can be used to collect person descriptions. For example, witnesses can write down their description (free recall instruction: 'Tell me all you can about the physical appearance of the criminal') or be administered a facial feature adjective list (FFAL; Ellis, 1986). The FFAL contains items where the participant rates individual facial features and shapes, with the option of responding 'Don't know' or 'Not applicable'. Simply by the nature of the task, the checklists, however, force the witness to consider a particular feature, even if they have no memory for it, by determining if it corresponds to a visual memory of the face. This is why a feature checklist produces more incorrect features than a free recall task (Wogalter, 1991; 1996). This method, although easy to use and appearing to be *a priori* common sense, is not compatible with the endeavours of law professionals because of the poor quality information obtained from witnesses. Although a feature checklist produces more exhaustive recall than self-generated descriptions, feature checklists lead to an increase in the error rate in comparison to spontaneous testimony (Stern, 1902; Borst, 1904; Whipple, 1909, 1913; Cady, 1924; Goulding, 1971; Dent & Stephenson, 1979). In addition, feature checklists may subsequently interfere with participants' ability to identify the target person (Wogalter, 1991, 1996; Demarchi, Py, Parain & Groud-Tan, 2006). The counterargument is that a verbatim free report is usually poor and ineffective in making an arrest (Lipton, 1977), despite a good accuracy rate.

The nature of the instructions given to the witness also modulates both the quantity and quality of descriptors produced by limiting, expanding or cautioning the participants on the information to be generated. For example, Meissner, Brigham & Kelley (2001) found that asking someone to 'be sure to report only those details that they are confident of, and do not attempt to guess at any particular feature' (*warning instruction*) significantly increases the overall description quality in comparison to a standard ('Describe in as much detail as possible the face you saw') or a *forced recall* ('It's important to report everything. Try not to leave out any details about the face even if you think they are not important'). Nevertheless, even when the warning instruction was used, the quality of descriptions was very poor.

Despite the crucial importance of a perpetrator's description in the investigative process, few studies have attempted to increase the completeness and quality of descriptions. Some researchers, for example, used the standard Cognitive Interview (CI) protocol (Fisher, Geiselman, Raymond, Jurkewich & Warhaftig, 1987; see Ginet & Py, 2001, for a French version of the CI) to enhance person recall. The CI incorporates four retrieval mnemonics: *report all*, *context reinstatement*, *change of order* and *change of perspective*. The results of several studies show that, despite these methods significantly increasing the completeness of descriptions, the information gain is weak (Geiselman, Fisher, Firstenberg, Hutton, Sullivan, Avetissian & Prosk, 1984). Nevertheless, some results lead us to conclude that particular instructions of the CI are more efficient for person description. For example, Boon & Noon (1994) and Clifford & George (1996) have shown that the *report all* and *context reinstatement* instructions were the more useful. These results, however, show that the

CI, even if it is a powerful tool in obtaining exhaustive event recall, had poor results concerning person recall.

However, removing the inappropriate instructions of the standard CI appears to increase the completeness of description. Finger & Pezdek (1999) eliminated the *change order* and *change perspective* instructions, and added a novel one, *imagery*, from which participants tried to visualize the face and mentally form an image of it. Results showed that the modified CI was more effective than a standard interview. Py & Demarchi (2006) obtained similar results in a field study in collaboration with police officers. They kept both the *report all* and the *context reinstatement* instruction, and added a *holistic processing* instruction (based Craik & Lockhart, 1972; Bower & Karlin, 1974). The modified CI, in comparison to a standard police interview, significantly enhanced both the completeness and the quality of physical information reported by participants about a person they had previously met informally (experiment 1). Compared to a standard police interview, it also permitted easier detection of the target person from an array of similar individuals (experiment 2). This research showed that a modified CI can enhance person recall, providing that new protocols are used to complement a standard CI for events and facts recall. Consequently, there is an increase in the time taken to conduct two CIs. There is a pressing need to produce a simpler method.

The person description interview (PDI)

One way to improve person descriptions is to take a similar approach to that used in the CI. A good understanding of episodic memory is required to create a tool compatible with memory processes. The method must be based on the following fundamental principles:

1. It is useful not only to ask someone to describe a person, but also to give instructions to facilitate the recall task.
2. In accordance with ergonomic practice, any tools or instructions must be adapted to the natural human process or strategy. An instruction based on an *unnatural* (or *reversed*) one could decrease the global quality of the response, in terms of increasing the total amount of errors, for example.
3. If only one strategy is spontaneously used to do a particular task, then a complementary approach should improve it, such as an inversed strategy (e.g. the *change of order instruction* in the CI). This is only relevant if the complementary approach does not have a disruptive influence.

Scientific literature contains little information about the cognitive processes or strategies involved in describing people and methods to improve them. Therefore, it is necessary to understand how person verbal recall is organized and structured before creating an interview method. Two preliminary studies were conducted to determine the strategies spontaneously used to describe a person. In study 1, participants met a man (target) informally. After a 10-minute delay during which they completed a filler task, they had to describe the target following a *standard instruction* ('Tell me all you can about the person you met'). Descriptive analysis showed that 84% of participants spontaneously reported general features first (age, height, weight, attitudes, etc.), and then carried on with more local traits (hair, eyes, etc.). We described this spontaneous strategy as *general to specific*. Half the participants continued to use a downward *top-to-bottom* descriptive strategy, where upper facial elements (e.g. hair) were reported first, followed by lower traits (eyes, nose, mouth, etc.). Finally, only 16% of the participants used no apparent strategy at all. In study 2, which concerned only face description, participants were presented with a single photograph of the same target man. All participants were given the same instruction as in study 1 and subsequently described the target. Descriptive analysis confirmed that the majority of participants (87%) used the *top-to-bottom* strategy to describe a face. In accordance with laboratory and real-life case studies, it was also observed that lower facial features were never recalled.

These observations lead to the conclusion that two instructions can be created (first fundamental principle presented above). The first one, related to the *general-to-specific* strategy, can be created which concerns all the physical and trait judgements (second fundamental principle), and the second one, related to the *top-to-bottom* strategy, which concerns only face description (third fundamental principle). This means that it is necessary to use two successive free recalls, each following an instruction. The first instruction aims to enhance the *general-to-specific* strategy, which seems to be the only spontaneously used method to describe a person, because, as in the experiments above, none of the participants started their spontaneous free recall by reporting details first. We've termed this strategy the *general-to-specific instruction* (or GSI) and is articulated as follows:

> Try to describe the person you saw. Be as complete as you can. Try not to provide only detail, and please begin your description by reporting general and global features of the person you saw, like silhouette, height, build, ethnicity, or personality, occupational impressions, etc., and carry on with facial or clothing details.

Our pilot studies suggest that this instruction must be given first. The second instruction was specifically designed to increase the number of facial descriptors, especially lower facial features. Neither a free recall instruction nor one based on a natural strategy would be sufficient to obtain lower facial descriptors. In order to solve this problem, a reverse-order descriptive strategy was used. We termed it the *down-to-up instruction* (or DUI). It is formulated as follows:

> Try to describe the face of the person you saw. Begin with the lower part of his
> face – such as his chin – and then go up to the top.

Because it is concerned with only face description, this instruction must be considered as complementing the first one and must be used after the initial description has been completed.

The efficiency of these instructions was tested in comparison with a *standard instruction* (Demarchi, 2003). Participants in this condition were presented with the following instructions:

> Please describe the person you saw. Try to be as complete as possible.

In the first experiment, the GSI used at the beginning of the interview obtained a 70% increase in correct information ($M = 12.35$) compared to the standard instruction ($M = 7.25$), without a significant increase in the number of errors. Results from the second experiment showed that the DUI, used after an initial free recall, led participants to reporting 242% more correct facial information ($M = 5.30$) compared to the standard instruction ($M = 1.55$), but also an 127% increase in errors (respectively $M = 1.10$ and $M = 2.50$ for standard and GSI instructions). In conclusion, the GSI led to more complete and accurate descriptions than a standard instruction, and the DUI provides more facial descriptors because participants were prompted to report lower facial features, which would not otherwise have been recalled. In fact, an optimal interviewing method for acquiring a person (or criminal) description consists of two consecutive free recalls each following a particular instruction: first, a GSI, and second, a DUI. We have termed this the *person description interview* (or PDI).

The laboratory test of the methods that comprise the PDI reported by Demarchi (2003) is very encouraging. However, it is essential that the combination of the two techniques used in the PDI is evaluated both in the laboratory and in the field, before any recommendation that the PDI should be used by the police. First, we examined the effect of the PDI protocol on completeness and accuracy of person description produced in the laboratory, in comparison to a control interview made up of two successive standard instructions and recall. This control interview began with a standard instruction ('Please describe the person you saw in as much detail as possible'). After this first description, the experimenter told the participant to describe he same target person again with the same standard instruction ('Now, describe the same person again in as much detail as possible'). Forty participants (all university students) were randomly assigned to one of two conditions, and were tested individually. They were shown a video of a target person performing routine activities. For external validity, we used 20 videos (same actions, scene, settings and view) with a different actor in each. No information about the aim of the experiment was given (incidental encoding). After watching the video, participants were given a 5-minute filler task and subsequently administered one of the two protocols.

Each interview was audio-taped and transcribed. All the descriptors reported by participants for the same target person were listed and distributed into several categories (facial elements, general components, clothes and subjective/attitudinal/behavioural details). Subjective details are those that refer to ambiguous qualities of face shape or personality/occupational impressions (Meissner *et al.*, 2001). Twenty students independently coded all the descriptive details recalled as either correct or incorrect.

Results showed that the descriptions obtained by the PDI contained significantly more correct information about general features ($M = 4.00$), facial features ($M = 9.25$), clothing ($M = 5.15$) and subjective/attitudinal/behavioural information ($M = 2.45$) than those obtained by the control interview (respectively $M = 2.60$, $M = 3.50$, $M = 3.10$ and $M = 2.45$), without an accompanying increase in errors, except for facial components (respectively $M = 4.25$ and $M = 2.45$ for PDI and control interview).

Ultimately, the PDI yielded more complete descriptions in comparison to a control interview. Nevertheless, before this method is employed in the field, it must be tested in collaboration with police officers because each professional, in their everyday job, could have some damaging practice which may decrease the efficiency of a new tool. There are also some informal institutional matters which are very difficult to detect in laboratory.

In our second experiment, we examined the effect of both the PDI protocol and the *standard French police interview for person description* (SFPIPD) on completeness and accuracy of person description produced in the field. When the SFPIPD is used, police officers usually begin with an open-ended instruction ('Give me all the details you can about the criminal'), and carry on with many questions about physical traits unreported by the witness or the victim.

The main procedural difference from the previous experiment was that all the interviews were conducted by police officers experienced and specializing in criminal investigation. All the interviews took place at a police station, in a police officer's office. Police officers were trained in the PDI protocol by an experimenter for approximately 20 minutes.

Twenty-eight university students were randomly assigned and were tested individually. They were shown one of the same videos as before. No information about the aim of the experiment was given. Consequently, they were not warned that their memory would be tested. After a 5-minute filler task, an experimenter told the participant that, if they agreed to take part, the next part of the study would take place in a police station. If the participant refused, their participation in the study ended. If they accepted, then the experimenter drove the participant to the police station. Immediately, a police officer would come and instruct the participant to accompany him to his office. Then, the interview would begin.

Results showed that the descriptions obtained by the PDI contained significantly more correct information about general features ($M = 5.93$), facial components ($M = 9.43$) and subjective information ($M = 3.29$) than those obtained by the SFPIPD (respectively $M = 3.50$, $M = 2.07$, and $M = 1.07$), without an accompanying increase in errors. The accuracy for these particular elements was significantly higher for the PDI than for the SFPIPD, respectively 90% and 71% for general features, 82% and 41% for facial components, and 96% and 56% for subjective elements. However, we did not observe any qualitative or quantitative difference between clothing descriptors reported by PDI or SFPIPD. Considering the total number of descriptors, we observed that the PDI obtained a 135% increase of correct information (respectively $M = 9.14$ and $M = 21.50$ for SFPIPD and PDI), with a 34% decrease in errors (respectively $M = 7.57$ and $M = 5.00$ for SFPIPD and PDI), and these significant differences led to more accurate descriptions (respectively 56% and 82% for SFPIPD and PDI).

Other results of interest to police officers concerned the proportion of witnesses whose description included each type of descriptor, which was equal to or higher for PDI compared to the SFPIPD (see Table 14.4). The PDI descriptions more frequently included ethnicity, forehead, chin, subjective information or face shape descriptors than those obtained by means of a SFPIPD. More important for the effectiveness of the investigative process is the significantly higher accuracy rate obtained with the PDI, particularly concerning

Table 14.4:   Occurrence and accuracy of descriptors

Descriptors	Occurrence (%)		Accuracy (%)	
	SFPIPD	*PDI*	*SFPIPD*	*PDI*
Gender	100	100	100	100
Height	100	100	44	80*
Age	93	100	41	81*
Ethnicity	79	100*	91	93
Build	71	93	82	94
Hair color	100	93	61	76
Hair length	100	100	35	75*
Forehead	0	29*	–	67
Eyes	100	100	40	55
Nose	43	93*	17	81*
Mouth	43	100*	17	93*
Chin	0	79*	–	86
Face shape	21	57*	25	77*
Other descriptors[a]	29	64*	75	93

Notes
'–' = unavailable or incalculable data.
a. Ears, attitudes, etc.
* Significant difference at $p < 0.05$.
SFPIPD = standard French police interview for person description; PDI = person description interview.

height or age, hair length, nose, mouth and face shape. Height and age are important descriptors used for a mug shot search, while the other descriptors are highly relevant for the construction of a facial composite.

Thus, police officers, when using the PDI, obtained more complete and more accurate descriptions of a target person than with their standard protocol interview. The superiority of the PDI is specifically prevalent in the most useful descriptive element categories, namely general features, facial descriptors (ideal for a mugshot search) and personality traits. For these categories, the SFPIPD not only provided fewer correct elements, but resulted in numerous errors. There is a potential explanation for this lower accuracy rate. The performance of police officers in this study resulted in completeness of the descriptions that were largely and significantly greater than those observed in archival study (Demarchi, 2003). There is a general ethos of evaluation in their everyday practice and they would have wanted to show that their standard protocols were effective ones. However, because they did not have any methods to increase the completeness of recalls, they must have used numerous closed questions which led to a decrease in the quality of the information reported (Stern, 1902; Borst, 1904; Whipple, 1909, 1913; Cady, 1924; Goulding, 1971; Dent & Stephenson, 1979).

The poorer performance obtained with the standard methods does not imply necessarily that the descriptions provided are less useful than those obtained with a PDI. For police officers, an efficient method must not only improve completeness and quality of perpetrators' descriptions, but also increase suspect detection and identification. As a result, there is a need to evaluate the efficiency of both the PDI and the SFPIPD in their relative ability to detect the target person. So we asked 60 participants to match target persons and their corresponding descriptions among a sample group of similar people (see Christie & Ellis, 1981, for a similar experimental procedure). The material consisted of descriptions obtained in the second experiment, and a set of 33 photographs of similar individuals (matched for sex, age, height, ethnicity, build, hair), which included the 20 target persons. Participants were provided with seven descriptions obtained from only one type of interview (SFPIPD or PDI), and their task was to pair all the descriptions with the corresponding people from the panel of photographs. Results showed that descriptions provided by the PDI led to a 50% increase in correct matches in comparison to SFPIPD. Nevertheless, the absolute matching rate (i.e., total number of correct matches divided by total number of matches) was low (0.12 for the FSPIPD and 0.18 to for the PDI).

To explain the superiority of the PDI in this detection task, we investigated the significant links between completeness, accuracy and correct matches. If PDI increases the detection frequency of a previously described person, it is first and foremost because it leads to more complete recall whilst keeping constant the overall quality. If the opposite phenomenon is observed with the SFPIPD, it is because this method decreases the recall accuracy as soon as the number of reported descriptors increases.

Conclusions and future directions

By using adapted instructions based on an analysis of spontaneous cognitive processes, with just 20 minutes' training, police officers can obtain descriptions which contain twice as many correct descriptors and half the number of errors than a standard police interview. These findings are in contrast to previous studies, which found that encouraging people to generate more complete descriptions, particularly facial descriptions, resulted in a greater proportion of inaccurate details. These quantitative and qualitative improvements are immediately translated into an improved ability to identify a potential suspect. From a research point of view, this finding showed that the efficiency of a physical description should not be measured only in terms of qualitative and quantitative aspects, but also through more concrete and ecological measures, such as the calculation of a matching score between the target person and its corresponding description among a definite population of similar individuals.

More important for professionals is the ease of learning and using the PDI protocol. The PDI training in France lasts approximately 20 minutes as in our second study: 15 minutes for theoretical and empirical concepts and 5 minutes of attempts to obtain correct recitation of the two instructions. In France, the PDI training is now incorporated into standard and CI training for experienced police officers. However, the PDI is not yet taught to novice police officers or investigators.

Police officers can use the PDI protocol in isolation or to augment a standard or a cognitive interview. Preliminary research suggests that when a CI framework is used, the best time to give the witness the PDI instructions is after the last witness's free recall which follows the 'change perspective' instruction, and before the questioning phase. This order appears to produce the most effective performance. Further research will address this issue.

Some issues that have implications for professionals need to be further explored. First, the impact of delay on completeness and accuracy of descriptions obtained by the PDI needs to be explored. Second, the ability of particular sub-populations (e.g. children, older people, learning disabled) to produce better descriptions with aid of the PDI should be investigated. Third, researchers must also investigate the possible interaction of the PDI with some potential adverse factors affecting person description, for example the *verbal overshadowing effect* (VOE; Schooler & Engstler-Schooler, 1990; Meissner *et al.*, 2001). The VOE is defined as impairment in recognition performance when people are required to provide a verbal description of a complex stimulus, such as the face of a perpetrator. Finger & Pezdek (1999) showed that the VOE does not appear if there is a sufficient delay (about 24 minutes) between description and recognition from line-ups or a photographs. Nevertheless, identification from a line-up can only be used after a suspect has been apprehended. Witnesses usually do not know the criminal and the investigation often includes an examination of mugshots. The latter would be selected from available databases using the description given by the witness. According to the French police investigative procedure, police must ask witnesses for a detailed description of a perpetrator and *immediately* present them with an album of photographs of suspects known to have committed a crime in the local area and whose descriptions fit the witness's account. Whether verbal overshadowing will occur when such procedures are used remains to be established. Demarchi, Py, Parain & Groud-Tan (2006) found that recognition performance from a mugshot search following a PDI or a SFPIPD was similar to the performance of a control group who did not describe the face prior to viewing the mugshots.

In conclusion, the PDI protocol, which allows the witness to recall pertinent information by using relevant instructions, promotes the completeness of a description of a person in the absence of social pressure or suggestive prompts for unrecalled information. Such a technique elicits more accurate descriptors and reduces the likelihood of contaminating subsequent attempts at verbal recall and perceptual identification from a line-up or a mugshot file.

References

Boon, J. C. W. & Noon, E. (1994). Changing perspectives in cognitive interviewing. *Psychology, Crime, and Law, 1,* 59–69.

Borst, M. (1904). Recherches expérimentales sur l'éducabilité et la fidélité du témoignage [Researches on educability and reliability of testimonies]. *Archives de Psychologie,* III.

Bower, G. H. & Karlin, B. M. (1974). Depth of processing, pictures of faces and recognition memory. *Journal of Experimental Psychology, 103,* 751–757.

Brown, C. & Lloyd-Jones, T. J. (2003). Verbal overshadowing of multiple face and car recognition: Effects of within- versus across-category verbal descriptions. *Applied Cognitive Psychology, 17,* 183–201.

Cady, H. M. (1924). On the psychology of testimony. *American Journal of Psychology, 35,* 110–112.

Christie, D. F. & Ellis, H. D. (1981). Photofit constructions versus verbal descriptions of faces. *Journal of Applied Psychology, 66,* 358–363.

Clifford, B. R. & George, R. (1996). A field evaluation of training in three methods of witness/victim investigative interviewing. *Psychology, Crime and Law, 2,* 231–248.

Craik, F. I. M. & Lockhart, R. S. (1972). Levels of processing: A framework for memory research. *Journal of Verbal Learning and Verbal Behavior, 11,* 671–684.

Davies, G. M., Van der Willik, P. & Morrison, L. J. (2000). Facial composite production: a comparison of mechanical and computer-driven systems. *Journal of Applied Psychology, 85,* 119–124.

Demarchi, S. (2003). Conception and evaluation of an interviewing method for person recall based on a social psychology engineering approach. Unpublished doctoral dissertation, Paris 8 University.

Demarchi, S., Py, J., Parain, T. & Groud-Tan, N. (2006). *Describe a person without prompt verbal overshadowing effect.* Proceedings of the 16th conference of the European Association of Psychology and Law.

Dent, H. R. & Stephenson, G. M. (1979). An experimental study of the effectiveness of different techniques of questioning child witnesses. *British Journal of Social and Clinical Psychology, 18,* 41–51.

Doob, A. N. & Kirshenbaum, H. M. (1973). Bias in police lineups – partial remembering. *Journal of Police Science and Administration, 1,* 287–293.

Ellis, H. D. (1986). Face recall: A psychological perspective. *Human Learning, 5,* 189–196.

Ellis, H. D., Shepherd, J. W. & Davies, G. M. (1980). The deterioration of verbal descriptions of faces over different delay intervals. *Journal of Police Science and Administration, 8,* 101–106.

Fahsing, I. A., Ask, K. & Granhag, P. A. (2004). The man behind the mask: Accuracy and predictors of eyewitness offender descriptions. *Journal of Applied Psychology, 89,* 722–729.

Finger, K. & Pezdek, K. (1999). The effect of cognitive interview on face identification accuracy: Release from verbal overshadowing. *Journal of Applied Psychology, 84,* 340–348.

Fisher, R. P., Geiselman, R. E., Raymond, D. S., Jurkewich, L. M. & Warhaftig, M. L. (1987). Enhancing enhanced eyewitness memory: Refining the cognitive interview. *Journal of Police Science and Administration, 15,* 291–297.

Geiselman, R. E., Fisher, R. P., Firstenberg, I., Hutton, L. A., Sullivan, S., Avetissian, I. & Prosk, A. (1984). Enhancement of eyewitness memory: An empirical evaluation of the cognitive interview. *Journal of Police Science and Administration, 12,* 74–80.

Geiselman, R. E., Schroppel, T., Tubridy, A., Konishi, T. & Rodriguez, V. (2000). Objectivity bias in eyewitness performance. *Applied Cognitive Psychology, 14,* 323–332.

Ginet, M. & Py, J. (2001). A technique for enhancing memory in eyewitness testimonies for use by police officers and judicial officers: the cognitive interview. *Le Travail Humain, 64,* 173–191.

Goulding, G. J. (1971). Facial description ability. *Police Research Bulletin, 19,* 42–44.

Green, D. L. & Geiselman, R. E. (1989). Building composite facial images: Effects of feature saliency and delay of construction. *Journal of Applied Psychology, 74,* 714–721.

Kuehn, L. L. (1974). Looking down a gun barrel: Person perception and violent crime. *Perceptual and Motor Skills, 39,* 1159–1164.

Laughery, K. R., Duval, C. & Wogalter, M. S. (1986). Dynamics of facial recall. In H. D. Ellis, M. A. Jeeves, F. Newcombe & A. Young (Eds.), *Aspects of face processing,* (pp. 373–397). Dordrecht: Martinus Nijhoff.

Lindsay, R. C. L., Martin, R. & Webber, L. (1994). Default values in eyewitness description: A problem for the match-to-description lineup foil selection strategy. *Law and Human Behavior, 18,* 527–541.

Lipton, J. P. (1977). On the psychology of eyewitness testimony. *Journal of Applied Psychology*, *62*, 90–95.

Meissner, C. A. (2002). Applied aspects of the instructional bias effect in verbal overshadowing. *Applied Cognitive Psychology*, *16*, 911–928.

Meissner, C. A., Brigham, J. C. & Kelley, C. M. (2001). The influence of retrieval processes in verbal overshadowing. *Memory and Cognition*, *29*, 176–186.

Pozzulo, J. D. & Warren, K. L. (2003). Descriptions and identifications of strangers by youth and adult eyewitness. *Journal of Applied Psychology*, *88*, 315–323.

Py, J. & Demarchi, S. (2006). Describe and detect criminal with the cognitive interview. *Revue Québequoise de Psychologie*, *27*, 197–215.

Py, J., Demarchi, S. & Ginet M. (2003). *'Who is the suspect?' A complementary instruction to the standard mock witness paradigm*. 2nd Psychology and Law International and Interdisciplinary Conference. Edinburgh.

Schooler, J. W. & Engstler-Schooler, T. Y. (1990). Verbal overshadowing of visual memories: Some things are better left unsaid. *Cognitive Psychology*, *22*, 36–71.

Sporer, S. L. (1996). Psychological aspects of person descriptions. In S. L. Sporer, R. S. Malpass & G. Köhnken (Eds.), *Psychological issues in eyewitness identification*. (pp. 53–87). Mahwah, NJ: Lawence Erlbaum.

Stern, L. W. (1902). Zur Psychologie der Aussage [On the psychology of testimony]. *Zeitschrift fuer die gesamte Strafrechtwissenschaft*, *22*, 315–370.

Tanaka, J. W. & Farah, M. J. (1993). Parts and wholes in faces recognition. *Quarterly Journal of Experimental Psychology, Human Experimental Psychology*, *46A*, 225–245.

Tollestrup, P. A., Turtle, J. W. & Yuille, J. C. (1994). Actual victims and witnesses to robbery and fraud: An archival analysis. In D. F. Ross, J. D. Read & M. P. Toglia (Eds.), *Adult eyewitness testimony: Current trends and developments* (pp. 144–162). Cambridge: Cambridge University Press.

Tunnicliff, J. L. & Clark, S. E. (2000). Selecting foils for identification lineups: Matching to suspects or descriptions? *Law and Human Behavior*, *24*, 231–258.

Van Koppen, P. J. & Lochun, S. K. (1997). Portraying perpetrators: The validity of offender descriptions by witnesses. *Law and Human Behavior*, *21*, 661–685.

Wells, G. L. & Bradfield, A. L. (1999). Measuring the goodness of lineups: Parameter estimation, question effects, and limits to the mock witness paradigm. *Applied Cognitive Psychology*, *13*, S27–S40.

Wells, G. L., Rydell, S. M. & Seelau, E. P. (1993). The selection of distractors for eyewitness lineups. *Journal of Applied Psychology*, *78*, 835–844.

Wells, G. L., Small, M., Penrod, S., Malpass, R. S., Fulero, S. M. & Brimacombe, C. A. E. (1998). Eyewitness identification procedures: Recommendations for lineups and photospreads. *Law and Human Behavior*, *22*, 603–653.

Whipple, G. M. (1909). The observer as reporter: A survey of the psychology of testimony. *Psychological Bulletin*, *6*, 753–770.

Whipple, G. M. (1913). Psychology of testimony and report. *Psychological Bulletin*, *10*, 264–268.

Wogalter, M. S. (1991). Effects of post-exposure description and imaging on subsequent face recognition performance. *Proceedings of the Human Factors Society*, *35*, 575–579.

Wogalter, M. S. (1996). Describing faces from memory: Accuracy and effects of subsequent recognition performance. *Proceedings of the Human Factors and Ergonomics Society, 40*, 536–540.

Yuille, J. C. & Cutshall, J. L. (1986). A case study of eyewitness memory of a crime. *Journal of Applied Psychology, 71*, 291–301.

Chapter Fifteen

Recent Developments in North American Identification Science and Practice

Steven D. Penrod

John Jay College of Criminal Justice
City University of New York

and

Margaret Bull Kovera

John Jay College of Criminal Justice
City University of New York

Mistaken eyewitness identifications

A number of scholars, beginning with Borchard & Lutz (1932), have studied the causes of erroneous convictions by examining errors in hundreds of criminal cases (see especially Frank & Frank, 1957; Brandon & Davies, 1973; Huff, Rattner & Sagarin, 1986; Rattner, 1988; Gross, Jacoby, Matheson, Montgomery & Patil, 2005; Garrett, 2008). It has long been clear that a principal source of the problem is mistaken eyewitness identifications. Gross *et al.* (2005), for example, examined 340 exonerations (327 men and 13 women) that occurred between 1989 and 2003. The cases included 121 rape exonerations (88% involving mistaken identifications), six robbery exonerations (all mistaken identifications) and 205 murder exonerations (50% involved mistaken identifications).

The prominence of mistaken identifications as a source of erroneous convictions has been powerfully reaffirmed by DNA exonerations evidence (Scheck,

Handbook of Psychology of Investigative Interviewing: Current Developments and Future Directions
Edited by Ray Bull, Tim Valentine and Tom Williamson
© 2009 John Wiley & Sons, Ltd.

Neufeld & Dwyer, 2000). Wells, Small, Penrod, Malpass, Fulero & Brimacombe (1998) looked at the first 40 exoneration cases and found that 36 (90%) involved mistaken eyewitness identifications by one or more eyewitnesses. One person was identified by five eyewitnesses. These results are confirmed in a study of the first 200 DNA exoneration cases by Garrett (2008), which revealed that (79%) were convicted, based at least in part on mistaken eyewitness testimony; in a quarter of the cases eyewitness testimony was the only direct evidence against the defendant. Eyewitnesses are not the sole problem: 55% of the cases involved defective blood, fingerprint or hair evidence. These DNA exonerations, like those studied by Gross *et al.* (2005), with which there is some overlap in cases, were predominantly rape (n = 141), rape-murder (n = 44) and murder (n = 12) cases.

Just how often do eyewitnesses make identification errors?

Archival studies of exonerations and DNA exculpations tell us that witnesses do make errors that result in erroneous convictions by juries and judges. Of course, these cases may be only the tip of a very large iceberg. Experimental psychologists who study eyewitness identification issues are certainly not surprised by the DNA exoneration results. These researchers have a variety of data sources that underscore the frequency of eyewitness error. They can point to data on accuracy rates of actual eyewitnesses that emerge from field studies of eyewitness identifications. In such studies researchers seek to reap the benefits of both laboratory experiments and realistic crime conditions by conducting well-controlled experiments in field settings. Cutler & Penrod (1995) assembled data from four such studies (Brigham, Maas, Snyder & Spaulding, 1982; Krafka & Penrod, 1985; Platz & Hosch, 1988; Pigott, Brigham & Bothwell, 1990) involving 291 eyewitnesses who were administered 536 separate identification tests. The average correct identification rate from presentations that included the target (i.e., the culprit) was 41.8%. In the three studies where the data are available, nearly a third of witnesses (31.5%) missed the target and picked a filler (or foil – one of the known innocents placed in arrays along with the suspect). False identifications in target-absent presentations, in which the culprit was not included, were assessed in two of the studies and over a third of the witnesses (35.8%) incorrectly chose an innocent filler. These results indicate that identifications of persons seen briefly in non-stressful conditions and after brief delays are frequently wrong – only two out of five guilty persons were correctly identified and an innocent person was falsely identified in about one in three arrays.

Meta-analytic research by Haber & Haber (2001) provides further evidence about witness accuracy rates in experimental studies and, at the same time, supports the conclusion that witnesses who believe that they have seen actual crimes perform similarly to witnesses who are aware that they are participating in experiments. Haber & Haber examined experiments in which witness-participants viewed a crime and later attempted to identify the perpetrator. In

23 studies the participant-witnesses watched a video, slide presentation or movie of a crime. In 14 of these studies, a crime was staged in the presence of participants. Later – before attempting identifications – these witnesses were informed the crime was staged. In seven studies, the witnesses believed they had seen a real crime and also believed the line-up presentation was real. As Table 15.1 shows, performance was quite similar (not significantly different at $p > 0.05$) across the three groups of studies, with about one in three positive identifications being an erroneous filler identification in target-present arrays and about 50% of decisions represent erroneous filler choices in target-absent arrays.

Larger-scale analyses of experimental studies yield very similar results. A meta-analysis by Ebbesen & Flowe (2001) also examined studies of correct and false identifications in studies using simultaneous and sequential procedures. Simultaneous presentations are the traditional method of presenting suspects and foils to witnesses – either in a line-up or a photo array in which the suspect and foils can be seen simultaneously. In sequential presentations the witness is shown one individual at a time. Depending on the sequential method used, the witness may be shown the individuals once or more than once, may be called upon to decide whether each individual is the perpetrator/ target on seeing each individual, or may have an opportunity to go back through the individuals before deciding. Another important variation in sequential procedures is whether viewings stop after a selection is made or the witness is permitted to continue looking at faces and make additional selections. The Ebbesen & Flowe sample of studies consisted of 113 experiments from 82 papers, with a total of 152 line-ups. The sample of 136 line-ups with adults included 11 sequential-only line-ups, 17 line-ups using both procedures and 108 simultaneous-only line-ups. Ebbesen & Flowe reported that in 114 simultaneous, target-present line-ups, the target was identified 49% of the time. In the 23 sequential target-present line-ups, a correct identification was made 45% of the time. The difference in correct identifications between simultaneous and sequential line-ups was not statistically significant. Unfortunately, they do not report filler identification rates in target-present arrays. In target-absent line-ups, witnesses made false identifications in simultaneous line-ups 49% of the time (n = 84), but only 29% of the time in sequential line-ups.

Table 15.1: Witness performance as a function of knowledge about real vs. demonstration studies

	Target Present			Target Absent		
	Hit	Foil ID	Miss	CR	Foil ID	Overall Correct
Demo Crime/Demo Line-up	43%	34%	24%	49%	51%	46%
Real Crime/Demo Line-up	52%	24%	24%	48%	52%	50%
Real Crime/Real Line-up	47%	24%	28%	53%	47%	50%

Sequential line-ups were associated with a marked reduction in mistaken filler identifications.

More informative data comes from a study by Steblay & Dysart (2008a), who report a meta-analysis of 46 papers with 70 comparisons of sequential and simultaneous procedures. These studies included judgements from over 10,000 research participants. Across 45 studies the correct identification rate for traditional simultaneous target-present photo arrays was 49%, the mistaken identification rate of fillers was 24% and the no identification rate was 26%. (The results of the sequential line-ups are discussed below.) In short, one in three positive identifications using the traditional simultaneous method was clearly wrong – the witness's 'guess' was wrong even though the target person was in the array. Experimental studies provide not only some insights into the rates of eyewitness error, they also provide some insights into methods that might reduce such errors. In the mid-1990s a set of recommended identification practices were formulated by experimental researchers. These recommendations have generated new policy debates and new research on eyewitness error rates.

Recommendations for collecting eyewitness evidence

Recommendations for how to conduct line-ups are not a new phenomenon, with the earliest published set of recommendations in the USA, produced by the District Attorney's and Public Defender's Offices of Clark County Nevada, appearing in 1967 (Procedure for line-up identification, 1967). More recently, in light of the evidence provided by the analysis of DNA exonerations that mistaken eyewitness identifications play a significant role in wrongful convictions and the burgeoning research literature assessing the efficacy of different line-up procedures, a number of groups began reconsidering best practices for the collection of eyewitness evidence. The two most influential sets of recommendations came from a group of scholars sponsored by the American Psychology-Law Society (Wells *et al.*, 1998) and a group of scientists, legal practitioners and law enforcement personnel convened by then Attorney General Janet Reno under the auspices of the National Institute of Justice (Technical Working Group for Eyewitness Evidence, 1999). Although there is substantial overlap between the documents produced by these two groups, there are some notable differences in the recommendations that may be the result of the different constituents of committees that drafted the recommendations.

In 1996, the Executive Committee of the American Psychology-Law Society (AP-LS; Division 41 of the American Psychological Association) appointed a subcommittee of scholars familiar with research on eyewitness identification to produce recommended guidelines for the collection of eyewitness evidence using line-ups or photo arrays. The resulting paper describing those recommendations (Wells *et al.*, 1998) was accepted as an official AP-LS Scientific

Review paper by a unanimous vote of the Executive Committee. The recommendations were fourfold. First, all line-ups should be conducted using a double-blind procedure in which neither the witness nor the line-up administrator knows the identity of the suspect. Second, the witness should receive instructions that the person who committed the crime may not be in the line-up or photo spread, and that the person administering the line-up does not know who the suspect is in the case. Third, the line-up should be constructed in such a way that the suspect is not salient in comparison to the other line-up members, based on the witness's previous description of the perpetrator or any other feature that may call undue attention to the suspect. Fourth, the line-up administrators should take precise statements of confidence from witnesses immediately after the identification and before providing any feedback to the witness about their confidence that the person that they identified is the actual perpetrator.

Two additional rules were considered by the subcommittee but they were not ultimately endorsed by the group. First, the group considered recommending that all line-ups be conducted using a sequential presentation of the line-up members rather than the traditional simultaneous presentation. Because of concerns that sequential line-ups may be more prone to influence from a non-blind administrator and perceived reluctance on the part of law enforcement to adopt double-blind procedures, the group did not include sequential line-up presentation among its recommendations (research on administrator influence is discussed below). Second, the group considered recommending that all line-up or photo-spread administrations be videotaped and provided to the court. Again, the group stopped short of recommending videotaping line-up administrations as a rule because of concerns that videotaping increases costs to law enforcement agencies coupled with fears that videotaping might not capture improper influence because of the low-quality of amateur video productions and the need to have cameras capture multiple viewpoints – i.e., the line-up, the witness, the administrator.

The NIJ guidelines were developed by the 34 members of the Technical Working Group on Eyewitness Evidence convened by NIJ to make recommendations about the collection of eyewitness evidence, including how to prepare mug books (photograph albums), develop composites, collect witness recollections of the event and conduct identification procedures. Of interest here are the recommendations that the working group made regarding the administration of line-up and photo-spread identification procedures.

As mentioned previously, many of the recommendations made by this panel were similar to those made by the AP-LS subcommittee, although they often include greater detail. For example, the guidelines additionally recommend that only one suspect should appear in each line-up or photo-spread and that fillers be chosen to match the witness's description of the culprit. The suspect should also not stand out from the fillers because of any unique features (e.g., tattoos, scars). In terms of instructions, the NIJ guidelines not only recommended that administrators instruct witnesses that the perpetrator may not be in the line-up, but also that it is just as important to clear innocent suspects as to convict guilty ones, the perpetrator's appearance may have changed since the time of the crime, and the police will continue to investigate the crime irrespective of whether the witness makes an identification. Finally, the NIJ guidelines, like those from the AP-LS subcommittee, recommended obtaining statements from the witness regarding their level of certainty in any identification made prior to providing them with feedback about their decision.

The researchers of the working group identified two major shortcomings of the guidelines (Wells, Malpass, Lindsay, Fisher, Turtle & Fulero, 2000). Unlike the AP-LS panel recommendations, the NIJ guidelines contained no recommendation for double-blind line-up administration. In the absence of such a recommendation, the guidelines did warn the administrator not to do or say anything to the witness that would influence his or her decision. Like the AP-LS recommendations, the NIJ guidelines also failed to recommend presenting line-up members sequentially rather than simultaneously, although both methods are described in the guide. Despite support from the social scientists for these recommendations, police officers and prosecutors voiced practical concerns, including the extra resources needed for double-blind administration and the potential for previous convictions obtained using simultaneous line-ups to be appealed, which prevented the inclusion of these line-up features in the NIJ recommendations (Wells *et al.*, 2000).

Does the available science, including the science produced since the publication of the AP-LS white paper and the NIJ guidelines, support the recommendations for conducting line-ups and photo-spreads that were made by these two groups? In the following sections, we review the literature related to the recommendations on line-up composition, witness instruction, sequential vs. simultaneous presentation of line-up members and double-blind line-up administration.

Line-up construction or composition

The composition of a line-up is important because the proper selection of line-up members can help control some of the damaging effects of witnesses guessing. If the suspect is the only line-up member, as when police conduct a show-up containing only the suspect, then witnesses who guess will necessarily pick the suspect. A line-up containing fillers (i.e., line-up members who are not suspects) helps to minimize bad outcomes from guessing in target-absent line-ups as guesses should be distributed equally among line-up members, assuming that the line-up is unbiased, with only a fraction of the guesses resulting in an identification of an innocent suspect. However, the choice of fillers can bias witnesses towards choosing the suspect if the suspect is the only line-up member who has features mentioned in the witness's description. Under these circumstances, although a line-up with one suspect and five fillers may have a nominal size of six, in effect, the suspect is the only viable line-up member for the witness to choose. Thus, the line-up becomes a test of the witness's recall of his or her description rather than a test of the witness's recognition of the perpetrator's face (Luus & Wells, 1991).

In recognition of these issues, both the AP-LS and NIJ guidelines recommended that a suspect should not stand out from the line-up distractors and that the decision about whether the suspect does stand out in problematic ways should be determined by comparing the line-up members to the description provided by the witness. Care should be taken to ensure that the suspect is not salient, as might be the case if the suspect is the only line-up member to possess a feature mentioned in the witness's description (Lindsay & Wells, 1980).

One way to examine the bias in arrays is to examine the rates at which 'designated innocent' individuals who resemble perpetrators/targets are chosen relative to the (other) fillers. In situations where one wants to assess line-up fairness in the absence of choosing data, the most common procedure begins by obtaining the witness's original description of the perpetrator and then presenting that description to 30 or more 'mock witnesses' (Doob & Kirshenbaum, 1973). These participants have not seen the crime or the perpetrator but are asked to make an identification from the line-up based on the description provided by the actual witness to the crime. If mock witnesses, who did not see the perpetrator, pick the suspect at levels greater than would be expected by chance (e.g., greater than 20% of the time for five-person line-ups and 17% of the time for six-person line-ups), then there is evidence that the line-up is biased against the suspect (Doob & Kirshenbaum, 1973). The functional size of the line-up, or the number of plausible line-up members, is obtained by dividing the number of mock witnesses by the number of suspect identifications (Wells, Leippe & Ostrom, 1979). For example, if 11 of 30 mock witnesses (37%) identify the suspect, then the line-up has a functional size of 2.73 (30/11). Other methods of assessing line-up fairness include effective size (Malpass, Tredoux & McQuiston-Surrett, 2007) and E' (Tredoux, 1998).

Studies of the fairness of line-ups used in actual cases suggest that many line-ups are biased against defendants. Brigham, Meissner & Wasserman (1999) tested the proportion of mock witnesses who chose the suspect in 18 US cases. Suspects were selected an average of 2.6 times as often as one would expect by chance alone. Wells & Bradfield (1999), in a study of ten photo arrays and line-ups from US cases, found suspects were selected, on average, more than 2.1 times as often as expected by chance. Of course, arrays in these studies were not randomly selected – they were from contested identifications – so may overestimate the level of bias in the majority of actual cases.

In a mock witness study of 25 actual five-person line-ups used in France, the observed proportion of mock witnesses who chose the suspect was 48% in contrast to the expected rate of 20% – nearly 2.5 times the chance rate (Py *et al.*, 2003). Similarly, Valentine & Heaton (1999) studied suspect bias using photographs of a representative set of 25 line-ups and 16 video parades from the UK. The video parades consist of 15-second clips of individuals and are selected from an archive of more than 15,000 clips. In live line-ups individuals are shown simultaneously; video clips are shown sequentially. All arrays contained nine members, with an expected guess rate of 11% per face. Mock witnesses selected line-up suspects 25% of the time, a rate 2.2 times chance, and video parade suspects 15% of the time, 1.4 times chance. The difference between line-ups and video parades might be attributable to the methods of filler selection (perhaps more fillers resembling witness descriptions are available in videos – a point noted by Valentine & Heaton, 1999), the method of presentation (simultaneous vs. sequential) or other factors. That the line-up multiplier is lower than in the USA may be attributable to the larger arrays, to fairer arrays or both.

Given that the line-ups used in actual cases appear to be relatively biased, is there an optimal strategy for choosing line-up fillers that will decrease the likelihood that an innocent suspect will be identified? There are two primary strategies for selecting fillers for line-ups or photo-spreads: match-to-suspect and match-to-description. The match-to-suspect strategy involves selecting fillers with features that are similar to the suspect's features. Although matching fillers to the suspect may appear to be a reasonable method, taken to the extreme the strategy would result in a line-up with a suspect and fillers that are indistinguishable from one another.

An alternative method for choosing fillers is the match-to-description (or match-to-culprit) strategy. With this strategy, line-up constructors choose fillers who share the features of the perpetrator that the witness mentioned in his or her description of the culprit but who vary on features that were not mentioned by the witness (Luus & Wells, 1991). So if the witness described the culprit as in his late twenties, 6 feet tall, medium build, with blond hair and light eyes, then all the fillers should share these features but could vary on whether their hair is curly or straight and whether their eyes are green or blue.

There is some research support for an advantage of the match-to-description strategy. For example, one study tested the rate of suspect identifications when fillers were selected from a pool of potential fillers using one of three procedures (Wells, Rydell & Seelau, 1993). In the mismatch-description condition, each filler violated the participant's description on at least one major feature (e.g., the filler had black hair but the participant described the thief as having blond hair). In the match-to-suspect condition, experimenters chose the fillers that most closely resembled the suspect. In the match-to-description condition, researchers discarded all the fillers that failed to match the witnesses' descriptions. From those photos that remained, the experimenters chose those that least resembled the suspect. Witnesses made more correct identifications from line-ups constructed using the match-to-description strategy than from the match-to-suspect strategy and made fewer mistaken identifications when line-up fillers were matched to description rather than mismatched. The match-to-description strategy also produced fewer filler identifications and more correct rejections. Other research, however, has not yielded an advantage for match-to-description (see, e.g., Tunnicliff & Clark, 2000; Darling, Valentine & Memon, 2008).

Line-up instructions to the witness

One recommendation that was made in both the AP-LS white paper and the NIJ guidelines was that witnesses should be instructed that the person who committed the crime may or may not be in the line-up. The purpose of this instruction is to reduce the pressure that witnesses may otherwise feel to choose someone from the line-up, even when they are not sure whether that person is the culprit. The AP-LS guidelines included an additional instruction to witnesses that the line-up administrator does not know which line-up member is the suspect. This instruction is necessarily absent from the NIJ guidelines, given that they do not include a recommendation that line-ups be conducted by administrators blind to the suspect's identity. We know of no published empirical research testing whether this instruction influences the accuracy of witnesses' identifications; however, there is a fairly substantial literature addressing the effects of warning the witness that the culprit may not be present in the line-up.

A meta-analysis of studies that manipulated whether line-up instructions were biased (e.g., that implied that the witness's task was to identify the perpetrator from the line-up) or unbiased (e.g., that reminded witnesses that the culprit might not be in the line-up) showed that participants who received unbiased instructions were more likely than participants who received biased instructions to reject a line-up if the perpetrator was absent (Steblay, 1997). There was no effect of instruction type on the rate of correct identifications. It was the case, however, that more people failed to make a choice from a target-present line-up when the instructions reminded witnesses that the perpetrator might not be present than when the instructions contained such reminder.

These findings – that a reminder that the culprit might not be in the line-up decreases mistaken identifications while leaving the rate of correct identifications unchanged – led some police departments to adopt the instruction. However, a recent reanalysis of the data from the Steblay meta-analysis by Steve Clark (2005) suggested that this asymmetry in the influence of biased instructions in target-absent vs. target-present line-ups may not exist. First, he argued that if one assumes that biased instructions increase false identifications by shifting downward the criterion that witnesses use to make a choice of a line-up member, then that criterion shift should also produce an increase in correct identifications. However, it is more difficult to demonstrate the influence of biased instructions in target-present line-ups than target-absent line-ups because increasing guessing through biased line-up instructions would produce asymmetrical effects in the two types of line-ups. In target-absent line-ups, for every new identification produced by guessing, there will be an equivalent drop in the correct rejection rate. In target-present line-ups, only a fraction ($1/k$, where k = the number of line-up members) of the identifications produced by guessing, namely the identifications of the target, will result in an increase in the correct identification rate.

Next, Clark scrutinized the studies including in the original Steblay meta-analysis (1997). Steblay reported that six studies found that biased instructions increased correct identifications, six studies found that they decreased correct identifications and three studies found no effect of biased instructions. Clark's reanalysis of these studies demonstrated methodological problems (e.g., ceiling effects in the unbiased instruction conditions) in several studies and he argued for a different categorization of some conditions into either biased or unbiased instructional conditions in other studies. The results of this reanalysis question Steblay's finding that biased instructions have a negligible effect on correct identifications. It appears that the size of the biased instruction effect in target-present line-ups is influenced by the correct identification rate in unbiased instruction conditions. When that rate is high, ceiling effects prevent the biased instructions from significantly increasing correct identifications. Further research should resolve the issue.

In addition to recommending that witnesses be instructed that the perpetrator may not be present in the line-up, the NIJ guidelines recommended that police include an instruction as part of their standard eyewitness identification procedure about the possibility that perpetrators have changed their appearance (Technical Working Group for Eyewitness Evidence, 1999). The guidelines provide the specific instruction to witnesses: 'Individuals depicted in line-up photos may not appear exactly as they did on the date of the incident because features such as head and facial hair are subject to change' (*ibid.*, p. 32). Charman & Wells (2007) questioned the guidelines' recommendation of the appearance-change instruction without theoretical and empirical evidence for its use. Among the possible hypotheses, they posited that the appearance-change instruction may be problematic if witnesses infer that perpetrators may no longer look like their memory of them and, therefore, reduce their criterion level for identification. In the only empirical examination of the effects of appearance-change *instruction* (as opposed to studies of the effects of appearance change itself), each participant witness was presented with four line-ups, two of which were target-absent and two target-present. All participants were instructed that the perpetrator may or may not be in the line-up, and half of the participants additionally received the appearance-change instruction.

The appearance-change instruction increased filler identifications in target-present line-ups and target-absent line-ups, but did not significantly increase correct identifications in target-present line-ups. Choosing rates were significantly higher in the appearance-change instruction conditions, supporting the hypothesis that the instruction results in witnesses lowering their response criterion. Response latency to make an identification decision was significantly longer for witnesses receiving the instruction, perhaps due to the lower criterion increasing the number of photos witnesses needed to consider before making their decision (Charman & Wells, 2007). Although it would be premature to make policy recommendations based on a single study, the results of this initial test of the appearance-change instruction suggest that the instruction may not have its intended effect. What is not yet clear is whether the presence of the appearance-change instruction interacts with the actual appearance change of the perpetrator such that the instruction increases correct identifications of perpetrators with changed appearance, but does not increase mistaken identifications when the perpetrator is not present in the line-ups. Although the Charman & Wells study included four perpetrators who varied in the extent to which their appearance changed between the event and the subsequent line-up, the extent of the appearance change differed among the perpetrators, making the results difficult to interpret. Thus, what is needed are studies that cleanly manipulate appearance change and the presence of the appearance-change instruction in a single study.

Simultaneous vs. sequential line-up presentation

In a simultaneous line-up, witnesses view all line-up members at the same time. In the sequential line-up, most often tested in psychological research, witnesses view each line-up member one at a time, making a yes/no decision after viewing that member as to whether he or she is the culprit (Lindsay & Wells, 1985; Lindsay, Lea & Fulford, 1991). If the witness indicates that the line-up member is not the culprit, the administrator presents the next line-up member. If the witness indicates that the line-up member is the perpetrator, the presentation ends. In contrast, the NIJ description of a sequential line-up procedure allows the administrator to continue showing the witness more line-up members even after the witness has made an identification, if it is consistent with departmental procedures to do so.

Although both the NIJ guidelines and the AP-LS white paper described the sequential line-up procedure, neither document recommended the procedure over the use of the simultaneous procedure despite research suggesting the superiority of the sequential procedure. A meta-analysis of 25 studies comparing the effects of simultaneous and sequential line-up presentation on eyewitness accuracy, combining the data from over 4,000 witnesses, concluded that sequential line-ups reliably and substantially reduce mistaken identifications in target-absent line-ups (Steblay, Dysart, Fulero & Lindsay, 2001) – a conclusion reaffirmed in the much larger meta-analysis by Steblay & Dysart (2008a). This effect has been dubbed the sequential superiority effect. Although this drop in mistaken identifications is laudable, there is also a smaller reduction in correct identifications, which concerns prosecutors and law enforcement officials.

There continues to be debate over why sequential line-ups produce fewer mistaken identifications than simultaneous line-ups. Some have argued that simultaneous line-up presentation encourages witnesses to make relative judgements among the line-up members and results in witnesses choosing the line-up member who looks most like the perpetrator (Lindsay & Wells, 1985; Gronlund, 2004). Assuming that, in target-present line-ups, the perpetrator will most closely resemble the witness's memory of the perpetrator, this relative judgement process should produce correct identifications when the target is present in the line-up. For target-absent line-ups, if an innocent suspect most closely resembles the perpetrator, perhaps because he became a suspect because of his physical resemblance to the perpetrator, one should expect an increase in false identifications. It is thought that sequential line-ups reduce these relative judgements, encouraging witnesses to make absolute judgements of similarity between each line-up member and their memory of the perpetrator. Other scholars have recently argued that rather than encouraging witnesses to shift from a relative to an absolute judgement process, sequential line-ups raise the criterion threshold that witnesses must cross before they are willing to make a choice from a line-up (Meissner, Tredoux, Parker & MacLin, 2005; Flowe & Ebbesen, 2007). Using a signal detection approach, Meissner and his colleagues demonstrated that indeed simultaneous presentation produces a lower criterion for choosing a line-up member than sequential presentation does.

In part because of this uncertainty about the psychological processes underlying the sequential superiority effect, some scholars have questioned the wisdom of making public policy recommendations to adopt the sequential line-up presentation as a preferred method of obtaining eyewitness identifications (McQuiston-Surrett, Malpass & Tredoux, 2006). These authors also argue that it is premature to recommend sequential line-ups because:

1. the Steblay meta-analysis contained many unpublished studies that do not meet the admissibility criterion of peer review promulgated in the *Daubert v Merrell Dow Pharmaceuticals* (1993) Supreme Court decision;
2. the body of research on which the meta-analysis rests is relatively small and therefore prone to unreliability; and
3. the results supporting the sequential superiority effect were obtained primarily from a single laboratory.

What is clear from this analysis is that more research is needed to understand what variables (e.g., culprit-suspect similarity, line-up construction method, double- vs. single-blind line-up administration) moderate the effects of simultaneous vs. sequential line-ups on identification decisions. The new meta-analysis by Steblay and Dysart offers rebuttals to all of these points.

One likely advantage of the sequential line-up is often overlooked by commentators and those who argue about the relative merits of the two procedures. The rates at which 'designated innocent' suspect fillers are chosen relative to the other fillers in experiments with target-absent conditions clearly indicates that the arrays used in those studies – like the arrays used in the real world – are biased against the designated innocent suspect and therefore likely to be even more biased against the actual suspect. The respective numbers from Steblay & Dysart (2008a) for simultaneous arrays was 23% for the designated filler vs. an average of about 7% for other fillers (a ratio of 3 : 1), which is on a par with the results from other studies of line-up bias that we noted earlier. In sequential arrays, Steblay & Dysart report that designated fillers were picked by 12% of witnesses vs. 7% for other fillers – a ratio of less than 2 : 1. These results may, indeed, arise because the sequential format makes it more difficult for witnesses to merely compare members of the line-up and pick the 'most similar' face.

Another way to look at bias in sequential and simultaneous arrays is to consider what the changes in choosing patterns are like when moving from target-present to target-absent arrays in simultaneous and sequential presentations. Here we focus on Steblay & Dysart's (2008b) results from 38 studies with complete data on identifications under both present/absent and procedure manipulations. Results from these studies indicate that 30% of the 47% (nearly two-thirds) of witnesses who seemingly correctly 'identified' the suspect in simultaneous target-present arrays would have guessed a filler in the target-absent condition, and a further 17% would have been correct in both types of arrays (see Table 15.2). For sequential arrays the respective numbers were 35% correct 'identifications', 24% fillers and 41% no choice in target-present conditions and 34% filler choices and 66% no choice in target-absent conditions. For target-absent arrays these numbers indicate that 10% of the 35% (less than one third) of witnesses who seemingly correctly 'identified' the suspect in target-present arrays would have guessed a filler in the target-absent condition, but 25% would have correctly rejected the line-up; those 25% appear to have a reliable memory vs. 17% in simultaneous arrays.

Sequential presentation thus appears to do more than simply reduce choosing by witnesses; it appears to be differentially effective at suppressing *guessing* by witnesses. Indeed, logic dictates that essentially all of the putative 'loss' in correct 'identifications' in sequential line-ups (47% vs. 35% in the studies considered here) is in the form of witnesses who guess the suspect in target-present arrays ('guess' insofar as their memory is not strong enough to avoid a filler identification with the perpetrator is not present). Given that not more than

Table 15.2: Steblay *et al.* meta-analysis of simultaneous presentations

	Target Present (N = 38)	Target Absent (N = 38)
No Choice	28%	45%
Identification	47%	–
Foil Choice	25%	55%

25% of witnesses seem capable of getting it right in both target-present and target-absent arrays (the best estimate of doubly-reliable witnesses is 21% if one also considers the 17% doubly-accurate rate in simultaneous arrays), we might well conclude that the 47% 'correct identification' rate in simultaneous target-present arrays is mostly lucky guessing by witnesses (around 26% of the 47%) confronted with biased arrays; so, it appears that most of those witnesses would pick a filler in a target-absent array, and, of course, those witnesses would be most likely to pick the similar-looking designated suspect in a similarly biased target-absent array rather than another filler.

In contrast, sequential arrays yield significantly fewer lucky guesses (10% of the 35% of 'correct identifications' in target-present arrays), substantially fewer erroneous filler choices (41% vs. 55%) and fewer designated innocent suspect choices (12% vs. 23%, although those results come from a somewhat different set of studies). The overall ratio of correct identifications to innocent suspect identifications may be far superior for sequential presentations (35/12 – about 3 : 1) than for simultaneous (47/23 – about 2 : 1).

Although some policy-makers may fret over the loss in accurate 'identifications' (we characterize them as lucky guesses) that can result from the sequential line-up, it should be noted that the odds of an identification of the suspect being accurate are substantially increased by the use of the sequential line-up in spite of some loss of identifications. In addition, it seems clear that policy-makers should not always favour a method of conducting line-ups merely because it yields more 'hits'. Consider, for instance, a method in which witnesses who claim that they do not recognize anyone are instructed to guess. This guessing method would certainly yield more suspect identifications than would a method that discouraged guessing, but it would also yield many more innocent suspect identifications. Under most circumstances policy-makers surely would not want to encourage a method that relies on guessing and generates more errors. We say 'most circumstances' because, as Penrod (2003) has noted, one can imagine a system in which investigators were forced to choose (prior to any identification test) how they were going to employ eye-witnesses. If they intended to use eyewitnesses and their identifications in court as evidence against a defendant, they might be pressed to use stringent procedures which maximize the diagnostic value of identifications (that is, increase the ratio of correct to incorrect suspect identifications). If, on the other hand, investigators needed the witness to assist them in generating investigative clues, they might wish to use procedures that encourage guessing and the generation of cues, but would be forced to do so at the cost of losing the witness as a source of 'identification' evidence at trial.

Double-blind vs. single-blind line-up administration

Although the NIJ guidelines stopped short of recommending double-blind line-up administration, in part due to concerns from law enforcement about the feasibility of finding sufficient administrators in small jurisdictions, the AP-LS white paper recommended double-blind line-up administration as best practice. What evidence is there that double-blind line-up administration reduces mistaken identifications or wrongful conviction? At the time these recommendations were made there was little direct evidence that the line-up administrator's knowledge of the suspect's identity would affect the reliability of an eyewitness's identification; however, there was initial support for the idea that administrator feedback about whether the witness had identified the suspect influenced witness confidence (Wells & Bradfield, 1998). Instead of basing this recommendation on the results of eyewitness research, scholars argued, based on the body of research on experimenter expectancy effects (e.g., Rosenthal, 1976; 2002), that administrator knowledge of a suspect's identity would lead the administrator to communicate behavioural cues that would influence witnesses' identification decisions and their reported confidence. Since that time, a significant body of research has examined the role of administrator feedback in the malleability of witness confidence and a smaller number of studies have examined the role of administrator knowledge on the accuracy of witness identifications.

Confidence malleability

When a line-up administrator knows which line-up member is the suspect, there is the potential for the administrator to provide witnesses with feedback about whether they have identified the suspect. If this feedback is provided prior to the witnesses expressing their confidence in the accuracy of their identification, it is likely that the feedback will influence their reported confidence in predictable ways. In one of the earliest studies of this phenomenon, pairs of witnesses viewed a staged theft (Luus & Wells, 1994). The witnesses then separately viewed a line-up that did not contain the suspect; almost all of them identified a member of the line-up as the perpetrator. Subsequently, eyewitnesses were given one of nine forms of feedback about the identification decision made by their co-witness and were interviewed by a confederate police officer who recorded their confidence in the accuracy of their identification. Witnesses who learned that their co-witness had identified the same line-up member were more confident in the accuracy of their identification than were witnesses who received no feedback. Witnesses who learned that their co-witness had identified a different line-up member or rejected the line-up were less confident than witnesses who received no feedback.

Gary Wells and his colleagues have conducted a number of studies demonstrating that feedback from a line-up administrator influences witness confidence (Wells & Bradfield, 1998; Bradfield, Wells & Olson, 2002; Wells, Olson & Charman, 2003). When line-up administrators provide confirming feedback (e.g., 'Good, you identified the suspect'), witnesses were much more confident than witnesses who received disconfirming or no feedback (Wells & Bradfield, 1998). This effect holds even when witnesses are instructed that the perpetrator may not be present in the line-up (Semmler, Brewer & Wells, 2004). Not only does confirming feedback from the administrator increase witness confidence, it also causes witnesses to report that they had a better view of the culprit and paid more attention to the culprit's face when observing the event (Wells & Bradfield, 1998).

A meta-analysis of 20 tests of the post-identification feedback effect on witness confidence, based on data from over 2,400 participants, demonstrated that the effect is robust and relatively large (Douglass & Steblay, 2006). In addition, confirming feedback had a significant impact on a variety of objective and subjective measures of the witnesses' experience, including how good a view they had of the perpetrator, their opportunity to view his or her face, how much attention they paid, whether they had a good basis to make an identification, how easy it was to make an identification, how quickly they made an identification, their willingness to testify, their memory for strangers and the clarity of their memory. These findings support the recommendations that witness confidence be collected immediately after an identification before any feedback about the identification decision is provided by the administrator.

Investigator knowledge effects on eyewitness accuracy

Despite the recommendation of the AP-LS subcommittee that line-ups be conducted by a blind administrator, only a handful of studies have directly examined the effects of administrator knowledge on the reliability of eyewitness identification decisions. These studies have produced mixed results in terms of the conditions under which the effects of administrator knowledge of the suspect's identity are obtained (Phillips, McAuliff, Kovera & Cutler, 1999; Haw & Fisher, 2004; Greathouse & Kovera, 2009) and whether the effect is obtained at all (Haw, Mitchell & Wells, 2003; Russano *et al.*, 2006). The first study to examine the influence of administrator knowledge empirically paired mock line-up administrators with mock witnesses who had previously viewed a live, staged crime involving two perpetrators (Phillips *et al.*, 1999). Phillips and colleagues manipulated whether the administrator knew the identity of the suspect, the type of line-up presented (simultaneous vs. sequential), as well as the presence of an observer during the line-up task. When the line-up was presented sequentially and an experimenter-observer was present, administrator knowledge influenced witnesses to choose an innocent suspect.

Additional support for the effects of line-up administrator knowledge was obtained in research manipulating the level of contact between administrators and witnesses (Haw & Fisher, 2004). For some witnesses, administrators had direct contact with them while administering the line-up. For others, administrators sat behind the witnesses out of their direct view, limiting their ability to communicate cues to the suspect's identity to the witnesses. When the administrator was permitted high contact with the witness and presented a target-absent simultaneous line-up, witnesses were more likely to identify the innocent suspect. In contrast, other studies have failed to find any influence of administrator knowledge on witnesses' identification decisions (Haw *et al.*, 2003; Russano *et al.*, 2006).

Given the variability in the influence of administrator knowledge on eyewitness decisions across studies, it is likely that previously unidentified variables moderate its effects. Greathouse & Kovera (in press) hypothesized that factors which lower the criteria that witnesses use to make a positive identification, such as the presence of biased line-up instructions or simultaneous line-up presentation, may moderate the effects of administrator knowledge. If a witness is presented with biased instructions (e.g., instructions that fail to remind the witness that the perpetrator may not be in the line-up), they may cue unsure witnesses to attend more to the investigator's behaviour, allowing single-blind administrators to wield more influence. To test this hypothesis, Greathouse & Kovera manipulated whether the administrator had knowledge of the suspect's identity, the type of line-up (simultaneous vs. sequential), the presence of the actual perpetrator in the line-up and the type of line-up instructions (biased vs. unbiased). In an attempt to ensure that the findings were not specific to a particular perpetrator or line-up composition, witnesses viewed one of two perpetrators committing a theft and then made an identification from a target-present or a target-absent line-up constructed for that perpetrator.

When the witnesses received biased instructions and simultaneous line-ups, they were more likely to make suspect identifications in single-blind than in double-blind line-ups (*ibid.*). The pattern of filler and suspect identifications in both double-blind and single-blind conditions suggests that this increase in mistaken identifications was the result of single-blind administrators influencing those who would have, under double-blind conditions, made filler identifications to make suspect identifications instead. This finding could be conceptualized as shifting unsure witnesses' guesses from filler identifications in the double-blind condition to suspect identifications in the single-blind condition. Line-up rejections did not significantly increase or decrease as a function of line-up administrator knowledge. Moreover, suspect identifications were twice as diagnostic for double-blind administrations as they were for single-blind administrations.

Thus, it appears from this research that double-blind line-up administration would protect against mistaken identifications, especially when witnesses' criteria for choosing are lowered; however, double-blind line-up administration also appears to decrease correct identifications. Moreover, it is not clear that even double-blind administration can protect against the administrator expectancy effect when the administrator conducts line-ups with multiple witnesses. There is evidence to suggest that the confidence of the witness from the first line-up administration influences the administrator's beliefs about the difficulty of the identification task. As a result, double-blind administrators who administered a second line-up to a different witness were more likely to steer the second witness to the photo chosen by the first witness when the first witness lacked confidence in his or her identification than when the witness was confident in their decision (Douglass, Smith & Fraser-Thill, 2005). Although double-blind line-up administration may not correct all problems associated with administrator expectations and their influence on witness behaviour, there is little evidence that it would produce harmful results. It is clear, however, that much more research is needed to understand how the influence of administrator knowledge of the suspect's identity operates in eyewitness identification tasks.

Eyewitness error rates in field studies using alternative identification procedures

The studies just reviewed were experiments – sometimes staged events, sometimes videotaped events in which the researchers knew the identity of the targets. That knowledge permits us to ascertain precisely when a witness has made an error. In studies of actual witnesses using police archives it is generally not known whether the suspect is the actual perpetrator, but it is still possible to gauge inaccurate identification rates by looking at filler identifications. For reasons that will be explained, the best archival studies come from the UK. These studies include Slater's (1994) examination of identification attempts by 843 British witnesses who viewed 302 suspects. Slater found suspect, filler and no identification rates of 36%, 22% and 42% respectively. Wright & McDaid (1996) examined identification attempts of 1,561 British witnesses who viewed 616 suspects in live line-ups and found suspect, filler and no identification rates of 39%, 20% and 41% respectively. Pike, Brace & Kynan (2002) reported a 49% suspect identification rate in 8,800 line-ups, a 39% suspect identification rate in a separate study of a video presentation system (940 witnesses) and a 35% suspect identification rate in 1,635 live line-ups (no information was provided on filler identification rates). Valentine, Pickering & Darling (2003) reported the results of identification attempts by 584 witnesses shown 295 live line-ups and found suspect, filler and no identification rates of 41%, 21% and 39% respectively. More recently Wright & Skagerberg (2007) reported suspect, filler and no identification rates of 58%, 21% and 21% respectively in a study of 134 witnesses shown video line-ups.

Although there are differences across these studies (some reported and some not known – e.g., it is possible that some datasets include identifications made in non-stranger cases), the general pattern that emerges is that *nearly one in three positive identifications made by witnesses in these cases is clearly wrong* as the overall weighted averages across the studies are suspect, filler and no identification rates of 45%, 21% and 40% respectively (numbers do not add to 100 due to missing data in the studies reported by Pike *et al.*, 2002). Note that it is likely that witnesses in most of these studies were confronted with nine-person arrays, the British standard. Given that 21% of witnesses in these studies were 'guessing' one of the innocent fillers (an average of 2.6% per filler), we would have to expect – assuming these arrays were all perfectly fair – that another 2.6% of the witnesses guessed the suspect by chance. Unfortunately, as we detail below, other evidence indicates arrays are not entirely fair; thus, a higher (perhaps much higher) percentage of witnesses may be guessing the suspect.

A body of research on actual witnesses is beginning to emerge in North America, though the studies to date all suffer from significant limitations. Tollestrup, Turtle & Yuille (1994) examined Royal Canadian Mounted Police records on 119 robbery and 66 fraud cases (42 and 45 files respectively were discarded because they lacked eyewitness descriptions or identification attempts) reported positive identifications of suspects in 31.7% of the Vancouver photo arrays (most with eight photographs) they studied (vs. 45% reported in the UK studies). Overall, 46% of robbery victims, 33% of robbery witnesses and 25% of fraud victims identified suspects. Unfortunately, the police records were incomplete and therefore did not permit the researchers to differentiate non-identifications from filler identifications:

> Identification outcomes were entered in the files in a variety of ways such as 'negative results,' 'unable to identify police suspect,' 'not in the line-up,' 'pointed out suspect and one other as looking like perpetrator,' 'positive ID,' and 'weak ID.' ... for the most part, we could not distinguish reliably between outcomes in which an eyewitness rejected the photo spread and those in which he or she failed to select the police suspect. (p. 153)

Studies in the USA are more recent. Behrman & Davey (2001) examined Sacramento, California-area police records for 271 cases involving 349 crimes (the vast majority were armed robberies). They examined a total of 258 field show-ups, 289 photographic line-ups and 58 live line-ups, and reported that 76% of witnesses who viewed show-ups made an identification and 48% of witnesses who observed a photographic line-up identified the suspect. However, because the police files were incomplete, Behrman & Davey (like Tollestrup *et al.*, 1994) could not determine how many identifications of known innocent fillers were made by witnesses viewing photo-arrays. In live line-ups, where the records did include reports of mistaken filler identifications, Behrman & Davey reported that 50% of witnesses identified the suspect (an unknown percentage of those identifications were errors); the rate of erroneous identifications of fillers was 24% and 26% of the witnesses did not make a choice. As in the UK archival data, about one in three positive identifications was clearly wrong and the average rate of guessing was 5% per filler, which might mean (per the suspect bias multiplier noted earlier) that 15% of suspect identifications were also guesses. Behrman & Richards (2005) also reported a study based on some of the data included in the Behrman & Davey (2001) project, but it appears that the 2005 data also do not offer a suitable basis for estimating overall witness error rates (selections of fillers). The 2005 study draws on 424 photographic line-ups (for which Behrman & Davey were unable to determine filler identification rates) and 37 live line-ups. The focus of the analyses is 238 suspect identifications vs. 68 filler identifications which the authors were able to identify.

Klobuchar, Steblay & Caligiuri (2006) reported the results of an unusual field study conducted in Minnesota in 2004, in which identification information was collected in 280 line-ups from 117 cases involving 206 eyewitnesses. The unusual aspects of the study were that the police used blind procedures (i.e., the line-up administrator did not know the identity of the suspect) and sequential line-ups when presenting arrays to witnesses. In the sequential procedure employed in Minnesota, photos were presented one at a time, with a decision made about each photo (witnesses were permitted to view the entire sequential display as often as desired).

In 178 line-ups the witnesses were looking for perpetrators who were strangers to them. In these line-ups 35% of witnesses picked the suspect and 11% picked a filler. Thus, about one in four positive identifications was clearly wrong, and the filler guessing rate was about 2% per filler. Assuming the suspect is identified three times more often than the fillers due to bias in the line-up, perhaps 6% of the 35% of suspect identifications were guesses. Overall, 53% made no choice. As noted above, sequential arrays have been shown to reduce choosing by witnesses, perhaps because they reduce witnesses' opportunity to compare the members of an array and possibly pick the face that offers the best match to the memory of the witness. In the Minnesota study about 46% of witnesses saw the sequential array more than once. For 33 witnesses who viewed the array only once, the rates of suspect and filler identification were 42% and 3% respectively compared to 32% and 13% for 31 witnesses who viewed the array twice and 43% and 29% for 14 witnesses who viewed it three times. Repeated views were thus associated with a significantly increased likelihood of a mistaken identification.

The results of a second large field study in Illinois were reported in 2006 (Mecklenburg, 2006). This study compared witness selections in non-blind simultaneous line-ups (i.e., the presenting officer knew the identity of the suspect) and blind sequential line-ups (the presenting officer did not know the identity of the suspect) in several jurisdictions in the Chicago area. Table 15.3 reports the results in cases involving 548 stranger-identification attempts.

Table 15.3: Effects of simultaneous vs. sequential presentation on identification rates

	Simultaneous	Sequential
(Number)	(319)	(229)
Suspect	59.9%	45.0%
Filler ID	2.8%	9.2%
No ID	37.6%	47.2%

The Illinois data were complemented by a report (p. 43 of the Illinois report) of suspect and filler identification rates in 2,677 simultaneous non-blind live line-ups conducted in Queens, New York during 2001–5. The overall suspect identification rate was 54% and the reported filler identification rate was 3%. Although the Illinois results have been claimed by some as evidence for superior performance in non-blind simultaneous arrays, the study has been criticized by leading psychologists (non-eyewitness researchers) Schacter, Dawes, Jacoby, Kahneman, Lempert, Roediger & Rosenthal (2008) for confounding blind and sequential vs. non-blind and simultaneous procedures. Schacter *et al.* note: 'Our reading of the materials forces us to conclude that the confound has devastating consequences for assessing the real-world implications of this particular study' (p. 4).

It will be apparent that the non-blind simultaneous filler identification rates from Illinois (3%) and Queens (3%) are markedly discrepant from those reported in the various UK studies (which averaged 21%) and the Behrman & Davey live line-up rate of 24%. Possible explanations for the discrepancy are buried in the Illinois report: the low number of filler identifications emerged from a non-blind simultaneous procedure in which it appears that the police could ignore identifications that did not meet their 'probable cause' standards (pp. iii–iv), a practice that seems akin to the Queens practice in which 'an identification [was recorded] only if it was based upon a high level of confidence', so that all tentative identifications were recorded as 'no identification' (p. 43). These practices raise two questions:

1. Are substandard suspect IDs ignored just as often as substandard filler IDs? Some might think that results in Illinois and Queens may be far more skewed by selective non-reporting of filler IDs in non-blind presentations than through any effort of the police to steer witnesses to suspects.
2. Does the failure to report even substandard IDs deprive defendants of information that may be useful in their defence? Jurors and judges may wish to know about such errors.

There are also indications that a substantial proportion of identifications in Queens are actually second/confirmatory identifications of suspects following photographic or other forms of identifications of suspects; this practice would also conceal foil or other forms of misidentifications prior to the confirmatory line-ups. Analyses by Wells & Lindsay (1980) and Clark & Wells (2008) underscore that in many situations filler identifications and non-identifications can be highly diagnostic with respect to the quality of witness memory and identification accuracy in single and multiple witness situations.

Unfortunately, it seems that legal decision-makers such as jurors may not be properly attuned to the diagnostic value of non-identifications. Even if the non-identifying witness is offered in court, McAllister & Bregman (1986) raise doubts about the ability of jurors to give effective weight to non-identification evidence. These researchers presented mock jurors with a series of one and two witness combinations of identification evidence. Their results, using ratings on a 1 (innocent) to 9 (guilty) scale, showed a reliable increase in guilt ratings for a single identifying witness (M = 6.64) relative to a non-identifying witness who neither identified nor rejected the defendant as the perpetrator (M = 5.14), but only a very slight and non-significant decrease in guilt ratings for a single witness who said the perpetrator was not in the line-up (5.06) relative to the non-identifying control. The results show that mock jurors believed the single identification to be diagnostic of guilt, but mistakenly believed the rejection of the line-up to have essentially no probative value.

As suggested above, filler identifications are important partly because they raise questions about the witnesses' memory, but also because filler identifications can serve as a basis for estimating the rates of innocent suspect identifications. If witnesses are 'guessing' fillers at a rate of 25%, as in Behrman & Davey's (2001) archival study or Steblay & Dysart's (2008a) meta-analysis, the average filler draws about 5% of witnesses selections in perfectly fair arrays, and 5% would have to be guessing the suspect. If the suspect is the perpetrator 80% of the time, then four of those five guesses would identify a guilty person (though based on somewhat questionable 'evidence') and one in five suspect guesses would identify an innocent person – the overall rate of mistaken identifications of innocent suspects would be 1 in 100 in this scenario.

Unfortunately, as we have noted, there is a growing body of research indicating arrays are biased against suspects. It is not implausible that 15% of witnesses (rather than 5% in this instance) are guessing the suspect; and, again, if 20% of suspects are innocent, then 3% of witnesses will identify an innocent suspect. And lest the point be lost, another 25% of witnesses would be guessing a filler, thus raising significant doubts about the quality of their memory and impugning the reliability of any subsequent identifications they might make.

The bottom line is that if we are interested in getting some sense of the number of innocent suspects chosen by witnesses with defective memories in field studies, we need to know the filler identification rates of witnesses and the degree of line-up bias. With this information a reasonable estimate of the rates of innocent suspect identifications can be made, which would be valuable to defendants to raise questions about the reliability of identifications by witnesses who have previously identified a filler.

The state of eyewitness identification science and practice

Although psychological research on the sources of eyewitness identification error started more than a century ago (Whipple, 1909, in the first of a series of reports on research mostly conducted in Europe, provides a succinct English language summary of the earliest research), and despite the fact that we have long had systematic evidence that eyewitness error is a primary source of erroneous convictions, it is only in the past two decades that the rapidly growing body of scientific research and practice has begun to converge. Several factors have provided an impetus to this convergence. Recent DNA exculpations and exploration of the causes of those exculpations have significantly raised public and criminal justice practitioner awareness of the important role that eyewitness errors play in producing erroneous convictions. Archival research, particularly from the UK, supplemented by research conducted in controlled settings, has provided further compelling documentation of the high rates of errors among actual witnesses who choose/guess foils. Decomposition of those errors indicates that the guessing rate is significantly higher than foil choices alone would indicate. In the past few decades scientific research on the sources of errors and the role that identification procedures and practices play in producing errors has matured to the point where it was possible, a mere decade ago, to advance a conservative set of practice recommendations (Wells *et al.*, 1998), based on a mix of scientific and logical analyses. Some of these recommendations were quickly embraced by policy-makers in the form of the NIJ guidelines on identification procedures.

Recommended practices – suspects should not stand out from foils in arrays, witnesses should be instructed that the person who committed the crime may or may not be in the line-up, confidence judgements should be collected and recorded at the time of an identification – found their way into the NIJ guidelines. Other recommendations were considered, but were not incorporated. The guidelines did not include the recommendation that identifications should be conducted double-blind. Nor did they include a recommendation for sequential line-ups, a practice that received favourable consideration by Wells *et al.*

In recent years there have been halting steps to evaluate the impact of these practices in field settings using experimental and non-experimental methods. Although the early studies have drawn significant criticism with respect to their designs and data-recording practices, further research – some employing stronger research designs – is under way. It is likely that in the next few years we will possess strong evidence about the ways in which the procedures recommended by research scientists play out in field settings. Arguments about such matters as blind and sequential presentation methods will likely shift from a consideration of *what* impact these procedures have on witness and system performance to policy questions concerning the precise manner in which procedures should be deployed.

References

Behrman, B. W. & Davey, S. L. (2001). Eyewitness identification in actual criminal cases: An archival analysis. *Law and Human Behavior, 25*, 475–491.

Behrman, B. W. & Richards, R. E. (2005). Suspect/foil identification in actual crimes and in the laboratory: A reality monitoring analysis. *Law and Human Behavior*, *29*, 279–301.

Borchard, E. M. & Lutz, E. R. (1932). *Convicting the innocent: Errors of criminal justice*. New Haven, CT: Yale University Press.

Bradfield, A. L., Wells, G. L. & Olson, E. A. (2002). The damaging effect of confirming feedback on the relation between eyewitness certainty and identification accuracy. *Journal of Applied Psychology*, *87*, 112–120.

Brandon, R. & Davies, C. (1973). *Wrongful imprisonment*. London: Allen & Unwin.

Brigham, J. C., Maas, A., Snyder, L. D. & Spaulding, K. (1982). Accuracy of eyewitness identifications in a field setting. *Journal of Personality and Social Psychology*, *42*, 673–681.

Brigham, J. C., Meissner, C. A. & Wasserman, A. W. (1999). Applied issues in the construction and expert assessment of photo line-ups. *Applied Cognitive Psychology*, *13*, S73–S92.

Charman, S. D. & Wells, G. L. (2007). Eyewitness line-ups: Is the appearance change instruction a good idea? *Law and Human Behavior*, *31*, 3–22.

Clark, S. E. (2005). A re-examination of the effects of biased line-up instructions in eyewitness identification. *Law and Human Behavior*, *29*, 575–604.

Clark, S. E. & Wells, G. L. (2008). On the diagnosticity of multiple-witness identifications. *Law and Human Behavior*, *32*, 406–422.

Cutler, B. L. & Penrod, S. D. (1995). *Mistaken identification: The eyewitness, psychology, and the law*. New York: Cambridge University Press.

Darling, S., Valentine, T. & Memon, A. (2008). Selection of line-up foils in operational contexts. *Applied Cognitive Psychology*, *22*, 159–169.

Doob, A. N. & Kirshenbaum, H. M. (1973). Bias in police line-ups ± partial remembering. *Journal of Police Science and Administration*, *1*, 287–293.

Douglass, A. B. & Steblay, N. (2006). Memory distortion in eyewitnesses: A meta-analysis of the post-identification feedback effect. *Applied Cognitive Psychology*, *20*, 859–869.

Douglass, A. B., Smith, C. & Fraser-Thill, D. (2005). A problem with double-blind photospread procedures: Photospread administrators use one eyewitness's confidence to influence the identification of another eyewitness. *Law and Human Behavior*, *29*, 543–562.

Ebbesen, E. E. & Flowe, H. D. (2001). Simultaneous v. sequential line-ups: What do we really know? Unpublished manuscript. http://www-psy.ucsd.edu/~eebbesen/SimSeq.htm. Accessed 6 June 2008.

Flowe, H. D. & Ebbesen, E. B. (2007). Effect of line-up similarity on recognition accuracy in simultaneous and sequential line-ups. *Law and Human Behavior*, *31*, 33–52.

Frank, J. & Frank, B. (1957). *Not guilty*. London: Gollancz.

Garrett, B. (2008). Judging innocence. *Columbia. Law Review*. *108*, 55–142.

Greathouse, S. M. & Kovera, M. B. (2009). Instruction bias and lineup presentation moderate the effects of administrator knowledge on eyewitness identification. *Law and Human Behavior*, *33*, 70–82.

Gronlund, S. D. (2004). Sequential line-ups: Shift in decision criterion or decision strategy? *Journal of Applied Psychology*, *89*, 362–368.

Gross, S. R., Jacoby, K., Matheson, D. J., Montgomery, N. & Patil, S. (2005). Exonerations in the United States from 1989 through 2003. *Journal of Criminal Law and Criminology*, *95*, 523–560.

Haber, R. N. & Haber, L. (2001). *A meta-analysis of 250 research studies of the accuracy of line-up identifications made by eyewitnesses.* Paper presented at the Annual Conference of the Psychonomics Society, Orlando, FL, November.

Haw, R. M. & Fisher, R. P. (2004). Effects of administrator-witness contact on eyewitness identification accuracy. *Journal of Applied Psychology, 89,* 1106–1112.

Haw, R. M., Mitchell, T. L. & Wells, G. L. (2003). *The influence of line-up administrator knowledge and witness perceptions on eyewitness identification decisions.* Poster presented at the International Congress of Psychology and Law, Edinburgh, July.

Huff, R., Rattner, A. & Sagarin, E. (1986). Guilty until proven innocent. *Crime and Delinquency, 32*(4), 518–544.

Klobuchar, A., Steblay, N. & Caligiuri, H. L. (2006). Symposium: Reforming eyewitness identification: Convicting the guilty, protecting the innocent: Improving eyewitnesses identifications: Hennepin county's blind sequential line-up pilot project. *Cardozo Public Law, Policy & Ethics Journal, 4,* 381–413.

Krafka, C. & Penrod, S. (1985). Reinstatement of context in a field experiment on eyewitness identification. *Journal of Personality and Social Psychology, 49,* 58–69.

Lindsay, R. C. L. & Wells, G. L. (1980). What price justice? Exploring the relationship between line-up fairness and identification accuracy. *Law and Human Behavior, 4,* 303–314.

Lindsay, R. C. L. & Wells, G. L. (1985). Improving eyewitness identifications from line-ups: Simultaneous versus sequential line-up presentation. *Journal of Applied Psychology, 70,* 556–564.

Lindsay, R. C. L., Lea, J. A. & Fulford, J. A. (1991). Sequential line-up presentation: Technique matters. *Journal of Applied Psychology, 76,* 741–745.

Luus, C. A. E. & Wells, G. L. (1991). Eyewitness identification and the selection of distractors for line-ups. *Law and Human Behavior, 15,* 43–57.

Luus, C. A. E. & Wells, G. L. (1994). The malleability of eyewitness confidence: Co-witness and perseverance effects. *Journal of Applied Psychology, 79,* 714–723.

Malpass, R. S., Tredoux, C. G. & McQuiston-Surrett, D. (2007). Line-up construction and fairness. In R. C. Lindsay, D. F. Ross, J. D. Read & M. P. Toglia (Eds.), *The handbook of eyewitness psychology. Volume II, Memory for people* (pp. 155–178). Mahwah, NJ: Lawrence Erlbaum.

McAllister, H. A. & Bregman, N. J. (1986). Juror underutilization of eyewitness nonidentifications: Theoretical and practical implications. *Journal of Applied Psychology, 71*(1), 186–170.

McQuiston-Surrett, D., Malpass, R. S. & Tredoux, C. G. (2006). Sequential vs. simultaneous line-ups: A review of methods, data, and theory. *Psychology, Public Policy, and Law, 12,* 137–169.

Mecklenburg, S. H. (2006). Report to the legislature of the state of Illinois: The Illinois pilot program on double-blind, sequential line-up procedures. http://www.chicagopolice.org/IL%20Pilot%20on%20Eyewitness%20ID.pdf. Accessed 6 June 2008.

Meissner, C. A., Tredoux, C. G., Parker, J. F. & MacLin, O. H. (2005). Eyewitness decisions in simultaneous and sequential line-ups: A dual-process signal detection theory analysis. *Memory and Cognition, 33,* 783–792.

Penrod, S. (2003). Eyewitness identification evidence: How well are witnesses and police performing? *Criminal Justice,* Spring, 36–47, 54.

Phillips, M. R., McAuliff, B. D., Kovera, M. B. & Cutler, B. L. (1999). Double-blind photoarray administration as a safeguard against investigator bias. *Journal of Applied Psychology, 84*, 940–951.

Pigott, M. A., Brigham, J. C. & Bothwell, R. K. (1990). A field study on the relationship between quality of eyewitnesses' descriptions and identification accuracy. *Journal of Police Science and Administration, 17*, 84–88.

Pike, G., Brace, N. & Kynan, S. (2002). *The visual identification of suspects: Procedures and practice.* Briefing Note No. 2/02. London: Home Office Research Development and Statistics Directorate, March.

Platz, S. J. & Hosch, H. M. (1988). Cross-racial ethnic eyewitness identification: A field study. *Journal of Applied Social Psychology, 18*, 972–984.

Procedure for line-up identification (1967). *American Criminal Law Quarterly, 6*, 93–95.

Py, J., DeMarchi, S, Ginet, M. & Wasiak, L. (2003). *'Who is the suspect?' A complementary instruction to the standard mock witness paradigm.* Paper presented at the American Psychology-Law Society and European Association of Psychology and Law Conference, Edinburgh.

Rattner, A. (1988). Convicted but innocent. *Law and Human Behavior, 12*, 283–294.

Rosenthal, R. (1976). *Experimenter effects in behavioral research.* New York: Irvington Publishers.

Rosenthal, R. (2002). Covert communication in classrooms, clinics, courtrooms, and cubicles. *American Psychologist, 57*, 839–849.

Russano, M. B., Dickinson, J. J., Greathouse, S. M. & Kovera, M. B. (2006). Why don't you take another look at number three: Investigator knowledge and its effects on eyewitness confidence and identification decisions. *Cardozo Public Law, Policy, and Ethics Journal, 4*, 355–379.

Schacter, D. L., Dawes, R., Jacoby, L. L., Kahneman, D., Lempert, R., Roediger, H. L. & Rosenthal, R. (2008). Policy forum: Studying eyewitness investigations in the field. *Law and Human Behavior, 32*, 3–5.

Scheck, B., Neufeld, P. & Dwyer, W. (2000). *Actual innocence.* New York: Harper.

Semmler, C., Brewer, N. & Wells, G. L. (2004). Effects of postidentification feedback on eyewitness identification and nonidentification confidence. *Journal of Applied Psychology, 89*, 334–346.

Slater, A. (1994). *Identification parades: A scientific evaluation.* London: Police Research Group, Home Office.

Steblay, N. M. (1997). Social influence in eyewitness recall: A meta-analytic review of line-up instruction effects. *Law and Human Behavior, 21*, 283–297.

Steblay, N. & Dysart, J. (2008a). Seventy tests of the sequential superiority effect: A meta-analysis. Unpublished manuscript.

Steblay, N. & Dysart, J. (2008b). Personal communication, 27 April.

Steblay, N., Dysart, J., Fulero, S. & Lindsay, R. C. L. (2001). Eyewitness accuracy rates in sequential and simultaneous line-up presentations: A meta-analytic comparison. *Law and Human Behavior, 25*, 459–473.

Technical Working Group for Eyewitness Evidence (1999). *Eyewitness evidence: A guide for law enforcement* (NCJ 178240). National Institute of Justice, US Department of Justice.

Tollestrup, P., Turtle, J. & Yuille, J. (1994). Actual victims and witnesses to robbery and fraud: An archival analysis. In D. F. Ross, J. D. Read & M. P. Toglia (Eds.),

Adult eyewitness testimony: Current trends and developments (pp. 144–160). New York: Cambridge University Press.

Tredoux, C. G. (1998). Statistical inference on measures of line-up fairness. *Law and Human Behavior, 22*, 217–237.

Tunnicliff, J. L. & Clark, S. (2000). Foils for identification line-ups: Matching suspects or descriptions? *Law and Human Behavior, 24*, 231–258.

Valentine, T. & Heaton, P. (1999). An evaluation of the fairness of police line-ups and video identifications. *Applied Cognitive Psychology, 13*, S59–S72.

Valentine, T., Pickering, A. & Darling, S. (2003). Characteristics of eyewitness identification that predict the outcome of real line-ups. *Applied Cognitive Psychology, 17*, 969–993.

Wells, G. L. & Bradfield, A. L. (1998). 'Good, you identified the suspect': Feedback to eyewitnesses distorts their reports of the witnessing experience. *Journal of Applied Psychology, 83*, 360–376.

Wells, G. L. & Bradfield, A. L. (1999). Measuring the goodness of line-ups: Parameter estimation, question effects, and limits to the mock witness paradigm. *Applied Cognitive Psychology, 13*, S27–S39.

Wells, G. L. & Lindsay, R. C. L. (1980). On estimating the diagnosticity of eyewitness nonidentifications. *Psychological Bulletin, 88*, 776–784.

Wells, G. L., Leippe, M. R. & Ostrom, T. M. (1979). Guidelines for empirically assessing the fairness of a line-up. *Law and Human Behavior, 3*, 285–293.

Wells, G. L., Rydell, S. M. & Seelau, E. P. (1993). The selection of distractors for eyewitness line-ups. *Journal of Applied Psychology, 78*, 834–844.

Wells, G. L., Small, M., Penrod, S., Malpass, R. S., Fulero, S. M. & Brimacombe, C. A. E. (1998). Eyewitness identification procedures: Recommendations for line-ups and photospreads. *Law and Human Behavior, 22*, 1–39.

Wells, G. L., Malpass, R. S., Lindsay, R. C. L., Fisher, R. P., Turtle, J. W. & Fulero, S. M. (2000). From the lab to the police station: A successful application of eyewitness research. *American Psychologist, 55*, 581–598.

Wells, G. L., Olson, E. A. & Charman, S. D. (2003). Distorted retrospective eyewitness reports as functions of feedback and delay. *Journal of Experimental Psychology: Applied, 9*, 42–52.

Whipple, G. M. (1909). The observer as reporter: A survey of the 'psychology of testimony'. *Psychological Bulletin, 6*, 153–170.

Wright, D. B. & McDaid, A. T. (1996). Comparing system and estimator variables using data from real line-ups. *Applied Cognitive Psychology, 10*, 75–84.

Wright, D. B. & Skagerberg, E. M. (2007). Post-identification feedback affects real eyewitnesses. *Psychological Science, 18*, 172–178.

Case

Daubert v Merrell Dow Pharmaceuticals, 509 U.S. 579 (1993).

Chapter Sixteen

Truthfulness in Witnesses' and Suspects' Reports

A. Daniel Yarmey

University of Guelph
Ontario

Although errors of omission and commission typically occur in eyewitness memory, it is often assumed by psycho-legal researchers that mistakes in eyewitness memory are *honest* errors that occur as a function of misperception, interference, retrieval failures, and so forth. In contrast, police often interview witnesses and suspects who are uncooperative and may, in fact, intentionally fabricate their testimony. Deception may be defined as 'a successful or unsuccessful deliberate attempt, without forewarning, to create in another a belief that the communicator considers to be untrue' (Vrij, 2000: 6). Although there has been substantial interest in the investigation of verbal and nonverbal correlates of deception (e.g., Vrij, 2000; Watkins & Turtle, 2003), and in determining the abilities of laypersons, police officers and psychologists to detect deception (e.g., Köhnken, 1987; Ekman, 2001), research on deception in an eyewitness memory paradigm is limited. Relatively little is known regarding the distortions that occur in eyewitness descriptions and identification as a function of witness deception.

The purpose of this chapter is to describe some recent studies from our laboratory that have addressed eyewitness memory and truthfulness/deception, with particular attention being given to the paper presented by myself and Elizabeth Wells and Linda Yuval at the 2nd International Investigative Interviewing Conference held at the University of Portsmouth, July 2006. Attention will be given to the following issues:

Handbook of Psychology of Investigative Interviewing: Current Developments and Future Directions
Edited by Ray Bull, Tim Valentine and Tom Williamson
© 2009 John Wiley & Sons, Ltd.

1. Based on common-sense understandings of eyewitness behaviour, how would men and women anticipate their likely responses as truthful or deceptive eyewitnesses when questioned regarding a violent crime?
2. What is the relationship between truthfulness/deception and eyewitness identification?
3. Can university students distinguish between deceptive and truthful eyewitnesses in their testimony?
4. Are there differences between deceptive (research) suspects and honest suspects in their repeated recall of real-world personal activities, including their participation in either a crime or non-crime incident, respectively?
5. Can duration estimations be used as an indicator of deception?

Common sense and deception in eyewitness reports

The objectives of police interviews are to determine whether a crime has occurred, to obtain accurate descriptions and evidence that can identify the individual(s) involved and to determine the credibility and truthfulness of the eyewitnesses and suspects (Gudjonsson, 1992; Kebbell & Wagstaff, 1997). Most deceptive witnesses, of course, will attempt to be persuasive and credible in their reports to the police. In contrast to the reports of truth-tellers, the reports of deceptive witnesses will probably be based in part on logical or common-sense understandings of eyewitness memory and on their beliefs about how they could best protect themselves from being found out. Previous studies of common knowledge of eyewitness memory have followed various approaches, including: the use of questionnaires (e.g., Kassin, Tubb, Hosch & Memon, 2001; Benton, Ross, Bradshaw, Thomas & Bradshaw, 2006); written descriptions of trials or videotaped trials (e.g., Hosch, Beck & McIntyre, 1980; Wells, Lindsay & Tousignant, 1980); prediction studies of the accuracy of eyewitness identification in staged crimes (e.g., Leippe, Wells & Ostrom, 1978; Kassin, 1979); and the cross-examination of eyewitnesses to staged crimes (e.g., Wells, Lindsay & Ferguson, 1979; Lindsay, Wells & Rumpel, 1981). These different procedures have found relatively consistent results, that is, laypersons (potential jurors), as well as police officers, lawyers and trial judges, have poor understanding of many issues involved in eyewitness memory.

Unlike the above studies, Yarmey (2004) asked participants how accurate/inaccurate they believe they would be as honest or deceptive eyewitnesses, respectively, in a criminal situation. Some 219 men and women in three Canadian cities were asked how they would respond if coerced to lie to protect a male perpetrator and female perpetrator, in contrast to being truthful and as accurate as possible. Participants were given a description of an armed robbery involving the shooting of a store worker, including a description of the persons involved. The incident was described as lasting either 15 seconds or two minutes, and participants were told to assume they were the sole eye-witness to the crime. Participants assigned to the deceptive condition were told to assume that they and their family would be harmed if they did not protect the perpetrator in their eyewitness reports. Participants assigned to the truthful condition were asked to respond as they would when trying to be as accurate as possible. Truthful and deceptive participants were instructed to state their expected accuracy/distortion of reports in estimating the height, weight and age of the two perpetrators, their estimation of the duration of the incident and their identification decision regarding a male suspect in a photo line-up.

The results indicated that both truthful and deceptive witnesses had a bias towards overestimation rather than underestimation of the height, weight and age of the two perpetrators. As expected, the bias was greater for deceptive witnesses than for truthful witnesses. Note, however, one interesting sex difference: the data indicated that if coercive threats were made to self and family, women in the deceptive condition would be more likely than their male counterparts to significantly distort their reports regarding perpetrator characteristics.

Prior to making their identification decisions, all participants were told to assume that the photo of the perpetrator was present in the photo line-up. Most truthful witnesses expected to be highly accurate (84% hits, 2% false alarms, 1% not there, 13% don't know) in their photo identification of the male suspect. In contrast, most deceptive witnesses indicated that they would say either that the suspect was not present in the line-up (31%), or that they did not know if he was present (37%), rather than falsely identify an innocent foil (4%). Truthful witnesses also expected to be significantly more confident in their identification decisions than deceptive witnesses. Contrary to expectations, a substantial minority (27%) of deceptive witnesses said they would correctly select the perpetrator in spite of possible retribution to both them-selves and their family. Deceptive witnesses, in contrast to truthful witnesses, reported significantly less confidence in their identification decisions. The reac-tion time to make identification decisions also revealed significant differences between truthful and deceptive witnesses. Truthful witnesses indicated that their identification decisions would be significantly faster than did deceptive witnesses.

Interestingly, participants on average in both the truthful condition and the deceptive condition indicated that they would overestimate the 15-second criminal event by 306%, and the two-minute incident by 88%, with no signifi-cant differences between truthful and deceptive participants. Of interest is the fact that several experiments show that short-duration events are significantly overestimated, and that women make significantly larger overestimations than do men (e.g., Loftus, Schooler, Boone & Kline, 1987; Yarmey & Yarmey, 1997). Consistent with the research literature, this study showed that women indicated that they would overestimate the duration intervals at better than a 2:1 ratio than would men. It appears that women more than men may both anticipate and then act in crime-like situations with the expectation that time will appear to move very slowly when they are witnesses to a highly emotional criminal event.

Truthfulness and deception in eyewitness identification

In a laboratory-designed experiment, Parliament & Yarmey (2002) presented undergraduate psychology students with a videotaped staged crime of a young man abducting an eight-year-old boy. Participants were randomly assigned to a deception group or a truthful group. Deceptive participants were instructed to lie to protect the perpetrator, whereas truthful participants were told to tell the truth and to identify the perpetrator to the best of their ability. One week later all participants were given either a seven-person sequentially presented suspect-absent photo line-up or suspect-present photo line-up. Of the 16 deceptive participants given the suspect-present line-up, 100% claimed the perpetrator was not there. In contrast, in the truthful group, 11 of 16 participants (69%) correctly identified the target, four identified foils and one said he was not present. Given a suspect-absent line-up, 14 of 16 deceptive participants (88%) said he was not present and two made false identifications. In contrast, seven of 16 truthful witnesses (44%) correctly rejected the line-up and nine (56%) made false identifications. Deceptive participants also made their identification decisions significantly faster than truthful participants in both the suspect-present and the suspect-absent line-ups.

In summary, these results suggest that deceptive eyewitnesses will behave significantly differently from truthful witnesses in their identification decisions and reaction times to make decisions. These results are interesting insofar as they suggest that eyewitness identifications are not consistent with how individuals believe they would behave in a traumatic criminal situation with respect to their identification decisions as either honest or deceptive eyewitnesses, as demonstrated in the questionnaire study on common sense just described. Future research is needed to determine the limits of these differences in a variety of situations.

Judgements of deception and accuracy of performance in eyewitness testimony

Can university students distinguish between eyewitnesses who were deceptive or truthful in their testimony, and either accurate or mistaken in their identification of a target in a photo line-up (Desmarais & Yarmey, 2004)? Participants, all of whom could be potential jurors, were shown videotapes taken from an unpublished study (Yarmey, 2003) of four truthful and four deceptive eyewitnesses as they were being interviewed about their descriptions and photo identification of a perpetrator in a field experiment. Two witnesses in each group were accurate and two were inaccurate in their line-up identification as determined by post-experimental analysis. (Note that two of the deceptive eyewitnesses were correct in their identification of the perpetrator in spite of their assigned role to 'protect' the suspect. This may have occurred because they forgot who the suspect was and mistakenly identified him, or refused to maintain their role as deceptive eyewitnesses and correctly identified the suspect.) Students rated each of the eight videotaped eyewitnesses on his or her accuracy of testimony, honesty, competence, confidence and credibility, and also indicated which verbal and nonverbal cues guided their ratings.

Participants' decisions regarding deception and accuracy of eyewitness identification were not significantly different from what would be expected by chance. However, participants were significantly better in detecting honesty in truthful eyewitnesses than they were in detecting lying by deceptive eyewitnesses. Also, participants were significantly better in detecting accurate eyewitnesses than inaccurate eyewitnesses.

In terms of subjective impressions, truthful eyewitnesses were perceived as more honest and more credible than deceptive eyewitnesses. Also, truthful eyewitnesses were perceived to be more honest and more credible when they were correct in their identification. In contrast, deceptive eyewitnesses were considered more honest and more credible when they were incorrect in their identifications. Thus, deceptive eyewitnesses appear to be able to project credibility and trust when they misidentify a target.

Participants reported that they relied on different verbal and nonverbal cues when judging truthful and deceptive eyewitnesses, and accurate and inaccurate testimony. For example, participants relied on pauses or hesitations in speech, frequent head movements and postural shifts to characterize deceptive witnesses. In contrast, truthful witnesses reportedly were discriminated by faster rates of speech, greater amounts of recalled details and higher frequency of smiles and laughter. Different cues also were used to differentiate between accurate and inaccurate eyewitnesses. Witnesses were judged more likely to be accurate if they spoke quickly, gave many descriptions, gave descriptions that were judged relevant and showed frequent arm and hand movements. In contrast, witnesses were judged to be inaccurate if they showed frequent pauses or hesitations in speech, admitted their forgetfulness or inadequacy and displayed frequent smiles and laughter. Eye contact or gaze were not said to be relied on to differentiate between truthful and deceptive eyewitnesses, whereas some studies have shown that liars engage in more eye contact than do truth-tellers (e.g., Vrij & Easton, 2002; Strömwall & Granhag, 2003).

It may be concluded that people use different verbal and nonverbal cues to differentiate between truthful and deceptive eyewitnesses, and between accurate and inaccurate eyewitnesses. However, these cues are not powerful enough to allow laypersons to differentiate between accurate and inaccurate testimony, or between truthful and deceptive eyewitnesses, beyond what would be expected by chance.

Deceptive suspects' event recall and duration estimates across repeated interviews

Consider the following scenario: Two men, John Brown and Joe Smith, independently find an unmarked envelope in a city street. Brown's envelope contains $25,000 in bank notes payable to the holder, whereas Smith's envelope contains some worthless advertisements. Brown realizes that the envelope has been lost and the proper thing to do would be to find its rightful owner by calling the police. Instead, he makes the decision to keep the money, knowing full well that, from this point onward, he will have to lie to protect himself if he is ever questioned about how he obtained this money. A day later the police contact both Brown and Smith because they were reportedly seen in the area where the money had gone missing. They are repeatedly questioned about their activities during the general time period when the bank notes were lost. Clearly, the two men have different motivations in describing their activities to the authorities. John Brown wants to keep the money and has decided to be deceptive in his reports, whereas Joe Smith, who has done nothing wrong, attempts to be accurate and truthful in his reports.

The research to be described in this section mimics the above scenario (Yarmey, Wells & Yuval, 2006). This experiment had two purposes: first, to explore the differences in reports of deceptive suspects and truthful suspects in their repeated accounts of personal activities, including a staged crime or a staged non-criminal incident, respectively; and second, to determine if time estimations may be used as an indicator of deception.

Truthful and deceptive persons do differ somewhat in their verbal reports. For example, in contrast to truth-tellers, liars tend to use fewer words and offer fewer details in their stories (Undeutsch, 1982; deTurck & Miller, 1985; Zuckerman & Driver, 1985; Miller & Stiff, 1993; Anolli & Ciceri, 1997; Yuval, 2003). This may be because of the ease with which fewer details can be stored and remembered when liars are asked to repeat their testimony (Vrij, 2000). Compared to truth-tellers, the stories reported by liars have been found to be less plausible but more structured in the chronological order of story-telling (i.e., this happened first followed by this, then that, and so forth) (Zaparniuk, Yuille & Taylor, 1995; Granhag & Vrij, 2005).

Granhag & Strömwall (2000) suggest that the 'repeat vs. reconstruct' hypothesis can account for the different strategies that liars and truth-tellers employ over repeated interviews. They argue that deceivers recognize that, in order to avoid detection, they have to retain a clear memory of what they said in previous accounts. Second, because memory is reconstructive (Loftus, 1979; Baddeley, 1990), individuals who are telling the truth will gain, lose and change information over time. Thus, deceivers will attempt to repeat what they have said in previous accounts, while truth-tellers will attempt to reconstruct an event they actually experienced. Because deceptive suspects possess the common-sense understanding that fewer details are easier to remember than multiple details, they will make their statements as short as possible in order to avoid contradictions and inconsistencies over repeated interviews. Thus, our first hypothesis was that deceptive suspects would give shorter statements and omit more details than truthful suspects across repeated interviews.

The second major interest of this research was the investigation of the impact of deception on recall time and duration estimates, a focus of interest that has yet to be empirically explored by researchers. An individual's ability to provide an accurate account of both where he or she was and the times or durations of these events has practical forensic implications (Loftus, *et al.,* 1987; Jackson, Michon & Melchior, 1993; Yarmey, 2000; Pedersen & Wright, 2002). If a suspect provides alibi evidence of a timeframe of a critical event that overestimates or underestimates the actual duration or conflicts with evidence from witnesses' duration estimates of the same event, police can use the temporal statement as an investigative tool. Theoretical and empirical investigation of duration estimations date back to the nineteenth century, with Vierordt's (1868) discovery that short intervals tend to be overestimated and longer ones underestimated. Consistent with Vierordt's Law, forensically related research has shown that witnesses tend on average to overestimate the duration of relatively short events lasting a few minutes or less (e.g., Loftus *et al.,* 1987; Yarmey & Yarmey, 1997) and underestimate relatively long events lasting 20 minutes and more (Yarmey, 1990).

People perceive and recall the duration of events subjectively and their estimations of time are influenced by cognitive, affective and subjective preference (Carmichael, 1997). Deceptive suspects have different purposes, goals and agendas from truthful suspects. That is, deceptive suspects probably wish to distort their time reports and distance themselves from the period in which the crime occurred. Deceptive participants in this study were told to be credible in their reports. As a consequence they would probably make duration estimations constrained somewhat by reality rather than construct fantasy-type fabrications (Johnson & Raye, 1981; Johnson & Sherman, 1990). Whereas the research literature would support the prediction that truthful participants would overestimate the duration of their involvement in short-term, mundane activities (see Yarmey, 2000), it was uncertain whether deceptive suspects would overestimate or underestimate the duration of both routine activities and the critical incident. It also was uncertain whether deceptive participants would differ from truthful participants in estimating the specific time in which the critical incident began.

Research participants and procedures

Nineteen men and women were randomly assigned to a truthful condition and 17 to a deceptive condition (overall *M* age = 27.61 years, *SD* = 10.34). All participants (14 men and 22 women) were city-dwellers and worked in different occupations (business, homemakers, educators, college students, and so forth). The experiment used a 2 (Group: Deceptive, Truthful) × 3 (Repeated interviews: one-day, one-week, two-week retention interval) mixed-group factorial design.

Two female psychology students acted as both observers and as mock police officers for the experiment. The observer accompanied the participant for a two-hour period during which time notes were taken of each change in an event or activity. Observations were done outside of normal working hours, but the participant was free to do any type of activity. Common activities included eating, household chores, and so forth. The observer did not interact with the participant during this period, except to announce that they were 'going for a walk'. The procedure involved taking on-the-spot records of behaviour as it occurred for two continuous hours. This record was then compared to the participant's later report of his or her activities in an attempt to establish the accuracy or distortion of time-delayed recall. The observer recorded all activities initiated by the participant and the amount of time engaged in each activity in chronological order. Timing of activities was rounded off and recorded to the nearest minute. The level of detail for an activity unit was to be such that someone reading the description could visualize the events as they occurred. An activity unit of behaviour was defined as a natural and meaningful action with a start and ending and which lasted approximately one minute or longer in duration.

Approximately 40 minutes into the observation session the observer announced that they were leaving the residence (assuming they were indoors at this time) and going for walk. Once outside the observer placed an envelope on the ground as if someone had dropped it. The participant had earlier been instructed to pick up the envelope, read its contents and then put the 'found' materials in their pocket or purse. Participants in the truthful condition found an envelope containing a one-page advertisement flyer. This was accompanied by a note stating that the participant was to read the ad for information purposes only, but was not expected to memorize it. Participants in the deceptive condition picked up an envelope containing a bank note worth $25,000 payable on demand to the bearer. An accompanying note informed the participant that 'although the money does not belong to you, you will keep it rather than trying to locate its owner or hand it over to the police. From this point on you realize that you must protect yourself. No one, particularly the police, should know that you have kept the money. When you are questioned about the lost note you will be trying to fool the interviewer (a mock police officer) but will try to be credible and convincing in your reports'.

After 'finding' the lost materials all participants were instructed to carry on their activities as they saw fit during the rest of the observation period. Participants also were told that the observer and mock police officer did not know which group they were in and they were not to reveal this information. The participants were interviewed one day, one week and two weeks later. The mock police officer told the participants that a witness had reported that they in the general vicinity of where the envelopes were lost and that the police wanted them to answer a few questions about their whereabouts at the approximate time of the incident. The participants were asked to put in writing all the activities they could recall engaging in during the two-hour observation period and the amount of time spent performing each one, or the time it started and stopped. They were told to recall those types of activities lasting approximately one minute or longer, or any activity they considered to be distinct or important, regardless of its duration. In order to allow participants to determine their own order of free recall, they were told that the chronological order of their recall was not important. When participants finished their report they were asked if they remembered being told by the observer: 'We are going for a walk'. If the participants said 'yes', they were asked to estimate the specific time of day that occurred.

Results and discussion

To summarize our findings, the analyses of free recall scores showed that, in contrast to truthful suspects, the reports of deceptive suspects declined significantly from the initial interview compared to one and two weeks later. Significant differences were found for: the total number of activities reported regardless of accuracy; the percentage correspondence of activities scores (that is, the agreement between the number of correct activities observed by the research assistant and reported by the participant converted into ratio scores); and the level of precision of details reported. Contrary to our expectations, truthful suspects did not show an increase in the amount of correct information reported across interviews (hypermnesia) or new information recalled across interviews (reminiscence effects). Furthermore, no significant difference was found between truth-tellers and deceptive suspects in the chronological structure of their free narrations of the two-hour observation period.

No significant differences were found between truthful suspects and deceptive suspects in their duration estimations for seven categories entailing routine mundane activities. However, on the critical event involving a walk, a significant difference in duration estimations was obtained. Whereas truthful suspects on average overestimated this short-duration event, deceptive suspects were highly consistent in significantly underestimating the duration of the critical event. These differences occurred in spite of the fact that no significant differences were found between the two groups in their estimation of the time when the walk event began.

In line with our interpretation of Granhag & Strömwall's (2000) 'repeat vs. reconstruct' hypothesis, this experiment showed that the number and percentage accuracy of activities and the number of details reported by deceptive suspects decreased across interviews. In order to remember what was previously said, a deceptive suspect probably would attempt to follow a remembered script. In subsequent interviews, deceptive criminal suspects are repeating an originally deceptive account rather than trying to *reconstruct* an account that actually occurred. Thus, they will use fewer words and give fewer details with repeated interviews in an attempt to ensure that their recall will appear accurate and credible. Coarsely grained but credible responses, as opposed to more specific responses, would appear to be the preferred and wiser choice for deceptive suspects. In contrast, because memory is reconstructive, it would be expected that truthful reports will gain, lose and change information over time and, in an attempt to be more informative, will show more fine-grained responses (Loftus, 1979; Baddeley, 1990; Goldsmith, Koriat & Weinberg-Eliezer, 2002).

The fact that the mean scores for *correspondence of activities* at one day were highly similar for both truthful and deceptive participants deserves particular consideration. Both truthful and deceptive suspects reported approximately one-third of the total possible number of activities observed by the research assistant. The 'repeat vs. reconstruct' hypothesis would predict that truthful accounts should contain more details than deceptive accounts. So what can account for these findings? As Granhag & Strömwall (2000) theorize in their own study, participants in the current study were asked to distort an original event rather than create a complete fabrication. Distortions may in general contain a greater number of details than pure fiction, potentially negating the effects of deception on the number of details initially reported by participants. Furthermore, in this investigation both truthful and deceptive suspects operated in the very familiar surroundings of their own home and nearby streets. The context of the events for both deceptive and truthful suspects would have been relatively similar in terms of visual, auditory and spatial details. Performing a mock crime in familiar surroundings would have been highly conducive for the construction of logical and well-rehearsed reports by the deceptive suspects. Such familiarity would facilitate credible and logical stories by both deceptive and truthful suspects.

Additionally, our findings support the basic premise of the hypothesis put forth by Undeutsch (1982), which argues that fewer details are provided by deceptive individuals because it is relatively easier to recall fewer details later. Thus, in actual forensic settings in which a criminal suspect is interviewed repeatedly, the number of details and the length of particular accounts over time may be important clues to veracity. Note that these are not absolute quantities but relative ones in which the point of comparison is the individual him- or herself. Individuals vary greatly in the number of words and details that they use in general, and this is based on a variety of factors, including intelligence, educational level and language proficiency. In an initial interview, it is thus difficult if not impossible to predict how many words and details might be used. But over time with repeated interviews one may see decreases in quantities and fine details, and these decreases can serve as important indicators of deception.

Interestingly, neither truthful nor deceptive suspects reported what they did during the walk, apart from stating that they were going for the walk. It is likely that no disclosures were given regarding activities undertaken during the walk because participants were repeatedly instructed by the research assistant not to reveal into which group they had been placed. These findings suggest that our participants were highly compliant in following the experimental instructions. Furthermore, the methodology used in this investigation (written free responses without direct questioning from the mock police officer) probably contributed to the lack of details reported by participants during the walk. Follow-up studies of the present investigation should investigate the differences between truthful and deceptive suspects as a function of type of interview and suspect responses.

This study provides preliminary support for the equal ease with which both deceptive and truthful participants can effectively account for their time during an event or series of events. Thus, asking a criminal suspect when an event took place or how long that event lasted may not be a reliable clue to deception if the act of deception has no differential effect on one's ability to estimate its duration. Recall of event duration is seen by legal experts to have potential significance in the courtroom. In her article directed to defence lawyers, Steele (2004) advises that attention should be paid to 'Event Duration ... for how long did the witness see the culprit? ... the witness' estimate is almost certain to be wrong; generally, the witness will overestimate durations' (p. 10). Although the witnesses referred to by Steele are victims of or bystanders to a crime, it is also true that guilty suspects are witnesses to their own involvement in a crime. In the present investigation truthful suspects and deceptive suspects did not differ in their duration estimations for routine, mundane events. However, deceptive participants in contrast to truthful participants significantly and consistently underestimated the duration of 'the walk' (the point during the study when participants were asked to go out and find either the bank note or advertisement). Note that the research literature on duration estimations for events lasting three minutes or less is highly reliable, that is, short-duration events are on average overestimated (see Yarmey, 2000). The implications of this finding are potentially considerable, particularly given the lack of significant findings for any of the other duration estimates. The key experimental manipulation of being assigned to either the truthful or deceptive condition is made most salient to participants when they are instructed to go out for the walk. Although they already know whether they will be behaving truthfully or deceptively, 'the walk' is the point at which these instructions actually become an event that the participants must act upon.

The practical psycho-legal implications of the current study centre on the number and accuracy of activities reported, including the level of precision and the durations estimates provided for the crime in question. First, deceptive criminal suspects use decreasingly fewer words and fine-grain details over time. Given that criminal investigations likely include repeated interviews of criminal suspects over time, it would be incumbent upon investigators to pay close attention to this indicator during an investigation. Ideally, recorded interviews would be coded for the number of details and words used by a criminal suspect. Practically speaking, however, limitations on time and resources may preclude this possibility. A reasonable alternative would have investigators reviewing recorded interviews collectively, making relative comparisons and agreed upon judgements about the length of suspect statements and accounts over repeated interrogations.

Second, deceptive criminal suspects only underestimate the length of time that occurs during the actual criminal event relative to their duration estimations for other activities surrounding the critical event. This is a compelling forensic indicator which can be assessed with relative ease in actual interrogation settings and does not depend on repeated interrogations. Investigators would simply need to compare the suspect's duration estimates with the victim(s) and other witnesses, particularly given that the study demonstrated that truthful individuals do not under- or overestimate any of the activities. Of course, this strategy assumes that both the victim(s) and other witnesses are themselves being truthful. This is a separate issue, and one that cannot be addressed by this study.

As with many psychological studies investigating behaviour in forensic settings, limitations of the current study centre on its ecologically validity. For both ethical and practical reasons, it is impossible to create an actual criminal situation in order to experimentally study deceptive behaviour. Given that key features of an actual, high-stakes criminal act were absent from the current study, in particular, the real-world consequences of getting caught or of succeeding and the accompanying emotions, such as guilt, fear or elation, one has to question the degree to which the current findings generalize to actual criminal suspects. Lying about a fake $25,000 bank note is not the same as lying about participating in an armed robbery. A related issue concerns the artificiality of role-playing. In the current study, we asked both the participants and the research assistants to assume very specific roles and then play them out (witness/criminal suspect and police officer, respectively). There is a contrived nature to this sort of role-playing that is necessarily absent from actual settings in which people *are* witnesses, suspects or police officers, arriving in these roles through a highly complex interaction of events, decisions and circumstance. Nevertheless, it is likely that there are features that are inherent to the deceptive act itself (regardless of what one is lying about or why) that are relatively robust across both real-world and artificial settings.

Future research should continue to investigate the effects of repeated recall over time on deceptive and truthful accounts. In addition, future studies should add to the research on the effects of deception and repeated recall over time on duration estimates. This is an understudied and potentially significant indicator which may eventually demonstrate high predictive value in investigative interviews.

Conclusion

Both laboratory-bound and field experiments on eyewitness behaviour may be conducted to explore the differences between honest and deceptive eyewitnesses, and honest and deceptive suspects. Common-sense or individuals' intuitions of how well they would perform as potential honest or deceptive eyewitnesses to a violent or serious crime are not predictive of actual eyewitness behaviours. Judgements of honesty/deceptive behaviours, as well as the accuracy/inaccuracy of eyewitnesses by highly educated lay-persons, are not significantly different from what would be found by chance. However, there are a number of subjective beliefs that are consistently held by observers regarding the behaviours of honest and deceptive eyewitnesses. Finally, it appears that duration estimations can be added to the list of indicators that may differentiate between truthful and deceptive behaviours.

References

Anolli, L. & Ciceri, R. (1997). The voice of deception: Vocal strategies of naïve and able liars. *Journal of Nonverbal Behavior*, 21, 259–284.

Baddeley, A. (1990). *Human memory: Theory and practice*. Hove: Lawrence Erlbaum.

Benton, T. R., Ross, D. F., Bradshaw, E., Thomas, W. N. & Bradshaw, G. S. (2006). Eyewitness memory is still not common sense: Comparing jurors, judges and law enforcement to eyewitness experts. *Applied Cognitive Psychology*, 20, 115–129.

Carmichael, A. R. (1997). Duration estimates: A potentially useful tool for cognitive ergonomists. In D. Harris (Ed.), *Engineering psychology and cognitive ergonomics. Volume 2: Job design and product design* (pp. 267–273). Aldershot: Ashgate.

Desmarais, S. & Yarmey, A. D. (2004). Judgements of deception and accuracy of performance in eyewitness testimony. *Canadian Journal of Police & Security Services*, 2, 13–22.

deTurck, M. A. & Miller, G. R. (1985). Deception and arousal: Isolating the behavioral correlates of deception. *Human Communication Research*, 12, 181–201.

Ekman, P. (2001). *Telling lies*. New York: Norton.

Goldsmith, M., Koriat, A. & Weinberg-Eliezer, A. (2002). Strategic regulation of grain size memory reporting. *Journal of Experimental Psychology: General*, 131, 73–95.

Granhag, P. A. & Strömwall, L. A. (2000). Repeated interrogations: Stretching the deception detection paradigm. *Expert Evidence*, 7, 163–174.

Granhag, P. A. & Vrij, A. (2005). Deception detection. In N. Brewer & K. D. Williams (Eds.), *Psychology and law: An empirical perspective* (pp. 43–92). New York: Guilford Press.

Gudjonsson, G. H. (1992). *The psychology of interrogations, confessions and testimony*. Chichester: Wiley.

Hosch, H. M., Beck, E. L. & McIntyre, P. (1980). Influence of expert testimony regarding eyewitness accuracy on jury decisions. *Law and Human Behavior*, 4, 287–296.

Jackson, J. L., Michon, J. A. & Melchior, K. (1993). Time meets crime: A search for a common theoretical framework. *Psychologica Belgica, 33,* 297–309.

Johnson, M. K. & Raye, C. L. (1981). Reality monitoring. *Psychological Review, 88,* 67–85.

Johnson, M. K. & Sherman, S. J. (1990). Constructing and reconstructing the past and the future in the present. In E. T. Higgins & R. M. Sorrentino (Eds.). *Handbook of motivation and cognition: Foundations of social behaviour* (vol. 2), (pp. 482–526). New York: Guilford.

Kassin, S. M. (1979). Unpublished study. Cited in G. L. Wells (1984). How adequate is human intuition for judging eyewitness testimony? In G. L. Wells and E. F. Loftus (Eds.). *Eyewitness testimony: Psychological perspectives* (pp. 256–272). New York: Cambridge University Press.

Kassin, S. M., Tubb, V. A., Hosch, H. M. & Memon, A. (2001). On the 'general acceptance' of eyewitness testimony research: A new survey of the experts. *American Psychologist, 56,* 405–416.

Kebbell, M. R. & Wagstaff, G. (1997). Why do the police interview eyewitnesses? Interview objectives and the evaluation of eyewitness performance. *Journal of Psychology, 13,* 595–601.

Köhnken, G. (1987). Training police to detect deceptive eyewitness statements: Does it work? *Social Behavior, 2,* 1–17.

Leippe, M. R., Wells, G. L. & Ostrom, T. M. (1978). Crime seriousness as a determinant of accuracy in eyewitness identification. *Journal of Applied Psychology, 63,* 345–351.

Lindsay, R. C. L., Wells, G. L. & Rumpel, C. (1981). Can people detect eyewitness identification accuracy within and across situations? *Journal of Applied Psychology, 66,* 79–89.

Loftus, E. F. (1979). *Eyewitness testimony.* Cambridge, MA: Harvard University Press.

Loftus, E. F., Schooler, J. W., Boone, S. M. & Kline, D. (1987). Time went by so slowly: Overestimation of event duration by males and females. *Applied Cognitive Psychology, 1,* 3–13.

Miller, G. R. & Stiff, J. B. (1993). *Deceptive communication.* Newbury Park, CA: Sage.

Parliament, L. & Yarmey, A. D. (2002). Deception in eyewitness identification. *Criminal Justice and Behavior, 29,* 734–746.

Pedersen, A. C. I. & Wright, D. B. (2002). Do differences in event descriptions cause differences in duration estimates? *Applied Cognitive Psychology, 16,* 769–783.

Steele, L. (2004). Trying identification cases: An outline for raising eyewitness ID issues. *Champion,* 8–18 November. http://www.nacdl.org/public.nsf/0/9973f3 ec244ba99685256f6a00558f39?OpenDocument

Strömwall, L. & Granhag, P. (2003). How to detect deception? Arresting the beliefs of police officers, prosecutors and judges. *Psychology, Crime & Law, 9,* 19–36.

Undeutsch, U. (1982). Statement reality analysis. In A. Trankell (Ed.), *Reconstructing the past: The role of psychologists in criminal trials* (pp. 27–56). Stockholm: Norstedt & Somers.

Vierordt, K. (1868). *Der Zeitsinn nach Versuchen.* [Empirical studies of time experience], Tübingen: H. Laupp.

Vrij, A. (2000). *Detecting lies and deceit: The psychology of lying and the implications for professional practice.* Chichester: Wiley.

Vrij, A. & Easton, S. (2002). Fact or fiction? Verbal and behavioural clues to detect deception. *Medico-Legal Journal, 70*, 29–37.

Watkins, K. & Turtle, J. (2003). Investigative interviewing and the detection of deception. *Canadian Journal of Police & Security Services, 1*, 115–123.

Wells, G. L., Lindsay, R. C. L. & Ferguson, T. J. (1979). Accuracy, confidence, and juror perceptions in eyewitness identification. *Journal of Applied Psychology, 64*, 440–448.

Wells, G. L., Lindsay, R. C. L. & Tousignant, J. P. (1980). Effects of expert psychological advice on human performance in judging the validity of eyewitness testimony. *Law and Human Behavior, 4*, 275–286.

Yarmey, A. D. (1990). Accuracy and confidence in duration estimates following questions containing marked and unmarked modifiers. *Journal of Applied Social Psychology, 20*, 1139–1149.

Yarmey, A. D. (2000). Retrospective duration estimations for variant and invariant events in field situations. *Applied Cognitive Psychology, 14*, 45–57.

Yarmey, A. D. (2003). *Eyewitness testimony and deception: A field experiment.* Paper presented at the International Conference on Psychology and Law, Edinburgh, July.

Yarmey, A. D. & Yarmey, M. J. (1997). Eyewitness recall and duration estimates in field settings. *Journal of Applied Social Psychology, 27*, 330–344.

Yarmey, A. D., Wells, E. C. & Yuval, L. (2006). Deceptive suspects' event recall and duration estimates across repeated interviews. *Canadian Journal of Police & Security Services, 4*, 200–210.

Yarmey, D. (2004). Effects of deception on eyewitness reports. *Canadian Journal of Police & Security Services, 2*, 199–207.

Yuval, L. N. (2003). *Uncovering the behavioural correlates of the deceptive eyewitness.* Unpublished master's thesis, University of Guelph, Ontario.

Zaparniuk, J., Yuille, J. C. & Taylor, S. (1995). Assessing the credibility of true and false statements. *International Journal of Law and Psychiatry, 18*, 343–352.

Zuckerman, M. & Driver, R. (1985). Telling lies: Verbal and nonverbal correlates of deception. In A. W. Siegman & S. Feldstein (Eds.), *Nonverbal communication: An integrated perspective* (pp. 129–147). Hillsdale, NJ: Lawrence Erlbaum.

Chapter Seventeen

Evaluating Truthfulness: Detecting Truths and Lies in Forensic Contexts

Barry S. Cooper

The Forensic Alliance
Forensic Psychiatric Services Commission

Hugues Hervé

The Forensic Alliance

and

John C. Yuille

The Forensic Alliance
University of British Columbia

Introduction

As Nietzsche (1967) asserted, lying is a fact of life. Indeed, on average, we all lie about three times a day and to about one third of the people with whom we interact (Ekman, 1992; DePaulo, Kashy, Kirkendol, Wyer & Epstein, 1996; Ford, 2006). Most lies are well intended, such as an omission (a type of lie) to spare someone's feelings or a fabrication (another type of lie) to make someone feel good (Ekman, 1992; Ford, 2006). Such lies could be viewed as altruistic in nature and as having evolved to facilitate socialization (Nietzsche, 1967). Less commonly, lies are markedly more self-serving (e.g., for self-protection), if not downright manipulative and/or malevolent (e.g., to avoid punishment and/or gain an underserved reward; Cooper & Yuille, 2006). Although less common in the general population, selfish lies, which could be viewed as a product of natural selection, are relatively prominent in forensic

Handbook of Psychology of Investigative Interviewing: Current Developments and Future Directions
Edited by Ray Bull, Tim Valentine and Tom Williamson
© 2009 John Wiley & Sons, Ltd.

contexts (Spidel, Hervé, Greaves, Cooper & Hare, 2003), where their impact can have disastrous effects (e.g., lead to the guilty being freed or the innocent jailed). Not surprisingly, lying in general and lying for selfish reasons in particular have received a great deal of scholarly attention throughout history.

The goal of the present chapter is to provide an overview of the research on skill-based, as opposed to technology-driven, methods for evaluating truthfulness (i.e., differentiating truths from lies via verbal and nonverbal channels) and to introduce an evidenced-based approach that promotes the state of the art in this area. First, the complex nature of distinguishing truths from lies is discussed, followed by a brief review of the extant approaches in this area. Next is an overview of the research on the topic, including its limitations. The focus then turns to a review of the research on individuals' abilities to distinguish truths from lies and a discussion of barriers that often prevent people from being able to reliably evaluate truthfulness. Following, evidenced-based components involved in improving individuals' capacity to distinguish truths from lies are presented. Finally, an approach to evaluating truthfulness is introduced, including its strengths and limitations. It is hoped that the chapter will provide a foundation from which to improve the capacity to reliably distinguish truths from lies.

The complex nature of evaluating truthfulness

Lying and its evaluation are an inherently complex topic. For example, what constitutes a lie depends largely on one's motivation, which itself reflects, at least in part, the triggering event and the context in which the lie occurs. Clearly, lying about not liking your partner's new hairstyle is emotionally less intense and cognitively taxing than lying to the police about your involvement in a murder (i.e., different triggering events). Similarly, a criminal lying to peers in a bar about some misdeed is likely to feel very different about the same lie committed in a court of law (i.e., different contexts). In other words, one's motivation not only defines the interaction (truth or lie), but also dictates how it will reveal itself, both qualitatively and quantitively.

For the purpose of the present chapter, a lie is defined as the deliberate intention to deceive another person without prior notification (Ekman, 1992). For example, a financial adviser who provides poor investment advice is viewed as lying if she or he knows their advice is poor yet represents it as good, but is not seen as lying if the advice is well intended and proves to be poor. As another example, a woman with a *bona fide* paranoid delusion, who states that she is Mary Magdalene, is not lying, while a woman deliberately feigning a delusion during a psychological examination is lying.

In order to detect lies, one needs to understand the nature of truth-telling, which adds to the complexity of evaluation. That is, one needs to gain knowledge and skills in two distinct but related areas: how to identify truths when they are present and how to detect lies when they are present. Expertise in only one of these areas will undoubtedly lead to many errors, with the *expert* truth-seeker missing many lies (i.e., false negatives) and the *expert* lie-catcher missing many truths (i.e., false positives). For this reason, we have moved away from the popular nomenclature of 'lie detection' or 'credibility assessment', choosing instead to describe the differentiation of truths and lies as 'evaluating truthfulness'.

The practice of evaluating truthfulness is inherently complex as it never occurs in a vacuum, in contrast to the vast majority of laboratory research on the topic. The focus of most research and practice in assessing truthfulness is usually in the context of some formal or quasi-formal assessment. This can be a police interview of a witness or suspect, a customs agent interviewing an incoming passenger, a salesperson talking to a potential client, a lawyer conducting a discovery or a mental health professional doing a forensic examination. Evaluating truthfulness in the context of an assessment involves multi-tasking as, in addition to evaluating truthfulness, the assessor is always involved in other tasks (e.g., forming the next question, listening to the interviewee, monitoring professional tasks). Multi-tasking inevitably makes the evaluation of truthfulness more difficult. Indeed, evaluating truthfulness is a difficult task by itself, something that is exacerbated whenever there are any distracters. Adding to its difficulty is the reality that evaluating truthfulness is dynamic in nature. That is, the task will change during a single interview, as well as across interviews: an interviewee may lie about a particular topic at one point but not at another, or may display a lie about a particular topic differently at different times (e.g., verbally at first but non-verbally subsequently). As is emphasized below, research indicates that there is no lie response and, therefore, truthfulness must always be inferred. Sometimes, what appears to be an indication of a lie may turn out to be in indication of something else; therefore, the accurate evaluation of truthfulness requires repeated reassessment of one's hypotheses and conclusions (see below).

The complexity of evaluating truthfulness is enhanced by the presence of both individual and cultural differences. For example, individuals differ in their motivations for lying and telling the truth (Ekman, 1992; Cooper & Yuille, 2006; Spidel et al., 2003), as well as their ability to deceive and/or detect deception (Ekman & O'Sullivan, 1991; Porter, Woodworth & Birt, 2000). In addition, although some of the clues to deception that are reviewed below are cross-cultural, others are culturally specific. For example, the facial expression of anger appears to be universal (Ekman, 2003), however, the triggers that cause anger are thought to be, at least in part, culturally determined. To complicate matters further, individual difference variables must always be interpreted in terms of context and a host of other factors. For example, just because a forensic assessor knows that she or he is dealing with an interpersonally gifted psychopath with a penchant for lying does not mean that everything that the psychopath says during the interview(s) is deceptive.

Clearly, the complex nature of conducting evaluations of truthfulness poses considerable challenges for both practice and research. That said, it is important to note that these challenges are not insurmountable obstacles but rather roadblocks to be carefully navigated. Before turning our attention to the impact of these obstacles, as well as ways around them, we briefly review a number of contemporary methods available for evaluating truthfulness.

Approaches to evaluating truthfulness

There is a long history associated with discriminating truth from lies. For example, Ancient Egyptian papyri, as well as records of classical Chinese courts, included hints or recommendations on how to discriminate a truth-teller from a liar (Ford, 2006). However, the twentieth century witnessed an explosion of both theory and technology related to evaluating truthfulness. The approaches that have developed can be classified into two basic types: those that are technology-based and those that are skill-based. Technology-based techniques for discriminating truth from lies can be classified as either psycho-physiological or neuropsychological in nature. The best known of the psycho-physiological techniques is the polygraph, which measures heart rate, skin conductance and respiration while a person is answering a number of questions. The polygraph is often mislabeled a lie detector test. The polygraph does not detect lies; it detects stress. Perhaps the most effective aspects of the use of the polygraph are the polygraphers, who are often excellent interviewers, and the fact that the polygraph detects change, a core aspect to our proposed approach to evaluating truthfulness (see below). The polygraph is a useful tool, but it has a focused use (e.g., criminal suspect investigations and national security) and can produce both false-positive and false-negative errors (National Research Council, 1996).

In terms of more recent technological advances, a number of companies have been promoting and selling voice stress analysers as lie detectors (for a review, see Vrij & Granhag, 2007). Such devices detect changes in the pitch and tension of the voice and there is no question that detecting change is an important aspect in evaluating truthfulness. However, although changes in the voice can be a clue to deception, voice characteristics are unreliable as a single basis for evaluating truthfulness (Vrij & Granhag, 2007), largely due to the fact that vocal changes can occur for a variety of reasons (see below). A more promising approach relies on thermal imaging, which measures temperature changes in the body. Not only has the technology evolved to allow for measures to be taken covertly at a distance, recent research suggests that there may be reliable thermal changes (e.g., on the face, particularly around the eyes) when a person is being deceptive (Vrij & Granhag, 2007). Research is also currently being conducted on the value of a functional magnetic resonance imaging (fMRI) and other techniques for assessing brain activity as a method for discriminating truth from lies (for a review, see Spence *et al.*, 2004). Although promising, it is important to note that these technological advances are in their infancy and require equipment that is intrusive, non-mobile and expensive. Accordingly, it would be premature to draw firm conclusions regarding the applied utility of such techniques.

Although technology-based approaches to evaluating truthfulness have their merits, there are a number of advantages of skill-based techniques. The main advantage of skill-based techniques is that they are extremely portable and unobtrusive. Skill-based assessment techniques typically fall into two general categories: those that rely on the assessment of verbal behaviour and those that focus on non-verbal aspects of behaviour. Verbal clues to truth and deception include the content of speech, the style of speech and voice characteristics (Horowitz, 1991; Porter & Yuille, 1996). Nonverbal clues are generally separated into those related to the face and those related to the rest of the body (Ekman, 1992; Ekman, O'Sullivan, Friesen & Scherer, 1991). The approach to skill-based assessment of truthfulness introduced in this chapter involves the integration of all of these channels of information, both verbal and nonverbal (see below).

As with technology-based approaches, there is no single verbal or nonverbal channel that clearly communicates deception. Rather, research and clinical-forensic experience suggest that it is the change in a particular channel and/or inconsistencies across channels that are particularly revealing (for a review, see Griesel & Yuille, 2007). Viewed in this context, research is beginning to demonstrate that skill-based approaches parallel technology-based approaches in terms of reliability and validity, without, however, the pitfalls associated with reliance on technology. Even proponents of technology-based approaches (e.g., polygraphers) understand the merit of skill-based methods.

Research on evaluating truthfulness

As noted above, the approach to evaluating truthfulness introduced in this chapter is research-based. Before this approach is outlined, it is important to discuss certain conceptual and methodological limitations inherent in this line of research. The basic difficulty in conducting research on evaluating truthfulness stems from the complexity of the topic itself (as defined above). In fact, we argue that current research methodology and associated statistical procedures cannot do the topic justice in terms of identifying and assessing clues to lies/truths and identifying how people evaluate truthfulness in the real world.

As with other areas in psychology, such as the field of eyewitness memory, most of the research that has been done on evaluating truthfulness is laboratory-based (for reviews, see DePaulo, Lindsay, Malone, Muhlenbruck, Charlton & Cooper, 2003; Griesel & Yuille, 2007). In a typical study, undergraduate volunteers are asked either to tell the truth or lie in highly controlled conditions. Often the motive for lying is weak (e.g., course credit, small monetary reward, praise) and the controls so stringent as to render the context psychologically sterile; thus, the generalizability of the findings to other contexts is limited. Indeed, one characteristic that discriminates relatively useful laboratory research from less useful research is the effort the researcher has put into developing effective or strong motivation for the participants in the laboratory study. Another factor is the multifaceted level attained by the mock design: the addition of variables often renders studies relatively more realistic. To approximate real-world scenarios more closely, we believe that research in this area should also attempt to vary the level of the participants' motivation according to the presence or absence of certain influencing variables. Evaluating truthfulness is both complex and dynamic; thus the research to support its techniques should be similarly complex and dynamic.

Field research (e.g., studies using tapes from criminal investigations; tapes from offenders discussing their crimes; tapes of people being interviewed at immigration entry points) generally does not have the motivational limitations of laboratory-based research (e.g., Cooper, Ternes, Griesel, Viljoen & Yuille 2007; Ternes, Cooper & Yuille, 2007). However, unlike laboratory studies, field research, although high in external validity, often lacks ground truth. Moreover, there is considerable variability in field research in terms of the manner in which ground truth is examined and measured. In other words, the nature and quality of the information determining ground truth is a major factor discriminating the scientific contribution of field research.

Irrespective of whether the research on evaluating truthfulness is laboratory- or field-based, research in this area has suffered from poor adherence to assessment training protocols. For example, one technique that is described in more detail below involves the assessment of the content of statements, i.e., Criteria Based Content Analysis (CBCA; Steller, 1989; Steller & Koehnken, 1989). It turns out that the response to training in this method is quite variable. In our experience, some trainees can learn this method and apply it reliably after two days of training, but others require weeks of training and practice before they are able to obtain the same degree of reliability. Some trainees, however, seem unable to acquire the methodology at all and research studies on this method of statement analysis have rarely taken this variability into account. Thus, researchers often end up with a mixed group of assessors rendering the study ineffective for evaluating the usefulness of the technique.

This area of enquiry is further limited by researchers' bias for quantitative research paradigms, often to the exclusion of qualitative approaches. To continue with the example of the CBCA, this approach to statement analysis is of a qualitative nature (Griesel & Yuille, 2007); however, researchers have shown a clear preference for statistical cut-off scores. Consequently, they often impose a quantitative structure on this qualitative assessment procedure, resulting in a distortion that often misrepresents research outcomes. As an aside, the same appears to be the case with structured clinical guidelines for the assessment of risk for recidivism. That is, even though it is the assessor's decision of the offender's risk level based on an overall evaluation of the risk factors examined that matters (Cooper, Griesel & Yuille, 2007), researchers have a preference to use numbers and cut-off scores to indicate low-, medium- and high-risk levels, which distorts the spirit of structured clinical judgement.

In addition to the methodological limitations reviewed above, this area of study is constrained by the limits of available statistical procedures. One of the main problems with applying traditional statistics to research on evaluating truthfulness is that statistics impose limits on the quality of the questions being answered. Indeed, while the practice of evaluating truthfulness is unique to the individual being assessed, it is often the case that researchers use group-based statistics that dilute these all-important individual differences. For example, some research suggests that examining body language has no or little valid role in helping evaluate truthfulness (DePaulo *et al.*, 2003; Vrij, Mann & Fisher, 2006). However, such research fails to consider the role of different types of body language (e.g., illustrators vs. manipulators vs. emblems), each having been found to relate to truthfulness differently (Ekman, Friesen & Scherer, 1978; Ekman, O'Sullivan, Friesen & Scherer, 1991). In fact, most research does not take into consideration the reality that, while certain types of body movements may increase in one person when he or she is lying, the same type of movement may decrease in another person when he or she is lying. Moreover, researchers build methodologies and thereafter rely on statistical procedures that assume that evaluating truthfulness is static in nature (i.e., is revealed at one point and/or consistently across lies/time) when in fact it is dynamic, changing within and across people and time. This raises another important point: although statistics appear to provide the context of objectivity and scientific integrity, the fact remains that the quality of the data that go into the analysis determines the quality of the results. No matter how sophisticated the statistical procedure employed, the above noted methodological issue will undoubtedly yield results of relatively limited practical utility. Accordingly, in reviewing the existing research, individuals are urged to do so cautiously and critically.

One potential solution to these problems is to employ a different method from that traditionally used in research on evaluating truthfulness: a series of case studies in which verbal and nonverbal behaviour are examined and determinations of truthfulness are made on an individual basis via an empirically-grounded and experience-informed approach (see below). With such an approach, quantitative and qualitative statistics could be utilized. While individual cases should be evaluated qualitatively, individual cases can thereafter be aggregated and analysed quantitatively. Not only would this approach serve to overcome the limitations discussed above, it would also help focus researchers on developing better-informed approaches to evaluating truthfulness as opposed to searching for the all-elusive 'signs' of deception. As expanded on below, such diagnostic signs have yet to reveal themselves and, moreover, are likely not to exist. Of course, single-case research designs come with their own complexities. That is, they are labour-intensive and costly, which may explain why this approach has never gained favour in such a competitive, publication-driven arena. Nevertheless, we argue that case studies will prove very useful in understanding how to evaluate truthfulness in applied contexts.

Pre-training accuracy in evaluating truthfulness

One of the major findings in the research on evaluating truthfulness is that it has been repeatedly demonstrated that most individuals, irrespective of professional background, are poor at distinguishing truths from lies. Ekman & O'Sullivan (1991) examined the ability of a large group of professionals and non-professionals, including police officers, secret service agents, polygraphers, psychiatrists and college students, to evaluate truthfulness by showing them a series of videos of individuals lying or telling the truth. Some video clips depicted individuals lying or telling the truth about their opinions on sensitive subjects, such as the death penalty, while others depicted individuals lying or telling the truth about their participation or non-participation in a mock crime. The researchers showed that there was no relationship between gender and the ability of the participants to tell who was lying and who was telling the truth. There was no relationship between years as an investigator/professional and the ability to evaluate truthfulness. There was also no relationship between confidence in one's ability to evaluate truthfulness and one's actual ability. Men have been found to be more confident in their wrong decisions (e.g., Porter, Woodworth & Birt, 2000), once again highlighting the importance of considering individual differences. The major finding from Ekman & O'Sullivan's (1991) study was that, as a group, participants were shown to be able to differentiate truth from lies only at chance levels. Only one subgroup, the secret service agents, was demonstrated to evaluate truthfulness at a level higher than chance (64%), although only marginally so and not to levels necessary for effective job performance. The flavour of Ekman & O'Sullivan's results has been replicated with different stimuli and participants, suggesting that most people, irrespective of profession and experience, cannot accurately evaluate truthfulness (Porter *et al.*, 2000).

Roadblocks to the accurate evaluation of truthfulness

Research has demonstrated that there are a number of roadblocks that prevent individuals from accurately evaluating truthfulness (Ekman, 1992; Hervé, Cooper & Yuille, 2008; Vrij, 2000). Heading the list is a lack of evidence-based knowledge and skills specific to evaluating truthfulness, which results in individuals relying on their 'experience' and/or popular myths (see below). More generally, another roadblock reflects a lack of critical thought. Critical thinking is a necessary, but not sufficient, component in conducting evaluations and to evaluating truthfulness within such evaluations. Each roadblock is discussed in turn.

In terms of lack of knowledge, research indicates that most individuals do not know what lies and truths look like (Akehurst, Kohnken, Vrij & Bull, 1996; Ekman & O'Sullivan, 1991; Porter *et al.*, 2000; Vrij, 2004). It is clear that people rely on certain clues related to what they think lies and truths look like; however, research indicates that, more often than not, such heavily relied upon clues (e.g., all liars will experience anxiety/fear and, therefore, avoid eye contact; Ekman, 1992) are wrong. Such clues are simply myths, often perpetuated in the media and in professional manuals, but lacking empirical support.

With regards to skills, if the skills required for the job are lacking in breadth and depth, the job cannot be performed adequately. For instance, if evidence-based approaches are not used for the assessment of risk for recidivism, there will be substantial false-positive and false-negative errors made (Monahan, 1981). The same is true with respect to evaluating truthfulness: if the right 'tools for the job' are absent, it is impossible to do that job. This is especially notable in this context given that the vast individual differences in how people reveal their lies dictates a need for a vast arsenal for detecting lies. Nevertheless, it is sometimes the case that, even if people have the right tools for the job, they are using them in the wrong way. For example, individuals could be trained in proven approaches for investigative interviewing and in evaluating verbal clues to credibility (i.e., two approaches integral to evaluating truthfulness), but such skills could still be poorly applied (i.e., rigidly rather than fluidly and flexibly). It is likely that this especially occurs over time; that is, too often individuals fall prey to drift, thus illustrating the need for practice and quality control. Finally, sometimes individuals fail to use the tools at all. The consequences of the first generation of risk assessments studies are a case in point. In this generation, clinicians relied on their clinical opinion as opposed to empirically validated risk inventories, and errors were made more often that not (Steadman & Cocozza, 1974; Thornberry & Jacoby, 1979; for a review, see Monahan *et al.*, 2001). A similar lesson has been learned in the area of evaluating truthfulness: empirically validated tools are needed for the job!

Another roadblock relates to failing to consider how knowledge and skills change over time. Within any area in psychology – and most other disciplines for that matter – knowledge and skills change, as the evidence to support them changes. Consistent with most assessment practices, the accurate evaluation of truthfulness requires individuals to stay up to date with the literature. Moreover, professionals have an ethical obligation to stay current in the literature related to their areas of practice. Keeping up to date with the literature and implementing suggestions into clinical practice will prevent drift and related problems.

Although proper knowledge and skills are clearly important, a lack of critical thought is arguably the major roadblock to accurately evaluating truthfulness. Unfortunately, it is not uncommon for individuals to fail to evaluate each case on its own merits and to adopt a 'cookie cutter' approach to the task at hand. Such lack of objectivity can frequently be traced to internal or external factors. In terms of the former, poor psychological and/or physical health and/or egos too often impact on evaluators' decision-making. With regard to external factors, individuals may be pressed for time because of an onerous workload or unreasonable deadlines. Moreover, lack of objectivity may relate to being biased *a priori* against the person being assessed. Lack of critical thinking also leads to a failure to consider alternative hypotheses. Just because a given question appears to be a 'no-brainer' does not mean that it should be treated as such. Indeed, the decisions that are made in the forensic arena affect the lives and well-being of many individuals and, therefore, alternative hypotheses must be considered before a conclusion is made. Finally, lack of critical thinking may lead to a failure to check and double-check conclusions drawn. The approach to evaluating truthfulness that is introduced in this chapter requires individuals to frequently re-evaluate their conclusions in light of the evidence that formed their conclusions. In fact, the business of evaluating truthfulness is so complex that it requires a conscientious, quasi-perfectionist approach.

The bottom line is that roadblocks to evaluating truthfulness need to be overcome. That is, individuals need to know about evidence-based practice in evaluating truthfulness. To this end, the following section outlines empirically-based training components for the accurate evaluation of truthfulness. These training components form the basis of the approach introduced in the following section.

Evidenced-based training components for the evaluation of truthfulness

A review of research on clinical decision-making in general and evaluating truthfulness in particular suggests that training in evaluating truthfulness involves four major areas: (i) bad habits need to be unlearned; (ii) evidence-based knowledge about evaluating truthfulness needs to be acquired; (iii) empirically-validated tools need to be learned and practiced; and (iv) a method that emphasizes critical thinking in evaluating truthfulness needs to be used; the latter of which is perhaps the most difficult area to train. Each component is discussed in turn below.

Unlearning bad habits

Unlearning bad habits requires knowledge. Without basic, empirically-based knowledge about evaluating truthfulness, individuals tend to make common errors. As some researchers have suggested that the state of the research in evaluating truthfulness is not yet adequate to support its use in practice (e.g., Vrij, Mann & Fisher, 2006), it is argued that, at the very least, individuals should be informed of the errors, or myths, that riddle their work, as well as methods to avoid committing such errors. Although many myths exist (see Ekman, 1992; Vrij, 2000), they can be broadly categorized as being either experiential or societal in nature, although these are not necessarily mutually exclusive categories.

Experientially-driven myths stem from individuals' personal experiences. For example, some people rely on what has been termed the 'me' theory of behavioural assessment (Ekman, 1992). That is, they assume people will behave as they do when telling the truth or lying. For example, when using the 'me' theory, if someone avoids eye contact when lying, this person will view others as lying when they avert their gaze. Unfortunately, this approach more often than not results in what has been termed the 'idiosyncratic error' – not taking into account the various unique behaviours of individuals (*ibid.*). Not only may individuals differ within a culture (e.g., some people often rub their noses; others manipulate the hair on their face routinely), research has begun to identify important cross-cultural differences as well (e.g., eye gaze has been found to vary across cultures; McCarthy, Lee, Itakura & Muir, 2006).

Some individuals, particularly those with experience in evaluating truthfulness, often rely on 'gut instincts' or on 'intuitions' about whether or not someone is telling the truth or lying. It is not suggested that individuals should ignore their instincts or intuitions; indeed, a recent review of research on intuition has demonstrated that, at least occasionally, intuition can point people in the right direction (Hodgkinson, Langan-Fox & Sadler-Smith, 2008). However, we suggest that instincts/intuitions should not be viewed as answers in and of themselves. Rather, they should be viewed as hypotheses to be tested against the available evidence. If the data do not support the person's intuition/instinct, there should be no reason for a conclusion to be made simply on intuition/instinct.

Another experientially-driven myth concerns the relationship between experience and accuracy in evaluating truthfulness. Regarding the findings on experience, the research has been mixed. Some (e.g., Ekman & O'Sullivan, 1991) report no benefit from experience, but others (e.g., Mann, Vrij & Bull, 2004) have shown a positive benefit from experience on detection of lies. Experience can also produce overconfidence, which unfortunately too often leads evaluators to become myopic and, therefore, to seek the same false clues time and time again. The research is clear: if people rely solely on their own idiosyncrasies and/or experiences as the basis for their judgements for evaluating truthfulness, they are likely to be wrong most of the time (see Ekman, 1992; The Global Deception Team, 2006).

Societal-driven myths reflect shared beliefs about 'the sign or signs' of deception or of truth-telling (Ekman, 1992; Ford, 2006). In terms of truth-telling, there are the common myths that maintaining eye contact and lack of observable anxiety are reliable signs of honesty. Conversely, there are the opposite myths that sweating, anxiety and/or fear are signs indicative of deception. This type of myth unfortunately results in what Ekman (1992) has termed the 'Othello error' (after Shakespeare's tragedy, *Othello*). Othello wrongfully believed that his wife, Desdemona, had been unfaithful to him. When he confronted her about her suspected infidelities, she presented as fearful. Desdemona had considerable reason to be fearful, as Othello had already murdered her suspected lover. Othello's error occurred when he misattributed Desdemona's fear of being disbelieved as evidence of her guilt. It is important to understand that fear of being disbelieved looks the same as fear of being caught in a lie. That is, spotting an emotion only informs us about its kind, not its source or cause (Ekman, 2003). Consequently, it is important to be mindful of the reasons why someone may be experiencing an emotion in a given circumstance.

Proponents of neuro-linguistic programming (NLP) suggest that looking up and to the left is associated with lying. However, there is no research to support this proposition. Not only does the research indicate that the direction of the eye gaze has no meaning, averting eye gaze could be a clue to concentration, could reflect one's attempt not to be influenced by the facial expression of interviewees/peers, and/or could be associated with lying. Again, the research is clear: there is no Pinocchio response indicative of deception (Ekman, 1992). That is, there is no particular physiological, physical or psychological response that individuals demonstrate when they lie that they do not also demonstrate when they are under stress and/or concentrating.

An error that reflects experiential influences but tends to be common within society, at least in Western culture, concerns the tendency to focus uncritically on verbal information to the detriment of nonverbal information, which appears to reflect the overemphasis on language development. Indeed, while children are known to be relatively proficient in nonverbal communication, adults – through socialization – have learned to focus more on the spoken word. As a result, facial expressions of emotions are, for example, usually ignored due to verbal overrides, particularly if the emotion displayed is at odds with what is being said. This speaks to the importance of active listening and actively observing simultaneously, another important aspect in the accurate evaluation of truthfulness.

Bad habits can also reflect ignorance about why truths and lies succeed, as well as why they fail. For example, although lies sometimes succeed in light of factors beyond evaluators' control, such as the liar's skill and preparation, lies too often succeed because of a lack of knowledge or skill in the recipient of the lie. Moreover, lies too often succeed because the recipient of the lie wants to believe the liar (i.e., collusion), has no baseline information about the liar or has failed to seek collateral information. It is extremely important to seek collateral information in order to confirm or disconfirm the information provided, particularly in forensic contexts. Understanding one's context is also important, as base rates of truth-telling/lying can also have a negative impact on one's decision-making, with environments characterized by high incident rates of lying (e.g., prisons) resulting in an over-sceptical viewpoint and relatively honest contexts (e.g., churches) creating an overly trusting attitude.

Clearly, the more one knows about his/her biases, bad habits and environmental influences, the better able one will be at avoiding bad practices when it comes to evaluating truthfulness. However, the best way to counteract these errors is to treat each case on its own merit by looking for behavioural change, that is, changes from how a person typically behaves when telling the truth (their baseline behaviour). Indeed, viewing changes from baseline is essential to the accurate evaluation of truthfulness and is a fundamental aspect to the approach introduced in the present chapter.

Acquiring evidence-based knowledge

Research suggests that a basic training component for evaluating truthfulness consists of the acquisition of empirically-derived knowledge. At the very least, individuals should learn about what causes people to lie or tell the truth and the typography of truths and lies. Research indicates that there are many motivations for lying – to avoid punishment, to obtain an underserved reward, to protect a loved one, for amusement or to reduce shame (Ekman, 1992) – and that personality may impact on one's penchant for particular motivations (e.g., Spidel *et al.*, 2003). Research also indicates that lies can vary in terms of their content. That is, people can misrepresent their emotional state, their opinion on a particular subject, factual information or their future intents. Knowing about the different content of lies will assist in the accurate evaluation of truthfulness.

In addition, research has identified different types of lies, including, but not limited to, concealment and/or falsification or fabrication, as well as telling the truth falsely and the incorrect-inference dodge (Ekman, 1992). Concealment lies are the simplest form but the most difficult to detect because the liar is not actively engaging in lying. The outcome is less data to evaluate truthfulness than would result from, for example, spinning an elaborate web of deceit. Falsification reflects a deliberate misrepresentation of information. It is harder for the falsification lie to succeed in comparison with the concealment lie, as the liar has – at the very least – to remember the false statement if asked again.

No less important, but often forgotten, is the need to learn about what the truth looks like. As suggested above, if individuals only know what lies look like, they are likely to become susceptible to not believing the truth when they see it. As the truth reflects the end-result of generic emotional and cognitive processes, evaluators must acquire this basic knowledge. For example, if investigating some past event, individuals should understand how memory works, as well as how stress and emotions can disrupt cognitive processes in general and memory functioning in particular (see Hervé, Cooper & Yuille, 2007). In short, it is important to know about the motivations, nature and types of truths/lies because they have different emotional and/or cognitive consequences for the individual and, therefore, will reveal important clues during evaluations of truthfulness.

To understand and appreciate the differential impact of emotions and cognitions on lying and truth-telling, one should gain knowledge about 'the psychology of lying and truth telling' (see Figure 17.1). As implied above, in

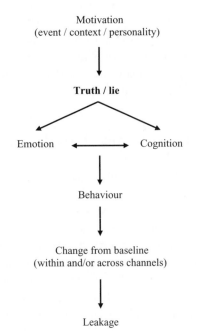

Figure 17.1: The psychology of truthfulness

order to understand the psychology of lying and truth-telling, background knowledge on how emotional and cognitive processes typically operate and how they impact on certain behavioural channels are required. As Figure 17.1 depicts, a person's motivation to lie or tell the truth must be taken into account, as well as the context of the assessment and knowledge about the personality of the person being evaluated (if available). These factors interact to delineate the particular psychological state of the individual being assessed.

When an individual lies or tells the truth, there will be emotional and cognitive consequences, which will, in some way, impact on their behaviour (Yuille, 1989; Ekman, 1992). The impact on their behaviour will be viewed as a change from baseline – that is, a change in how the individual typically behaves (e.g., in their facial expression, eye gaze, body language) and/or contradictory behaviours that occur simultaneously or in close succession (e.g., head shake indicating 'no' but answering 'yes'). When someone demonstrates a change from baseline via a behavioural (i.e., observable) channel, the result is leakage. That is, in effect, the change from baseline leaks out (Ekman, 2003; Hervé, Cooper & Yuille, 2008). Identifying leakage via active listening and observing is crucial to the process of evaluating truthfulness. That is, behavioural change is not random; it occurs for a reason (see below for further details).

Skill acquisition

In addition to empirically-based knowledge, the literature indicates that training in evaluating truthfulness should involve the development of specific, evidenced-based skills. The knowledge base discussed above would form the foundation for the development of certain skills and, more importantly, for the appropriate application of these skills. One skill involves identifying leakage (i.e., emotional or cognitive leakage), that is, how lies leak out through non-verbal channels (e.g., facial expressions and body language) and verbal channels (e.g., verbal style and content). In order to identify leakage, attention should focus on what people do and say and how they do it and say it. In other words, for leakage to be identified, 'active listening' and 'active observing' must occur simultaneously. Through active listening and observing, emotional and cognitive leakage can be observed through a number of observable behavioural channels.

Emotional leakage can be viewed through a number of observable channels, such as the face or voice and via body language. The face, however, is the primary and clearest channel through which to observe emotional reactions, and it is also the most researched (for a review, see Ekman, 2003). Ekman has demonstrated that there are seven universal facial expressions of emotion that can be observed – fear, sadness, disgust, happiness, surprise, contempt, anger – research suggests that they appear in all cultures regardless of language. It has been shown that, by developing the skill of observing the facial representations of these seven basic emotions, one's ability to identify different emotional states accurately can be increased (Frank & Ekman, 1997).

Most of the time, when a facial expression of emotion is observed, it is a macro-expression, that is, it is full and relatively long-lasting (>1 second) (Ekman, 2003). However, macro-expressions of emotions are usually ignored due to verbal overrides (see above) and, more importantly, are relatively easily faked. In addition to facial macro-expressions of emotion, subtle and micro-expressions have been identified (Ekman, 2003). In general, subtle or micro-expressions of emotion reflect attempts to conceal the emotion to one's self or to others (Ekman, 2003). A subtle expression is a partial facial expression of emotion resulting from one's inability to fully control emotional expression. A subtle expression may also occur when an emotion is just beginning to develop. Micro-expressions are full expressions of emotion that occur fleetingly, typically between 0.04 and 0.2 of a second (Ekman, 2003). Most people miss micro-expressions in their day-to-day interactions, however, training in their detection in the context of active observing can improve individuals' ability to detect them (Frank & Ekman, 1997). Training can also improve an individual's ability to detect subtle expressions. Although identifying micro- and subtle expressions can inform individuals as to the emotional state of others, on their own, they cannot inform individuals of why that emotional state is being felt (see below).

Another channel that has been heavily researched is verbal content (Yuille, 1988), a domain in which cognitive leakage could be observed. Although cognitive reactions to lying and truth-telling can be observed across a number of behavioural channels, verbal content is, however, the primary and clearest channel with which to observe such cognitive reactions. The analysis of verbal content stems, in part, from the assumption that, in general, it takes more mental effort to lie than it does to tell the truth. That is, lying causes more cognitive load than does truth-telling (Yuille, 1989; Vrij & Granhag, 2007). Indeed, as a liar does not have a memory of a false account of an event, it takes more cognitive capacity for him or her to keep the story consistent. In contrast, a truth-teller can rely on his or her memory when relating an event. Thus, an increased cognitive load is one of the factors that may betray a liar. Based on factors associated with memory and cognition, such as cognitive load, Undeutsch (1989) formulated a hypothesis, which essentially posits that memories of experienced events differ in quantity and quality from memories of invented experiences. The Undeutsch hypothesis formed the basis of Statement Validity Analysis (SVA), which has received empirical support (Horowitz, 1991). The core of SVA is CBCA, criteria that research has demonstrated to be more likely to be found in credible accounts as opposed to non-credible accounts of events (e.g., Lamb *et al.*, 1997; Colwell, Hiscock & Memon, 2002). Research indicates that CBCA is a complex qualitative assessment procedure and should be combined with the other skill-based components to evaluating truthfulness (Cooper *et al.*, 2007; Cooper, Hervé & Yuille, 2007). Unlike many other skills associated with the evaluation of truthfulness (e.g., the ability to detect micro-expressions), CBCA focuses on factors associated with truth-telling and, therefore, nicely complements other approaches or skills that focus on detecting clues associated with lying.

Although there is extensive research support for facial expressions and verbal content in evaluating truthfulness, other important evolving areas include reading the face together with body language and detecting changes in the voice and verbal style (Ekman *et al.*, 1991). In terms of the former, changes in body language are complex and can betray both the emotional and cognitive aspects of lies. For example, research indicates that knowing the baseline of use of different types of gestures (e.g., emblems, illustrators and manipulators) is important to detect change in these gestures (Ekman *et al.*, 1978; Ekman *et al.*, 1991). For example, one person may show a decrease in illustrators (i.e., hand movements used to illustrate speech) when he or she has an increase in cognitive load, yet another person may show an increase in illustrators when their cognitive load has been taxed. Detecting change within a given individual is crucial to the evaluation of truthfulness.

In terms of detecting changes in the voice, this can betray emotional and, to a lesser extent, cognitive aspects of lying (Ekman *et al.*, 1978; DePaulo, 1992; 1994). For example, the voice may get softer when someone is lying, however, a softer/lower voice can also reflect sadness, which highlights the importance of always considering alternative hypotheses before making a decision about the significance of what has been heard and/or observed (i.e., using a hypothesis-testing approach). As indicated above, some companies advertise voice-based lie detectors but, as these devices measure changes in voice pitch, they are not lie detectors but change detectors. Change can be due to lying but can also be due to many other factors, which once again highlights the need to utilize a hypothesis-testing approach.

Finally, it has been demonstrated that verbal style can leak both emotional and cognitive aspects of lying. Such would include increased duration of pauses or greater use of filled pauses, changes in pronoun use or responding without answering the question. For example, if a suspect in a robbery, during the recounting of his or her version of events in the first person pronoun, pauses at the point of entering the location of the robbery and then drops the use of the first person pronoun ('I'), the change may reflect a lie of omission – more may have transpired than what was being revealed. It should be noted, however, that the change does not imply that the person committed the robbery. Rather, it highlights a point in the account that should be reviewed again, as a significant change in verbal style has been observed (i.e., a significant change from baseline verbal style).

Although implied throughout this chapter, it is nevertheless important to highlight the reality that none of the aforementioned channels are in and of themselves clues to deception; they are clues of importance. As noted above, changes in these channels simply reflect a change in emotional and/or cognitive load. At times, the channels may be revealing different messages, thereby suggesting internal conflict. These changes and inconsistencies are important in conducting evaluations of truthfulness, not because they necessarily reveal lies but because they reveal topics that need further exploration; hence the need for a method by which to conduct such evaluations.

Method

Research and practice suggest that an evidence-based method that helps evaluators organize the information collected and, thereafter, make an informed decision is a vital component of clinical decision-making in general (see Monahan *et al.*, 2001) and evaluating truthfulness in particular (Hervé, Cooper & Yuille, 2008). At the very least, this method should promote critical thinking – the objective evaluation of data in the context of multiple hypothesis-testing. We believe that using a 'single case design' can help evaluators achieve this goal. With this design, each case can be evaluated on its own merits. This design not only advocates collecting data rich in quantity and quality (as detailed above), it also emphasizes the importance of considering multiple hypotheses; that is, using a hypothesis-testing approach, both when considering the meaning of particular data points and when making overall decisions. The evaluator is encouraged to check and double-check his or her hypotheses against the available evidence – changing/updating hypotheses as the evidence to support the hypotheses changes. Even when the issue at hand appears to be quite simplistic, multiple hypotheses should be considered. As noted above, instincts or intuitions should not be viewed as answers in and of themselves but as hypotheses to be tested via critical thinking. Once all the data have been collected and alternative hypotheses considered, decisions could be drawn based on the balance of probabilities (Hervé, Cooper & Yuille, 2008). That is, a conclusion of whether someone is telling the truth or lying in a given situation should be based on the balance of probabilities. Of course, the particular threshold for decision-making will largely be dictated by contextual factors, with lower cut-offs being used for screening purposes (e.g., individuals being screened for further evaluations, such as employees in airport security) and higher cut-offs being used for final decisions (e.g., individuals being excluded from flying).

In addition to promoting critical thought, we advocate that any decision-making model should be objective, fluid and ethical. It should be standardized, yet flexible enough to be tailored to individual cases, much akin to using structured clinical guidelines in the assessment of risk for recidivism and CBCA in the assessment of verbal content. Moreover, the approach should be transparent so that it can stand up to scrutiny by others – a criterion that is inherently met if the aforementioned criteria are also met. As with many types of assessments, as long as the recommendations and conclusions stem logically from the body of the report, the method in question should be relatively 'bullet-proof'. The same is true with the evaluation of truthfulness.

Generalizing from the classroom to the real world

Although unlearning bad habits, acquiring knowledge and skills, and using the right method for evaluating truthfulness are necessary to conducting such evaluations effectively, it is important to note that these steps are not sufficient. Indeed, there is a growing body of research in the education literature that suggests that learning does not generally translate well to real-world settings without both practice and support (see Bransford, Brown & Cocking, 1999). With regard to practice, the old edict still, in part, applies: practice makes perfect! Practice becomes especially important when unlearning bad habits, as this involves fundamentally changing one's beliefs about and approach to evaluating truthfulness. At the 2nd International Investigative Interviewing Conference (2006), one attendee highlighted that, at the very least, professionals involved in conducting evaluations of truthfulness should learn about their own bad habits and how to counteract them (we agree fully with this proposition). The bottom line is that without focused practice, people simply tend to revert to old patterns, including bad habits (smoking being a case in point).

Unfortunately, when it comes to evaluating truthfulness within professional settings, the amount and type of practice available to individuals are often constrained by environmental demands (e.g., from caseloads to outdated regulations). For example, while videotaping interviews can prove very valuable in terms of practice and conducting evaluations, many jurisdictions/organizations still shy away from videotaping. Moreover, new approaches to evaluating truthfulness, particularly those akin to the one proposed in this chapter (see below), often require not only time to learn but more time than previous, outdated approaches. Indeed, there is no question that relying on instinct alone is much quicker than collecting high quantity and quality data, which is constantly evaluated via a hypothesis-testing approach. However, if accuracy and resistance to challenges/scrutiny are the objective, we suggest that the latter, more time-consuming approach should be employed.

Given the additional demands associated with practicing new skills or methods in general and a specific approach to evaluating truthfulness in particular, we strongly believe that the generalization of information from the classroom to the real world will depend not only on practice but also on the amount of support received by the sponsoring agency/supervisors. Ultimately, for training to be successful, trainees will need the support and guidance of those around them, including superiors. In addition to providing tangible support (e.g., smaller caseload; videotaping capabilities), having a supervisor who is knowledgeable and skilled in evaluating truthfulness allows for a mentoring approach to training, thereby ensuring that bad habits are replaced with evidence-based practices. This approach can also help protect against drift over time, that is, the re-emergence of old or emergence of new bad habits.

An evidenced-based approach to detecting truth and lies

Grounded in the research noted above, an approach to evaluating truthfulness was developed to blend empirical evidence with the experience of clinical-forensic mental health professionals and law enforcement professionals. The mix of science and practice produced an approach to evaluating truthfulness that is evidenced-based, user-friendly and ethical in nature. As can be seen in Figure 17.2, this approach is rooted in the psychology of lying and truth-telling (see Figure 17.1).

When a person tells a lie or the truth, it can lead to emotional and/or cognitive consequences that are leaked behaviourally (see Figure 17.2). That is, when a person tries to lie about an emotion or has an emotion about lying, that emotion will leak out (i.e., an observable change will occur). When someone lies about their thought process or is thinking about lying, that too will leak out. Although not commonly discussed in the deception literature, as noted above, truth-telling can also result in leakage. A person telling the truth, for example, may leak emotions that reflect contextual factors (e.g., anxiety about the consequences of telling the truth, such as returning to jail; fear of being disbelieved, as displayed by Desdemona in *Othello*), the topic under discussion (e.g., during a murder investigation, an interviewee may display sadness or anger at the loss of a friend), and/or factors unrelated to either the topic or the context (e.g., during an investigation, an interviewee may display anger or sadness associated with the fight he or she had with his

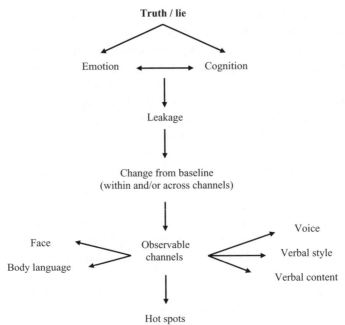

Figure 17.2:   Model for evaluating truthfulness

or her partner that morning). Similarly, the truthful person may have particular thoughts regarding the context or more unique views about the topic under discussion. The bottom line is that someone can have emotional and cognitive reactions when telling the truth, reactions that should not be confused with signs of deception. Consequently, it is extremely important to consider alternative hypotheses when conducting evaluations of truthfulness.

When a lie or a truth affects or changes one's psychological state, be it emotional or cognitive, there will be some consequence of this change: leakage. It has been demonstrated that lies can leak out through a variety of channels or aspects of behaviour. The channels depicted in Figure 17.2 were chosen for the present model for two reasons: (i) they have been found to be valid indicators of leakage (i.e., evidenced-based); and (ii) they are easily observable in interviews without the use of equipment/technology (i.e., are user-friendly), unlike, for example, techniques that measure physiological changes (e.g., heart rate).

The easiest way to detect leakage is through a change in baseline (i.e., how the person typically behaves). That is, it is easier to detect leakage in what someone says if it is known how that person says things when not lying and/or influenced by factors known to affect their psychological states when telling the truth (see above). Similarly, it is easier to detect a leak through body language if you have some knowledge of the baseline body language of the person. At times, collecting such baseline information might reveal a 'tell' (the term 'tell' is used by poker players to refer to a behaviour that gives away, or 'tells', that a player has a good hand or is bluffing). Note that this is not a 'universal' sign but a sign that applies 'only' to the individual in question and likely inconsistently, that is, it is a person-specific leakage that the person typically displays when lying. Baseline information is also crucial in evaluating how a person typically responds when telling the truth, which can then be contrasted with their reactions when lying.

It is important not to assume automatically that the identified leakage is a sign of deception. Indeed, leakage, be it emotional or cognitive, can reflect lying or truth-telling. Accordingly, we urge people to adopt a new term when observing leakage: a 'hot spot'. A hot spot is any significant change in a person's baseline behaviour within or across one or more observable channels. Inconsistencies between channels are particularly significant hot spots, such as when the person says, 'No, I didn't do it' all the while nodding 'yes'. Clearly, when one's nonverbal behaviour perhaps unconsciously contradicts one's verbal content, evaluators can – at the very least – be confident that the topic under discussion is creating internal/psychological conflict for the interviewee and, therefore, should be followed up. It is theoretically appealing that such inconsistencies are especially meaningful and more likely to be associated with lying than with truth-telling. Indeed, not only is truth-telling likely to lead effortlessly to the coordination of channels in such a manner as to lead to consistency across channels, the monitoring and coordination of multiple channels is inherently harder for liars to achieve than the monitoring and controlling of only one channel. This phenomenon is akin to juggling: it is simply easier to juggle one or two items than four or five. Unfortunately, the same can be said of evaluators. That is, it is harder to learn to monitor multiple channels in others than only one or two, again highlighting the importance of training and practice in active listening and observing across multiple behavioural channels.

The bottom line is that, when a change occurs in, or there is an inconsistency across, a person's face, body language or voice pitch, this is meaningful: change and/or inconsistencies do not occur randomly. Again, a hot spot is not a clue to lying; rather, it is a clue to importance. A hot spot may occur for a variety of reasons, of which lying is only one possibility (others include thinking about something off-topic, truth-telling). This highlights the importance of knowing about the nature of truths and lies and using a hypothesis-testing approach to evaluating truthfulness.

Step-wise approach to evaluating truthfulness

Although the model outlined in Figure 17.2 and described above provides the foundation from which to gain knowledge and acquire skills specific to evaluating truthfulness, it does not provide a method for implementation. We therefore suggest the following step-wise approach to evaluating truthfulness in clinical-forensic practice:

Seek background information

If possible, the evaluator/investigator should prepare for the interview/interaction by collecting background information. This will help define and identify the central issues, as well as other topics of interest. Evaluating truthfulness is akin to conducting other types of assessments in clinical-forensic contexts: professionals should never enter such contexts with patients/client/offenders blindly (i.e., before reading institutional/case files or discussing the case with the referral source). The more information that is attained, the better position the professional will be in to evaluate the interviewee. It is crucial that interviewers review as much information as possible before interviews, as this will help them develop interview strategies, will facilitate their ability to develop alternative hypotheses and will help them better evaluate the baseline of the interviewee. For example, at the time of the interview, interviewers can ask questions about known topics, which will allow them not only to collect baseline information (how the person behaves when telling the truth and/or lying), but to begin to develop an idea of the response style the interviewee is adopting (e.g., positive vs. negative impression management). Of note, if the interviewee is from another culture, background information on culture-specific topics related to the issue at hand (e.g., attitude to crime, mental health, business process and organizational structure), expected social conduct (e.g., social hierarchy and related interpersonal expectations, shameful behaviour) and behavioural idiosyncrasies (e.g., body language, eye contact, emotional expression) should be collected. Such information will prove crucial in assisting evaluators to avoid culturally-based idiosyncratic errors.

Establish baseline

The more baseline information obtained, the better position the evaluator will be in to detect changes from baseline. Again, by baseline we are referring to how someone typically behaves under certain conditions (e.g., when telling the truth, when lying; when happy, when sad). When using our model, or any other behaviourally-based model, we suggest that evaluators seek baseline information about all five channels depicted above (see Figure 17.2) – from facial expressions, eye contact, eye movement, gestures, voice characteristics, and verbal style and content. The establishment of a baseline can be made by discussing the person with others (e.g., case managers, front-line staff), through recordings of the person or in face-to-face conversation. If using the last approach, the collection of baseline data can easily be accomplished during the rapport-building phase of the interview. It is important to note that the rapport phase should also focus on making interviewees relatively at ease, as this serves to decrease anxiety stemming from issues unrelated to the topic at hand that too often result in hot spots unrelated to deceit. In essence, the goal is to calibrate the situation (i.e., relax the interviewee) in such a way as to decrease the noise-to-signal ratio (topic-unrelated hot spots/topic-specific hot spots), not unlike that accomplished by polygraphers during their rapport-building phase of the pre-polygraph interview.

Observe hot spots

With baseline information in hand, the interviewer should actively observe and listen in order to be alert for changes within a channel or inconsistencies across channels, as well as for any signs that suggest the person is being truthful. To facilitate active listening and observing, it would be wise to remove any potential distracters such as those that are psychological (e.g., unresolved issues about the case, context or personal topic), physical (e.g., fatigue and/or hunger) and/or environmental (e.g., noise and/or visual barriers) in nature. Any significant change from baseline is a hot spot and the topic that produced the change should be noted. The hot spot should be used to determine if the observed change was due to emotional or cognitive reasons. If possible, the topic should be raised later to see if it again produces a similar hot spot. If the hot spot occurs consistently, one can be relatively confident that it was produced by the topic under discussion, as opposed to some unrelated issue.

Evaluate alternative hypotheses

As discussed above, knowing that a particular topic consistently gives rise to a hot spot only provides information indicating that a topic of importance has been identified. Determining what the hot spot actually signifies requires, among other things (e.g., adept interviewing skills), the consideration of alternative hypotheses. As noted above, the topics in question may raise issues in the interviewee but not bear on his or her guilt, such as when someone is interviewed about the disappearance of a close friend. In other words, alternative explanations for a hot spot should always be entertained before making a determination of its probable cause. In fact, we promote the consideration of multiple hypotheses (e.g., guilty vs. not guilty but knowledgeable of topic vs. innocent), not just two (e.g., guilty vs. innocent). As with other types of assessments and interviews in forensic contexts, the final conclusions should be data-driven. Indeed, by gaining the right knowledge, empirically-validated skills and a structured method that stresses critical thinking, one no longer needs to interject biases or rely solely on intuitions when making decisions. Rather, one can let the data speak for themselves. Only high quantity and quality data that are evaluated and re-evaluated against alternative hypotheses can lead to accurate decision-making – the closer one comes to this ideal, the more confident one can be about one's conclusions.

Conclusions

The goal of this chapter was two-fold: first, to discuss the literature on evaluating truthfulness; and second, to introduce an evidence-based and practically-informed approach to the topic. As emphasized throughout this chapter, the proposed technique was developed by combining research with the field experience of law enforcement and forensic mental health professionals in order to develop a user-friendly, transparent and ethical procedure that is skill-based and portable. Of course, this model and related training programmes will evolve, as will the science and practice of evaluating truthfulness.

As the model was built on known psychological process, we believe that it applies across cultures. That is, although we are cognizant that there are cultural differences regarding baseline behaviour and why and how lies and truths leak out, the main part of this framework (i.e., going down the centre of Figure 17.2) is hypothesized to apply to all individuals, irrespective of culture: when someone tells a lie or the truth, it may lead to emotional and/or cognitive consequences that leak out in observable behaviour, resulting in a hot spot to be followed up. Given the strengths and applicability of this model, we have seen a growing attention in this and related approaches (e.g., Porter, Woodworth & Birt, 2000) in recent years, with interest spanning a variety of disciplines (psycho-legal, law enforcement, homeland security, airport security, customs and border control, the corporate world).

It should be noted that, although the individual components of the present approach have been empirically supported (see above), the entire model has yet to be completely validated. To a large extent, this is due to the research limitations addressed above (e.g., imposing a quantitative structure on a qualitative procedure). These limitations notwithstanding, research has found that training in verbal and nonverbal channels significantly improves (from 40% to 70%) people's ability to evaluate truthfulness (Porter *et al.*, 2000). Further, there is evidence that individuals who are naturally adept at evaluating truthfulness (i.e., individuals who attain accuracy rates over 80% with little training; O'Sullivan & Ekman, 2004) use approaches that are not unlike that reported in the present chapter. Although promising, this line of research constitutes only indirect evidence. Consequently, we are evaluating the present approach through a series of real-life case studies and are dedicated to the process of evaluation through pre- and post-studies (i.e., before and after the training). We invite others to test the present approach to evaluating truthfulness independently and hope that, in doing so, they will take into consideration the previously outlined limitations regarding the state of research in this area.

It is important to highlight that the evaluation of truthfulness is usually not a stand-alone procedure; rather, it is typically embedded as part of a bigger package. For example, the accurate evaluation of truthfulness involves the use of a high-quality, semi-structured, non-leading, non-suggestive interview (Yuille, 1988). We do not promote the use of deception and/or torture in interviews, as we believe such techniques are not only unethical but lead to too many errors and, therefore, detract from the task at hand: the search for knowledge. Further, the interview requires a fair bit of preparation so that it can be tailored to the individual and the topic(s) in question. Indeed, at least within clinical-forensic populations, individual differences far outweigh individual similarities. The context (e.g., assessment vs. treatment; police vs. correctional interview) must also be taken into account, as well as the triggering event (i.e., what led the interviewee to be interviewed), as these factors may impact on the psychological state of the interviewee, and possibly the interviewer, thereby affecting the evaluation.

Evaluating truthfulness depends, to a large extent, on the quality and quality of the available evidence, data or information. If enough high-quality information by which to evaluate truthfulness is not obtained, the task cannot be completed. It is akin to trying to conduct a risk assessment without any collateral information or relying solely on clinical judgement: poor decisions will be made.

Acknowledgement

We would like to acknowledge The Ekman Group: Training Division, and in particular Dr Paul Ekman and John Yarbrough for their integral contributions to the approach to evaluating truthfulness that is introduced in this chapter.

References

Akehurst, L., Kohnken, G., Vrij, A. & Bull, R. (1996). Lay persons' and police officers' beliefs regarding deceptive behavior. *Applied Cognitive Psychology*, *10*, 461–471.

Bransford, J., Brown, A. & Cocking, R. (1999). *How people learn: Brain, mind, experience, and school.* http://stills.nap.edu/html/howpeople1/ Accessed 4 October 2000.

Colwell, K., Hiscock, C. K. & Memon, A. (2002). Interviewing techniques and the assessment of statement credibility. *Applied Cognitive Psychology*, *16*, 287–300.

Cooper, B. S. & Yuille, J. C. (2006). Psychopathy and deception. In H. F. Hervé & J. C. Yuille (Eds.), *The psychopath: Theory, research and practice* (pp. 487–503). Mahwah, NJ: Lawrence Erlbaum.

Cooper, B. S., Hervé, H. F. & Yuille, J. C. (2007). *Evaluating truthfulness in offenders of violent crime: Verbal clues to credibility.* Paper presented at the 4th Annual Forensic Psychiatry Conference, Mental Health and the Justice System across the Lifespan, Victoria, BC, March.

Cooper, B. S., Griesel, D. & Yuille, J. C. (2007). Clinical-forensic risk assessment: The past and current state of affairs. *Journal of Forensic Psychology Practice*, *7*(4), 1–63.

Cooper, B. S., Ternes, M., Griesel, D., Viljoen, S. & Yuille, J. C. (2007). *An examination of the credibility of Canadian offenders' accounts of instrumental and reactive homicides.* Invited paper presented at the 30th International Congress on Law and Mental Health, Padua, Italy, June.

DePaulo, B. M. (1992). Nonverbal behavior and self-presentation. *Psychological Bulletin, 111*(2), 203–243.

DePaulo, B. M. (1994). Spotting lies: Can humans learn to do better? *Current Directions in Psychological Science, 3*(3), 83–86.

DePaulo, B. M., Kashey, D. A., Kirkendol, S. E., Wyer, M. M. & Epstein, J. A. (1996). Lying in everyday life. *Journal of Personality and Social Psychology, 70*, 979–995.

DePaulo, B. M., Lindsay, J. J., Malone, B. E., Muhlenbruck, L., Charlton, K. & Cooper, H. (2003). Cues to deception. *Psychological Bulletin, 129*(1), 74–118.

Ekman, P. (1992). *Telling lies: Clues to deceit in the marketplace, politics, and marriage.* New York: W. W. Norton.

Ekman, P. (2003). *Emotions revealed: Recognizing faces and feelings to improve communication and emotional life.* New York: Henry Holt and Co.

Ekman, P. & O'Sullivan, M. (1992). Who can catch a liar? *American Psychologist, 46*, 913–920.

Ekman, P., Friesen, W. V. & Scherer, K. R. (1978). Body movement and voice pitch in deceptive interaction. *Semiotica, 16*(1), 23–27.

Ekman, P, O'Sullivan, M., Friesen, W. V. & Scherer, K. R. (1991). Face, voice, and body in detecting deceit. *Journal of Nonverbal Behavior, 15*, 125–135.

Ford, E. B. (2006). Lie detection: Historical, neuropsychiatric and legal dimensions. *Internal Journal of Law and Psychiatry, 29*, 159–177.

Frank, M. G. & Ekman, P. (1997). The ability to detect deceit generalizes across different types of high-stake lies. *Journal of Personality and Social Psychology, 72*, 1429–1439.

The Global Deception Team (2006). A world of lies. *Journal of Cross-Cultural Psychology, 3*, 60–74.

Griesel, D. & Yuille, J. C. (2007). Credibility assessment in eyewitness memory. In M.P. Toglia, J.D. Read, D.F. Ross & R.C.L. Lindsay (Eds.), *Handbook of eyewitness psychology. Volume I, Memory for events* (pp. 339–370). Mahwah, NJ: Lawrence Erlbaum.

Hervé, H., Cooper, B. S. & Yuille, J. C. (2007). Memory formation in offenders: Perspectives from a biopsychosocial theory of eyewitness memory. In S. A. Christianson (Ed.), *Offenders' memories of violent crimes* (pp. 37–74). Chichester: John Wiley & Sons.

Hervé, H. F., Cooper, B. S. & Yuille, J.C. (2008). *Assessing credibility in correctional and forensic psychiatric contexts: An empirically-based practical approach.* Paper presented at the American Psychology and Law Society's conference, Jacksonville, FL, March.

Hodgkinson, G. P., Langan-Fox, J. & Sadler-Smith, E. (2008). Intuition: A fundamental bridging construct in the behavioural sciences. *British Journal of Psychology, 99*, 1–27.

Horowitz, S. W. (1991). Empirical support for statement validity assessment. *Behavioral Assessment, 13*, 293–313.

Lamb, M. E., Sternberg, K. J., Esplin, P. W., Hershkowitz, I., Orbach, Y. & Hovav, M. (1997). Criterion-based content analysis: A field validation study. *Child Abuse & Neglect, 21*, 255–264.

Mann, S., Vrij, A. & Bull, R. (2004). Detecting true lies: Police officers' ability to detect suspects' lies. *Journal of Applied Psychology, 89*, 137–149.

McCarthy, A., Lee, K., Itakura, S. & Muir, D. W. (2006). Cultural display rules drive eye gaze during thinking. *Journal of Cross-Cultural Psychology, 37*, 717–722.

Monahan, J. (1981). *The clinical prediction of violent behavior.* Washington, DC: Government Printing Office.

Monahan, J., Steadman, H. J., Silver, E., Appelbaum, P. S., Robbins, P. C., Mulvey, E. P., Roth, L. H., Grisso, T. & Banks, S. (2001). *Rethinking risk assessment: The MacArthur study of mental disorder and violence.* New York: Oxford University Press.

National Research Council, Division of Behavioral and Social Sciences and Education (1996). *The polygraph and lie detection: Committee to review the scientific evidence on the polygraph.* Washington, DC: The National Academies Press.

Nietzsche, F. (1967). *Will to power.* New York: Random House.

O'Sullivan, M. & Ekman, P. (2004). The wizards of deception detection. In P. A. Granhag & L. Strömwell (Eds.), *Detecting Deception* (pp. 269–286). Cambridge: Cambridge University Press.

Porter, S. & Yuille, J. C. (1996). The language of deceit: An investigation of the verbal clues to deception in the interrogation context. *Law and Human Behavior, 20*, 442–458.

Porter, S., Woodworth, M. & Birt, A. R. (2000). Truth, lies and videotape: An investigation of the ability of federal parole officers to detect deception. *Law and Human Behavior, 24*, 643–658.

Spence, S. A., Hunter, M. D., Farrow, T. F. D., Green, R. D., Leung, D. H., Hughes, C. J. & Ganesan, V. (2004). A cognitive neurobiological account of deception: Evidence from functional Nneuroimaging. *Philosophical Transactions of the Royal Society of London, 359*, 1755–1762.

Spidel, A., Hervé, H. F., Greaves, C., Cooper, B. S. & Hare, R. D. (2003). Psychopathy and deceptive motivations in young offenders. In M. Vanderhallen, G. Vervaeke, P. J. Van Koppen & J. Goethals (Eds.), *Much ado about crime: Chapters on psychology and law.* Brussels: Politeia.

Steadman, H. J. & Cocozza, J. J. (1974). *Careers of the criminally insane.* Lexington, MA: Lexington Books, D. C. Heath & Co.

Steller, M. (1989). Recent developments in statement analysis. In J. C. Yuille (Ed.), *Credibility assessment.* Dordrecht: Kluwer Academic.

Steller, M. & Koehnken, G. (1989). Statement analysis: Credibility assessment of children's testimonies in sexual abuse cases. In D. C. Raskin (Ed.), *Psychological methods in criminal investigation and evidence.* New York: Springer.

Ternes, M., Cooper, B. S. & Yuille, J. C. (2007). *Verbal clues to credibility in male offenders' memories for violent crime.* Paper presented at the 4th Annual Forensic Psychiatry Conference, Mental Health and the Justice System across the Lifespan, Victoria, BC, March.

Thornberry, T. P. & Jacoby, J. E. (1979). *The criminally insane: A community follow-up of mentally ill offenders.* Chicago, IL: University of Chicago Press.

Undeutsch, U. (1989). The development of statement reality analysis. In J. C. Yuille (Ed.), *Credibility assessment* (pp. 101–120). Dordrecht: Kluwer Academic.

Vrij, A. (2000). *Detecting lies and deceit: The psychology of lying and the implications for professional practice.* Chichester: Wiley.

Vrij, A. (2004). Why professionals fail to catch liars and how they can improve. *Legal and Criminological Psychology, 9*, 159–181.

Vrij, A. & Granhag, P. A. (2007). Interviewing to detect deception. In S. A. Christianson (Ed.), *Offenders' memories of violent crimes*, (pp. 279–304). Chichester: John Wiley & Sons.

Vrij, A. Mann, S. M. & Fisher, R. P. (2006). *An empirical test of the behavior analysis interview*. Paper presented at the 2nd Conference on International Investigative Interviewing, Portsmouth, July.

Yuille, J. C. (1988). The systematic assessment of children's testimony. *Canadian Psychology, 29*(3), 247–262.

Yuille, J. C. (1989). *Credibility assessment*. Dordrecht: Kluwer Academic.

Index

Note: Page numbers in italics refer to tables. Abbreviations used: CI for Cognitive Interview; ID for identification